Coastal Seas

British Wildlife Collection 16

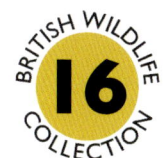

Coastal Seas

Frances Dipper &
Paul Naylor

BLOOMSBURY WILDLIFE
LONDON • OXFORD • NEW YORK • NEW DELHI • SYDNEY

BLOOMSBURY WILDLIFE
Bloomsbury Publishing Plc
50 Bedford Square, London, WC1B 3DP, UK
Bloomsbury Publishing Ireland Limited,
29 Earlsfort Terrace, Dublin 2, D02 AY28, Ireland

BLOOMSBURY, BLOOMSBURY WILDLIFE and the Diana logo are trademarks of
Bloomsbury Publishing Plc

First published in the United Kingdom 2025

Copyright © Frances Dipper and Paul Naylor, 2025

Frances Dipper and Paul Naylor have asserted their right under the Copyright, Designs and Patents Act, 1988,
to be identified as Authors of this work

For legal purposes the illustration credits on page 360 constitute an extension of this copyright page

All rights reserved. No part of this publication may be: i) reproduced or transmitted in any form, electronic
or mechanical, including photocopying, recording or by means of any information storage or retrieval
system without prior permission in writing from the publishers; or ii) used or reproduced in any way for
the training, development or operation of artificial intelligence (AI) technologies, including generative AI
technologies. The rights holders expressly reserve this publication from the text and data mining exception
as per Article 4(3) of the Digital Single Market Directive (EU) 2019/790

Bloomsbury Publishing Plc does not have any control over, or responsibility for, any third-party websites
referred to in this book. All internet addresses given in this book were correct at the time of going to press.
The author and publisher regret any inconvenience caused if addresses have changed or sites have ceased
to exist, but can accept no responsibility for any such changes.

A catalogue record for this book is available from the British Library
Library of Congress Cataloguing-in-Publication data has been applied for

ISBN: HB: 978-1-3994-0476-1; ePDF: 978-1-3994-0478-5; ePub: 978-1-3994-0475-4

2 4 6 8 10 9 7 5 3 1

Design by Susan McIntyre
Jacket artwork by Nik Pollard

Printed and bound in Dubai by Oriental Press

To find out more about our authors and books visit www.bloomsbury.com and sign up for our newsletters
For product safety related questions contact productsafety@bloomsbury.com

HALF TITLE: Common Octopus *Octopus vulgaris*.
FRONTISPIECE: Hydroid medusa *Neoturris pileata* above a kelp forest.

Contents

	Preface	6
	Part One: Shallow seas	**10**
1	A different world	12
2	Immersing yourself	52
	Part Two: Habitats and communities	**80**
3	Forests beneath the sea	82
4	Reef life	104
5	Sand, mud and maerl	136
6	Underwater meadows: seagrasses	160
7	The open sea	188
	Part Three: Species	**212**
8	Fish tales	214
9	Invertebrate variety	252
10	Cunning cephalopods	274
11	Living together: shared lives and unwelcome lodgers	296
	Part Four: Conservation	**320**
12	Protecting our seas	322
	Acknowledgements	354
	References and further reading	355
	Illustration credits	360
	Index	361

Preface

When holiday-makers stand on a beach, pier or seaside esplanade around the British Isles, perhaps with a comforting coffee or ice cream in hand, many will gaze out to sea and appreciate its beauty. However, they may know very little of the vibrant life hidden beneath the rather chilly-looking surface, and are often astonished to hear that dazzlingly colourful fish, exotic-looking corals, octopuses and thousands more sea creatures all live within a few hundred metres of our shores. The shoreline around the British Isles provides tantalising, twice-daily glimpses of this world, especially on the lowest tides (spring tides), but reveals almost nothing of the fascinating behaviour and interactions of the animals, plants and other organisms living just out of sight in hugely varied and often picturesque habitats.

However, things are changing, and in addition to the increasing number of universities and colleges now offering marine courses, there is a growing enthusiasm amongst individuals, wildlife groups, societies and organisations to 'spread the word' about the wealth of marine life around the British Isles. In the terrestrial environment, nature and wildlife are easily visible, and appreciation of the importance of conserving and enhancing it, not least for our own well-being, is becoming well established. It is vital that the same happens in our shallow seas, but how can you be enthusiastic about something you can't see? We have both been lucky enough to have spent our lives watching, studying, photographing, filming and learning about this amazing world. We want others to venture into our shallow seas, literally or figuratively, and our aim in this book, the 16th in the British Wildlife Collection, is to stimulate an interest and passion for this vital realm, by providing an accessible introduction to the habitats and wildlife found there. In this way we extend the

OPPOSITE PAGE:
Male and female Black-faced Blennies *Tripterygion delaisi* among sponges and sea squirts on a leg of Swanage Pier, Dorset.

footsteps of John Archer-Thomson and Julian Cremona down from *Rocky Shores* (No. 7) into the shallow seas.

We both started down the 'natural history' route and ended up studying marine biology at university, in different ways. Although it is by no means a prerequisite, growing up in the deep Warwickshire countryside surrounded by farmland, with lambs, cows, guinea pigs and geese for companions (not to mention five annoying brothers), gave Frances an affinity with the natural world. She blames a seaside holiday diet of hauling up crabs and shrimps from the Cobb in Lyme Regis and finding glistening 'fool's gold' ammonite fossils, along with weekends at home watching underwater explorers Hans and Lotte Hass in glorious black and white on television, for her initial interest in marine life. This eventually led her to the Isle of Man to research the biology of wrasses for her PhD and to learn to dive. She survived home-made wetsuits, twin-hose regulators and 'horse-collar' style life jackets, before moving on to work with the then Nature Conservancy Council on early baseline marine survey work. A family move to Southeast Asia was an entry point to voluntary coral-reef work and the start of her life as a self-employed marine biologist and author.

As for Paul, it was his first snorkelling experiences as a teenager on the Norfolk coast that set him on the marine biology path, as we describe in Chapter 2. Paul's PhD, looking at the responses of bivalve molluscs to metal pollution, led to a career in environmental regulation but he continued his enthusiasm for marine animals with underwater photography and filming. Paul has always been passionate about using his material to raise awareness of the wonderful creatures of our seas. He is continually encouraged by encounters with interested members of the public, such as when fellow train passengers see the colourful images he is compiling for a presentation on his laptop, ask him what exotic foreign location he has returned from, and are utterly astonished when he tells them they were all taken within a few metres of our coast. Or the person who commended his footage of a nest-building wrasse being shown at a Bioblitz in Devon, but then politely added that the event should only include films of local wildlife, and not tropical fish.

Frances has the same passion for 'spreading the word' through her writing, and it was that shared goal that led to our collaboration on this book. We are also united in the belief that, for all the visual colour of our marine life, their fascinating behavioural stories are even more

Preface

impressive and striking. Past tales of mermaids and monsters abound around our shores: mysterious selkies in remote areas of Scotland that shed their seal skin to become human, and don it again in order to return to the sea; sinuous sea serpents as long as a ship; and bulbous-headed monsters with sucker-arms reaching up for terrified sailors. Whilst such legends probably arose from rare sightings of large sea creatures such as Oarfish *Regalecus glesne*, 11m long with a bright red 'mane' of a dorsal fin, and Giant Squid *Architeuthis dux*, brought up from the depths, the colourful lives led by the inhabitants of our coastal seas are often even stranger. That is what we have been keenest to show in this book.

LEFT: Frances taking her nephew for his first dive in the 1980s.

RIGHT: Paul aged 14, kitted up for snorkelling on the Norfolk coast.

Part One
Shallow seas

A different world

chapter one

The ocean is a very different environment from the one we are used to living in. Imagine drifting along in a watery world, with no visible reference points to tell you which way is up or down. Or moving around terrain where almost irresistible forces can sweep you away, visibility can vary dramatically and some of the 'scenery' might eat you. Perhaps you are one of the creatures rooted to the seabed, unable to move to find food, friends or a mate – or maybe you are an expert swimmer but must surface to take a breath. Jacques Cousteau called it a 'silent world' in his 1953 book of that title, but you can sense vibrations in the water or hear faint snaps, crackles and pops all round, though it is difficult to tell which direction the sounds are coming from.

For the myriad wonderful and often surprising animals and plants that live and thrive in the shallow seas around the British Isles, this is the norm. The physical conditions and restraints that marine organisms experience in the ocean are different to those on land and allow for some very different ways of life. In some cases, it can even be difficult to tell animal from plant, as many animals break the accepted custom of moving from place to place and eating other organisms. Some familiar organisms even turn out to be neither plant nor animal (see *Seaweed colours*, page 31).

So, in this first chapter, we set the scene by describing the underwater environment that allows for these differences and that shapes and influences marine life, both in our shallow seas and further afield. In subsequent chapters we describe the variety and wealth of shallow-water habitats found around the British Isles and the animals and plants that live there; those that divers, snorkellers, swimmers, canoeists and coastal and shore walkers might encounter, as we have done ourselves over the years. The ocean is a truly three-dimensional environment, and a multitude of animals and plants live out their

PREVIOUS PAGES:
Evening sunshine lighting up the underwater world; sandeels swim above swaying seaweed in shallow coastal water.

OPPOSITE PAGE:
A rich variety of colourful but sedentary animals including sponges, sea anemones, hydroids, bryozoans, tubeworms and sea squirts inhabit these rocks in Plymouth Sound.

lives floating and swimming in the water above the seabed, whilst others live on and within the rock and sediment below. The use of the water above the seabed (the water column or pelagic environment) expands the living space and habitats available to marine organisms by many fold. In the terrestrial environment, in contrast, only a very few specialist birds, such as Swifts *Apus apus*, and a number of tiny insects are able to spend almost their entire lives airborne.

Animals and plants that are suspended in the water and drift with it are known as **plankton**, and this includes everything from tiny single-celled organisms to large jellyfish. Fish, mammals and other animals that swim purposefully through the water are called **nekton**. The myriad seaweeds, seagrasses and animals that live on and in the seabed are called the **benthos** and inhabit the benthic environment. Benthic organisms living on hard or soft seabeds are referred to as **epibenthic** (the **epifauna** and **epiflora**) and, logically, benthic animals such as clams and worms that live within the seabed comprise the **infauna**.

In this book we cover mainly benthos and nekton. The majority of planktonic organisms are too small to observe easily or see at all when out diving and snorkelling. However, plankton sometimes makes itself obvious in the form of wonderful phenomena such as phosphorescence and less welcome 'red tides', as well as occasional painful or beautiful encounters with jellyfish and other gelatinous plankton. We describe our experiences with these, as well as coastal mammals, birds and open-water fish, in Chapter 7.

Shallow coastal seas defined

'Shallow' in the context of this book means within normal recreational diving depths down to about 40m, an area often referred to as the shallow sublittoral (littoral = shore) or shallow subtidal, where we have both spent a considerable part of our lives. This excludes the seashore, in itself a fascinating but challenging environment, where conditions can be harsh for animals and plants living between the tides. The seashore around the British Isles is an environment that can be accessed relatively easily, and rocky shores and pools in particular are a firm favourite with visitors of all ages. A fascinating account of rocky shores around the British Isles and the marine life to be found there is given by John Archer-Thomson and Julian Cremona (2019) in a companion book in this series. They quote the much-bandied-about fact that everyone in the British Isles is within about 113km of the coast. Which means that the shallow sublittoral is within the same reach. Incidentally, this figure is derived by finding the habitation furthest from the coast, a small village called Coton in the Elms in Derbyshire.

Whilst many seashores around our islands are rich in marine life, it is in our shallow coastal waters, beyond the shore and out to the edge of the continental shelf, where the greatest biodiversity and productivity are found. The shelf borders the whole of Europe's coastline as well as the British Isles and is a gently sloping area of seabed that extends to a variable distance offshore and a depth of approximately 200m. Most other continents have a similar shelf. Beyond this, the seabed drops away relatively steeply down the continental slope, away into the depths. The continental shelf may be shallow in ocean terms, but anything below about 40–50m depth is beyond direct exploration without the use of specialist deep-diving equipment and breathing gases, submersibles or remote techniques such as drop-down cameras.

Shifting baselines

There are very few terrestrial places and habitats in the British Isles that can truly be called 'wild' and that have persisted within living memory with no, or very little, management or agriculture. Fields, hedgerows, grazing land, woodlands and freshwater lakes have all been created, modified or heavily managed and influenced by human activities, and may have been so for thousands of years. Even our wild upland moorlands are often maintained and groomed for activities such as grouse shooting. So far the same is not true of our marine habitats. With the exception of small restoration projects such as the planting of kelp (Chapter 3) and seagrasses (Chapter 6), and some reclamation or conversely re-creation of maritime land, we have not so far planted and cultivated crops on the seabed. Therefore, the underwater landscape features we see when diving or snorkelling have not resulted from human cultivation and habitation efforts, as they have on land. With the exception of marine aquaculture (for example the cultivation of mussels and farmed fish such as salmon), we are still hunter-gatherers as far as the sea is concerned. It is wonderful to think when you are snorkelling or diving, even close to a crowded holiday beach, that you could be looking at a landscape that has changed little in terms of its character or inhabitants for millennia.

The key word in that optimistic sentence is 'could'. It does not mean that the seabed and marine life around our coastline have not changed dramatically through our activities. For example, the majority of shallow sediment seabed around our shores is heavily and regularly trawled for fish, effectively ploughed up without anyone ever seeing it. Sand and gravel extraction, as well as dredging and subsequent dumping of sediments, has radically changed the types of sediment habitat over extensive areas. In general, rocky areas, where such activities are impractical, fare a bit better, but the removal of animals by fishing and spread of non-native species (Chapter 12) can have a dramatic effect on all marine communities.

So, when studying and recording marine life and assessing the condition of marine habitats, it is important to remember that the original baseline condition may have changed. An area seemingly in good condition today may actually be rather poor or at least very different when compared with what it was like in the past. The 'shifting baseline syndrome' describes the tendency for marine scientists to fail to recognise the magnitude of change from one generation to the next. Rich beds of native European Flat Oyster or Edible Oyster *Ostrea edulis*, for instance, used to carpet firm seabed areas in estuaries and along coasts throughout the British Isles. They were so common that they were considered 'food for the poor', and in Victorian times oyster pie was a staple food for the 'lower classes'. The seabed in such areas today may look (and be) healthy but the biodiversity associated with the oyster beds has been lost. The term 'shifting baseline' was first coined by fisheries scientist Daniel Pauly in 1995, and has recently been explored by a group of international scientists to help inform responses to global environmental change (Alleway *et al.* 2023).

Rooted to the spot

As mentioned in the introduction to this chapter, it can be surprisingly difficult to distinguish many marine animals from plants. A first snorkel or dive into the seas around our coastline can therefore be a rather confusing experience. Yes, you will see fish, crabs and many other mobile animals swimming and scurrying about their business amongst forests and meadows of seaweeds, but there are also lumps,

A different world

LEFT: A collection of filter-feeders: Edible Mussels *Mytilus edulis* pumping water over food-trapping gills via intake (frilly) and outflow (smooth) siphons; a Common Hermit Crab *Pagurus bernhardus* catching food particles in its mouthparts; and barnacles on the crab's shell sweeping the water with feathery limbs.

clumps, crusts and tufts that are animals masterfully masquerading as plants. These are so-called 'sessile' animals, permanently attached to rocks or anchored in sediment, at least for their adult lives. They must somehow gather food and reproduce from one fixed spot. Some, such as mussels and barnacles, are a familiar sight on rocky seashores, whilst others are far less so. How and why do they live their lives like this?

Animals on land are surrounded by a relatively sterile medium – air – and most of them move around to get their food, whether by grazing plants or pursuing other animals. By contrast, animals in the sea live in what is a relatively rich suspension of food, carried and delivered by water currents. For many of them it therefore makes energetic sense to stay in one place, or move very little, and simply eat what plankton and other drifting material they can sieve or catch from the seawater. Most of the major invertebrate animal groups or phyla (singular phylum) have members who follow this lifestyle, including molluscs, arthropods, annelid worms and the less familiar sponges, cnidarians, bryozoans and invertebrate chordates (particularly sea squirts). We introduce the basic biology of these static animal groups below, as they feature widely in the following chapters.

Sponges: filter-feeders extraordinaire

Sponges are almost exclusively filter-feeders, meaning they draw in water to extract food particles. Most people associate sponges with tropical reefs and atolls, where indeed they proliferate. However, newcomers to our waters are often surprised by their abundance and variety, with about 400 species found around the British Isles, although many are difficult to differentiate without microscopic examination of their internal structure. The most easily recognised species form specific shapes such as attractive fan-like structures, and globular masses or mounds, whilst many others encrust hard surfaces and are more difficult to identify. Some of the latter live on the armour or shells of other animals, and we explore their intriguing relationships in Chapter 11. The sponge phylum is named Porifera, which means 'pore bearer' and refers to the way the surface of a sponge is covered in tiny openings through which water is drawn in, before particles are filtered out within the body cavity and the water is expelled, usually through a few much larger openings or vents (oscula). Sponges really can be accurately described as 'animated filters', and one just a few centimetres across or tall can filter 20 litres of seawater in a day.

BELOW: A typical large sponge known as a Sea Orange *Suberites ficus*, with a few prominent water-outlet 'chimneys' (oscula) and numerous much smaller pores for water intake.

Mussel power

Another very different group of animals that pump and filter impressive volumes of water are the bivalve molluscs. They also demonstrate the amazing flexibility of the molluscan body plan. Whilst one subgroup of molluscs are the 'go-faster' brainy cephalopods (to which we devote Chapter 10), the bivalves have an apparently much less demanding existence. It would be rather unfair, however, to think of them simply as the couch potatoes of the mollusc world, because they are highly specialised and very good at what they do. Contained within their two-part shells are extensive gills that create a powerful feeding current and trap any food particles that are drawn in, as well as carrying out the normal gill function of gaseous exchange for respiration. Bivalves are often not completely sessile like sponges, but are generally immobile unless

A different world

threatened by predators. Many live buried in sand or mud and draw in their water through siphons that extend up to the seabed surface; they can be abundant and are hugely important members of soft-seabed communities (see Chapter 5).

A well-known bivalve species, the Edible or Common Mussel *Mytilus edulis*, lives anchored to firm surfaces using strong byssus threads (the 'beard' that must be removed before cooking them) planted by its own foot. It is widespread, easy to collect and has a tendency to concentrate waterborne contaminants in soft tissues (thanks to its efficient pumping and filtration), so it has long been widely used in environmental pollution monitoring programmes and related research. This led to the one-time Institute of Marine Environmental Research (IMER) in Plymouth being rather unkindly known as the 'Institute of Mytilus Edulis Research' by staff at other establishments.

Paul's undergraduate project at Liverpool University bore witness to the mussel's prodigious filtering power. A disused city dock had been turned into a mussel farm, and the mussels were so efficient at filtering out plankton and suspended silt that a beautifully clear environment for snorkelling and studying ecology was created in the heart of the murky Mersey Estuary. Paul's only regret was that he never properly saw 'Goliath', a legendary but shy cod that had entered through a narrow water-exchange gap in the dock gate and grown to such an enormous size that it could never leave. Even on a small

BELOW: Bed of Edible Mussels *Mytilus edulis* busily filter-feeding in the calm shallows of a sea loch.

scale, filtration by the mussels was impressive. Paul attempted to quantify their performance by putting a few in a laboratory aquarium with a suspension of cultured plankton and measuring the gradually decreasing turbidity of the water at intervals. Having set up the experiment, he retired to the pub and came back two hours later to take the first sample. The water was already crystal-clear, so a much larger volume of water or a more diligent approach was required!

Oysters are another notable group of bivalves that are rooted to the spot. At one time, highly productive and biologically rich reefs composed of the native European Flat Oyster covered large areas of seabed around the British Isles. The reefs and their decline – and exciting proposals for their recovery – are described in Chapter 4.

Little squirts

Sitting in one spot and filter-feeding might seem like a laid-back lifestyle, but its exponents are vulnerable to being outcompeted by others for space or suspended food, or simply being smothered by them, a major factor in the sad fate of our oysters. The most important competitors with the Mersey mussels studied by Paul, and a concern for the mussel farm operators, were sea squirts. These strange animals belong to the phylum Chordata (chordates), as do fish, birds, reptiles and us mammals. This is indicated by the presence of a rudimentary 'backbone' called a notochord in their mobile, tadpole-like larva, that supports the tail and helps the animal to swim more effectively. The notochord is present in all chordates, including ourselves, in early embryonic development. In sea squirts it disappears later when the larva settles and develops into an adult sea squirt that is truly rooted to the spot. An individual adult sea squirt is, in essence, a U-shaped tube through which water is pumped in at one end, filtered and expelled at the other end. There are many variations to this theme, including colonial species where individuals group together within a common leathery tunic (sea squirts are also called 'tunicates') and have separate water intake openings, but share a combined water outlet.

While filter-feeders typically do best where strong currents constantly renew their supply of plankton and other suspended food, sea squirts can thrive in relatively sheltered habitats within harbours, docks and sea lochs. Here, their highly efficient filtration can combine with an ability to generate a water current for themselves and help a species such as the Yellow-ringed Sea Squirt *Ciona*

A different world

LEFT: Yellow-ringed Sea Squirts *Ciona intestinalis* (here with sea anemones and brittlestars) have an obvious pair of siphons for water intake and expulsion.

intestinalis to outcompete other filter-feeders and dominate all the available surfaces. The dominance is hardly surprising when a single individual can pump up to three litres of seawater in an hour and extract particles as small as one micron across.

Stinging batteries and boxes

The sponges, bivalves and sea squirts that we have described so far all filter-feed by pumping water through a body cavity that houses apparatus for capturing suspended particles and plankton. Many other animals use an external mechanism, held out into the water to ensnare passing food. The most prominent of these are the cnidarians (phylum Cnidaria): animals such as sea anemones, corals and hydroids, which use tentacles armed with batteries of stinging cells. Many of these are colonial animals, made up of numerous interconnected individuals. Their dominance over large areas of rocky reef that are too deep or too shaded to support seaweed growth (see *Light underwater*, page 27) produces some of the most beautiful underwater vistas around the British Isles, and we describe this further in Chapter 4.

Less showy and colourful than the cnidarians are the bryozoans (phylum Bryozoa), sometimes called sea mosses, another example of marine animals being given plant-like names because their immobile

Coastal Seas

RIGHT: Life in miniature: the feeding tentacles of a single polyp of a cnidarian, the Oaten Pipes Hydroid *Tubularia indivisa*, with two amphipod crustaceans.

lifestyle belies their status as animals. The bryozoan known as Hornwrack (yet another plant-like name) *Flustra foliacea* looks just like dried seaweed when found on the strandline but, when examined closely, reveals its true nature. Its surface is a mesh made up of tiny rectangular boxes: bryozoans are colonial animals, and each tiny member of the colony (a zooid) lives in its own box, with a ring of tentacles around its mouth for catching food. Bryozoan colonies can cover large stretches of seabed, as well as encrusting surfaces such as kelp fronds, and are an important part of the benthic community.

Barnacles and others

Just as bivalves are the filter-feeding specialists within the molluscs, so too are barnacles within the crustaceans. They catch suspended food by combing the water with what looks like a little net, but are actually feathery limbs that they extend from a trap door opening at the top of their shell 'house', cemented permanently to the substratum. Approach a rock pool cautiously, or lean quietly over the side of a pontoon, and you may be able to enjoy the elegant sight of barnacles effectively sweeping food towards their mouths with their feet.

The segmented worms (annelids) and the echinoderms are yet further animal phyla that are not exclusively filter-feeders but, within their ranks, contain many that are. Filter-feeding worms typically have attractive fans of tentacles that are extended from tubes in which they reside permanently; indeed some of the tubes are cemented to the seabed. Like the gills of bivalve molluscs, the worms' tentacles do more than one job, with responsibility for both respiratory gaseous exchange and snaring food particles. Some worms, including the aptly named Sand Mason *Lanice conchilega*, display great resourcefulness by using inedible captured material, such as sediment grains, for building or maintaining their tubes. Being held out into the water column means that the tentacles of worms are also the ideal location for sense organs that can detect vibration and light. Although any eye spots are rudimentary in terms of vision, many divers are convinced that they have an uncanny knack for spotting an approaching camera, given the rapidity with which such worms can withdraw their tentacle fan when the photographer is poised to take a perfect picture. Actually, vibrations from a diver's air bubbles may also be to blame. One species of tubeworm, *Acromegalomma vesiculosum*, possesses particularly large and obvious eyespots for a sedentary worm and has been used in studies of visual development in annelids; so we think that usage of its occasional, but very suitable, common name of Sentinel Fan Worm should be encouraged.

Echinoderms (starfish, brittlestars, sea urchins, featherstars and sea cucumbers) are almost all mobile animals, though some are much faster than others. Nevertheless, some do employ filter-feeding techniques, using modified tube feet, the structures generally used to haul themselves along. Brittlestars are actually the speediest

BELOW: Common design: a sea fan (left) and featherstars (right) are very different animals but share a similar approach to catching suspended food, maximising the exposure of their particle-trapping appendages to the current.

echinoderms and can 'outrun' their predatory starfish relatives, but nevertheless some species raise their arms up to capture food particles, a dramatic sight when thousands occur together in 'beds' (see Chapter 9).

Reproduction and long-distance relationships

If you are an animal stuck in one spot, then there is another problem to overcome aside from gathering food, and that, of course, is reproduction. Unlike their mobile crab relatives, barnacles cannot go in search of a mate, but overcome this by having a famously long penis, possibly the longest in the animal kingdom relative to their size. Barnacles are hermaphrodites (an individual is both male and female) and often live close to others of their species, so may not have to reach too far, but a more typical approach involves the release of sperm or both eggs and sperm into the water. Most sponges use the former strategy, with sperm produced within one sponge being released in its out-flowing current into the seawater, from where it can enter another sponge via its in-flowing current. Fertilisation of an egg and subsequent development of a larva then typically occur within that sponge before the larva is released into the sea, where it drifts until settling and developing into a new sponge. Interestingly, while sponges are generally hermaphrodite, each individual produces eggs and sperm at different times to avoid self-fertilisation.

RIGHT: The barnacle at the bottom of this photograph cannot move, and so fertilises its neighbour's eggs using a very long penis.

A different world

LEFT: Many marine animals have rather remote relationships. This Common Starfish *Asterias rubens* has crawled up the kelp to release its cloud of spawn, which will drift away in the current and meet with that released by other starfish.

Some sea squirts reproduce in a similar way, with sperm released into the water and fertilised eggs brooded within the adult before a free-swimming larva is released. The beautiful Light-bulb Sea Squirt *Clavelina lepadiformis* has a transparent tunic (which gives rise to its common name), so the eggs of this species are easily visible within its body. Other sea squirts, such as *Ciona intestinalis* mentioned earlier, do what many marine animals do and release both eggs and sperm, with fertilisation and development taking place in open water. Animals that use this apparently haphazard process offset the risk of many eggs remaining unfertilised, or being eaten, by producing vast numbers of eggs. A mussel, for example, may release 10 million eggs during its spring breeding season. Optimising timing is also important, and responses to different prompts such as changes in water temperature, day length, phases of the moon and thus tidal flows can all help synchronisation of egg and sperm release. In his book *Moonstruck*, Professor Ernest Naylor gives a fascinating account of how lunar cycles affect life, and gives many examples of marine invertebrates that spawn during particular lunar phases (Naylor 2015).

A chaste approach

Given the difficulty of close encounters for animals that are rooted to the spot, and the waste of resources involved in what is sometimes called a 'squirt and hope' strategy, it is not surprising that many sedentary animals have evolved to reproduce without sex at all for much of the time. The majority of sponges, sea squirts, bryozoans and sessile cnidarians (corals, sea anemones and hydroids) can reproduce asexually by processes such as budding and fission, where an individual (or individual zooid in colonial species) splits to form two new ones. This can lead to a colourful tapestry of sessile animals covering rocks, as we discuss in Chapter 4.

Moving on

Whether their eggs are fertilised within their bodies or 'alfresco', most sessile and sedentary animals rely on drifting or free-swimming larvae to reach and colonise new locations. The length of time the larvae of different species remain in the water column can vary from minutes to weeks. A shorter larval life in open water represents a safer bet for the animal in terms of finding suitable habitat, but a less ambitious attempt to spread its distribution. A good example of such variation is apparent on far-out North Sea gas platforms, situated as much as 75km from the coast, that are devoid of certain barnacles found in similar situations closer inshore because their larvae cannot survive the long journey. Instead, the platforms may be well colonised by mussels, whose larvae can drift for weeks with the aid of special long threads.

A wide range of factors affect where larvae settle, and their response to different environmental cues can change during their brief existence. Many larvae swim up towards brighter light when first released, to aid dispersion, then swim down away from light at a later stage when they are ready to settle. There can be useful combinations – so if a larva tends to swim upwards, but simultaneously away from light, it may well end up underneath a rocky overhang or on the roof of a cave, both good places to avoid being crowded out by seaweed. Larval behaviour on first 'landing' can also vary, with sponge larvae, for example, crawling about to explore a surface before fixing themselves, but sea squirt tadpoles attaching the moment they touch a solid surface.

Specific cues can encourage settling in certain spots, and most larvae are more likely to attach to surfaces that have a bacterial film. The larvae of some common bryozoan species appear to be particularly discerning and prefer to settle on Serrated Wrack *Fucus serratus* than on many other species of seaweed if given the choice, presumably in response to the chemical nature of its surface. For the larvae of many animals, including barnacles, oysters and tubeworms, the presence of adults of the same species is a major incentive to settle down. Being close to others rather than living in isolation will always maximise the potential for reproduction, and is absolutely essential for barnacles because of the relatively intimate way that they fertilise one other.

It is clearly necessary to consider the longevity and behaviour of larvae when studying the distribution of any species or, importantly, assessing its ability to recover from physical damage, habitat loss or pollution in different locations.

Light underwater

Climb to the top of a mountain or hill, or even the Shard in London, and unless the cloud base is very low, or air pollution is bad, you should be able to see for many miles. The same is not the case underwater, and divers can rarely see anything in front of them beyond about 30–40m, even in tropical waters. Around the British Isles coastline, underwater visibility is generally considerably less than this, due to suspended silt or plankton blooms. As you dive down from the surface, the light fades rapidly and a torch is often necessary to see details, even when visiting sites only 5–10m below the surface. One reason for this is that the sunlight that strikes coastal water at the latitude of the British Isles (50–60°N) is never directly overhead and therefore does so at an oblique angle and is reflected back. This can be seen by peering into a rock pool on a still, windless day, when it is easy to see your reflection, but much less easy to see or photograph the pool inhabitants.

In addition, the light that does penetrate below the surface is rapidly absorbed as it passes through seawater, to a much greater degree than when passing through air. The water molecules themselves absorb light, but suspended material such as silt and plankton also reduces light penetration. This affects how deep seaweeds can grow in different areas. It also makes it more difficult for divers trying to record marine life. This became very obvious to Frances in the 1980s when trying to carry out visual diving surveys at sediment-laden sites such as the Wash, the Bristol Channel and the outer reaches of the Thames Estuary. With a visibility of only about a metre, diving these sites was rather like driving a car in a pea-souper fog. Taking photographs under such conditions is

Coastal Seas

ABOVE: On a sunny day, the visibility on land can stretch for many miles, as here at Old Harry Rocks in Dorset.

particularly challenging, and as an underwater photographer Paul is acutely aware of this. Particles in the water not only reduce the amount of light from flashguns or video lights reaching the subject, but they reflect it back at the camera lens. Without careful positioning and angling of lights, photographs from even what seems like reasonably clear water can look as though they were taken in a snowstorm. Nevertheless, underwater visibility in many places around the British Isles, especially those facing the Atlantic, can be very good. In St Kilda, the most far-flung island group in the British Isles, over 60km west of the Outer Hebrides and a place rarely visited by divers, the clear waters allow seaweeds to flourish down to 50m depth, whereas around most of our coastline, 15–20m would be the more normal limit.

However, it is not only the quantity of light that is restricted underwater, but also the quality. Sunlight consists of different wavelengths of light, perceived by us as different colours. This is clearly demonstrated in a rainbow, because raindrops act as prisms, splitting sunlight into its constituent spectrum of colours. Red light has the longest wavelength of visible light and sits at one end of this spectrum. Blue light has a short wavelength and sits near the other end. Long-wavelength light is the first to be absorbed by water,

A different world

ABOVE: Even in clear water, visibility is much reduced compared to that on land. This diver appears indistinct in the gloom, although he is only a few metres away. The colours of the marine life in the foreground are only revealed thanks to the photographer's lights.

and consequently red light does not penetrate much below about 10m, whilst blue and green penetrate the deepest. For a diver or snorkeller descending into the depths, colours start to disappear rapidly and everything begins to take on a rather monochrome blue or green hue. This was well demonstrated to Frances when taking close-up photographs on a coral reef in the Maldives, whilst running a marine biology course. She inadvertently strayed over the entrance to a moray eel's home and the owner promptly emerged, bit her thumb hard and instantly disappeared back again. The consequent trail of blood appeared in a particularly fetching royal blue-grey colour, and instead of the blood splashing to the floor under gravity, water currents carried it upwards, spreading out as it went. That was the end of that dive, presumably much to the moray's satisfaction.

It is also interesting to see how the human brain interprets information from the eyes and tries to compensate for the way water absorbs light of different colours. The white light of an underwater torch appears distinctly pink at depth, for example, and Paul knows only too well how what look like well-balanced neutrally coloured images on his camera screen during a dive, still have a very greenish hue requiring correction on his computer once back on land.

Coastal Seas

ABOVE: Bright sunlight in shallow water enables forests of seaweed to thrive.

BELOW: Here, at a depth of over 30m, there is insufficient light for seaweed growth and the scenery is dominated by sea fans, soft corals and other sessile animals. The inquisitive fish is a female Cuckoo Wrasse *Labrus mixtus*.

Depth and zonation

Seaweeds and seagrasses are photosynthetic organisms and as such depend on sunlight for their survival. Like terrestrial plants, some species have higher light requirements than others. Therefore, as the quantity and quality of light decrease with depth, so too do the abundance and biodiversity of seaweeds. Along rocky coastlines in many parts of the British Isles, this often leads to an easily discernible vertical zonation of seaweeds in the shallow sublittoral. This is most clearly visible along areas of rocky coastline with stable bedrock sloping away below the low water mark and where wave action is moderate. Here, conditions allow the growth of perennial kelp forests (see Chapter 3), typically dominated by Forest Kelp *Laminaria hyperborea*.

These large seaweeds can easily reach 0.5–1m tall and have a high light requirement, so they are limited to about 10–15m depth around most of the British Isles. In exceptionally clear waters, such as those around remote offshore islands along the west coast of Scotland, the forest may extend to around twice this depth, provided a suitable bedrock substratum continues. In areas where the water is habitually turbid, such as the upper reaches of the Bristol Channel, there is little or no kelp even in potentially suitable bedrock areas.

A different world

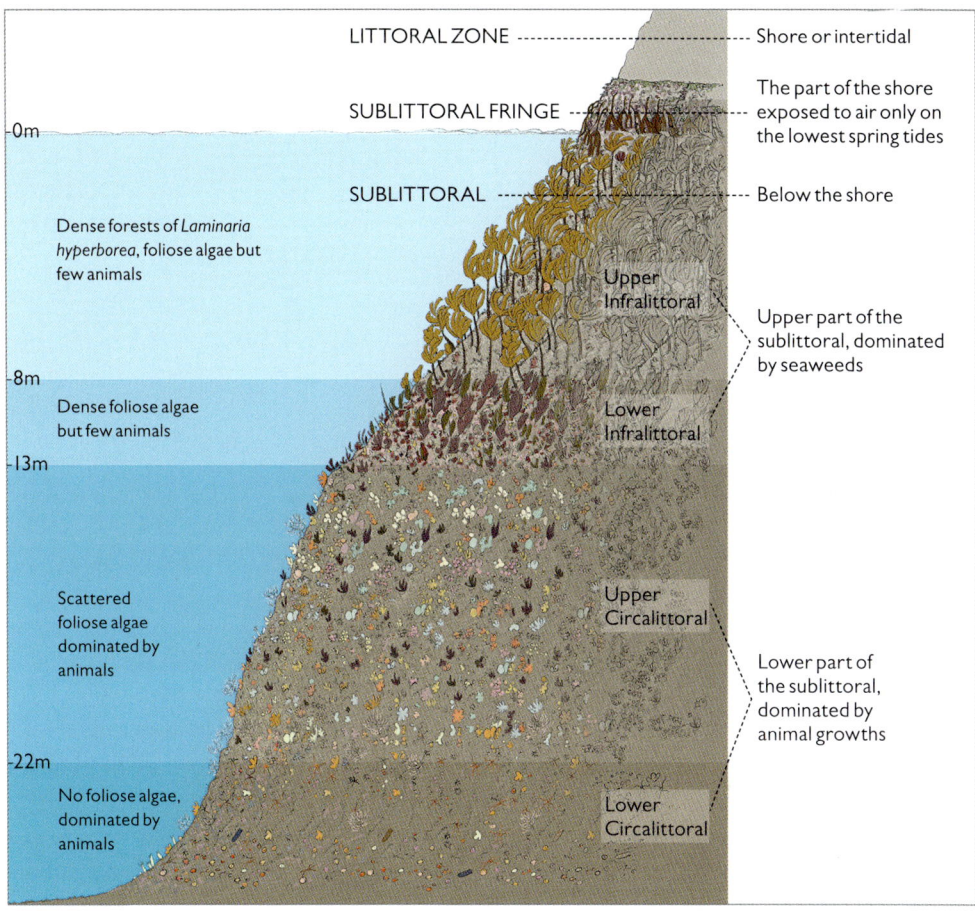

ABOVE: A typical zonation of seaweeds and animals resulting from the decreasing light gradient with depth, off a moderately exposed rocky coastline. From Dipper (2016).

As the kelp forest peters out with depth and there is little or no shading from the kelp canopy, smaller foliose seaweeds come into their own and can form a dense 'turf'. Eventually, however, there is too little light for photosynthesis, seaweeds decline, and sessile animal growths such as bryozoans and hydroids predominate.

Seaweed colours

When the Ford Motor Company first started car production, customers could only choose between a limited range of colours, and from 1908 to 1914 the Model T Ford famously came only in black. With seaweeds, the colour choice is slightly greater, but still limited to various shades of three colours: green, brown and red. Looking at terrestrial plants, we are used to seeing predominantly green foliage, because the photosynthetic pigment of plants is chlorophyll and

Coastal Seas

ABOVE: Seaweeds thrive in shallow, sunlit water. Representatives of all three groups of seaweeds, browns, greens and reds, are present in this unusually deep rock pool on Little Colonsay, a small Hebridean island near Mull.

chlorophyll is green. Seagrasses and green seaweeds are green for the same reason. Red and brown seaweeds also use chlorophyll for photosynthesis, but the green is masked by additional photosynthetic pigments. These help the seaweeds to utilise the restricted wavelengths of light available well below the water surface. In general, red seaweeds can live at greater depths than green or brown, but whilst they may be more efficient at using deeper-penetrating, short wavelengths of light, they are basically able to tolerate lower light conditions than browns or greens; in other words, they are shade-tolerant. This must be one reason why they are the most numerous of the three groups. There are more than 350 red seaweeds around the British Isles, compared to around 180 browns and 110 greens. Red seaweeds also have the longest fossil record, with one Canadian species dating back 1.2 billion years. Modern taxonomic techniques have thrown up the interesting fact that whilst seagrasses, green seaweeds and red seaweeds are all included within the plant kingdom (Plantae), brown seaweeds are classified as chromists (Chromista), a separate kingdom that also includes many planktonic microalgae, such as diatoms and dinoflagellates.

An excellent account of the natural history of seaweeds around the coastline of Britain and Ireland is given in the book *Rocky Shores* (Archer-Thomson and Cremona 2019).

Water currents

Water throughout the world's oceans is constantly moved from place to place by major currents, some of which circulate throughout entire oceans. The British Isles benefit from the warmth of the Gulf Stream, a slow current that flows across the North Atlantic from subtropical areas near the Gulf of Mexico, reaching as far as the English Channel. Without this current, the waters around the British Isles would be considerably colder and London would experience similar winter temperatures to Moscow, which is on a comparable latitude. In some years fingers of warm water extend right up to the west coast of Scotland, bringing unusual plankton with it. In one memorable dive off Lewis in the Outer Hebrides in the 1970s, Frances remembers surfacing from a dive through a swarm of palm-sized salps (Thaliacea) of a type normally found much further south, their transparent, rubbery bodies bouncing away with every fin kick. Salps are planktonic relatives of the more familiar sessile sea squirts.

In addition to such major, wind-driven ocean currents, local tidal currents occur along coastlines, created by horizontal movements of water as the tide rises and falls. In the shallow waters around the complex coastline of the British Isles, such currents can be very strong. The Severn Estuary has the second-largest tidal range (the difference in height between high and low tides) in the world at around 12m. All that water has to flow in and out of the estuary in only a few hours, creating strong currents. Such water movements can also be particularly strong where incoming or outgoing water is channelled through narrow gaps, swirls around headlands or is deflected by underwater rocky reefs and pinnacles.

Tidal currents along stretches of open coastline, with no restrictions to water flow, are considerably weaker. Why is this important? Tidal currents play a major role in determining the abundance and biodiversity of marine benthic communities. Calm seas and no currents may provide ideal conditions for easy diving and snorkelling, but do not make easy living for marine life. As we describe on page 16 (*Rooted to the spot*), anemones, hydroids, sponges and other sessile filter-feeding animals rely on local water currents and waves to bring them food in the form of plankton and drifting organic matter. They also rely on currents to disperse their eggs and larvae in much the same way that many terrestrial plants rely on wind currents to spread pollen and seeds. Moderately strong tidal currents are also beneficial to seaweeds and seagrasses, which never lack for water, but need essential nutrients, carried to them by water movements. Therefore, as long as the tidal flow is not so strong that it scours rock surfaces or dislodges sediment, then areas of strong tidal movement will often be rich in benthic, sessile animals.

Currents could be described as subject to the 'Goldilocks effect', where something is in just the right place or condition. In his exploration of Britain's seabed habitats, veteran diver and marine biologist Keith Hiscock describes currents up to about 3 knots as the most beneficial, whilst at 3–6 knots fewer species can thrive. Extremes of over 6 knots only allow a few specialist species to survive, ones that can retract or hide during the strongest flow times (Hiscock 2018). The same sort of thing could be said of divers, though the 'just right' bit is at much lower current speeds. A current of even 1 knot is tiring to swim against, but by keeping close to the seabed and hiding behind boulders and rock outcrops it is possible to minimise drift, take photos and make records.

Tidal rapids

Strong currents can be hazardous for divers, snorkellers and swimmers, but the abundant marine life associated with such areas can also be a draw. Tidal rapids and races are areas of particularly strong current flow, found where water is channelled through narrow passages. There are numerous examples found around the British Isles, running between adjacent islands or between mainland and island. Many Scottish sea lochs have narrow entrances and often submerged sills that channel and obstruct water flow, resulting in tidal rapids. With careful planning many such tide-swept areas can be dived at slack water, which is the time when the current is minimal, usually (but not always) when the tide is turning. If the current is not too extreme, a drift with the current, carrying a surface marker buoy, can work well as long as the cover boat remains attentive or the flow ends at a planned safe exit spot.

Depending on the strength of the current, depth and geology, rock surfaces in tidal rapids can be covered by spectacular and colourful growths of soft corals, anemones, sponges, hydroids, tubeworms and mussels, especially on steep rock surfaces. In many cases, whilst rock lines the edges of a channel, flatter areas in the middle are

ABOVE: Abundant and varied animal life in the tide-swept narrows of a sea loch includes sea anemones, soft corals, tubeworms and brittlestars.

floored with clean sediment. Provided it is not too deep and there is sufficient light, the nutrient- and oxygen-laden currents encourage the growth of maerl beds, growths of free-living, calcareous red seaweeds (Corallinaceae) that look more like knobbly twigs of coral than seaweed. Diving or snorkelling over a well-developed maerl bed is always a joy, and we explore these further in Chapter 5.

Fierce currents also encourage the growth of luxuriant seaweeds along the shallow rocky edges of tidal rapids. Seaweeds do not have roots, but cling to rock with a strong attachment called, appropriately enough, a holdfast. This produces a tough glue-like chemical to help attachment. However, seaweeds with broad fronds (a frond is roughly equivalent to a leaf) risk being torn away as they present considerable resistance to flowing water. So it is mostly species with finely divided fronds that thrive here. Large brown kelp seaweeds (Chapter 3) have finger-like divisions to their fronds and slippery surfaces to lessen water resistance. Those growing in rapids (and wave-exposed areas) have much finer divisions, whilst those growing in the still waters of sheltered sea lochs have hardly any. This same technique is used by many river plants such as water crowfoots *Ranunculus* spp., which have finely divided submerged leaves, but can at times (often when flowering) produce intact floating leaves with a greater photosynthetic surface area.

Regional tidal rapids

There are a number of tidal rapids and races that we have visited (though not always dived) around the British Isles over the years and that have stuck in our memories for one reason or another. Some are relatively mild and shallow, such as the narrow entrance to landlocked Lough Hyne in Ireland (see *Red-mouthed Goby* box in Chapter 8 for our description of diving here), but others are extreme and only for very experienced divers or snorkellers. However, some of the latter, such as the Gulf of Corryvreckan, are worth a visit just to stand on the shore and experience their power and beauty. Large tidal races can be very hazardous for yachts and small boats, especially when there is a strong wind blowing in the opposite direction to the tidal current. This can create large, steep and unpredictable waves, another reason why such areas are difficult to dive and survey, and why many are littered with shipwrecks. However, wrecks such as the MV *Lucy*, which sank in 1967 in Jack Sound, between the island of Skomer and mainland Wales, are a draw for divers and diving naturalists, as they make excellent artificial reefs (Chapter 4).

Gulf of Corryvreckan

This notorious, deep (up to 200m) Hebridean tidal sound runs for just over 3km between the north end of Jura and the island of Scarba. The strongest currents run in excess of 12 knots. Its infamous swirling whirlpools towards the western end are created by a complex hydrodynamic flow through the sound and around obstructions including 'the Pinnacle'. This rocky obstruction, better described as a wall, rises up from the seabed and its top (30m down) has only ever been dived by a few very experienced divers. A fascinating account of one such visit is given by intrepid underwater explorer Rod Macdonald in chapter 7 of his 2011 book *The Darkness Below*. He describes the top of the rock as scarred and pitted by potholes, refuges for the few crabs able to make a living there, amongst a low cover of small anemones, sponges and soft corals. Whilst neither of us has dived there, some of our marine biologist colleagues have, but along the edges, well away from the whirlpool areas.

Falls of Lora

Most people, ourselves included, admire the turbulent tidal waters that flow in and out of Loch Etive, Scotland, by driving over the Connel Bridge on the way to and from Oban. However, experienced

A different world

divers can enjoy an exhilarating drift dive here. On spring tides, current speeds can reach 6 knots and sometimes considerably more, so careful timing and planning is needed. The reward is the sight of dense growths of tough filter-feeders that can tolerate very strong currents, including Breadcrumb Sponge *Halichondria panicea*, large barnacles *Balanus crenatus* and the tough wiry Oaten Pipes Hydroid *Tubularia indivisa*.

Menai Strait

This narrow body of water between the Isle of Anglesey and mainland Wales is famous for its rich marine life. Visibility can be poor, but when the water is clear a wonderland of enormous sponges, lush bryozoan 'turf', groups of beautifully coloured Dahlia Anemones *Urticina felina* and numerous marauding crabs is revealed. The timing of dives here is not straightforward, because slack water does not correspond with high water as it does in many tide-swept locations. Paul once got a painful reminder of the importance of location-specific planning when he kitted up in what he thought was good time before high water at Menai and waited for the current to ease. Instead, he watched in frustration as the current strengthened dramatically and diving had to be abandoned, a lesson learned!

BELOW: The Menai Strait between Anglesey and mainland Wales supports rich benthic animal communities, well studied by the nearby Bangor University School of Ocean Sciences.

INSET: Strong tidal currents in the Menai Strait buffet these Peacock Worms *Sabella pavonina* and a Dahlia Anemone *Urticina felina* but also bring them plentiful supplies of suspended food.

Loch Sween

Loch Sween is a 16km-long sea loch on the eastern side of the Sound of Jura in southwest Scotland, designated as a Marine Protected Area or MPA (see Chapter 12) in 2014. Linne Mhuirich and Caol Scotnish, two arms branching off the western side and running parallel to the main basin, both have narrow entrances and channels that restrict tidal flow. This results in interesting rapids areas. Diving in Caol Scotnish in 1985 as part of a Nature Conservancy Council (NCC) survey team, Frances was delighted to find herself drifting over a seabed consisting almost entirely of a beautiful bed of ball- and twig-like growths of Northern Maerl *Lithothamnion glaciale*. Maerl thrives in clear water with moderate tidal flows. Maerl beds are also present in Linne Mhuirich, but consisting of the more widespread and common Celtic Maerl *Phymatolithon calcareum*.

Severn Estuary

Near the top of the extensive Severn Estuary, between England's southwest peninsula and Wales, fast incoming spring tides are constricted so much where the estuary narrows and shelves upwards into the River Severn, that a dramatic wave of water can be created. When it occurs, this 'tidal bore' attracts hundreds of board-surfers to ride it for as far as several miles up the river. The wider Severn Estuary's silt-laden waters offer virtually no visibility for divers or snorkellers, but support productive feeding grounds of international importance for wading birds and an unusually rich assemblage of fish species. The latter includes those that migrate up the River Severn and its tributaries to spawn, such as Atlantic Salmon *Salmo salar*, Sea Trout *Salmo trutta*, River Lamprey *Lampetra fluviatilis* and rare Twaite Shad *Alosa fallax*.

Waves

It is a rare day when a visit to almost anywhere along the British Isles coastline shows a glassy calm sea with no waves at all. Indeed, our entire coastline has been and continues to be shaped by the pounding and erosive action of waves. Norfolk and Suffolk are often in the news as more and more homes tip over soft, eroding cliffs and are lost. Communities of marine plants and animals on shores also bear the brunt of the waves, and wave exposure has a major controlling effect on just what can live and grow there.

Beyond the seashore in shallow water, the waves may still be violent enough to prevent much animal or seaweed growth, but a relatively short distance down, the movement is reduced sufficiently for even delicate sessile animals to flourish. There is negligible wave movement below a depth that is half the surface wavelength (the distance between successive wave crests). We both know this well, because provided divers can be dropped in and found and picked up safely (which is often a big if), they can descend to the seabed below this depth in fairly rough weather and experience a perfectly peaceful dive. Meanwhile those in the surface cover boat will not be having such a good time and will be worrying about getting the divers back on the boat and returning to safe and calm waters.

With the notable exception of tsunamis, waves result from the effects of wind blowing across the water surface and setting it in orbital motion. The size of the waves (before they hit the shore) depends largely on the strength of the wind, how long it continues to blow, and the fetch, which is the uninterrupted distance of ocean over which the wind can act. With our prevailing winds being west to southwesterly, it is unsurprising that Atlantic-facing coasts of the British Isles, such as those off Shetland and Orkney in Scotland and the southwest peninsula in England, experience the most wave-lashed conditions.

Waves bring with them both oxygen and food for sessile animals and seaweeds, but too much of a good thing means that surging and breaking waves limit what can live and grow on shallow, wave-exposed

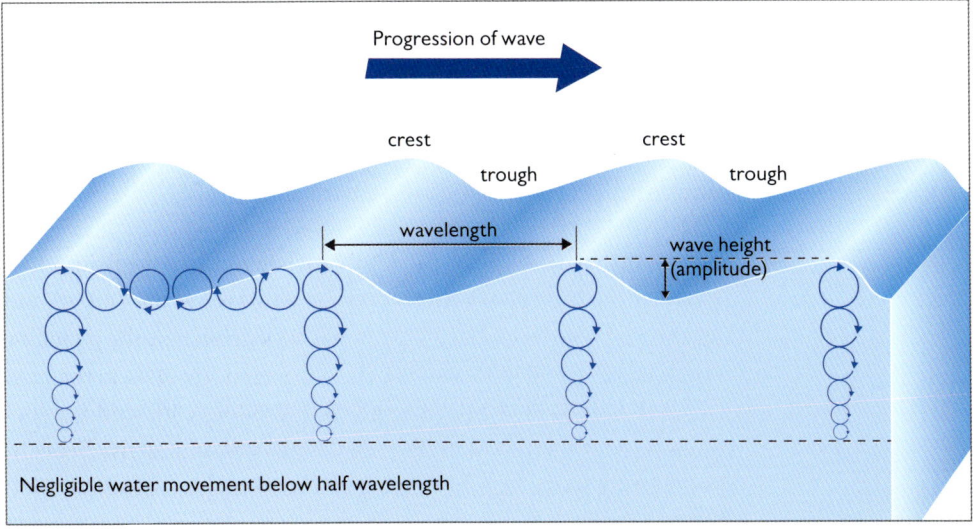

BELOW: Diagrammatic representation of water movement within and between waves, showing decrease of water movement with depth (not fully to scale). From Dipper (2016).

rocks and in regularly churned-up sediment. On rock, low-growing, tough species such as Jewel Anemones *Corynactis viridis* (Chapter 4), encrusting sponges, encrusting sea squirts and sublittoral barnacles such as *Balanus crenatus* can thrive. Dabberlocks *Alaria esculenta*, a kelp with a single long, strong stipe (stem) and frond, thrives in wave-exposed conditions in shallow water. In calm summer weather it can be difficult to estimate how wave-exposed a dive site is, but a forest of *Alaria* suggests that a return visit in winter might be difficult.

Wave surge

In exposed areas, such as are found along Atlantic-facing coastlines particularly in Scotland and Ireland, waves surging along and around steep bedrock cliffs, through steep-sided rocky gulleys and into and out of submerged caves can mimic the beneficial effects of tidal currents by carrying abundant food with them. Some species do particularly well in wave-surge areas, protected from the most destructive wave action, and can regularly be found in such situations. One such is the White Lace Sponge *Clathrina coriacea*, which often grows on the vertical sides of surge gullies and in the backs of caves in association with dense sheets of a small, red sea squirt, *Dendrodoa grossularia*. This defines a biotope recognised as '*Dendrodoa grossularia* and *Clathrina coriacea* on wave-surged vertical infralittoral rock' in the Joint Nature Conservation Committee (JNCC) Marine Habitat Classification for Britain and Ireland. Used in this sense, a biotope is a well-defined area with specific ecological conditions that support the organisms living there. Frances first came across this stunningly colourful association in the late 1970s when diving surge gullies off an exposed headland at Griminish, North Uist, with an NCC team. After a wave-jostled, hard-work dive the team were invited back to Callernish House by the then laird and owner of North Uist, the fifth Earl Granville, to get warm and dry before further warmth from large Scottish whiskies. This association (the sponge, not the whisky) has also been recorded from other sites in northwest Scotland including Shetland and Orkney, as well as the Isle of Man, Anglesey and England's southwest peninsula.

A community that survives rather than thrives in wave-scoured areas is an ephemeral, seasonal collection of seaweeds living attached to pebbles and cobbles covering a predominantly sediment seabed. Winter storms toss and turn over the rocks, and the seaweeds are

A different world

ABOVE: White Lace Sponge *Clathrina coriacea* and Baked-bean Sea Squirt *Dendrodoa grossularia* form a distinctive community on the walls of shallow surge gullies and caves, here seen in Kinlochbervie, Scotland.

therefore mainly annuals, or perennials that die back to a persistent remnant. Visiting such a site in summer reveals dense growths of tough, straggly brown seaweeds, especially the perennial Desmarest's Prickly Weed *Desmarestia aculeata*, also colourfully known as Landlady's Wig. The annual seaweed Desmarest's Flattened Weed *D. ligulata* also grows well in this habitat, and both are found throughout the British Isles. The latter has flattened, much-branched fronds and makes an excellent seaweed pressing. Exquisite translucent red Scinà's weeds *Scinaia* spp. grow almost exclusively on cobbles, pebbles and shells, whereas *Desmarestia* species also live on bedrock and boulders.

Supported by salt

Staring down at the enormous (and very smelly) remains of a dead baleen whale stranded on a beach in the Outer Hebrides in 1978 left Frances wondering how such a gigantic animal could swim so easily and hang around so effortlessly out at sea – and also, of course, why it stranded in the first place. She never did find the answer to the second question, but the first is more easily explained.

Seawater provides support, as anyone who has visited the Dead Sea (actually a lake) and tried floating in it will well know. It is virtually impossible to sink in its salt-laden waters, which contain around 340g of salt per kilogram of water. Most seawater contains far less than this (an average of about 35g per kilogram), but it is still sufficiently dense to support the bulk of a Blue Whale *Balaenoptera musculus* – very occasionally seen off the British Isles. Any stranded whale, let alone a Blue Whale, may easily die of asphyxiation because on land its huge weight compresses and can even break its ribcage and body organs. As far as is known, no animal this large has ever lived on land, though some dinosaurs reached impressive sizes. Minke Whales *B. acutorostrata* are regularly recorded off the west coast of Scotland and in the North Sea, and Fin Whales *B. physalus*, Humpbacks *Megaptera novaeangliae* and Sperm Whales *Physeter macrocephalus* all make occasional appearances.

At the other end of the size scale, our shallow seas teem with minute plant and animal plankton, again supported by the water. The microscopic scale of these organisms means that to them seawater appears a much more viscous medium than it does to us. They can float and drift without having to spend much energy to keep themselves from sinking.

Immense shoals of fish such as Cod *Gadus morhua*, Herring *Clupea harengus* and Sardine *Sardina pilchardus* live and swim permanently in mid-water around our shores, rarely if ever coming into contact with the seabed. The water provides support, especially since most open-water fishes have a gas-filled swim bladder within their bodies to help them stay neutrally buoyant. In saltwater fishes this generally takes up less space than in freshwater fishes, due to the extra support provided by the greater density of seawater.

Hard and soft living

The geology of the British Isles is complex, and in the terrestrial environment plays a significant role in determining soil type and therefore what the vegetation will be like or what a farmer can grow. The biodiverse grass and flower community that is found only in chalk areas such as the South Downs shows this to good effect. In shallow coastal waters, the underlying geology is also important, but in a different way and primarily in terms of whether the seabed is rock or sediment. If rock, then the importance lies mostly in how hard it is and how stable, rather than the actual rock type. If it is sediment, then the grade of sediment, from fine mud to coarse sand, is the main factor that determines what can live in it.

We have snorkelled, dived, swum or sailed in various far-flung parts of Britain and Ireland and never cease to be amazed at the complexity of different shallow-water habitats available. A dive might start near the shore, sloping down over a broken bedrock platform, then over a steep bedrock or boulder slope, and out gradually or abruptly into a sediment plain. Or rock may continue and predominate way below diving depths. Swimming out through a sandy bay, seaweed-covered rock might appear out of the gloom, or the sediment may continue way out to sea. This great variety of available habitats and microhabitats, often within a small area, is one of the underlying reasons for the rich biodiversity found in our shallow seas.

There are, however, significant differences in the proportions of hard and soft substrata that predominate in the shallow sublittoral around the British Isles. Frances has lived most of her life in land-locked Cambridgeshire, and her nearest coastline is East Anglia. From Lincolnshire south through Norfolk, Suffolk and Essex there is a distinct lack of rocky substrata, with just a few notable exceptions such as the chalk reef off Norfolk (see *Regional reefs*, Chapter 4). In contrast, the rocky coastline of Devon is Paul's stamping ground. Most of the southwest peninsula of England, the Welsh coastline and the west coasts of Scotland and Ireland have an abundance of rocky sublittoral areas. Sediments floor the large and well-known bays and estuaries found all around the British Isles, many of which are vitally important feeding grounds for overwintering populations of waterfowl and wading birds. The numerous long and complex lochs of Scotland and loughs of Ireland are fascinating for their combination of steep sublittoral rocky edges and soft sediment floors.

Rock

Epibenthic animals and seaweeds living on hard seabeds sport a plethora of different ways by which they can attach themselves firmly to rock surfaces, from the sticky byssus threads of mussels to the suction power of a limpet's foot and the complex holdfasts of seaweeds. So, provided other factors such as food supply are favourable, horizontal and vertical rock surfaces alike provide good living space for sessile animals and seaweeds. In contrast, in the terrestrial environment, steep cliff faces and crags – at the coast or inland – lack soil and are mostly devoid of plant growth and therefore of any associated animals.

Coastal Seas

Very hard rock such as granite is less easily eroded by wave action, or by the blasting effect of water currents laden with sand grains and the erosive activities of marine organisms. It will therefore have fewer holes, cracks, crevices and overhangs than softer rock. The more irregularities in the rock surface, the more easily seaweeds and sessile animals can grip on and the greater the variety of microhabitats available for small fish, crustaceans and other mobile animals to call home.

Boring animals

A seabed of soft chalk, such as that found off the north Norfolk and Dorset coastlines, does not provide a very stable platform for attachment of large seaweeds and long-lived colonies of animals like sea fans and large sponges. Chalk and limestone are easily eroded and broken by storms and strong currents. However, along with consolidated mudrock and sandstone, chalk is one of the rock types soft enough for boring animals such as piddocks (Pholadidae) to live in it. These bivalve molluscs bore into the rock, using the serrated ends of their shell valves to grind the rock away. They start this process when young, enlarging the burrow as they grow and becoming permanently entombed in the process. However, they can still extend their tube-like siphons beyond the burrow to draw water in and out for feeding and breathing.

BELOW: Areas of soft mudstone rock at Pett Level in Sussex are riddled with piddock holes. These weaken the rock, which breaks off more easily, adding to the erosion along this coastline. Empty holes provide refuges for other small invertebrates.

Some specialist worms such as *Polydora ciliata*, sponges and even a few red algae also bore into rock using chemical means, but only into calcareous rock and similar material such as empty mollusc shells. In spite of its name, the Boring Sponge *Cliona celata* is a fascinating animal. When divers come across yellow hillocks of this sponge underwater, they may be seeing only a small part of it. Rather like a toadstool, much of its mass can be hidden within the rock it is sitting on. The way some forms of the sponge bore into limestone is reminiscent of a

> **Piddock pranks**
>
> The Romans enjoyed their seafood. Middens of old oyster, limpet and whelk shells are often found during archaeological excavations of the remains of Roman habitation, particularly near to coasts. At some sites near Lyme Regis in Dorset, the remains of piddock shells have also been found. Apparently the Romans relished eating them, though it must have been hard work excavating and shelling them. They also appreciated the fact that the Common Piddock *Pholas dactylus*, widespread on the shore and in the shallow sublittoral around the British Isles, glows in the dark. Piddocks exhibit bioluminescence, that eyrie greenish light produced by a wide variety of mainly deep-sea organisms (see *Lighting up the sea*, Chapter 7). The Romans apparently entertained themselves by splattering each other with (presumably pre-masticated) piddock juice during late-night feasts, something commented on by the philosopher Pliny the Elder. Whilst neither of us has ever tried this, Frances recalls attaining a similar fun effect in her misspent youth by dispensing the contents of a 'glow stick' over a colleague's diving equipment prior to a night dive (do not try this at home).
>
> On a more serious note, the protein pholasin, responsible for bioluminescence in piddocks, can be used for the diagnosis of various diseases and conditions because reactive compounds of oxygen in white blood cells activate pholasin so that it glows.

mining operation in miniature, with special cells undercutting, surrounding and breaking away tiny chips of rock with an acid by-product of respiration. These rock fragments are then transported to the surface of the sponge and 'spat out' by its water current.

Sediment

The shifting surface of underwater sediments makes them a difficult place for sessile epibenthic animals and seaweeds to live and grow. Many of those that manage to thrive in this environment are attached to stones and shells lying on the surface or buried beneath it. In shallow water, stones can be picked up and moved by wave and current action, and it is not unusual to find long strands of seaweeds, such as the bootlace-shaped Mermaid's Tresses *Chorda filum*, cast ashore still attached to pebbles or cobbles. Some seaweeds benefit from this as a means of vegetative dispersal.

Coastal Seas

ABOVE AND BELOW: Two different forms of the Boring Sponge *Cliona celata*: a prominent yellow mass and much less conspicuous stud-like projections, with most of the sponge hidden within the rock, on which a Black Goby *Gobius niger* is resting.

By far the most numerous and biodiverse sediment dwellers are infauna that live a permanently buried existence. The majority of these are 'worms' belonging to various phyla, plus bivalve molluscs, and both groups are well adapted to a sedentary lifestyle. However, there are also mobile animals, including sea urchins, crabs and sea snails, that burrow and tunnel through sediment in search of prey, rather like moles on land. Our encounters with many of these are described in Chapter 5, which covers life in sand and mud.

Seasons in the sea

Around the British Isles the seasons on land provide an ever-changing landscape, a kaleidoscope of different colours, wildlife spectacles, varied animal behaviour and arrivals and departures. The BBC television series of *Spring-*, *Autumn-* and *Winterwatch* brings it all to the fore. The programme occasionally touches on what is going on in the seas around our coasts, but the colder water and more frequent storms in winter mean that many divers and snorkellers only ever venture into the sea during the warmer summer and autumn months. So it can come as a great surprise when a winter visit to a familiar site shows a substantially different scene to summer.

Yes, there are seasons in the sea, including a wonderful renewed burst of life in the spring and early summer. Many seaweeds are annuals or die back and overwinter in a reduced form. Forest Kelp *Laminaria hyperborea*, our nearest marine equivalent to trees, forms dense perennial forests (described in detail in Chapter 3) and drops its leaf-equivalent fronds annually. These either break off in winter storms, having become laden with epiphytic growths of bryozoans by the end of the summer, or are finally pushed off by the growth of a new frond from below, around March or April.

As winter approaches and planktonic food becomes scarce, colonial animals such as the soft coral Dead Man's Fingers *Alcyonium digitatum* withdraw their attractive feeding tentacles and hunker down as unappealing blobs. Their appearance can therefore be dramatically different according to season. In the spring and summer, hungrily extended translucent feeding tentacles give the fingers a fetchingly 'furry' appearance, but the colonies fall dormant in the autumn and winter. The fingers then look rather bare and unattractive, especially if they are discoloured with algae, and can certainly evoke thoughts of a deceased person's digits, particularly when washed up on the shore.

The Football Sea Squirt *Diazona violacea* and many others do the same, whilst feathery hydroids can become mere bare stalks.

Whilst different species respond to different cues, the most obvious seasonal controlling factors are water temperature, light and food availability, just as they are on land, but because water has a much higher capacity to hold on to heat than air does, the overall sea temperature lags well behind air temperature. In the British Isles the sea is generally coldest around March time and warmest in September. For human sea swimmers this means that, while they receive more plaudits for their Christmas Day dips, they actually have to be hardier to venture into the sea at Easter. More importantly, it means that much of the springtime burst of activity shown by seaweeds and other algae and by animals in our seas is occurring when the water is at or close to its coldest. For many seaweed species, this is because an increase in day length and light intensity, rather than temperature, is the important factor in getting them growing.

A beautiful example of early growth is Thong Weed, *Himanthalia elongata*. In January, it can be seen as a neat, button-like structure before starting to sprout its long, strap-like frond from the centre of the button (see photos on page 95). The frond, which is the reproductive part of the seaweed, grows, branches rapidly into two, and can reach 20cm in length in February, 60cm to 1m by March, and up to 2m by the late spring and summer. Rich, yellow-green Thong Weed 'forests' are thus formed on shallow rocky reefs in many areas around our coasts, and they can even be too dense to swim through, particularly around low tide. When late-summer and autumn storms take their toll, huge tangled masses of Thong Weed straps pile up on local beaches and the reefs become relatively bare.

Many animal species also start to increase their growth and activity early in the year, again when the water is still cold. This applies to sedentary filter-feeders such as soft corals, sea anemones and hydroids as well as mobile animals such as fish. For the filter-feeders it means they are 'up and running' to take maximum advantage of the spring plankton bloom that typically occurs in April and May. In fish such as the Tompot Blenny *Parablennius gattorugine*, a start to egg-laying in March helps to ensure a long breeding season. For benthic animals that release eggs or larvae into the water column, early egg production and hatching maximises the time the larvae have to feed and develop in plankton-rich water

A different world

LEFT: Dead Man's Fingers *Alcyonium digitatum* in July with most, but not all, colonies actively feeding (top), as seen in close-up (centre); and in October, when many more are withdrawn (bottom).

before finding a safe place to start their adult life. By the height of summer, much animal breeding activity has been successfully completed, in time for the resulting youngsters to sit out the autumn and winter storms.

Prolific seaweed growth in spring and summer means that sunlit rocky areas become a seaweed-searcher's paradise, especially beyond the shade cast by kelp forests. Up in the water column there may be significant numbers of jellyfish near the coast. Fish are very active and it is a good time to watch them feeding in shallow water among that tall seaweed. Also, by very late summer, keen eyes can spot the tiny juveniles of fish such as blennies, gobies and wrasses starting to gather around rocky reefs, along with juvenile flatfish settling onto sandy areas, having developed from their larvae in open water.

Obvious animal activity generally reduces in the autumn, despite there often being a further (smaller) plankton bloom. Autumn and winter storms churn up the sea and, in combination with muddy run-off from heavy rain, can reduce underwater visibility near the coast to almost zero, even in places with generally clear water. Occasionally, however, a spell of high pressure and calm weather in the depths of winter can produce wonderful water clarity because of the lack of plankton. It is then rather an eerie experience to snorkel or dive in an area which is familiar from summer exploration. The reefs are bare of tall seaweed and the swirling, swooping fish are mostly absent, having either moved offshore or hidden away in sheltered holes and crevices.

Our sea life's seasonal changes also affect us when we watch and record it. For an underwater photographer such as Paul, keen to film and document animal behaviour, the early spring is often the most important time of year. The water is cool but long dives are needed to capture all the activity that is going on, so a warm drysuit is essential. Frustratingly, plankton blooms can be another challenge in the spring because they are often densest when there is most to see. Many of Paul's potentially best images of courting and egg-laying cuttlefish, for example, are swamped by telltale green 'blobs' of blooming (in both senses) phytoplankton.

A different world

It is hardly surprising that early Victorian naturalists mistook anemones, hydroids, sponges and other static, unmoving and colourful animals for plants. Once their true nature was discovered, such animals were dubbed zoophytes (animal-plants). Even today those unfamiliar with such organisms could easily make the same mistake. It is hard to shake off the ingrained teaching centred around the terrestrial environment, that animals must move around to find their food. As we stated in the opening sentence to this chapter, the marine environment is very different physically from the terrestrial one. Our aim in this first chapter was to describe these differences and so allow an understanding of this and other unfamiliar animal (and plant) ways of life. In the second chapter we explore how to get immersed (figuratively and literally) in this unfamiliar world.

ABOVE: Springtime on a Devon reef: active filter-feeders including sponges, sea anemones, corals, hydroids and sea squirts under the watchful eye of a female Cuckoo Wrasse *Labrus mixtus* as she swims past.

Immersing yourself

chapter two

Few people forget the first time they look beneath the surface of the sea. Even in the shallowest water, and whether by snorkelling or scuba diving, it is an eye-opener in the true sense. For both of us, newly purchased face masks allowed us to see first-hand the marine life that provides so much joy and lifelong fascination. However, getting underwater is not for everyone, and there are many other ways of immersing yourself and appreciating the immensely varied watery world of our shallow coastal seas. Wander along a beach's strandline, gaze into a rock pool or out to sea from a clifftop, visit a public aquarium or even delve into the wealth of images, footage and information available online and on paper – all these we still do on a regular basis, and there is always something new to capture the imagination.

In our case we both ultimately became professional marine biologists, but whatever the incentive, making observations, writing records, taking photographs and sometimes (restrained) specimen collection can provide valuable scientific data as well as personal satisfaction. This chapter explains some of the ways such information can be collected by anyone who is interested.

Beach detectives

Beachcombing is a time-honoured occupation providing mementoes, material for those with an artistic bent, and even perhaps income for metal detectorists searching for lost coins and jewellery. However, it can also provide an intriguing glimpse into the underwater world and useful information on animals and plants living below the shoreline and far out into the open ocean. Both of us have collections amassed over the years that range from ancient glass fishing-net floats adorned with large barnacles, to dried-up pipefish and sponges and piddock-drilled rocks. Some of the most common

OPPOSITE PAGE:
Scuba diving does not have to be deep; could the safety procedure for an air-supply problem here be 'stand up'?

ABOVE: Peter Tinsley from the Dorset Wildlife Trust, with Porcupine Marine Natural History Society (PMNHS) volunteers searching for cast-up shells at Studland Bay.

INSET: PMNHS citizen scientists staying dry while recording the abundant seaweeds, anemones, hydroids and sea squirts growing on pontoons at the Marine Institute, University of Portsmouth, and checking for non-native species.

finds around our shores are empty mollusc and crustacean shells, cast-up seaweeds, hydroids and bryozoans and various tough egg cases. An excellent book by passionate beachcombers and photographers Steve Trewhella and Julie Hatcher (2015) provides a guide to what may be found, and a few of our favourites are described below. On occasion, more exotic finds land on our shores, including a variety of plant beans and seeds from the Caribbean – and even coconuts.

Local intelligence

The washed-up empty egg cases of skates and sharks, often known as 'mermaids' purses', can give us useful information on local populations of these fishes, and are much easier to spot than the enigmatic animals that produce them (though Frances did once find a Small-spotted Catshark *Scyliorhinus canicula* in a rock pool). This has led to a popular and successful 'citizen science' project that collects data on the increasingly pressured populations of these species, as described in Chapter 8.

Another common find is the obvious white 'cuttlebone' left after cuttlefishes, charismatic cephalopod molluscs (see Chapter 10), have died and decomposed. Not a bone, but their equivalent of a shell and a specialised internal float that helps the animal adjust its buoyancy. Cuttlebones have often just been regarded as calcium-providers for pet birds or for polishing jewellery, but it is now realised that they can tell us a lot about the animals' size and distribution. Equally common and intriguing are the dried-up crispy, cereal-like masses of empty Common Whelk *Buccinum undatum* egg cases. Each capsule will have contained up to a thousand eggs, with most going to feed the small proportion that hatch into miniature versions of the adults. These egg masses are sometimes known as 'sea-wash balls' because sailors are said to have used them for soaping down.

Further intriguing insights into the life histories of some marine animals come from moulted skins and exoskeletons. What are often thought of as 'dead crabs' on the beach, for example, are actually the armour suits that crustaceans have to shed in order to grow. These moults are astonishingly complete, and if you find a freshly shed one that has not spent much time tumbling in the surf, it will still include

ABOVE: Norfolk's sandy shores offer excellent beachcombing opportunities, providing plenty of clues to the marine life in deeper water: oyster, razor and cockle shells, whelk eggs, hydroids and Hornwrack *Flustra foliacea*.

INSET: Common Whelks *Buccinum undatum* congregating to lay their eggs. After hatching, the empty egg cases wash up on the beach as distinctive crispy cereal-like masses known as 'sea-wash balls'.

Coastal Seas

ABOVE: Shells bearing the telltale holes bored by predatory sea snails: (left) small clams collected from a sandy beach plus their nemesis, a necklace shell *Euspira* sp.; (right) an Edible Mussel *Mytilus edulis* shell, still attached to the rock, bored by a Dog Whelk *Nucella lapillus*.

the delicate coverings for eyes, mouthparts and antennae as well as the obvious body, claws and legs. A look inside the body of the armour will show that even some of the animal's gill structures remain, in an act of escapology which is difficult to visualise. Frances once watched a Common (or European) Lobster *Homarus gammarus* in an aquarium undergo this laborious procedure. Fifty years later she still has the cast shell, which, although slightly battered, still fools people into thinking it is the complete animal. Occasionally, a crab suit might be much heavier than a typical moult and will smell dreadful. This really is a dead crab. Finding the armour of a Spiny Spider Crab *Maja brachydactyla* is particularly interesting, as you can often see it has been 'decorated' by its owner with seaweed and other items; we say more about this process in Chapter 9.

Mollusc shells are always worth a good look because some carry indications of how the animal met its end. A small, round and very neat hole in a limpet or mussel shell indicates that it has fallen victim to a Dog Whelk *Nucella lapillus*, the well-known 'driller-killer' of rocky shore and shallow rock habitats. The shell penetration, achieved with a combination of chemical (acidic) softening and mechanical scraping, is not rotational, so the action is more properly described as boring, but 'borer-killer' does not have quite the same ring! However, barnacles are the easier and preferred prey, so on some rocky shores there are no bored mollusc shells despite the presence of numerous Dog Whelks. The less common European Sting Winkle *Ocenebra erinacea* leaves similar holes, but small bivalve shells found on sandy shores with a neat bevel-edged borehole in them indicate that the culprit is the Common Necklace Shell *Euspira catena*. We describe this predatory snail and its impressive adaptations in Chapter 5.

Rocky shores and pools

As the tide changes and water drains away from a rocky shore, life suddenly becomes a lot harder for the inhabitants, exposing them to the air and to extremes of temperature and drying winds. However, from a visitor's and naturalist's point of view, low tide provides (relatively) easy access to at least a small segment of our shallow seas, without the need to get wet, although, admittedly, we have both on occasion arrived back home wetter than after diving or snorkelling. Rock pools in particular provide a window into deeper water, miniature aquariums where fish, crabs, prawns, molluscs and others can be watched close up. Although the species mix will differ between the intertidal and sublittoral zones, seashores provide excellent outdoor classrooms and plenty of clues as to what lies in deeper water. The ecology of rocky seashores is fascinating in itself, and the coastline around the British Isles has an exceptional range and variety – see *Rocky Shores* (Archer-Thomson and Cremona 2019).

Because nets damage pool habitats unless they are used with great care, the best way to observe most rock-pool species is simply to sit quietly and watch on a still day. However, if you don't mind getting a wet head, then using a facemask, or the dry option of a 'rock-pool viewer' with a clear plastic base, gives good results. The ultimate dry viewing option is a glass-bottomed boat, widely used

BELOW: In rock pools, even small nets can cause damage, and their use is best avoided. However, netting along the sandy edges of the Gannel Estuary in Cornwall allowed Frances to find juvenile flatfish, shrimps and even a Lesser Weeverfish *Echiichthys vipera* without harming the habitat.

in the clear waters over tropical coral reefs, but not often an option around the British Isles. At least one operation, however, is running successfully by taking advantage of particularly clear and sheltered water off the west coast of Scotland. When Paul visited with his family, he especially enjoyed the opportunity it gave to readily share underwater views with young children.

Perhaps the most important essential for any shore visit is a tide table, a predictor of the extraterrestrial assistance we get from the moon (and to a lesser extent the sun), whose gravitational influences drive the tides.

Taking the plunge: snorkelling

Whatever the fascination of beachcombing, rock-pooling or (as we describe later) remote sampling, there is something very special about actually getting into the water and observing marine life in its own habitat. If there is one message we really want to get across here, it is that this can be experienced by many more people than just those who train as scuba divers and use relatively expensive and complicated equipment. Also, that it can often be enjoyed close to home without needing to travel to the sort of wilderness locations regularly featured in TV wildlife programmes (though visiting such places has been an enjoyable part of both of our lives). The straightforward joy of putting your head into (even cold) water and seeing this hidden world and its myriad species first-hand is immense, memorable and, for some, literally life-changing. It certainly was for Paul. As a teenager on holiday in Norfolk, he badgered his parents to get him snorkelling equipment to make long days on the beach more interesting. Whilst the sea where they went was often too silt-laden to see much, Paul found clear water in sand-bottomed coastal lagoons left by the dropping tide. These were typically barely a metre deep but, once immersed, he remembers immediately seeing numerous Shore Crabs *Carcinus maenas* – and, best of all, the crabs were actively 'doing things'. Whether they were digging up worms, trying to pounce on Brown Shrimps *Crangon crangon*, or fighting each other over a mate, Paul was immediately captivated. An enduring love of the sea, marine life and biology was the natural result and has dominated the path of his life ever since.

As well as setting a path to deeper adventures, snorkelling brings joys and opportunities all of its own. A particular delight is being

Immersing yourself

ABOVE: Paul's partner Teresa equipped with the basics for underwater exploration (mask, snorkel and swimming costume) in a giant rock pool near Marazion, Cornwall.

LEFT: Pugnacious Shore Crabs *Carcinus maenas* 'squaring up', the sort of sight that so intrigued Paul when he first started snorkelling.

able to walk along a stretch of coast and choose freely where to enter the water. When encumbered by heavy scuba gear, you rely on a boat journey or staggering to a spot close to where you can park a vehicle. However, for those who prefer to remain dry as well as unencumbered, there are commercial wildlife tour boats that target iconic open-water species such as Basking Sharks *Cetorhinus maximus* and Blue Sharks *Prionace glauca* as well as seabirds and cetaceans. In Cornwall, where Blue Sharks are regularly sighted, local tour boats know the best times and places to see them, by swimming or snorkelling.

Coastal Seas

Going deeper: diving
Air and treacle needed

One of the first scientists to appreciate and put into practice the benefit of getting underwater to study marine habitats was John (known to colleagues as Jack) Kitching. There are wonderful stories of how, in 1932, he recorded the encrusting life in a patch of rocky seabed near Wembury, Devon, that is still known by diving biologists who have followed in his footsteps as 'Kitching's gulley'. Jack Kitching used a diving helmet that was basically a bucket with a window and had air pumped down to him through a pipe by assistants on the rocky ledge above. This 'umbilical', as we would now call it, also incorporated a telephone line so Jack could relay details of the species he was observing – at least that was the theory. In practice, the only messages that came up it were heartfelt pleas to the pump operators for 'more

RIGHT: In Jack Kitching's footsteps ... Paul in full scuba gear photographing life on the wall of the Devon gulley first surveyed by Kitching in 1932.

air, more air!' With no wetsuit, let alone a drysuit, he attempted to keep warm by wearing thick jumpers and reportedly eating a tin of treacle before immersion. We can't ascertain whether this helped, but we certainly empathise with a desire for frequent sugary snacks when working in cold water.

The bliss of scuba: becoming 'self-contained'

Fortunately, when we want to go deeper and spend longer submerged than is possible when snorkelling, we have it much easier than Jack Kitching. While surface-supplied diving (with breathing gas pumped down from above) is still used for some specialised work, standard diving equipment enables us to move freely underwater and enjoy the 'SC' of scuba (self-contained underwater breathing apparatus). Many people say that diving is the closest we can get to flying, and it certainly feels like that when gently finning or gliding past an underwater cliff adorned with colourful sea anemones and watching fish swim above, below and next to us. Standard 'open-circuit' scuba equipment is still similar in principle to the Aqualung invented by Jacques Cousteau and Émile Gagnan in 1943, but sophisticated rebreathers, where exhaled air is recycled rather than simply released as bubbles, are now becoming more widely used by working and recreational divers. Neither of us, nor many biologists, have yet taken on the considerable extra expense and training required for

BELOW: Seasearch divers and a pile of their air cylinders and other equipment on the Ulva ferry slipway at Mull.

rebreather diving, although advocates of the technology keep telling Paul how much more easily he could observe and film fish behaviour without the noisy disturbance of his exhaled air bubbles. Fortunately for Paul, blennies (see Chapter 8) seem insensitive to this noise, unlike some of the wrasses and many other species.

Gearing up

This book is not the place for reviews of the plethora of today's modern snorkelling and diving gear, but one item worth particular mention is the mask. It is the catalyst for any underwater exploration because our eyes cannot focus when in direct contact with water and need the pocket of air provided by a mask in order to see properly. We would therefore certainly recommend taking the time to find a good-quality mask that is comfortable and fits well. If you need glasses, it is also well worth considering the admittedly expensive step of having one fitted with your optical prescription. We have never known anyone regret doing this, but plenty who wished they had done it years earlier (including Frances) as everything swims back into glorious focus.

Training up

Around the UK and Ireland, diving (or snorkel) qualifications have traditionally been gained either via an intensive course at specialised commercial centres, run by a variety of organisations such as PADI (Professional Association of Diving Instructors) or through a local branch of the British Sub-Aqua Club (BSAC). 'Beesack', as it is affectionately known, has a worldwide reputation for the high quality of its training, and great numbers of divers thrive in the BSAC system, but a club-based approach may not suit everyone and other qualifications are equally valid. There are also now various combinations of the two approaches available through different organisations, including BSAC, to give people more flexibility. Something worth remembering is that a short diving course taken abroad in clear, warm waters may not equip you fully with the skills needed in more challenging home conditions, where the water is colder and the weather more variable. Extra training and more diving experience may be needed. In the UK, anyone who receives payment for diving, even for scientific research purposes, must gain a Health and Safety Executive (HSE) professional diving qualification.

ABOVE: The changing character of the sea: Wembury in Devon in perfect conditions for snorkelling or diving; and (inset) in a less hospitable mood when only brave surfers (black dots on the right of the picture) enter the water.

Keeping calm

In our opinion one of the most important pieces of advice for anyone ready to start exploring the marine habitats in the shallow waters around our coastline is to wait for the right, calm conditions before taking the plunge. It is so disheartening to see someone emerge from a choppy sea and complain that 'there was nothing to see' when you know a visit in calm conditions would have had them enthusing about a wonderful new experience. Waves and swell not only make snorkelling or shallow-water scuba diving uncomfortable in itself, they also stir up the seabed and suspend seaweed fragments and other material in the water, which can greatly reduce visibility. The difference to the whole experience in a glassily calm sea is immense.

Picking a windless day or a beach where the wind is blowing offshore will maximise your chances of calm conditions, although large swells arising from storms far offshore can sometimes provide a nasty surprise. Websites with information for surfers can be helpful in this regard, and one obvious rule is that if you see surfers congregating and looking happy, go somewhere else, wait for another time or swap your mask and snorkel for a surfboard for the day.

Recording what we see underwater

Making records of what you see when diving and snorkelling is little different from doing so on the shore or on land. A notebook, pencil and preferably a camera are essentially all that is needed. However, as we both discovered early in our careers, water and paper notebooks don't go well together. On the shore, plastic weather-writers can protect your notes from rain, but even 'waterproof' paper crumples. For us in early cash-strapped student days, a simple and cheap solution was to make an underwater writing slate from two pieces of white Formica laminate stuck back-to-back, complete with attached pencil and a snap hook to affix to yourself. Today, plastic writing slates can be bought ready-made, and these are the most widely used way for divers to record what they see underwater.

When working on early dive surveys in the 1990s, Frances and colleagues experimented with tape-recorders in waterproof housings using behind-the-ear bone microphones to pick up the speech. With teeth clenched around the diving regulator mouthpiece, the result was anything but clear. Sophisticated underwater communication systems now exist, employing full face masks that allow divers to speak freely to one another and record, but these are expensive and their use needs extra training.

The revolution in digital photography has greatly facilitated the development of natural history recording schemes in both the terrestrial and marine environments. In particular, digital

RIGHT: Our friend and colleague Paula Lightfoot using her underwater writing slate to record Seasearch data on species and habitats.

photographs can be easily uploaded to various platforms for species verification by experts, or often just for opinions from colleagues and friends. However, underwater photography has its own set of problems, some of which we explore below.

Whether on 'paper' or photograph, records are only of wider use to the scientific and conservation communities if they are sent in to appropriate organisations or data centres. For recreational divers and snorkellers around Great Britain, the Seasearch programme provides an easy way to make sure that records are collected and collated in a structured and useable format. The impressive Seasearch system is something we both keenly support, and we list this and a selection of other popular and more species-specific recording schemes in the table on page 71. The majority of such schemes make their datasets publicly available via the National Biodiversity Network (NBN) Atlas.

The challenges of underwater photography

The old adage 'a picture is worth a thousand words' is most certainly true underwater, where time is strictly limited. However, notetaking is also important, especially to capture habitat details such as depth and substratum as well as behaviour, all essential for species and habitat records to be of maximum use. Underwater photography has moved on in leaps and bounds since we first started along this road and is now both accessible and reasonably affordable. It does, however, have its own challenges, both in terms of keeping saltwater away from expensive electronics and the very different light conditions found underwater. Whatever the challenge, and whilst many might disagree, we think that almost any photo is better than no photo; even the tail of a fleeing fish might allow identification. However, knowing what features are needed for an accurate identification of, say, a fish and ensuring photographs show these is certainly helpful, as is remembering that not everything can be identified from photos.

Water clarity

Even in the clearest-seeming seawater, visibility is considerably lower than on land for reasons that we describe in Chapter 1. Awaking to a dense fog and visibility of 100m on land, most people would put their camera firmly away, or at the very least not attempt to photograph anything more distant than a couple of metres. Being able to see 100m underwater would be miraculous. Regardless of the conditions, a big ingredient of success underwater is always to minimise the amount of water between your camera and subject, by getting as close to it as possible.

The fact that sitting far away with a long telephoto lens is not an option means that there is then a potential conflict between getting the desired photographs and not causing stress to shy animals. The best way to resolve this is with patience and consideration, and the knowledge that an animal's response to your presence will vary greatly between species and even within species, depending on their personality and activity. Assigning 'personality' to some animals may seem fanciful, but it has a scientific basis and simply means that behavioural differences amongst individuals of the same species remain consistent over time. Cuttlefishes provide an excellent example of how an animal's reactions can also vary with the situation; they are often shy around divers but, at dusk, may actually follow them closely to use their lights for spotting prey (see Chapter 10).

The digital difference

Underwater photography used to be a specialist activity undertaken by a very small clique of divers, but it is now commonplace, and the advent of digital photography has been a major factor. We both remember vividly the irritation and frustration of being limited to 24 or 36 shots (the normal number of exposures on a roll of 35mm film) on a dive. Quickly snapping in a new roll of film is not an option underwater, and we both remember the pre-digital dilemma about 'blowing' our last few shots on an intriguing subject when an even more interesting one might be just about to swim or crawl round the corner.

A second huge advantage of digital is the facility to check that you have captured what you want or need whilst you are still on the spot and make changes there and then. Collecting a developed film from the shop was always exciting, but sometimes disappointing after a non-repeatable expedition. Because many of the first underwater cameras lacked direct viewing, this could even include leaving the lens cap on, or in Frances's case, not checking there was actually a film in the camera. However, animals do seem to have an innate sense of when they are being watched or filmed, so are liable to do the most interesting things when you are busy checking the quality of your last photo.

Choosing a camera

We both started out on underwater photography with the basic, but very effective and much-loved, Nikonos system. These were self-contained underwater cameras, waterproof to the maximum normal scuba diving depth, and there are no current equivalents. However, there are now some very capable compact cameras, waterproof without a housing down to about 15m depth and small enough to go in a pocket. They are great for rock pools, snorkelling and shallow dives but, for those wanting to venture deeper or dive with it regularly, a camera in a dedicated waterproof housing is more reliable, if bulkier. A rude shock here, though, is that top-quality housings can cost more than the cameras inside them.

Underwater housings are available for a great variety of cameras, whether SLR (single lens reflex), 'mirrorless' or compact, and also increasingly for smartphones. Despite that range, we have found that it is always best to check housing availability before you choose the camera. On camera choice, Paul's personal experience is that the quality of his still photographs is determined much more by what lighting he uses, water clarity, his patience and the behaviour of the subjects than by the camera. In contrast, with underwater video, he finds that camera technology plays a much bigger part in the final result.

LEFT: Paul photographing a Lion's Mane Jellyfish *Cyanea capillata*. An SLR camera in a housing with twin flashguns on extendable arms can give excellent results but is bulky to carry and cumbersome to use underwater.

Coastal Seas

ABOVE: A housed compact camera with a small but powerful torch, as used here by a diver surveying marine life at Lundy, can be a good alternative to a large housed SLR.

It is also worth bearing in mind the additional bulk that even the best-designed housings entail. A full-frame SLR, for example, might look reasonably compact on land but will become quite a monster when housed, especially with additional lighting and the large port that is required for a wide-angle lens to be used.

Lighting the way

Underwater lighting has come a long way since the flashbulbs that Frances used with her early edition of the Nikonos, but it can still provide plenty of headaches. Any additional lighting, whether electronic flash or video lights, has to be carefully positioned and directed in a way that illuminates the subject, but with as little water in front of the camera lens as possible. In even apparently clear water, failure to do this results in stills or video that look as though they have been taken in a snowstorm, because light is reflected straight back into the camera from even the tiniest particles. One option in shallow water is to use no artificial light at all and rely on camera settings (the so-called 'white balance') or a filter to remove or reduce the colour-shifting effect of the water described in Chapter 1 (see *Light underwater*, page 27). This reliance on 'available light' alone is becoming more feasible as digital cameras are developed to function in ever-lower light levels, and it is essential for imaging animals such as seahorses that are thought to be adversely affected by any artificial light.

Marine citizen scientists

The UK and Ireland have a long legacy of 'amateur' studies in marine natural history, stretching back to the beginning of the nineteenth century. Philip Gosse (1810–1888) is one of the best-known of these early self-taught biologists, a favourite naturalist and author of ours and remembered particularly for his wonderfully illustrated monograph *Actinologia Britannica: a History of the British Sea-Anemones and Corals* published in 1860. He was a skilled artist and, even today, reproductions of his drawings adorn coffee cups and coasters, as found by Frances, to her great pleasure, for sale in the Cambridge University Zoology Museum shop. In contrast, marine biology as an academic

discipline only started to come into its own in the 1880s, but it has since expanded greatly and become mainstream in universities. Now marine 'citizen science' is well and truly back, but this time, with diving a relatively easy option for anyone interested in getting underwater, it is no longer confined to the seashore.

The number of recreational divers in the UK has risen steadily since BSAC was founded in 1953, and whilst it is difficult to find accurate statistics, BSAC alone has around 28,000 members. There may be as many as 100,000 divers and snorkellers throughout the British Isles, and a conservative estimate of the number of sport dives made yearly through any agency in the UK is around two million. That is a lot of eyes underwater even if only a fraction are interested in marine natural history recording. David Bellamy realised the potential of this 'army' of underwater explorers as recorders in 1967 when he organised the first UK environmental science project using volunteer divers. Dubbed 'Operation Kelp', it involved more than 250 BSAC members who collected kelp samples as a means of checking pollution levels in the North Sea. Ten years later, in 1977, saw the launch of 'Underwater Conservation Year', in which Frances was involved as a project leader, the beginning of a rise in interest by divers wanting to take part in marine recording projects. Ultimately this morphed into the current Marine Conservation Society and Seasearch recording.

ABOVE: Activity at a marine 'Bioblitz' (recording the species in a small area over a set period – such as 24 hours) in Plymouth Sound, with volunteers exploring the shore and snorkelling. The canoeist was providing safety cover for the snorkellers.

INSET: A scuba diver at the same marine Bioblitz, downloading information to a colleague and handing over a sample.

The sponge enigma

Sponges come in a wonderful variety of colours, shapes and sizes but can be difficult to identify, especially in their natural underwater environment. Many species are naturally variable or adopt different growth forms depending on environmental conditions. Early classification and species identification relied almost entirely on museum specimens, collected from the shore or by dredging and then preserved or dried. In this state, sponges have little colour or form because they shrink down, losing their shape. However, what almost all sponges do have, and which can be seen under a microscope in preserved material, is a diffuse, fibrous skeleton made of a substance called spongin, plus additional microscopic skeletal elements called spicules. Seen under high magnification, these slivers of silicon or calcium carbonate have intricate shapes, ranging from stars and crescents to long thin barbed rods. Each sponge species has a specific complement of these spicules and different arrangements of spongin.

Once scuba diving and underwater photography became realistic options for scientists, it became apparent that the shape, form, size, colour and surface texture of sponges could allow accurate *in situ* species identification of many (but by no means all) sponges. First came the huge task of matching known species identified from their preserved skeletal elements to what they actually look like in life. Around Britain and Ireland this process was initiated in the early 1970s by a small number of interested 'amateur' divers, encouraged and helped by staff from the Natural History Museum in London. So began a project, subsequently taken up by the Marine Conservation Society, to produce an accessible identification guide, *The Sponges of the British Isles*. Photographs of individual sponges were taken by divers, and that same specimen (or part of) collected, preserved and identified from its spicules. The resulting printed, loose-leaf guide was based on 'mini-print' photographs stuck in by hand, alongside a full description (including spicule complement) of each species. It was further developed, and expanded editions produced, through to the early 1990s. The final *SPONGE V* came out in 1992 and, with input from the Ulster Museum and Queen's University, Belfast, covered 103 species (Ackers *et al.* 1992).

In 2018 the Seasearch book *Sea Squirts and Sponges of Britain and Ireland* was published (Bowen *et al.* 2018), covering 61 sponges considered distinctive enough to be identified by non-specialists on the shore or underwater by snorkellers and divers, without reference to their spicules. This whole decades-long process is one of the most significant collaborative efforts between sport divers (citizen scientists) and professional biologists in marine natural history that we know of.

Today, marine citizen science opportunities around the British Isles encompass a very wide variety of coastal, seashore and sublittoral recording and conservation projects, with involvement from numerous organisations and people of all ages and from all walks of life. For example, the Great Eggcase Hunt recorded over 370,000 shark and skate egg cases to January 2023. For anyone interested in the marine world and recording, it has never been so easy to get involved (see table opposite).

A selection of marine citizen science recording projects currently (2025) running in the UK and Ireland

We have contributed to all of these, and would recommend them all. The main participant groups and project focus are shown in the first column. Visit the relevant websites to find out how to participate, and to explore the data generated.

Project	Date started	Lead organisation(s)	Website or Contact
Individual marine records; PMNHS field trip records (shore, snorkellers, divers)	1970s	Porcupine Marine Natural History Society (PMNHS)	records@pmnhs.co.uk
Seasearch (divers, snorkellers)	Mid-1980s	Marine Conservation Society (MCS)	www.seasearch.org.uk
Beachwatch (shore)	1994	MCS	www.mcsuk.org/beachwatch-app
Marine Strandings Network (shore)	1990s	Cornwall Wildlife Trust	strandings@cornwallwildlife.org.uk
Shoresearch (shore)	2003 (relaunched 2019)	The Wildlife Trusts	Your Shore Network on Facebook
Great Eggcase Hunt (shore)	2003	The Shark Trust	www.sharktrust.org/greateggcasehunt
Cornwall Seal Group Research Trust (shore and boats)	2004	Cornwall Seal Group Research Trust	seals@cornwallsealgroup.co.uk
Big Seaweed Search (shore)	2009	Natural History Museum and MCS	www.mcsuk.org/bigseaweedsearch
Seaquest Southwest (marine megafauna sightings) (shore and boats)	2016	Cornwall Wildlife Trust	seaquest@cornwallwildlifetrust.org.uk
Project Sepia (snorkellers, divers)	2023	Cuttlefish Conservation Initiative	www.cuttlefishconservation.com

Gathering information

In England a communications-based initiative, South-West Marine Ecosystems (SWME), was set up in 2007 by Dr Bob Earll. This has since evolved as an informal partnership, now supported by a team with a wide range of marine interests. It aims to collate annual information on changes in natural marine ecosystems through a series of thematic topics covering various important habitats, such as seabed and seashore, species groups including fish, marine mammals and seabirds, and conservation management in areas such as fisheries and plastic pollution. Information from the public, professional and citizen scientists, universities, conservation bodies and others is brought together and disseminated through an annual conference and annual *State of the South-West Seas* report, webinars and social media. The value of this system in drawing information from such a broad span of sources and making it visible relatively quickly to scientists and administrators involved in conservation has been widely recognised. As a result, an equivalent EAST Marine Ecosystems (EASTME) has been initiated, and it held its first conference in May 2024.

'Hotspots' for observing marine life

Here, we have listed some of our favourite places for spotting and watching marine life, with a few notes and pointers about what makes them special to us. It is simply meant to provide some ideas for visits, is very far from exhaustive, and will undoubtedly not include many reader favourites. There is also always more to discover! The emphasis of regional underwater guides is often on shipwrecks but particularly good books for wildlife enthusiasts diving from the shore or snorkelling are *Top 100 British Shore Dives* by Anita Sherwood (2017) and *Snorkelling Britain* by Emma and Gordon Taylor (2025). Both include excellent practical details for many of these selected locations plus scores of others. Local Wildlife Trusts are a good source of information about where and how to go rock-pooling, and many organise public events for this purpose.

Our anticlockwise tour starts in North Devon, proceeds around Cornwall to South Devon where Paul is based, and then eastwards past Frances's base in East Anglia before finishing in Ireland.

North Devon
Lundy
This dramatic island at the entrance to the Bristol Channel has been at the vanguard of British marine conservation and seems an appropriate place to start our whistle-stop tour. We describe its history in Chapter 12.

Cornwall
Porthkerris
Renowned as one of the best shore dive sites in the southwest, this is an excellent place to see a wide variety of animals in a small area, including cuttlefishes, octopuses and a great range of fishes. Species not usually encountered when diving from the shore, such as Cuckoo Wrasse *Labrus mixtus* and Pink Sea Fan *Eunicella verrucosa*, are regular sights here thanks to the relatively deep water close to the beach. Other dive-friendly features are its position on the east side of the Lizard Peninsula, meaning it is sheltered from the prevailing winds,

ABOVE: Encounters with cuttlefish are common when snorkelling or diving at Porthkerris. Here, two Common Cuttlefish *Sepia officinalis* are each showing a large black spot on their back; they often make this signal of annoyance when a Ballan Wrasse *Labrus bergylta* (as here) is nearby.

and the fact that the beach gives unusually easy access to the water at all states of the tide. Paul has been able to get some of his best fish behaviour photographs here over the years, probably because the fish have become accustomed to the presence of divers.

Helford Estuary
This is a wonderfully picturesque setting for sheltered snorkelling over beautiful seagrass meadows and is a Marine Conservation Zone.

Hannafore Point, Looe
Also part of a Marine Conservation Zone, extensive intertidal areas, including many rock pools and lagoons, are exposed on low spring tides, when it even becomes possible to wade over to nearby St George's Island, owned by the Cornwall Wildlife Trust. A flat concrete path down the shore gives unusually easy access to snorkelling over interesting rocky and sediment areas. There is also an excellent café nearby.

South Devon
Wembury
This bay close to Plymouth was established as a Marine Conservation Area in 1981 and is famous for rich and varied marine life and the education and research that is carried out here. In addition to famous rock-pooling, snorkelling and shallow diving over the rocky reefs can be excellent, but it is very exposed to the south and west so it can be difficult to get calm conditions, as testified by its popularity as a surfing location – always a warning sign.

Thurlestone

This beach, also known as South Milton Sands, has wonderful rocky reefs for snorkelling with a very distinctive rock arch at the end of one of them. In the Second World War, a Belgian freighter trying to avoid U-boat attack came too close to shore and was wrecked on the reef at the other end of the beach. As the beach is exposed to the west, the wreck is quite broken up but can be easily visited by diving from the shore and has abundant fish life. It seems to act as a popular 'cleaning station' where small wrasses remove parasites from their larger relatives (see Chapter 8).

Torbay

A large bay, generally sheltered from prevailing winds, with numerous spots for exploring the shore, snorkelling and diving. There are several areas with seagrass meadows. Babbacombe, technically just 'round the corner' from the bay itself, is one of the most reliable spots for seeing Common Cuttlefish *Sepia officinalis* breeding and Spiny Spider Crabs congregating to moult.

Dorset

Lyme Bay

Dive boats visit various low rocky reefs offshore which support rich growths of sea fans and sponges. The stretch of coastline from Lyme Regis to Seatown is a mecca for finding loose fossils on the seashore. Well prior to its current popularity and designation of the Jurassic Coast as a World Heritage Site in 2001, it was even possible to find marine reptile remains, as Frances (or rather her parents) did in the 1960s; the plesiosaur backbone currently resides in her study.

Chesil and Portland Harbour

In front of the famous shingle beach, when the sea is calm, there is excellent diving at Chesil Cove, with unusually varied fish life close to shore. Behind its protective barrier is the large Fleet Lagoon, a Marine Protected Area (MPA) that supports a wide variety of habitats and rare species. Within the shelter of Portland Harbour is a good place for a leisurely search for small gobies, blennies and other bottom-living fishes. Note that diving is only allowed in some areas.

Kimmeridge
An underwater nature trail for snorkellers is in place in the summer, to help them enjoy seeing different types of habitat in the bay.

Swanage Pier
A justifiably famous location for divers, especially underwater photographers. We give more details under *Pier approval: Swanage and Brighton*, Chapter 4.

Isle of Wight
Bembridge
At Bembridge, on the east side of the island, there is a large area of limestone and chalk bedrock supporting diverse algae (including Peacock's Tail *Padina pavonica*, a delicate, fan- or funnel-shaped southern seaweed), invertebrates and shoaling fish. Seagrass beds are found here and elsewhere around the island.

Sussex
Brighton Pier
Less well known for marine life than Swanage Pier, but a great place for watching fish, including a particularly vibrant Tompot Blenny *Parablennius gattorugine* population. See *Pier approval: Swanage and Brighton*, Chapter 4.

Norfolk
Sheringham
In calm spring or summer conditions, the only time when the water is clear enough, snorkelling and diving over the chalk reef habitats can be wonderful. We describe the Norfolk chalk reef in Chapter 4. There is a short but excellent snorkel trail off the shore.

West Runton
This is worth a visit as one of the very few rocky shores in East Anglia as well as the location where a nearly complete fossilised mammoth skeleton was found.

Tyneside
Whitley Bay
An educational rock-pool project aiming to inspire children about marine life is based here.

Berwickshire

St Abbs

An attractive harbour with some of the UK's best shore diving within reach of a short swim. Underwater scenery includes a famous double archway, known as Cathedral Rock, that is festooned with sea anemones and soft corals. This site is also well known for resident Wolf Fish *Anarhichas lupus*, more usually found in deeper water, and it was here that we both first saw their rather gnarled-looking faces peering out from large crevices. St Abbs was Scotland's first voluntary marine nature reserve, and a marine station is located in the harbour.

Ross and Cromarty

Loch Carron

Another mecca for shore divers with a rich variety of attractive habitats including Flame Shell *Limaria hians* reefs, maerl beds and current-swept narrows.

Inverness-shire

The Small Isles

Canna, Rum, Muck and Eigg make up this island group just south of Skye that now forms part of a Marine Protected Area. The Small Isles Community Council and the Scottish Wildlife Trust recently (2024) produced a snorkel trail leaflet for this area. Whilst neither

BELOW: Loch Carron photographed from a viewpoint near Stromeferry, where a famous sign proclaims 'Strome Ferry (no ferry)'.

of us has tried this out, Frances remembers epic dives here during early surveys in the 1980s. Rum was the site of the first successful reintroduction of White-tailed Eagles *Haliaeetus albicilla* to Britain, in 1975.

County of Argyll
Oban
A resort town rather than a particular diving location, Oban is surrounded by stretches of sea and islands that are excellent for underwater exploration. Some of the most attractive and well-known shipwrecks in the British Isles lie in the nearby Sound of Mull. The wreck of the SS *Breda* in Ardmucknish Bay was the site where Frances first recorded the Sea Loch Anemone *Protanthea simplex* in the 1980s, its identity confirmed by anemone expert R. L. Manuel.

County of Bute
Arran
In addition to having an impressive variety of marine habitats including maerl beds and seagrass meadows, Arran is an inspiration to marine conservationists. Following 13 years of campaigning, a no-take zone in Lamlash Bay was designated in 2008 by a local community group called the Community of Arran Seabed Trust (COAST). This then became part of a larger Marine Protected Area in 2016 (see *Arran* in Chapter 12).

Anglesey
The coastline around the Isle of Anglesey in Wales is indented by numerous bays that give easy access to good snorkelling and diving. Most of the coastline is designated as an Area of Outstanding Natural Beauty (AONB), a designation that changed name to National Landscapes in 2023. We describe the species-rich, tide-swept Menai Strait in Chapter 1.

Pembrokeshire
A Marine Special Area of Conservation (SAC) encompasses the coastline and shallow seas here and contains a huge variety of reef, sediment and estuary habitats, plus major colonies of seals and seabirds. As an actively managed Marine Protected Area, the waters around Skomer Island support rich and diverse marine communities, and we cover this further in Chapter 12.

Portrait of a Marine Station

Early marine research around the British Isles was centred around a series of 'marine stations', many set up in the late 19th century when interest from scientists, students and lay people started to expand. Most had humble beginnings, set up in areas known to be rich in marine life, but went on to become major players attracting scientists, naturalists and students. The Port Erin Marine Laboratory (PEML) on the Isle of Man was one of the earliest, opening in 1892 and running as an independent marine station until 1919 when it became part of the University of Liverpool. The first undergraduate marine biology honours course in Great Britain was started by the university in 1970, with the students spending their final year in Port Erin. Like so many similar iconic institutions, it finally fell victim to cost-cutting and closed its doors in 2006, more than 100 years since its inception.

Frances first arrived at the laboratory on a cold and gusty October day in 1973 as a prospective PhD student, the start of her long adventure in marine biology and natural history. Sadly, the buildings were badly damaged by fire in 2016 and eventually demolished before the site was sold for redevelopment.

Port Erin Marine Laboratory in 2006, the year of its closure.

Ireland

A wide variety of marine habitats and species are found in the shallow seas around the varied 3,000km shoreline of the island of Ireland. However, since neither of us has dived extensively there, we only describe two personally memorable sites.

The Skelligs

These small uninhabited rocky islands off County Kerry, best known for important seabird colonies and an early Christian monastery, also have superb underwater scenery and rich marine life for diving adventures. Paul only made a few dives there but found the vistas of rock – carpeted with Jewel Anemones *Corynactis viridis*, Plumose Anemones *Metridium senile* and soft corals, and dotted by huge sponges – a wonderful spectacle in the clear Atlantic water. Their combination with ravines lined by richly coloured Dahlia Anemones *Urticina felina*, numerous wrasses 'on patrol' and the occasional visit from a curious Grey Seal *Halichoerus grypus* left him with special memories.

Roaringwater Bay and Sherkin Island

This large bay with its many islands in County Cork is a good place to explore sheltered habitats such as the maerl and seagrass beds. Rare Stone Rose Maerl *Lithophyllum dentatum*, described under *Maerl* in Chapter 5, is found at some sites here. Sherkin Island is a 15-minute ferry ride from Baltimore. Frances remembers it as a beautiful and unspoilt place to visit with an excellent pub and only a tractor for transport, though there are now buses. She spent a week there in the 1980s as part of a diving survey on behalf of the then recently established Sherkin Island Marine Station, a private enterprise. The station ceased research and monitoring in 2015 but is currently compiling datasets for publication online. Under the right conditions, the island is easily accessible by relatively small dive boats from the mainland.

While we have ended this chapter with a list of some favourite locations to whet the appetite of readers for exploration, our main aim here has been to show different approaches to observing, appreciating and studying the wildlife of our coastal seas. Scuba diving is an obvious and enthralling way of physically entering the underwater world, but the 'lower-tech' alternative of snorkelling has its advantages too. There are even plenty of possibilities for 'immersion' in terms of gaining understanding of marine life that don't involve getting wet. We hope we have shown that however observations are made, whether by professional scientists or by members of the public (often described as 'citizen scientists'), they have the potential to provide valuable information about this fascinating but relatively little-known environment.

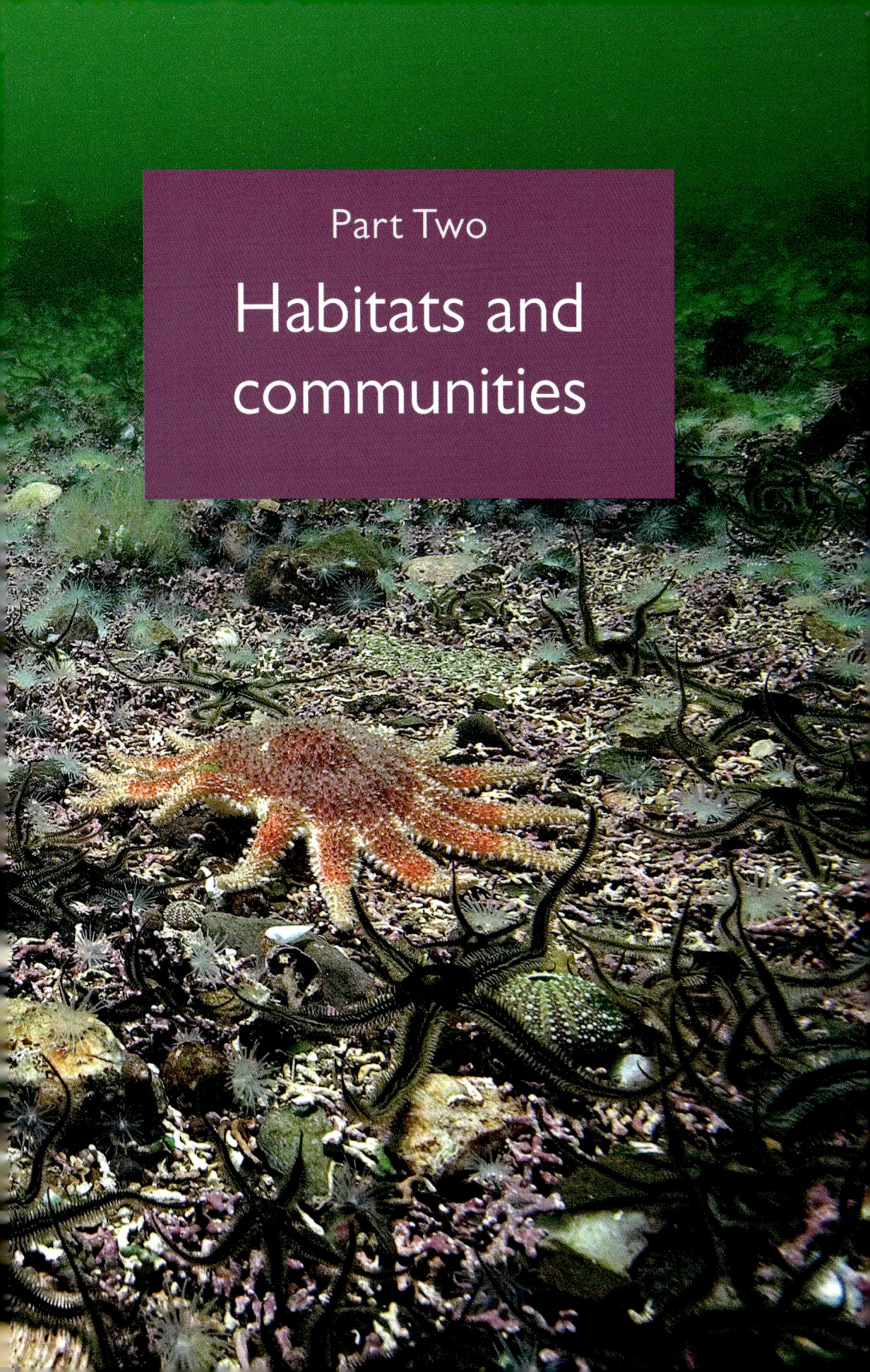

Part Two
Habitats and communities

Forests beneath the sea

chapter three

History relates that around 360 BC, the Greek philosopher Plato told the story of Atlantis, a fabled city with a utopian civilisation and great naval power, supposedly lost forever beneath the waves during a cataclysmic event. Whilst there are no lost cities beneath the waters around Great Britain (though many coastal villages destroyed by erosion), there are great forests, albeit of a lower stature than those on land, populated by a multitude of marine denizens. Statuesque kelp and other seaweed forests fringe much of our rocky coastline, though now to a far lesser extent than was once the case – and, like Atlantis, these too could be lost without due care.

Kelps are large brown seaweeds belonging to the order Laminariales, and the principal forest-forming species around the British Isles is Forest Kelp *Laminaria hyperborea*. Growing to 3.5m tall, it forms dense forests on stable, sublittoral rock in clear coastal water and is rarely exposed on even the lowest tides. In its place in shallower water, growing on the lowest parts of rocky shores, are forests of smooth, shiny Oar Weed *L. digitata* that can be seen exposed and flopped over on low spring tides. Tantalising glimpses of the tops of this species, just breaking the surface, can also be seen on less extreme tides, a wet-wellingtons lure to explore further.

Kelp forests provide a permanent structural habitat, and Forest Kelp can live for 10 years or more, shedding their fronds and growing new tops from the perennial stipe (stem) each year. This allows the development of a complex and productive ecosystem with a high biodiversity.

With a high light requirement, dense kelp forest generally does not extend much below 10m and thins out to well-spaced individuals forming a 'kelp park' as light levels decrease with depth, which can be something of a relief when towing a recalcitrant surface marker

PREVIOUS PAGES:
Abundant and varied animal life on this current-swept maerl bed in Loch Carron includes a large Common Sunstar *Crossaster papposus*, a Common Sea Urchin *Echinus esculentus* plus numerous Black Brittlestars *Ophiocomina nigra* and Sea Loch Anemones *Protanthea simplex*. Looking closely, there is an animal from virtually every major phylum.

OPPOSITE PAGE:
Small-spotted Catshark *Scyliorhinus canicula* in a thriving kelp forest.

Coastal Seas

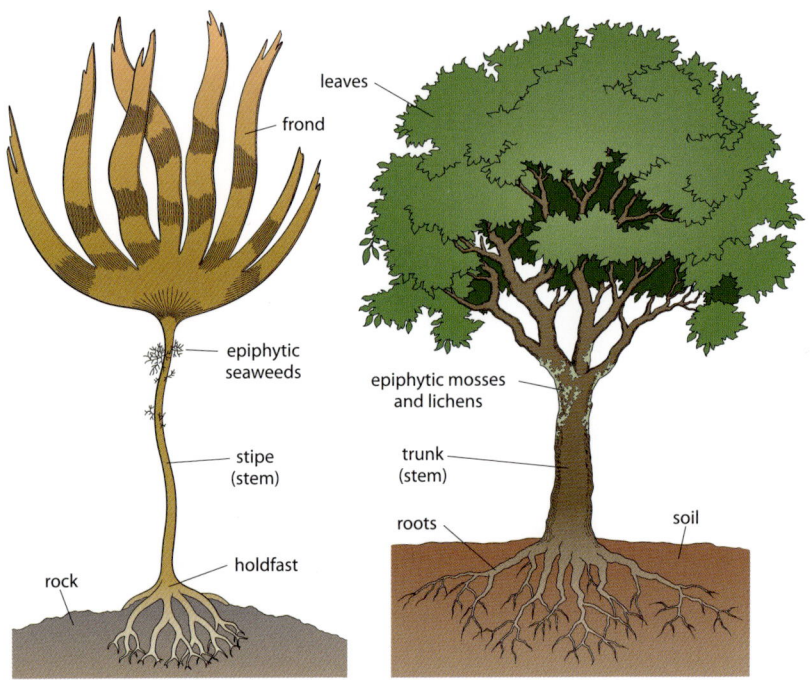

ABOVE: Comparison of the parts of a seaweed, Forest Kelp *Laminaria hyperborea*, with a woodland tree.

buoy behind you for the dive boat to follow. This is in contrast to a terrestrial forest, where trees tend to thin out with higher altitude as temperatures drop and soils become poorer. While there can be an increase in number and variety of understorey seaweeds within the kelp park as the shading effect of the kelp canopy diminishes, these too lessen with the overall fading light at greater depths.

Apart from their innate attraction as a beautiful and biodiverse habitat, kelp forests provide important 'ecosystem services'. Like their counterparts on land, healthy kelp forests are a key element in the fight against global and ocean warming, locking away considerable quantities of carbon on a long-term basis. They are also excellent 'storm breakers', dissipating wave energy and so lessening the impacts of waves crashing against cliffs and onto shores.

High-rise living

There is something mesmerising about diving through a kelp forest, finning between or gently pushing aside the tall stipes, as shafts of sunlight dapple the seabed. Kelp sometimes gets a 'bad press' from divers when they descend onto an extensive and superficially uniform landscape instead of the colourful rock pinnacle or shipwreck they

Forests beneath the sea

were expecting, but, as so often, a closer and more careful look is needed. A well-developed kelp forest has a tiered structure superficially similar to that of a terrestrial woodland or forest. Up above is a thick canopy of photosynthetic fronds, acting as the equivalent to leaves, supported and held up to the light by stipes like miniature tree trunks. Kelp has no need for the extensive root systems so vital to trees, as it is immersed in nutrient-containing water. Instead, each kelp is attached firmly to rock by a claw-like structure, the holdfast, a very appropriate name since that is exactly what it does. Fronds, stipe and holdfast each provide different habitats and feeding opportunities for other species, greatly increasing the biodiversity.

ABOVE: The dense canopy of a mature kelp forest cuts down the amount of light reaching the seabed and limits the growth of understorey seaweeds.

INSET: The stipes of kelp can be tall enough to give the feel of a forest and here they provide a foothold for a featherstar *Antedon* sp. A strong holdfast ensures each kelp plant is held firmly in place on the rock.

Epiphytes

The relatively rigid stipes of Forest Kelp have a rough surface that provides an excellent foothold for epiphytic red seaweeds as well as a variety of hydroids, bryozoans and encrusting sponges, all benefiting from their elevated position above the seabed. Older mature kelps

Coastal Seas

ABOVE: The branches of this ancient oak tree in the New Forest provide a sunlit home for epiphytic ferns and mosses (left). In the same way the rough perennial stipes of Forest Kelp *Laminaria hyperborea* provide an elevated position for red seaweeds (right).

carry more epiphytes than young ones, in much the same way as the splayed branches of an ancient oak become covered in ferns, mosses and lichens. One of the commonest stipe epiphytes is Dulse *Palmaria palmata*, an edible red seaweed also found growing on rocks on the shore. It has a high light requirement and so grows better held up off the darker seabed.

Among the epiphytic animals that find a home on kelp are lacy networks of bryozoans such as the Sea Mat *Membranipora membranacea* that in a single season can spread over entire fronds, turning them from brown to white. Dense bunches of small thread-like hydroids also benefit from high-rise living, where their alternative group name of sea firs seems particularly apt, though in this case more like fur than fir. If hanging around watching kelp fronds sway slowly back and forth with wave action doesn't make you feel seasick, then it is well worth examining the bryozoan expanses and hydroid clumps for colourful predatory nudibranchs or sea slugs. Munching their way across the Sea Mat, we often find *Polycera quadrilineata*, a translucent white species, dashingly marked with bright yellow spots and lines. The similarly coloured Orange-clubbed Sea Slug *Limacia clavigera* prefers another kelp-encrusting bryozoan, *Electra pilosa*. Like caterpillars, sea slugs are often specialist feeders, preferring one or only a few food sources. By the end of the growing season, kelp fronds may be so well covered by various growths that their photosynthetic capacity is considerably reduced. However, as described when discussing seasons in the sea in Chapter 1, Forest Kelp solves this problem by shedding its fronds each year.

Forests beneath the sea

LEFT: Orange-clubbed Sea Slug *Limacia clavigera* feeding on the bryozoan *Electra pilosa* encrusting a kelp frond in the Minard Isles, Loch Fyne, Scotland.

In contrast to the encrusting overload on Forest Kelp, its lookalike, Oar Weed, remains pleasingly clean, principally due to the smooth and slippery surface of its stipes and fronds. Exposed to the rough and tumble of waves around the low water mark on rocky shores and just below, the fronds act like newly conditioned hair, sliding easily over each other and remaining untangled and intact.

An eye on the next meal

An elevated position among the kelp can provide predators with a useful vantage point for ambushing their prey. Long-spined Sea Scorpions *Taurulus bubalis* are small fish that sometimes lurk among folds in the fronds, although you must be sharp-eyed to spot them because they camouflage themselves in kelp-colour to match their background. This location probably gives them an excellent chance of darting out, with surprising speed given their ungainly appearance, to grab Two-spotted Gobies *Gobiusculus flavescens* that like to hover in their small shoals around the kelp forest.

A more surprising predatory opportunity among kelp seems to be enjoyed by *Hyas araneus*, whose common names of Great Spider Crab and Sea Toad are both misleading as it is much smaller than the Spiny (or Common) Spider Crab *Maja brachydactyla* and looks nothing

Coastal Seas

ABOVE: A Long-spined Sea Scorpion *Taurulus bubalis* (left), matching its colour with the kelp for camouflage, waits to ambush passing prey. Eckström's Topknot *Zeugopterus regius* (right) on a kelp frond. We think this rarely seen fish may use the elongated fin ray by its mouth to lure small prey in a similar way to angler fish.

like an amphibian. On visits to Scottish sea lochs, particularly in Loch Carron, Paul saw these crabs climb up kelp stipes while also noting they sometimes ate pieces of jellyfish, and wondered if there was a connection. His suspicions were confirmed when he eventually came across a crab standing on the very top of a kelp frond, making grabs with its claws for small 'low-flying' jellyfish as they swept by in the current.

Crustaceans with something to fear from their seabed-bound colleagues can also use elevation to lessen the risk of becoming

RIGHT: Spider crabs *Hyas araneus* can sometimes be seen climbing up kelp to grab at passing jellyfish. The kelp here is covered with hydroids.

Forests beneath the sea

LEFT: Pair of Shore Crabs *Carcinus maenas* in pre-mate embrace, where a male waits for a female to moult her armour and become receptive. Pre-moult females release a chemical detected by males, and an elevated position in the kelp may help to minimise intrusion from competitors.

someone else's meal and to gain privacy, such as a pre-mate pair of Shore Crabs *Carcinus maenas* where the female is about to moult and will be soft and vulnerable.

Just as larger crustaceans gain advantage from clambering up kelp, caprellid shrimps (often called 'ghost' or 'skeleton' shrimps) benefit from lofty positions in turfs of smaller algae or on animals like erect hydroids and bryozoans. Beautifully adapted for this niche with an ultra-slim body, some species cling on with their rear pair of appendages, lean out into the current and extend rather sinister-looking hooked front appendages in the manner of a praying mantis, ready to grab animals such as even smaller crustaceans as they drift by.

Forest-floor refuges

The tangled multi-claw holdfasts of Forest Kelp branch out from the base of the stipe and always remind Frances of the above-ground buttress roots of some rainforest trees, which help support the great weight of the tree above. Kelp holdfasts have more to do with gripping the rock substratum, however, helped by a glue-like substance. Their complex structure provides numerous cracks and crevices in which small invertebrates such as Broad-clawed Porcelain Crabs *Porcellana platycheles* find homes and refuge. These tiny flattened crabs have the habit of clinging upside-down in such crevices or under

ABOVE: The knobbly holdfast of this Furbellows kelp Saccorhiza polyschides was home to a small clingfish (Gobiesocidae) guarding its eggs.

rocks, and if gently held on the palm of your hand, will scuttle over the edge and hang on underneath. Early surveys of kelp holdfasts by the well-known botanist David Bellamy found hundreds of individual animals and a wide variety of species associated with a single holdfast. As well as the mobile residents, this number also included numerous sessile sponges, bryozoans, hydroids and sea squirts living attached to the undulating and rough landscape of the holdfast surface.

The strangely named Furbellows *Saccorhiza polyschides* is another large kelp, easily recognised from its flattened, strap-like stipe and hollow, knobbly holdfasts. The latter make an ideal home and nursery for small clingfishes (Gobiesocidae) that slip in through damaged areas and then lay and guard their eggs there. This kelp is largely annual, the stipe and fronds torn away in winter storms, sometimes leaving the holdfasts behind as real estate for these and other small fishes.

Furbellows often grows mixed in amongst Forest Kelp but can predominate in areas of mixed sand and rock. Frances always looks through cast-up holdfasts or occasional live ones found on low spring tides, and was once rewarded by finding a beautiful Shore Clingfish *Lepadogaster purpurea* clinging on tightly with its modified pelvic-fin sucker. The two bright blue spots that adorn the head of these fish look for all the world like an extra pair of eyes staring up at you.

Munchers, crunchers and grazers

Kelp forests support a range of herbivores, chief amongst which are sea urchins and gastropod molluscs, particularly limpets and lookalike coat-of-mail chitons (Polyplacophora). However, there are far fewer direct grazers feeding on the live kelp than might be expected and no real equivalent to the hordes of spring- and summertime caterpillars that devour tree leaves on land. However, the fronds provide an ample food supply to detritovores. Forest Kelp fronds grow continually until they are finally shed, but the ends fray and break off as they whip back and forth with wave and current action. This provides a constant stream and an annual bonus of seabed (and strandline) detritus, avidly consumed by a wide variety of small invertebrates, including amphipods, isopods and a variety of worms.

The beautifully patterned and aptly named Blue-rayed Limpet *Patella pellucida*, with its delicate shell adorned with electric-blue lines, is a muncher extraordinaire of kelp and other large brown (and a few red) seaweeds. Groups of small individuals can often be found by a diligent search of larger, lower rocky-shore seaweeds or on freshly broken-off and washed-up kelp. At only 2cm long they can be difficult

BELOW: Blue-rayed Limpets *Patella pellucida* on kelp; the photo on the right shows the pits they excavate while feeding.

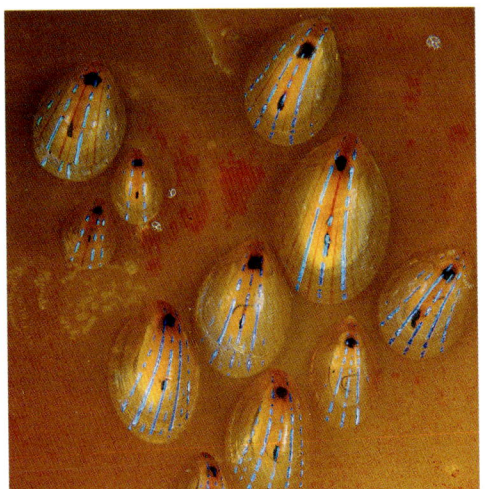

ABOVE: Large Common Sea Urchins *Echinus esculentus* browsing in the understorey of a kelp forest. There are small cup corals and other encrusting animals on the rock, with a Ballan Wrasse *Labrus bergylta* cruising past.

to spot when snorkelling or diving, but are well worth looking out for. Juveniles are most often found on the fronds and older adults on the stipes and in holdfasts, down onto which they crawl before the kelp sheds its annual frond. Holding on tightly with the strong suction grip of its foot, the limpet is able to rasp away at the kelp tissue, digging itself into a shallow pit such that it is both fed and protected. Large cavities excavated in kelp holdfasts and stipes can cause enough damage for the whole kelp, or part of it, to break off.

Limpets (and other gastropods) have a formidable grazing weapon in the form of a tongue-like radula, whose surface when viewed under a high-power microscope looks like a cheese-grater. Sea urchins have an equally potent feeding apparatus known as Aristotle's lantern, after the polymath of ancient Greece who was the first to describe it. This complex of hard skeletal elements and muscles looks rather like the 'chuck' or clamp of a power drill when its five teeth are closed. With this apparatus, sea urchins are perfectly capable of crunching their way through a kelp holdfast or scraping almost anything edible from a rock surface. In large numbers, the Common or Edible Sea Urchin *Echinus esculentus* can keep rock surfaces clear from all but tough crusts of calcareous seaweed and can easily prevent the growth of young kelp 'saplings'. Kept in check by the predatory activities of connoisseur seals and larger fish, they also suffer from human exploitation of their shells for the curio trade. In western Ireland numbers of the (still relatively) common Purple Sea Urchin *Paracentrotus lividus*, which is capable of boring into soft rocks, have been reduced by commercial harvest for its succulent roes.

Forests beneath the sea

LEFT: The complex feeding structure of a sea urchin (Aristotle's lantern) can be seen in place in the specimen on the left, with another removed and sitting upside down on the right. These were dead, stranded (and rather smelly) individuals.

Lower living

Whilst kelp forms permanent forests of some stature in shallow sublittoral waters, other brown seaweeds known generically as wracks (Fucales) provide shrubby, smaller-scale seaweed habitats on the lower shore and just below. Chief among these is Egg (or Knotted) Wrack *Ascophyllum nodosum*, a species that covers sheltered rocky shores with a tangled mat of leathery, centimetre-wide branches. Held up not by strong stipes but by air-bladders, these only 'come alive' and turn into magical forests when the tide is in. Then, instead of slipping and stumbling over rock-burying masses when searching beneath the heavy tresses for hidden crustaceans and molluscs, it becomes a delight to snorkel over and through the now elegant fronds rising up to 2m high. This is a long-lived perennial seaweed (the holdfasts can persist and develop new fronds for several decades), but it is surprisingly easily damaged by trampling and has low recruitment, something to bear in mind when visiting rocky shores. The heavy tresses of Egg Wrack are easily damaged by strong waves, and at more exposed sites the shorter Bladder Wrack *Fucus vesiculosus* forms miniature copses (see page 94).

Thong Weed wonders

Thong Weed *Himanthalia elongata* grows even taller, often to 2m, and can create dense forests on the lower shore and in the shallow sublittoral zone around much of the British Isles except (as with kelp) the southeast. Although it is a 'brown' seaweed, the strap-like fronds can appear almost yellow in the sunlight. On much of the rocky coastline of Devon and Cornwall, the forests combine with an understorey of pink encrusting algae and sometimes dense groups of large Snakelocks Anemones *Anemonia viridis*. When covered by enough tide and seen with colourful wrasses and other fish sweeping around and through the forest, this underwater scenery can be breathtaking and wonderful to explore. On a calm, sunny summer day, it is Paul's firm favourite for snorkelling. Occasionally, however, dense Thong Weed can be 'too much of a good thing', as Frances found out when swimming from a shore in St Agnes, Isles of Scilly, its entangling fronds reaching up to the surface and proving a nightmare to get through.

On a winter shore walk or snorkel, depending on the tide, it is easy to see distinctive green-brown, stalked globules or buttons of seaweed on the rocks and not appreciate their relationship with the dense yellow-brown Thong Weed forests you enjoyed the previous summer. The buttons can be seen at any time of the year, whilst the long straps that grow out of the centre of the buttons are reproductive bodies, which are formed in autumn then grow most rapidly between the following February and May. These die once the gametes have been released in the summer, through until the start of winter. The structures that produce the gametes appear as little dark spots on the strap when they are ripe (see also *Seasons in the sea*, Chapter 1).

BELOW: A shallow forest of Bladder Wrack *Fucus vesiculosus*, buoyed up by its bladders in the shallows of Loch Fyne, Scotland.

Forests beneath the sea

ABOVE: Forest of Thong Weed *Himanthalia elongata*, kelp and other algae in sunlit shallow water.

BELOW: Long strap-like reproductive fronds grow up from the centre of Thong Weed 'buttons' (inset).

Variations on a theme

Around the coast

Long, trailing kelp fronds exert considerable drag, and stable bedrock or large boulders are generally a prerequisite for the growth of a well-developed kelp forest. Consequently, whilst Forest Kelp is found all round Britain and Ireland, substantial kelp forests are not a feature where soft chalk predominates or there is a shortage of stable rock habitat. With some exceptions, therefore, there is a dearth of kelp in shallow sublittoral areas along the southeast and east coasts of England and parts of eastern Scotland. In contrast, the rocky coastlines of western Scotland, Wales, the southwest peninsula of England and the west coast of Ireland all support dense kelp forests. Kelp is largely lacking in the Bristol Channel, even in those parts where stable rock exists, primarily due to the high turbidity of the estuary. We discuss the relatively recent loss of kelp forest along the Sussex coastline later in this chapter.

Variations in form

The shape and form of many terrestrial trees and other plants can vary dramatically according to prevailing conditions such as light, altitude and wind exposure. Forest-forming kelp species also show such observable variations with environment (phenotypic variations). Classically the wide fronds of Forest Kelp and Oar Weed are divided into flat, strap-like or finger-like sections (described as digitate). This helps to prevent damage to the fronds under strong wave or current action, but it reduces the frond area available for photosynthesis. Under very sheltered conditions, such as those found near the head of a sea loch or in a very enclosed bay, these kelps grow with wide, undivided fronds. In similar circumstances, the always undivided fronds of Sugar Kelp *Saccharina latissima* expand laterally – and it becomes very difficult to tell these three kelp species apart without a close look at the stipe and holdfast. Diving over a kelp forest in one such Scottish sea loch had Frances metaphorically scratching her head over which species she was looking at, and with time short, the resulting record was simply kelp, Laminariales. The expansive fronds of kelp under these still conditions can provide an excellent platform for gastropod molluscs, such as topshells and periwinkles, that graze on an all but invisible film of diatoms coating the fronds.

Forests beneath the sea

In contrast, at very wave-exposed sites the only kelp to thrive in the sublittoral fringe and shallow water is Dabberlocks *Alaria esculenta*. This has a long, thin frond that provides little resistance to the water and is supported by a strong, tear-resistant midrib. The small rocky island groups of St Kilda and Rockall off the west coast of Scotland are exposed to extremes of wave action, and here Dabberlocks is the predominant kelp in the sublittoral, occasionally found as deep as 30m.

Back to those extremely sheltered heads of Scottish sea lochs – these often have variable salinity due to freshwater input from surrounding high ground. Under these circumstances Egg Wrack can be found growing as unattached mounds, lying loose on mixed mud and stone shores and in shallow water. Lacking its characteristic egg-shaped bladders and with short, fine branches, it looks nothing like its 'normal' self. In this state it is known as Crofter's Wig or Wig Weed *Ascophyllum nodosum* ecad *mackaii*. Individuals grow from fragments of the normal form broken off from nearby rock-attached individuals and carried in by wind and tide. The term 'ecad' is used to denote that the variation in morphology is induced purely by environmental influence. In its 'wig' form this seaweed modifies the sediment surface habitat, providing structure and protection for a variety of other species where there was little before. This uncommon community is always well worth a close look, as Frances found many years ago when a European Eel *Anguilla anguilla* slithered out from its humid and protective pile of seaweed.

ABOVE: Forest Kelp *Laminaria hyperborea* growing under wave-exposed conditions at St Abbs, Scotland, have clearly divided fronds (left), contrasting with the undivided 'cape' form of Furbellows kelp *Saccorhiza polyschides* in a very sheltered part of Kinlochbervie, Scotland (right).

A golden opportunity

The aptly named Golden Kelp *Laminaria ochroleuca* is a southern European species that today can be found as an alternative dominant in some forests in the southwest of England and in the Channel Islands. Whilst it has so far not been recorded further north than Lundy in the Bristol Channel, it appears to be spreading and becoming more abundant in response to warming seas. In Ireland there is a single, genetically confirmed record from the Mullet Peninsula on the west coast (Schoenrock *et al.* 2019). The record was made during a joint Porcupine Marine Natural History Society and Seasearch field trip in 2018, of which Frances was lucky enough to be a part (though not with the divers who found it). The common name of Golden Kelp comes from the golden sheen that suffuses the base of the blade. As it starts to thrive further northward, it may displace Forest Kelp in some areas, a concern as Golden Kelp forests are known to support much less biodiversity, partly because their smooth stipes and fronds are unsuitable for epiphytic growths.

New forests

Wireweed *Sargassum muticum* is a non-native brown seaweed in the same order (Fucales) as the common wrack species of our shores. Since its accidental introduction in the 1970s it has spread widely around the south and west coasts of Britain and all round Ireland (see also Chapter 12, where we discuss non-native species in more detail). This elegant, much branched species grows up to 2m tall (5m in suitable sheltered habitats) and can form dense stands in shallow water and rock pools. It can be a menace to boats and a nuisance to swimmers in shallow confined waters such as harbours. Its fast growth rate puts it in competition with similar-sized but slower-growing native seaweeds such as Thong Weed. However, one of the main reasons why it is so successful is that, during sexual reproduction, one plant can produce both ova (eggs) and sperm and can self-fertilise. The resulting germlings stay attached to the mature seaweed as they develop and only drop off when ready for rapid growth. They quickly fix onto the seabed and soon reach the stage when they are too big to be eaten by grazers such as limpets, and so survival of young plants can be high. Luckily it does not like being exposed to the air for any length of time, but we have often seen it filling permanent rock pools at most tide levels. However, like native

Egg Wrack and Thong Weed it too can form attractive understorey-style mini-forests and provide habitat and feeding grounds for a variety of animals.

Like Wireweed, the kelp Wakame *Undaria pinnatifida* comes from the Pacific around Japan, China and Korea; it was first recorded in 1994 in the Solent. Whilst it has since spread along the south coast of England, into Wales and the east coast of Ireland, with one record from Scotland in the Firth of Forth, it seems so far to be confined to artificial structures such as pontoons in harbours and estuaries and has not formed the dense forests found in its native areas. It has a known ability to spread around the world on the hulls of ships and more locally between marinas on small boats. Frances first came across Wakame in a marina in Portsmouth in 2015; she finds that it is always worth lying down and peering over the side of such structures, though she does get some strange looks.

ABOVE: The non-native Wireweed *Sargassum muticum* can form beautiful forests, its long straggling fronds held up by numerous small gas bladders.

Destruction, exploitation and reparation

'Natural' destruction

The hurricane-force winds that swept through the British Isles in 1987 and 1990 caused widespread destruction in mature forests, woodlands and arboretums. Frances well remembers the 1990 storm, as she had to drive back through the chaos from Heathrow to Cambridge with two small children on board. Kelp forests can be similarly affected by violent, storm-induced wave action. With its rigid stipes, Forest Kelp is more susceptible to snapping off during high-intensity storms than is Oar Weed, which has flexible stipes allowing it to bend over without breaking when exposed on very low tides. Storm Arwen in 2021 caused considerable damage to kelp forests in the Farne Islands.

Since about the 1970s, overgrazing by sea urchins has resulted in extensive 'barrens' in Norway, where kelp forests and other seaweeds are completely stripped away, in this case by the cold-water sea urchin *Strongylocentrotus droebachiensis*. In the British Isles, this species is not common and is mostly confined to northern Scotland. Norway supports what is thought to be the largest continuous area of Forest Kelp forest in Europe and this is a serious issue, thought to have been initiated by historical overfishing of urchin predators. Whilst grazing by our larger Common Sea Urchin certainly curtails seaweed and kelp growth in many areas, similar devastating grazing-pressure events have not so far been apparent around the British Isles. However, kelp forest has been and continues to be lost or reduced in some areas, such as along the Sussex coastline.

Forest Kelp is also called Northern Kelp; it thrives in cold, clear water, its preference reflected by its distribution, which extends from the British Isles north to Norway and Iceland, but only just reaching south to mid-Portugal. So the Sussex coast of England would not be an ideal habitat, compared to somewhere like the northwest coast of Scotland. Nevertheless there is plenty of suitable habitat along this stretch, and yet no real kelp forest. This was not always the case, and before the 1980s Forest Kelp and Oar Weed covered large areas of suitably stable rock from Selsey Bill to Shoreham. Whilst it would be easy to blame global warming, this loss appears to have much to do with destructive fishing practices and lowered water quality from historical sediment dumping.

Restoration

March 2021 saw the start of an ambitious 'rewilding' scheme on the Sussex coast, the Sussex Kelp Recovery Project, with the implementation of a Sussex Nearshore Trawling Byelaw that now protects an area of over 300km^2 out to 4km offshore from seabed trawling. This is very much a citizen science project, with input from professionals and volunteers alike, including the fishing community, to provide baseline data and monitor for signs of natural recovery.

As well as projects like this one aiming to allow natural recovery by removing identified pressures, there are now initiatives in various parts of the world attempting to actively restore damaged or lost forests. Restoration projects, whether for kelp, seagrass (Chapter 6) or native oyster habitats (Chapter 4), need a clear understanding of the aims and potential benefits, for example preventing coastal erosion, mitigating climate change, maintaining or increasing biodiversity and, of course, community education and involvement. The Kelp Forest Alliance has produced a *Kelp Restoration Guidebook* (Eger *et al.* 2022) with worldwide examples of best practice.

Kelp and seaweed harvests

Whilst we are used to seeing seals, people, dogs and even foxes and deer (which can swim well) on seashores, cows and sheep are a much rarer and perhaps surprising sight. It is on both of our 'bucket lists' to visit North Ronaldsay, the northernmost of the Orkney islands, where drystone walls keep sheep not in the fields, but out of them on the seashore. The original wall was built in 1832 to encircle the entire 5km (3 mile) long island, and this tough but rare breed of sheep has since adapted to survive and thrive on a diet of seaweed, including kelp cast up by storms. The wall hasn't done so well, but since 2019 the island now has a fulltime warden who coordinates locals and visitors as volunteer repairers. Farm ruminants, including sheep but particularly cattle, are a well-known source of methane emissions, thus contributing to global warming, but experimental supplementation of cattle feed with certain types of seaweeds has been shown to reduce these emissions. It would be interesting to know whether North Ronaldsay sheep are likewise naturally less 'windy'.

Large brown seaweeds, including kelp, have been traditionally harvested at a small scale around the British Isles for centuries. Frances remembers meeting a tractor and trailer loaded to the gunnels with Egg Wrack on a narrow road in South Uist, Outer Hebrides, in the 1980s. In Ireland, significant quantities of Egg Wrack are still harvested from rocky seashores for commercial processing, with a recent report from Munster Technological University citing 33,000 wet tonnes collected in 2020. Currently kelp has a far smaller role, harvested live or collected from the strandline mostly for local use by farmers and horticulturalists (MTU, 2022).

As far back as the 16th century, kelp and other seaweeds were collected and burnt to produce soda (sodium compounds) and potash (potassium compounds) used in soap, glass-making and fertiliser. The seaweeds that could be used in this way and the ash they produced were referred to as kelp (why, we don't know) and the name later became associated with the larger brown seaweeds in the order Laminariales because they produced the most useful ash. Even later it was used in gunpowder production, and this prompted an upsurge of interest and research into kelp forests worldwide prior to and during the First World War. Kelp and other seaweeds are still used in a wide variety of products, although no longer for glass-making or gunpowder production.

Kelp farming

Seaweed farming is big business in East Asian countries such as Japan and the Philippines, but is currently only an emerging industry in Britain and Ireland. There is no doubt of the ecological importance and beauty of kelp forests, but there is also no doubt that kelp and other seaweeds have potentially sustainable uses on a much larger scale beyond their current food, fertiliser and pharmaceutical ones, for example in alternative packaging and textiles. In particular, as large, productive species, kelps and wracks could be used in biofuel production. To be sustainable, this would have to be sourced from marine farms, and as yet the biofuel industry around the British Isles does not have a seaweed-based component. There are, however, a number of small, established or pilot kelp farms, including off the

BELOW: A successful kelp harvest in Japan.

Norfolk and Yorkshire coasts. Their products are currently mainly used as natural fertiliser in agriculture, and for the cosmetic and food industries.

The relatively short-lived Sugar Kelp grows particularly well attached to lines, the most common way to grow such seaweeds. Frances has seen farms successfully growing local seaweeds in this manner off the east coast of Sabah, Borneo, using simple ropes and string held up with empty plastic water bottles. In Scotland, the Scottish Association for Marine Science (SAMS), based near Oban, is researching the best species, techniques, environmental conditions and pathogen-control methods, and has two nearby experimental farms off the islands of Kerrera and Lismore, growing Sugar Kelp, Forest Kelp, Dabberlocks and some smaller seaweeds. Their research includes the potential use of Sugar Kelp to produce bioethanol.

Although not on the same height scale as a Californian Giant Kelp *Macrocystis pyrifera* forest, the tiered 'woodlands' of Forest Kelp and other large brown seaweeds that fringe our rocky coastline are impressive enough. Occasionally such forests are formed of several different kelp species, but the aptly named Forest Kelp stands out, frequently forming a 'monoculture' that can exceptionally reach 3.5m high. Through exploring the structure of kelp forests in this chapter, we have shown how this and other similar species transform what might be relatively barren rocky slopes into a structural habitat and home fit for a myriad of other seaweeds and animals.

Seaweed forests are more than just highly productive, and when a kelp forest is lost, the high biodiversity of the rocky areas in which they live is lost too. Attempts to restore kelp to areas where it was known to be historically present are both laudable and feasible, but it might be many decades before such 'new forests' support anywhere near the same number of species as an undisturbed 'ancient' marine forest. Fringing our coastline, mature kelp forests also sequester carbon and provide protection from storm waves. Individual Forest Kelps can live for upwards of 20 years, but such forests may have been in place for hundreds, and in our opinion they are as worthy of protection as ancient forests on land.

Reef life | chapter four

When the word 'reef' comes up in conversation, it usually conjures up visions of sunshine holidays and colourful coral reefs in the tropics, or for sailors and seamen the terror of failed engines and jagged rocks. This use is backed up by dictionary definitions that refer to areas of rock, coral and sand near or just emerging above the surface of the ocean and so a potential danger to shipping. In the Marine Habitat Classification for Britain and Ireland, reef categories all refer to deep-sea cold-water coral or other animal-created biogenic reefs. However, divers and marine biologists often use the term 'reef' less formally to refer to any submerged rocky outcrop, ridge, cliff or expanse of rock. This prosaic description does no justice to the wealth of habitats provided by rocky reefs around the coasts of the British Isles, or the mesmerising diversity of organisms that live on them.

Rocky reefs can be just as colourful and biodiverse as coral reefs, and the reason for this, as described in Chapter 1, is that many marine animals live an immobile life permanently attached to rock or other hard substrata. At sunlit depths, seaweeds also thrive attached to rocky reefs, creating habitats such as kelp and Thong Weed *Himanthalia elongata* forests, described in Chapter 3. However, in this chapter, we are concentrating on reef habitats that are rich in animals or actually formed by animals.

Animal-dominated reefs occur mainly where light levels or other environmental conditions are unsuitable for large seaweeds, so such reefs are often in relatively deep water (although still classed as shallow in the oceanic sense), or on vertical and otherwise shaded surfaces.

OPPOSITE PAGE:
Exotically colourful, this reef at Sula Sgeir (a small, uninhabited island off the northwest of Scotland) is covered in soft corals, sea anemones, sponges and more.

Colourful scenery

The bright colours and varied forms of sessile animals and the attraction of myriad crevices and hidey-holes for fish and other mobile animals make rocky reefs very appealing to divers wanting to explore and photograph spectacular underwater scenery. Perhaps the greatest contributors to the brightness of the scenery are the cnidarians (Cnidaria), including anemones, soft corals, sea fans and hydroids. These in turn provide food for another equally colourful group, nudibranchs or sea slugs (Nudibranchia), described in Chapter 9.

The universal feature of cnidarians is the possession of stinging cells called cnidae, sometimes still referred to as nematocysts. Imagine yourself as a small shrimp or a larval fish approaching a steep reef covered in cnidarians, and you could consider this a 'wall of death'. The description might sound over-dramatic, but that is what these reef surfaces, covered with hungry mouths surrounded by tentacles armed with batteries of stinging cells, must represent to any small creature that ventures too close. It is worth bearing this in mind when considering the number of progeny that marine animals with planktonic life stages must produce in order to 'beat the odds' and reproduce successfully. It also helps to explain the numerous mechanisms that have evolved to keep planktonic larvae in the water column until it is time for them to 'land' and start adult life as we described in Chapter 1.

Jewels in the sea

If you were to single out one species that makes a major contribution to this scenery, particularly around the south and west of the British Isles, it would probably be the Jewel Anemone *Corynactis viridis*. Although called an 'anemone', it belongs to a small order of so-called mushroom anemones (Corallimorpharia), rather than true sea anemones (Actiniaria), and is very much like a stony coral (Scleractinia) in terms of its anatomy, just lacking the hard chalky skeleton. All three orders are classed together as hexacorals (Hexacorallia). Jewel Anemones also share another quality with corals in that, although they do not create reefs, they make their big impact when present in huge numbers. Individual Jewel Anemones are small, about a centimetre across and not easily spotted without

ABOVE: Colourful patchwork of Jewel Anemones *Corynactis viridis* created by their prolific asexual reproduction.

a close look, but dense groups can cover large areas of rock face, especially vertical and steep surfaces, in a riot of colour.

The secret behind these tightly packed aggregations is the way the anemones reproduce asexually, with individuals stretching themselves then splitting across the middle to form two new anemones of equal size in a process known as longitudinal fission. What makes them spectacular is that the anemones occur in a variety of vibrant colours, including pink, purple, yellow and gaudy green to name a few, often with contrasting colours to body and tentacles, and the reproductive cloning process leads to large patches of anemones dressed in the same colours. With their knob-tipped tentacles they remind us of carnivorous sundew plants *Drosera* spp. found in boggy areas on land. Both they and Jewel Anemones use their tentacles to capture food.

Picturesque, but not peaceful

The much larger Plumose Anemone *Metridium senile* is another animal that creates fabulous scenery on rock faces and, because of its liking for vertical surfaces elevated above the seabed, it often adorns shipwrecks and other man-made objects too. With its tall column, topped with an elegant parapet and plume of tentacles, it resembles

Coastal Seas

ABOVE: The small individuals at the base of this group of Plumose Anemones *Metridium senile* will have been produced by pieces splitting away from the base of larger ones.

BELOW: Pretty but not peaceful: Plumose Anemones on a reef will attack their neighbours unless they are siblings (clonemates) or potential mates.

an ancient Corinthian column. Mind you, if you think a rock face adorned with Plumose Anemones swaying gently in the current or swell is a tranquil scene, then think again; there is warfare – including tribal conflict – under way. In addition to the tentacles they use for catching food, these anemones are armed with special 'catch tentacles' that carry densely packed stinging cells. These are used to sting and drive away potential rivals for space and food, including other species of sea anemones. This helps to explain why this species can dominate large areas of reef. Even neighbouring Plumose Anemones can be subject to strikes, but this is not indiscriminate, with clonemates safe from each other's attacks. Like Jewel Anemones, Plumose Anemones reproduce prodigiously by asexual means. They often do this by a process called basal or pedal laceration, where a piece at the base of the anemone's column splits away and develops into a new, smaller anemone. This means that groups of individuals on the rock face are often clones of each other, in other words genetically identical. For the Plumose Anemone,

Reef life

then, a gene that programmed its owner to attack neighbours which carried identical genes would not be successful.

However, the even more interesting aspect of the Plumose Anemone story, as revealed in early research, is that, as well as leaving clonemates in peace, they do not attack non-clonemates of the opposite sex (Kaplan 1983). On the contrary, having demonstrated the phenomenon, Kaplan also speculated that gentle stroking with catch tentacles between a neighbouring female and male, as distinct from attack, might be a type of courtship that synchronised the release of their eggs and sperm to maximise the chance of successful fertilisation.

Elegant by name …

Another sea anemone that can cover significant areas of rock face is *Cylista elegans*, the aptly named Elegant Anemone. It occurs in five distinct colour varieties that could be mistaken for different species. Like the Plumose Anemone, it can reproduce by basal laceration, so you often find groups of the same variety in patches, and a typical habitat for them is on the upper part of rock faces that are otherwise covered in Jewel Anemones.

BELOW: Clone groups of Elegant Anemone *Cylista elegans* varieties on a shipwreck: *venusta* (centre) and *miniata* (top right).

Colonies and coral

Like their sea anemone relatives, soft corals can produce their own brand of scenery on the faces of rocky reefs. Soft corals are colonial cnidarians with many individual anemone-like polyps joined together and, as their name suggests, with no supporting hard skeleton. Their soft bodies are, however, given some support by slivers of calcium carbonate called sclerites. They belong to a class of cnidarians called octocorals (Octocorallia), so named because each individual polyp has eight tentacles. The principal species, found all around the British Isles, is *Alcyonium digitatum*, known as Dead Man's Fingers (see photographs on page 49). It is notably dominant around popular diving sites on northern North Sea coasts, such as at St Abbs and the Farne Islands, splashing rocky reefs a white or pale orange colour. It is also often abundant on the west coast of Scotland, particularly around the entrances to sea lochs where strong water flow brings plentiful plankton food.

An impressive nudibranch sea slug, the largest in our waters, specialises in preying on these soft corals. Despite its size, *Tritonia hombergii* can be hard to spot because its orange colour and the branched protrusions that cover its body help it to blend in well among its favourite food.

Red Sea Fingers *A. glomeratum* is a second species of *Alcyonium* with an orange or sometimes more dramatic and photogenic blood-red body and contrasting white polyps, generally found tucked away from any wave action. It is far less widespread than Dead Man's Fingers, occurring mainly in the southwest of Britain and Ireland but extending north to western Scotland.

The Pink Sea Fan *Eunicella verrucosa* is a yet more visually striking octocoral. Sea fans most commonly grow as branching fan-shaped colonies, the branches supported by a central axis made of a flexible protein, gorgonin. This often survives long after the animal's death, and such 'skeletons' are occasionally washed ashore. Whilst sea fans are common in warmer waters,

BELOW: Rich animal life in a small area of reef, including a colony of soft coral Red Sea Fingers *Alcyonium glomeratum* (centre), Sunset Cup Corals *Leptopsammia pruvoti* (left) and Yellow Cluster Anemones *Parazoanthus axinellae* (right).

this is one of only two species found around the British Isles within diving depths, and it has a restricted distribution. This is reflected in its status as a nationally protected species under the Wildlife and Countryside Act 1981. It is very vulnerable to seabed trawling because it often grows on low, horizontal rocky reefs, but it can be abundant in some areas in the southwest of the British Isles. Sea fan 'forests' are a wonderful sight, with the fans usually all orientated in the same plane, aligned across the current to maximise feeding opportunities for their polyps. Such a vista also portrays a healthy, undisturbed habitat because a large fan may be over 50 years old. Once a young sea fan develops beyond a 10cm tall 'twig' and starts to branch, it may grow as little as 1cm a year.

A specialist nudibranch, *Candiella odhneri*, lives and feeds on sea fans and is extremely well camouflaged, with external gills perfectly resembling the sea fan polyps' tentacles. Its distinctive coils of eggs wrapped round the fan's branches are easier to spot, and it is often these that alert an observer to the presence of the slugs themselves. Around the British Isles the much smaller, white Northern Sea Fan *Callistephanus pallida* (previously *Swiftia pallida*) is only found on the west coasts of Scotland and Ireland. Whilst not individually protected, the habitat in which it most usually occurs, defined as 'Northern Sea Fan and sponge communities', falls within Annex 1 ('reefs') on the EU Habitats Directive.

BELOW: A forest of Pink Sea Fans *Eunicella verrucosa* mostly orientated in the same plane across the current on a reef near Plymouth.

ABOVE: A silt-covered reef in the Isles of Scilly dominated by a rich variety of sponges.

Sponge reefs

When we show images of colourful, sponge-dominated rocky reefs to interest groups, especially non-divers, there is often great surprise at the sheer number and variety of sponges found around Great Britain. We have already introduced sponges in Chapter 1, and there is no doubt of their importance as major filter-feeders within some shallow-water rocky reef communities, including the Northern Sea Fan community just described above. Though well below the limits of normal scuba diving and therefore beyond the scope of this book, it is still worth mentioning that in deeper water there are habitats where sponges are the key component, forming dense and long-lived sponge reefs. With their varied shapes, sizes and textures, such deep-sea sponges provide the basis for a high biodiversity of other animals, both invertebrates and fishes. Whilst we ourselves would never expect to see such a reef first-hand, the use of camera-armed submersibles is now bringing their beauty and complexity to a wide audience. Along with deep-water coral (*Desmophyllum pertusum*) reefs, new 'sponge cities' in the North Atlantic are now coming to light through exploratory projects such as ATLAS, which explored deep-sea ecosystems there between 2016 and 2020.

Sea caves

Over thousands of years, storms and strong wave action around the coastline of the British Isles have resulted in a plethora of intertidal caves. Cut into rocky shoreline cliffs, these are often completely or partially submerged at high tides, a fact not always appreciated by unwary beach walkers, but happily used by Grey Seals *Halichoerus grypus*. Historically, these caves were often used by Cornish and Welsh smugglers as a place to unload and hide their contraband. Smuggling was at its peak in the 18th century, but was declining fast by the late 18th and early 19th century, as government taxes on precious commodities such as tea, wine and spirits were reduced, making the risks less worthwhile.

Far less common around our shores are permanently submerged sublittoral caves, their walls providing a type of specialist, steep reef habitat. Whilst we have both explored intertidal caves on foot or by snorkelling (always making a careful check of tide time first), neither of us has had much opportunity (at least in this country) to visit deeper-water caves. Intertidal and shallow caves can be exposed to scour from bottom sand or cobbles that may limit what grows there, but strong water movement brings abundant food and oxygen, allowing rich growths of encrusting sponges, hydroids, sea squirts and cup corals to develop in many caves. The common Beadlet Anemone *Actinia equina* smothers the walls of some wave-exposed caves on Sark (one of the Channel Islands), its delicate appearance belying its tough nature, adapted as it is to survival on wave-tossed, rocky shores. Wave surge without the crashing action of breaking waves results in the development of some specific communities, such as the sponge and sea squirt association described in Chapter 1 and found both in caves and surge gullies.

Sublittoral caves and the walls of caves that remain largely or partly filled at all states of the tide are one of the best places to look for Pink Soft Coral or Pink Sea Fingers *Alcyonium hibernicum*, a pretty but diminutive and scarce soft coral with a patchy distribution along the southwest and western coasts of Britain and Ireland. The Sugarloaf caves near Port St Mary on the Isle of Man are a boat-accessible, popular dive site where this species thrives. It also grows well in the shade of extensive overhangs that provide similar cave-like conditions.

Caves and overhangs are also good places to search for one of our favourite small fish, the Black-faced Blenny *Tripterygion delaisi*. This

ABOVE: Divers exploring a sublittoral cave below one of the rocky stacks that abound in the St Kilda archipelago.

delightful but uncommon species has been recorded along the southwest coast of England as far east as Dorset, and also in the Channel Islands (see page 6). It has a tenacious habit of hanging around upside down on overhead rock or head-down on sloping overhang tops where there is little silt to obscure its courtship dance or smother its eggs laid onto the rock. In the summer months, we have watched breeding males, bright yellow with contrasting black heads, perform elaborate fin-flicking displays around a visiting female, enticing her to lay her eggs so that he can fertilise them. In the winter months, the males seem to disappear but in reality they have swapped their bright breeding garb for the camouflage brown, mottled colouration sported all year round by females and juveniles. Our recent observations suggest that, even within the breeding season, a male changes his colour from a 'routine' bright yellow to an even more vibrant hue when a female is in the vicinity.

In deep-penetrating freshwater cave systems and aquifers around the British Isles, a variety of small invertebrates, particularly crustaceans, are found only in these habitats. With a lack of any equivalent marine cave systems, there appear to be no cave-endemic marine species around the British Isles.

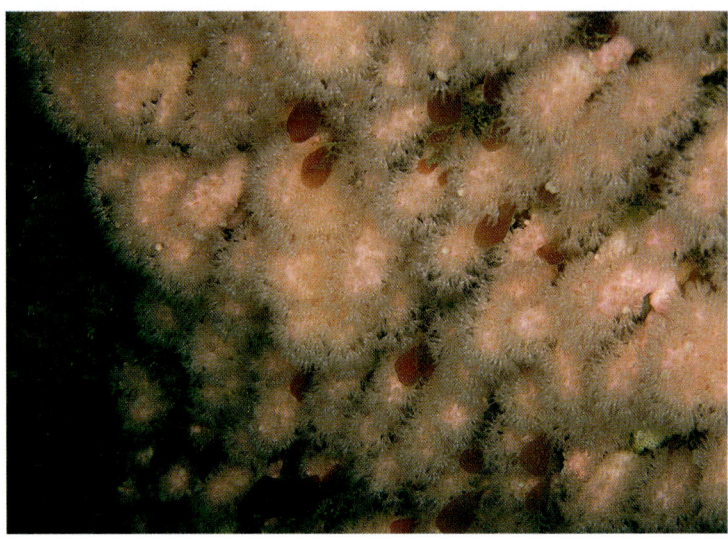

RIGHT: Extensive growth of the scarce soft coral *Alcyonium hibernicum* in a sea cave on the Isle of Man.

St Kilda

Lying just over 60km out into the Atlantic from North Uist in the Outer Hebrides, St Kilda is a remote archipelago whose several islands and sea stacks sport dramatic, rugged terrain and towering cliffs. Today, in the breeding season, it is home to a million or so seabirds that once sustained a small but hardy community of people until the final 36 inhabitants asked to be evacuated in 1930. Historical and archaeological remains indicate habitation going back 2,000 years, with recent research extending this to periodic habitation as far back as 4,000 years ago. St Kilda's unique history and culture, along with its outstanding natural environment and wildlife, both above and below the water, earned it UNESCO World Heritage status in 1986. Allowing for the dictates of the weather, St Kilda, which is owned and managed by the National Trust for Scotland (NTS), can be visited via boat tour companies or on your own (good-sized) boat. The NTS website gives very useful information on visiting the main island of Hirta, where there are basic facilities, seasonal rangers and volunteers.

The steep sea cliffs making up most of the coastline continue deep underwater, revealing a wealth of sublittoral caves and tunnels that have resulted from extreme wave action at sea level and subsequent subsidence of these once volcanic islands over geological time. An early pioneering diving survey described the islands as remarkable in the number and variety of these features (Howson and Picton 1985). The remote location and relatively pristine marine environment have encouraged many dive expeditions and surveys over subsequent years, in spite of the logistical difficulties inherent in such visits.

The archipelago was designated a Special Area of Conservation (SAC) in 2005 with reefs and sea caves as two of the main qualifying features. A recent marine survey carried out by Herriot-Watt University for Scottish Natural Heritage (now NatureScot) concentrated principally on sea caves, but the report provides a comprehensive summary of this most fascinating far-flung outpost of the British Isles (Harries et al. 2018).

A drone's-eye view of the St Kilda archipelago, with Boreray, Stac an Armin and Stac Lee in the foreground and the main island of Hirta in the background.

Busy neighbourhoods and 'blocks of flats'

The biodiversity of animal-dominated reefs around the British Isles varies depending on a multitude of environmental factors. However, the geology of the rock can play a major role, because it is not just the outer surfaces of our rocky reefs that support thriving life. Crevices, cracks, caves and other cavities in a reef are perfect places for numerous mobile animals to evade predators, find food, hide, rest between hunting expeditions, hold breeding territories, lay eggs and even build nests. We have both spent many cumulative hours crevice-watching, a rewarding pastime provided you have a patient diving buddy. A single crevice may house a single occupant, such as a sombre-looking Tadpole Fish *Raniceps raninus* that will only emerge at night, or it can be home to numerous animals from a wide variety of different phyla. In a single, metre-long crevice, for example, obvious inhabitants may include several species of crab, prawn and squat lobster, a sea cucumber wedged into the fissure with its feathery tentacles extended to catch food, fish such as blennies or rocklings, and a topshell feeding on encrusting sponge.

That is just the crevice-dwellers that can be seen with a casual eye and a diving torch, but there could be many more hidden away. A rock face may have numerous adjacent crevices with a variety of occupants coming and going, reminiscent of a busy block of flats or a close of houses. Neighbours sometimes get on whilst others quarrel, and it can be the same on a busy reef. Arguments can be mere bickering if between two Spiny Squat Lobsters *Galathea strigosa*,

BELOW: Spot the residents. This crevice contains Velvet Swimming Crabs *Necora puber*, Spiny Squat Lobsters *Galathea strigosa*, a Green Sea Urchin *Psammechinus miliaris*, a Cushion Star *Asterina gibbosa* and a Tompot Blenny *Parablennius gattorugine*. There will be many more animals hidden from view.

for example, or much more impressive if a Conger Eel *Conger conger* and Common Lobster *Homarus gammarus* are the protagonists. Paul describes his long-term observations of the varied and mesmerising interactions between individual crevice-occupying Tompot Blennies *Parablennius gattorugine* in Chapter 8.

Holes and crevices can also house sessile animals whose larvae settle out of the plankton into such protective spaces. A drab-looking, fissured rock face may suddenly flower with colour as tube-building polychaete worms extend their feeding fans, swiftly withdrawing again if they perceive threatening shadows or vibrations. Crevice sea cucumbers *Aslia lefevrei* and *Pawsonia saxicola* live with their sausage-shaped bodies hidden in cracks and crevices, so that all that can be seen of them is their branched, bush-like feeding arms or tentacles. Softer rocks such as chalk and sandstone allow specialised polychaete worms, bivalve molluscs and even sponges to bore or dissolve their own holes, ending up permanently entombed.

Regional reefs

The wonderful surprises that await anyone exploring the shallow undersea world around the British Isles are a recurring theme of this book, and the innumerable and varied rocky reefs that occur throughout our waters provide some of the most fabulous scenery. A few of these stand out as particularly good regional examples, often recognised as such by their inclusion in Marine Protected Areas. We describe two of our particular favourite reefs below.

Norfolk's 'Great Barrier Reef'

Stroll along the East Anglian coastline, and while the above-water scenery and dramatic skies may be beautiful, the sea often looks the uninviting colour of a milky coffee. This is caused by high levels of suspended silt in inshore waters – but, when still conditions or an offshore (southerly) breeze result in a flat-calm summer sea on the north Norfolk coast, there is a dramatic change. Then the lack of wave action combines with a hard seabed to produce clear water, and the unusual and impressive Norfolk chalk habitat can be explored and appreciated. An extensive exposure of chalk, sometimes described as Norfolk's Great Barrier Reef, runs for over 32km along the coast from Weybourne in the west to Cromer, with some patches well beyond there to the east. The easiest access points for snorkelling, and for scuba diving out to some of the best areas, about 200m offshore, are from the beach at Sheringham. Aside from its beauty, the reef is an unusual and precious environment, as recognised by the designation of the Cromer Shoal Chalk Beds Marine Conservation Zone (MCZ) put in place in January 2016 and covering over 300km^2 between Weybourne and Happisburgh. The chalk provides a foothold for seaweeds and sessile animals on an otherwise predominantly sediment coastline, and erosion of its relatively soft surface has resulted in a varied topography.

In the sunlit shallows, and easily appreciated by snorkelling, colour is provided by rich growths of red seaweeds and encrusting sponges. One particular sponge found on the reef, belonging to the subgenus *Hymedesmia* (*Stylopus*) and recorded by local Seasearch divers, is believed by sponge specialists to be new to science. It even gained fame beyond marine biology when a competition was held to give it a common name, won by a local school pupil with the entry of 'Parpal Dumplin', one that the judges felt perfectly reflected its colour and Norfolk heritage.

The reef is also home to a wide variety of sea anemones, hydroids, molluscs, bryozoans and fishes, with a particularly striking feature being the abundance of crustaceans, an unusual number of them being 'out and about' during the day. This has allowed fascinating aspects of their behaviour to be observed. It is for example the only place where Paul has been able to photograph a crustacean moult in the wild, with the exception of Spiny Spider Crabs *Maja brachydactyla*, which are very unusual in shedding their armour 'in public' (see Chapter 9). The Norfolk instance recorded by Paul involved a female Shore Crab *Carcinus maenas* being guarded by a male, who was waiting for her to moult so that he could mate with her. Even allowing for his protective custody, it was still a great surprise to find this risky procedure being undertaken in the open, rather than hidden away in a rocky crevice. On another occasion at Sheringham, Paul came across a newly moulted Brown or Edible Crab *Cancer pagurus* that, without any protection from its surroundings or a partner, was quickly and gruesomely ripped apart by a marauding Shore Crab. It is indeed quite common on the Norfolk reef to see crabs walking along carrying the remains of other crabs that, as can be judged from the texture and colour of the fragments, have just moulted. The frequency of such attacks could simply be due to the density of the crab population, but

LEFT: On the Norfolk reef, a moulting female Shore Crab *Carcinus maenas* emerges from her armour while being protected by her mate. It is very unusual to see such an event out in the open.

LEFT: This photograph of Brown Crabs *Cancer pagurus* on the Norfolk chalk reef shows what crabs normally do: moult safely hidden away in a crevice. The paler 'crab' in the centre of the photo is the female's discarded armour suit, and the newly moulted female is tucked underneath her protective male partner.

a shortage of crevices suitable as moulting shelters on the chalk reef, in comparison to the more permanent fissures of harder rock reefs, may well also be a contributing factor.

Associated with the hazards of moulting, there is one fascinating aspect of crustacean behaviour on the Norfolk reef that Paul has observed. Crabs of all the main species as well as Leach's Squat Lobster *Galathea squamifera* can all be found scraping at the chalk with their claws. On one memorable evening dive, Paul encountered dozens of small Brown Crabs *Cancer pagurus* in several areas on top of the reef, all busily scraping away at the chalk. It has generally

ABOVE: At certain times, large numbers of Brown Crabs can be found scraping at the chalk of the Norfolk reef. It is usually assumed that they are excavating worms, but they sometimes appear to ingest fragments of the chalk itself.

been thought that crustaceans do this to extract burrowing *Polydora* worms from the soft rock, but Paul has seen crustaceans scraping at apparently worm-free patches of chalk and ingesting chalk particles, so he has suggested there may be a different explanation. By eating the chalk itself, they could be boosting their body calcium concentration and thus speeding up the hardening of their new exoskeleton after they have emerged from the old one at a moult. As shown by all the crabs carrying pieces of their soft relatives, crustaceans are in great danger from predation after moulting. Not only do they lack their hard protective armour, they also cannot move properly because they have lost the firm anchoring points for their muscles (akin to us having rubbery bones). Any strategy that shortens this hazardous interlude would have a significant selective advantage. However, there are doubts amongst those marine physiologists that Paul has consulted as to whether such a mechanism could exist, so he intends to watch the Norfolk crabs' activities even more closely to try and find out what is going on.

In addition to its special ecology, the Norfolk chalk-reef area supports a small-scale but locally important fishery for 'Cromer Crab' (Brown Crab) and Common Lobster, using pots laid down in long lines. Potting is normally regarded as a relatively benign fishing method, causing less collateral damage to habitats and non-target species than other methods such as bottom trawling or dredging. In

Reef life

LEFT: Spot the prawn – the biodiverse fauna of the Norfolk reef includes this tiny, colourful amphipod *Iphimedia* sp. and a larger, very well-camouflaged prawn hanging over it, both clinging to the tube of a Peacock Worm *Sabella pavonina*.

Norfolk, however, conservationists are very concerned that the soft rock is uniquely vulnerable to damage caused by the lines of pots being hauled up and moved around by wave action in such shallow water. They note that ropes in the potting lines, when mobilised in this way, can act like cheese-wire and cut through chalk features such as small pinnacles and arches, so gradually levelling and seriously degrading the chalk reef.

Lyme Bay Reefs, Dorset

Lyme Bay and Lyme Regis in particular are world-famous for their Jurassic geology and wealth of marine fossils. However, far fewer people are aware of the colourful and biodiverse mudstone reefs found offshore, supporting exceptionally high numbers of Pink Sea Fans. The reefs can only be appreciated by boat diving (or on film) as they occur offshore and are too deep for snorkelling.

Finning and hovering above this fragile landscape is like looking down on a forest of miniature pink trees, interspersed with orange 'anthill' mounds, in reality head-sized colonies of Potato Crisp Bryozoan *Pentapora foliacea*. Bright orange 'anemones' on shaded rock surfaces turn out to be Sunset Cup Corals *Leptopsammia pruvoti*, the largest of three rare cup corals found within diving depths around southwest Britain. Lyme Bay, Lundy and the Isles of

Scilly are the only well-known sites to see this spectacular species, although it has been recorded from a few other places in Devon and Dorset. The other two smaller species are the Scarlet and Gold Star Coral *Balanophyllia regia* and the Southern Cup Coral *Caryophyllia inornata*. In contrast, in spite of its vernacular name, the Devonshire Cup Coral *C. smithii* is common on rocky reefs almost all round the British Isles.

Lyme Bay Reefs are now part of a Marine Protected Area (MPA), the Lyme Bay and Torbay SAC. These low reefs, interspersed with sediment areas, present no barrier to bottom trawling for scallops, and the eventful history of conservation measures, habitat recovery and monitoring in Lyme Bay is described in Chapter 12. In addition to trawling, Pink Sea Fans face further challenges here and in other areas, including a disease that causes fans to die back. In the winter of 2014/15 (and in subsequent winters), people walking across beaches in southwest England found them littered with 'sea fangles', essentially ripped-off sea fans bound up with plastic debris including fishing lines and party balloons. Researchers at Plymouth University have demonstrated that the likely origin is from sea fans torn away by 'ghost fishing', due to lost fishing gear drifting over reefs (Sheehan *et al.* 2017).

BELOW: A dense array of Pink Sea Fans *Eunicella verrucosa* and branching sponges thrives in this protected area of reef in Lyme Bay.

Animal-constructed (biogenic) reefs

In certain locations, animals do not just dominate the scenery, they build it. The most obvious example is a tropical coral reef, built up from the limestone exoskeletons secreted by colonial, reef-building (hermatypic) hard or stony corals. Corals are not the only animals to build reefs, though they are by far the most industrious and productive in terms of the sheer size and longevity of the resultant structures. The shallow waters around our coastline are too cold and turbid for reef-building corals, which depend on helpful, single-celled photosynthetic algae (called zooxanthellae) living within their cells to produce the extra food, hence energy, needed to build their skeletons. However, hidden away in the shallow waters around our coastline are other types of reef created mainly by certain species of bivalve molluscs and tubeworms, which on a smaller scale are dramatic in their own right. The hard shells of tightly packed oysters and Horse Mussels *Modiolus modiolus* covering soft mud and sand seabed provide a rock-like platform on which hydroids, bryozoans, sponges and algae can settle and grow. Crevices and holes between them provide refuge for a variety of mobile invertebrates and fishes.

Oyster reefs

Reefs formed from oysters are now considered to be one of the most seriously threatened marine habitats in the world, and across Europe populations of our native European Flat Oyster *Ostrea edulis* have declined by 95 per cent since the 1800s. In many parts of the British Isles it is even worse, with their abundance considered to be around 1 per cent of its former level. The principal reason for the dramatic decline has been massive overexploitation, but other factors such as pollution, disease and competition from invasive species, such as the Slipper Limpet *Crepidula fornicata*, have made the situation worse.

As well as losing the oysters themselves, we have lost the enormous gains that their massed ranks bring to shallow water and estuarine environments. In the same way that beavers are described as 'ecosystem engineers' in the terrestrial and freshwater environment, oysters richly deserve that accolade in the sea. Over a large reef area, their prodigious filtering activity removes many tonnes of suspended sediment, greatly increasing water clarity and light penetration. Water quality is also improved by their removal of nitrogen compounds, a significant boon in areas affected by the eutrophication that can be caused by agricultural run-off. Along with the increase in seabed stability that the oysters also provide, these enhancements can allow other habitats such as seagrass to flourish. The combination of those habitats with the oyster reefs themselves then provides valuable attachment points and shelter for a wealth of other organisms, including small fishes.

As well as enhancing local sustainable oyster fisheries, it is these big benefits that have encouraged projects by a range of organisations to re-establish oyster reefs in historical locations such as the Solent on the south coast of England, the Blackwater Estuary in Essex, Conwy Bay in North Wales and the Clyde in Scotland. Techniques employed include placing cages full of mature oysters ready to release larvae naturally in suitable positions such as hanging under pontoons, or releasing oyster larvae generated in nursery areas. Suitable seabed sites where natural beds once flourished are also 'seeded' with juvenile oysters (spat), often in conjunction with laying down material such as old oyster shells (called cultch) that helps to stabilise the seabed and encourages oyster settlement and reef formation.

Mussel reefs

Edible (or Common) Mussels *Mytilus edulis* are a familiar sight covering intertidal rocks at wave-exposed locations around our coastline. However, less well known is their much larger relative the Horse Mussel *Modiolus modiolus* that forms sublittoral, reef-like beds on soft sediments in sheltered coastal areas and sea lochs. These large filter-feeders thrive where there are sufficiently strong currents to supply them with abundant plankton. At 10cm long (sometimes 20cm) and living for 20 or more years, these large bivalves can form a reef well above the sediment if undisturbed, providing habitat for a wide diversity of other immobile and mobile species, including brittlestars. Frances well remembers collecting individual, sea-cleaned shells off the sandy beaches in Norfolk as a child and revealing their delicately muted purple colours in jam jars of fresh water.

Horse Mussels prefer cooler water, and whilst individuals are found all around Britain and Ireland, extensive reefs have only been documented northward from the Irish Sea and from the Humber Estuary. One of the largest is found within the Berwickshire and Northumberland Coast SAC. Horse Mussel beds within Scottish

MPAs include Sullom Voe (Shetland), Sanday (Orkney), the Small Isles (Inner Hebrides) and the loch systems Laxford; Dornoch Firth and Morrich More; Duich, Long and Alsh; Sunart; Creran; Upper Loch Fyne and Loch Goil. In Wales there are extensive beds off the north side of the Llŷn Peninsula.

Many mussel beds, small and large, have been badly degraded or destroyed by intensive dredging and trawling for scallops. Frances once dived a well-known reef in the current-swept entrance to Strangford Lough in the 1980s, but even then, in more easily dredged areas further within the lough, once-extensive beds were apparently a shadow of their former glory. Similar extensive reefs have been lost off the south of the Isle of Man. Once physically damaged, recovery can be slow or non-existent.

Flame Shell reefs

The saying 'All that glitters is not gold' is often appropriate to divers exploring shipwrecks, but for us on several occasions the reverse has been true: 'All that does not glitter may be gold.' Gaping File Shells *Limaria hians*, also known as Flame Shells, have a wide fringe of golden orange tentacles that project permanently from between the two halves of their shell. This flamboyance ought to make them stand out like a sore thumb, but each small 3–4cm long bivalve mollusc lives a hidden life amongst coarse gravel, shell sand and stones. Searching just such a seabed during a Scottish sea-loch survey many years ago, Frances was astounded to uncover such brilliance hidden beneath a rather drab seabed, having never encountered this species before. Flame Shells secrete sticky byssus threads, similar to those that anchor mussels to rock, and use them to bind shell gravel, stones, maerl or similar hard materials together, enclosing themselves in a protective tent or 'nest'. In a few increasingly rare places, such as Loch Carron and Loch Creran on the west coast of Scotland, extensive areas of seabed are bound together by several hundred adjacent individuals per square metre, effectively forming a low reef, perhaps better described as a bed. One of the first clues to such a hidden gem is the presence of mounded-up material, often with a covering of seaweeds or hydroids, raised above the normally flat sediment seabed and punctured by dark holes through which water can circulate.

Unsurprisingly, Flame Shell beds are very vulnerable to damage and destruction from trawling and dredging, and whilst individual

Coastal Seas

RIGHT: This flamboyant Gaping File Shell or Flame Shell *Limaria hians* is just one of many forming a bed or reef, and was excitedly photographed by Sarah Bowen on a Seasearch trip to Loch Fyne in 2024.

Flame Shells are not an uncommon find, only a few extensive reefs remain, most of them in Scotland. However, in his 2018 book, seabed habitat expert Keith Hiscock describes how targeted surveys undertaken since 2000 indicate that there has been a significant increase in the extent of such beds and the number of locations where they occur. This particular bright flame is perhaps not about to go out, but he also points out that in some areas, such increases have been to the detriment of maerl beds by consolidating sediments and allowing smothering seaweeds to grow.

Loch Carron

In April 2017 local Loch Carron Seasearch divers were horrified to find dead and broken Flame Shells scattered at a favourite dive site near the islet of Sgeir Bhuidhe in the outer loch, which they knew had been undamaged on previous recent dives. The evidence pointed to the probability that a scallop dredger had been through the area (not illegal at the time), and this was reported to Scottish Natural Heritage (now called NatureScot), prompting surveys that confirmed the damage. The area was quickly given a temporary protection order to allow time for further surveys. By the end of the year, these confirmed the presence of three Flame Shell beds around Sgeir Bhuidhe, all around 7ha in extent, plus an astounding and unimpacted 194ha bed in the Strome Narrows, now thought to be the largest known throughout this species' range. Flame Shell beds are one of 81 Priority Marine Features, a list of habitats and species produced to help focus and guide marine conservation.

Two years later, in May 2019, the Loch Carron MPA was made permanent. It now encompasses the Strome Narrows and outer reaches of Loch Carron, south to the Lochs Duish, Long and Alsh MPA and protects both Flame Shell and maerl beds from bottom-towed fishing gear and other damaging activities. Scottish Natural Heritage report number 1038 (Moore *et al*. 2018) gives full details.

Worm reefs

The structure of reefs built by serpulid worms is interestingly different from those formed by oysters and mussels. The tubeworm in question is *Serpula vermicularis*, which unlike our native European Flat Oyster is widespread around all coasts of the British Isles and often abundant, but reef constructions are extremely rare. The worms secrete and live in a hard calcareous tube, extending a feathery crown of tentacles to trap planktonic food. Under very wave-sheltered conditions, in certain Scottish and Irish sea lochs, their long chalky tubes become intertwined and they form fabulously complex structures. These reefs, often well described as 'towers', can be over a metre across and nearly as tall. When the worms' bright red tentacle fans are extended, they give the reefs a beautifully exotic appearance, but the slightest disturbance makes the fans withdraw and the reefs instantly look a rather more ghostly white. A wealth of other animals live around and among the worm tubes. The most obvious tend to be brittlestars, small sea urchins, squat lobsters, crabs and sea squirts, but there are many more. The reefs are fragile and easily damaged by storms, fishing gear, boat anchors and the carelessly placed fins of visiting divers. There also seem to be natural cycles of growth and collapse and sensitivity to water quality and changes in water flow, all poorly understood at present.

BELOW: A 'tower' of Organ Pipe Worms *Serpula vermicularis*, and a close-up showing their fan of tentacles and the distinctive trumpet-like plug that closes the tube when they withdraw.

Shipwrecks and other man-made reefs

There are estimated to be approximately 50,000 shipwrecks around the UK coastline, a staggering number even after you have considered the British Isles' rich maritime history, our dependence on seaborne trade and the numerous conflicts that have added to all the tragedies caused by accidents, breakdowns, human error and adverse weather.

Shipwrecks are the focus of a great deal of recreational diving activity, and non-divers are sometimes surprised by the number of divers for whom wreck exploration is their main interest. Diving clubs are often said to be split between those enthusiastic for 'rust' and artefacts and those for whom 'squidgy stuff' (i.e. marine life) is the attraction, but there is less of a divide than one might suspect, especially nowadays. This is because shipwrecks generally provide a home for rich marine life, as well as the interest of the wreck itself, and can be surprisingly beautiful places.

Many wrecks have great cultural and historic significance and are protected under the Protection of Wrecks Act 1973. The wrecks in Scapa Flow, Orkney, for example, are a world-class dive site with a renowned maritime history. Seven ships remain of the German High Seas Fleet, taken there for internment in 1918 but scuttled by the fleet commander to prevent their possible reuse by the British. Other ships of the sunken fleet were salvaged, and some of their steel has had an intriguing second life. The metal was cast before the invention of atomic weapons and does not contain any of the radioactive elements that were released into the atmosphere from their use or testing. It is therefore highly valued as shielding for radiation-detection instruments, where even minuscule amounts of man-made contamination in their casings would affect readings. Further wrecks around Orkney include two British battleships designated as protected war graves.

Shipwrecks large and small provide all the benefits of a natural reef, including elevated surfaces that give sedentary plankton-feeders good access to passing currents, numerous nooks and crannies for crevice-dwellers, and plenty of shelter for fish. Indeed, when navigating to a wreck underwater, the first reassuring sign that you are getting 'warm' tends to be the increasing number of fish that you meet. Some fish are naturally attracted to solid objects, a trait called thigmotropism that helps them find protective cover appearing on new wreck sites within just a few days. Shipwrecks, however, have ecological benefits beyond simply providing additional reef habitat. A 2023 study by Plymouth University and the Blue Marine Foundation demonstrated that some

have acted as effective sanctuaries for marine life by preventing the use of bottom-towed fishing gear in the areas that immediately surround them (Hickman *et al.* 2024). As the study emphasises, many wrecks have been in position for well over a century and, in areas of heavy fishing pressure, have thus protected their local spots from decades of damaging trawling. For example, in parts of the seabed within a 50m radius of studied wreck sites, the average density of marine life was found to be 340 per cent greater than in control sites accessible to fishing.

ABOVE: Something for everyone: a shipwreck such as the *Hispania* in the clear water of the Sound of Mull provides beautiful scenery, historic interest and plentiful marine life, with the steamship's steel structures making ideal elevated habitat for sea anemones.

Wrecks and piers as artificial reefs

Shipwrecks can be thought of as a type of artificial reef, along with other man-made hard constructions such as piers and oil-rig legs. Given the right conditions and timing, such structures provide opportunities for researching marine natural succession, following the order and changes in the organisms and communities that colonise them. In the terrestrial environment, succession is relatively easy to study and has been well documented for a variety of ecosystems, especially important because an understanding of it can be essential for effective conservation management. This is well shown in wetland areas such as Wicken Fen National Nature Reserve in Cambridgeshire and the Norfolk Broads, both nearby favourites of Frances. Here, for example, there are clear demonstrations showing that, if left unmanaged, reedbeds, so important to birds such as Bearded Tits *Panurus biarmicus*

Liberty Ships

The Second World War created a huge need for cargo ships to carry war supplies, and a large number were provided to the British by the USA Emergency Fleet Program. These were the Liberty Ships, simple, standardised cargo steamers that could be produced quickly and cheaply. Two hundred of the 3,000 or so produced were lost during the war, and one of these, the SS *James Eagan Layne*, has become perhaps the most iconic and most visited of shipwrecks around the British Isles. Lying upright in only 20m of water on a sandy seabed in Whitsand Bay near Plymouth, the wreck is still providing divers with an array of nooks and crannies to explore and a wealth of marine life to appreciate, even after 80 years. The ship was torpedoed in 1945 (with no loss of life) only three short months after her initial launch, and although much of her cargo was salvaged at the time, she herself sank when being towed to safety. However, whilst her war service was short, her life as a productive artificial reef has been long. Time is now taking its toll, and the ship is gradually breaking up as she is battered by storms and currents – but the purposeful scuttling of the HMS *Scylla* in 2004 about 500m away (see opposite) has created new artificial reef habitat in this area. The 70th anniversary of the sinking of *James Eagan Layne* was in 2015, and a project to document her history provides many more fascinating details given on the SHIPS Project website.

In total contrast, the wreck of another Liberty Ship, the SS *Richard Montgomery*, lies just out to sea off the Isle of Sheppey in Kent. Frances remembers gazing out to sea from Sheerness during childhood visits to her grandmother and seeing the three masts sticking out of the water, as they still do today. The ship was carrying 7,000 tons of munitions when she dragged her anchor and grounded on a sandbank in 1944 and sank before all of it could be salvaged. The ship remains there with 1,400 tons of explosive still inside, any approaches strictly prohibited and an exclusion zone in force, with the fate of the town's windows easily imagined if the wreck became unstable and blew up. An artificial wreck maybe, but not one that can be studied and appreciated.

The three masts of SS *Richard Montgomery*, which sank in 1944, are still visible from the shore at Sheerness on the Isle of Sheppey in the outer Thames Estuary.

Reef life

and Bitterns *Botaurus stellaris*, would naturally progress from open water to wet fen woods and finally climax dry woodland. Less is known of settlement and succession in the marine environment. A new shipwreck within diving depths, hopefully a non-disastrous one, provides an ideal opportunity to follow marine succession and to compare the communities that develop on it with nearby natural rocky (or coral) reefs.

In 1987 Frances was presented with just such an opportunity when a cargo vessel called the *Mare* sank when being towed for repairs, several nautical miles off the coast of Dubai, settling in 20m of water. Living there at the time, she was able to make regular visits with her local diving club to document its colonisation by marine life (Dipper 1991). This of course was an accidental sinking in the warm waters of the Arabian Gulf, but a recent purposeful sinking near Plymouth has provided an exciting similar opportunity much nearer to home.

ABOVE: Shipwrecks often attract large shoals of fish, such as these Bib *Trisopterus luscus* on the wreck of the *Persier*, Devon.

INSET: At the smaller scale, wrecks provide crevice homes for large animals like Conger Eels *Conger conger*, Crawfish *Palinurus elephas* and a host of smaller creatures as here on the *N.G. Petersen*, Cornwall.

Sinking of the *Scylla*

The deliberate and careful sinking of the Royal Navy frigate HMS *Scylla* in 2004 is, to date, the biggest project of its kind in European waters. *Scylla* was launched in 1968, the last warship to be built at

Devonport Dockyard. She had a varied life around the world that included serving as a protection vessel in the Icelandic Cod War of the 1970s, participating in Queen Elizabeth II's Silver Jubilee and suffering a collision with a ferry near Devonport that led to her captain's court martial. She was decommissioned in 1993 and laid up at Portsmouth.

The concept of using a shipwreck to create another artificial reef close to the famous, but disintegrating, wreck of the Second World War Liberty Ship *James Eagan Layne* on the flat seabed of Whitsand Bay, to the west of Plymouth, was originally a brainchild of local divers. The idea then came to life when the National Marine Aquarium obtained funding to purchase and prepare HMS *Scylla* in 2003. Work was carried out on the ship, at this point back at Devonport Dockyard, over several months. This was to make it environmentally safe by removing any materials that might cause pollution or harm marine life, and to ensure it was safe for visiting divers by improving or blocking access points and eliminating snagging hazards. Finally, in late March 2004, around 50 explosive charges were fitted. Once the wreck was in position in Whitsand Bay, these were fired to make holes in the hull and *Scylla* descended to start her new life on the seabed.

Colonisation of the *Scylla* by marine life has been fascinating, with developments monitored by local scientists and Seasearch divers: see Hiscock *et al.* (2010) and also Keith Hiscock's book on *Exploring Britain's Hidden World* (2018), where a summary of developments is illustrated by numerous colour photographs. Five years after sinking, the wreck supported what is regarded as a mature steel-wreck community, with extensive coverage by species such as Plumose Anemones and Dead Man's Fingers. During the first two years, there were some large fluctuations, with surprising influxes from species such as Green Sea Urchins *Psammechinus miliaris* and Queen Scallops *Aequipecten opercularis* (which are rarely seen in the area otherwise), as well as more expected settlers like tubeworms, barnacles and Common Starfish *Asterias rubens*.

As in any newly established community, there were interactions between sequential arrivals, so the urchins removed many of the tubeworms and barnacles until they themselves fell prey to arriving wrasses, and the starfish quickly consumed any settling mussels. Then, from the two-year mark, most species that would be dominant or representative after five years had arrived. Species continued to arrive after five years, but it is interesting and very relevant to marine conservation to note that many species characteristic of nearby reefs

Reef life

have not yet settled on *Scylla*. These include branching and some cushion-like sponges and the beautiful Yellow Cluster Anemone *Parazoanthus axinellae*. This shows that, while artificial reefs can provide very valuable new environments, they should not be regarded as replacements for lost or damaged natural habitats.

Pier approval: Swanage and Brighton

Unlike most shipwrecks, which require a boat journey to access them, the numerous seaside piers of the British Isles provide artificial reef habitats that can be visited straight from shore. Two famous examples on the south coast of England at Swanage and Brighton are very different in character and the way that they are used. Swanage Pier,

LEFT: At Brighton, there are busy and fascinating worlds to explore both on the pier above and in the sea below.

in Dorset, is in a bay that shelters it from the prevailing southwest winds, so often has clear conditions and is a huge draw for divers and snorkellers. On summer weekends, there is often a queue of divers' cars snaking back from the pier long before it opens. If they get to park on the approach to the pier as they hope, divers can walk fully equipped from their car to some very convenient stone steps and, a few kicks from their fins later, be beneath the platform of the pier and surrounded by fish. Countless British divers remember Swanage Pier as the place they first entered the underwater world and fell in love with it.

The Palace Pier at Brighton, East Sussex, is massively popular for the amusements and entertainment along its length but is used far less by snorkellers and divers. Paul is an enthusiastic visitor, but hardly ever meets other divers, and as he enters the water with his diving partner they are more usually watched by surprised onlookers enjoying their ice creams – whereas divers don't warrant a second glance at Swanage. It is presumably Brighton Pier's position on the open south-facing coast, making sea conditions far less reliable, combined with the much longer swim needed to access its most interesting parts, that explains its relative lack of popularity.

Both piers are excellent places to watch marine animals go about their business. At Swanage, fish in particular are varied and prolific along the whole length of the pier. Numerous Ballan *Labrus bergylta* and Corkwing Wrasse *Symphodus melops* feed on encrusting life on the pier legs. In the spring and summer, the Corkwings use crevices in the pier's structure as the basis for their intricate nests of seaweed (see *Corkwing nests*, Chapter 8). Because seaweed growth around the nests is limited by the pier's shade, it is easier to appreciate the extent of this conscientious constructor's handiwork than it often is on sunlit reefs. Common Dragonets *Callionymus lyra*, gobies and other bottom-living fish dart around on the sand between the legs of the pier, and this site is also one of the best places to find the elusive and distinctive John Dory *Zeus faber* and the Black-faced Blennies mentioned earlier in the chapter. Shoals of Bib *Trisopterus luscus* hover in the gloom under the broader platform at the pier's seaward end, and around its better-lit margins there are often large shoals of Sand

BELOW: A John Dory *Zeus faber* swimming serenely between the supports of Swanage Pier, belying its ability to stalk and almost instantaneously suck in unsuspecting small fish from the shoals that shelter here.

Smelt *Atherina presbyter*. On one memorable early morning dive, Paul watched the Sand Smelt being chased by hungry Bass *Dicentrarchus labrax*. The combination of dramatic predatory pursuit and swirling silvery fish caught in shafts of sunlight around the pier was stunning. Intense diving activity and rich marine life at Swanage Pier are also a recipe for sightings such as the first Anemone Shrimp *Periclimenes sagittifer* recorded on mainland Britain (see Chapter 11).

A notable feature of the equally rich, but different, marine life beneath Brighton Pier is the dense encrustation of Edible Mussels. They are food for hordes of Common Starfish and numerous crustaceans such as Spiny Spider Crabs, Brown Crabs, Velvet Swimming Crabs *Necora puber* and Shore Crabs. Other sessile invertebrates live on or among the mussels, including sponges, oysters and many attractive White-striped Anemones *Actinothoe sphyrodeta*, while shoals of fish, such as small Bib, circulate between the pier's dense forest of legs. Bulky metalwork on the seabed beneath the pier, which is a much more imposing structure than at Swanage, provides hiding places for the crabs and amazingly abundant Tompot Blennies. The blennies seem to obtain at least some of their living by stealing the crabs' food, and their readily observed behaviour (see Chapter 8) is the main reason for Paul diving here. There are also plenty of refuges for Conger Eels and European Eels *Anguilla anguilla*, the latter being seen by divers only very rarely elsewhere.

Whether they are formed by geology, constructed by marine animals or made by humans, the reefs of our coastal waters are special places. Although they vary greatly in terms of origin, extent and character, they share important qualities such as hard surfaces to which seaweeds and sessile animals can attach. Those static organisms gain sustenance from nutrients and plankton in the seawater surrounding and passing over the reef, and they in turn provide shelter and rich feeding grounds for other creatures, as well as being attractive in their own right. Supplementing the hard surfaces, many reefs also possess crevices and holes where further animals can anchor themselves or hide, hunt, breed and hold territories. Healthy reefs are thriving communities that can be imagined as bustling natural 'cities' in the sea.

Sand, mud and maerl

chapter five

Who doesn't remember building sand castles on holiday beaches, and who hasn't heard the idiom 'don't bury your head in the sand'? The sea is within easy reach of nearly all of us in the British Isles, and coastline sand plays a part in many of our lives. There is certainly plenty of it to choose from, with many miles of sandy beach exposed at low tide and much more hidden below the shoreline. Seaside holiday-makers enjoying the sun rarely find it boring, but swim out from the shore and attitudes change. Recreational divers and snorkellers tend to choose rocky areas or wrecks to explore, assuming that there will be more to see there. In some ways they are right, because, with some spectacular sediment-surface exceptions, such as the serpulid worm reefs described in Chapter 4 and maerl beds in this chapter, much of the interesting natural history is hidden from view beneath the surface.

Much of the work done examining sediment communities involves boat-operated grabs and dredges that bring up a 'bite' of mud or sand, subsequently sieved to reveal the animals living within it (the infauna). This can range from a disappointing catch to a stunning variety and number of bivalve molluscs, worms, brittlestars and crustaceans, depending on the type of sediment and its location. Samples taken at different depths down into the sediment can provide additional information. The composition and richness or poorness of the community will be obvious, but its three-dimensional structure is more difficult to work out. The same problem faces terrestrial soil biologists. However, for us and other divers the main interest is the natural history of the many and varied animals living on the sediment surface, or that appear magically before our cameras from hidden tubes and burrows.

OPPOSITE PAGE:
Bright orange Norway Lobster *Nephrops norvegicus* and large Fireworks Anemones *Pachycerianthus multiplicatus* show how spectacular life can be in muddy habitats such as here in a Scottish sea loch.

Dredging, diving and snorkelling are not the only ways to explore sediment communities. In today's age of remote technology, underwater drones can be 'flown' over a flat seabed to film the extraordinary animals found there, without stirring up clouds of mud as the older technology of sledge-mounted cameras can do. A rather more daunting, long-ago experience for Frances was being towed from an inflatable boat hanging onto a simple, wooden 'sledge' that rode just above the seabed. All fine until large boulders started looming out of the gloom.

Just as the wind creates and sculpts sand dunes and deserts on land, currents and wave action shape and shift sediment underwater. Animals living on and within it create mounds, excavate holes and burrows, sift the sediment surface for detritus and deposit characteristic piles of uneaten material and faeces. Although there are extensive plains of apparently flat, featureless sediment, especially at greater depths, all this physical and biological activity generally leads to much more interesting undulating, uneven and pitted sediment surfaces, crossed by numerous tracks and feeding trails. Some species, such as the Gaping File Shell or Flame Shell *Limaria hians*, are important in stabilising and binding sublittoral sediments. This fascinating bivalve mollusc can form living reefs and is described in Chapter 4. In very wave- or current-exposed areas, coarse sands may only have a limited fauna but can build up into an impressive scenery of underwater 'dunes'.

Unfortunately, it is difficult to find shallow sublittoral sediment areas around the British Isles that have rarely or never been disturbed by trawling or other mobile fishing gear or boat anchors and mooring chains. Disturbing sediments, especially repeatedly, is a serious problem, not least because, once disturbed, sediments release stored carbon. Even Marine Protected Areas (MPAs) are far from immune to such activities, but there are a few exceptions where divers and snorkellers can explore largely undisturbed sediment habitats. One such is around the island of Skomer in Wales where the seabed has been protected for upwards of 30 years, as described in Chapter 12. Another example also described in Chapter 12 is the No-Take Zone (NTZ) within the Lundy Marine Conservation Zone, which is largely sediment and has remained undisturbed since 2003, the year that the NTZ was established.

It is not our intention to describe the many different grades and types of sediment habitat and their associated communities that cover the majority of the shallow seabed (in fact most of the continental shelf)

ABOVE: An extensive expanse of sandy seabed in the shallows of a sea loch, dotted with the tubes of Sand Mason Worms *Lanice conchilega*. Numerous pockmarks and tracks indicate the busy wanderings of hermit crabs, whelks and other mobile animals.

around the British Isles, but instead to highlight what we consider the most interesting and important and the most easily appreciated by divers and marine naturalists. As already mentioned, the majority of species found in sediment areas live beneath its surface as infauna and so require techniques other than diving and photography to appreciate them. Nevertheless, it should be remembered that sediment communities can be extremely rich in terms of numbers of individuals and species of animals. For example, a survey and mapping of sediments from around all of Lundy undertaken in 2007, using sediment grabs operated from a survey vessel, identified 478 invertebrate taxa (identified to species level where possible) from the nearly 50 stations it covered (Smith and Nunny 2012).

Chapter 6 expands on this chapter's theme by covering seagrass, a vitally important community growing in shallow sand and muddy sand areas.

A muddy life

The west coast of Scotland is studded with long fjordic sea lochs, mostly of glacial origin. Dive down to the seabed in one of these, or in the many other sheltered bays, estuaries and other marine inlets around the British Isles, and mud is likely to be what you will find – not perhaps everyone's choice of an interesting dive or snorkel site. However, whilst we have both dived in ultra-sheltered places where the bottom is so soft you are enveloped in it as you arrive, there are many more where stable muddy sediments and light water currents

Coastal Seas

support rich communities of burrowing animals. This is the realm of tube anemones, sea pens, Norway Lobster *Nephrops norvegicus*, sea cucumbers and strange mound-creating 'worms'. The animal communities present at each site differ principally with the stability and consistency of the sediment and the depth and the strength of water currents that sift and shift sand and mud and bring in food for filter-feeders. With their varied topography, and often stretching far inland, Scottish sea lochs provide the ultimate in wave-sheltered environments and are home to a host of species with otherwise restricted distributions around our coastline.

Fireworks and flamboyance

Sea anemones seem eminently unsuited to living in mud, and most are found with the bases of their soft bodies attached to rock and other hard substrata, where many provide dramatic and colourful displays (Chapter 4). So it can come as a bit of a surprise to find some of the most spectacular species thriving in squelchy mud. The Fireworks Anemone *Pachycerianthus multiplicatus* is one such, and it is the largest and most flamboyant of all the 60 or so anemones and their close relatives found around the British Isles. This species and other tube anemones (Ceriantharia) create and live inside a parchment-like tube up to a metre long, buried in soft sediment and into which they can withdraw very rapidly if danger threatens. The alternative strategy,

RIGHT: Fireworks Anemones *Pachycerianthus multiplicatus* can reach a height of 30cm above the seabed. The base of the anemone is in a tube that is buried as far as 1m into the seabed.

employed by most rock-living anemones, is to withdraw the tentacles down into their soft column body, so that they resemble a nondescript blob, something tube anemones cannot do.

With up to 200 long, white or banded tentacles spanning as much as 30cm, Fireworks Anemones only adorn the soft bottoms of very sheltered, fjordic sea lochs on the Scottish and Irish west coasts. Like all tube anemones they also have an inner ring of short labial tentacles, in a contrasting colour. Thriving particularly where there are land-based inputs of organic matter such as from freshwater streams, significant populations have been recorded during Seasearch surveys from Lochs Shira, Duich, Goil and Upper Loch Fyne in Scotland. Searching out Fireworks Anemones is a fairly niche activity, but the much smaller Burrowing Anemone *Cerianthus lloydii*, whilst not as spectacular, is a common and widespread tube anemone that can easily be seen when snorkelling or diving over suitable sediment sites round most of the British Isles.

Sea pens belong to a class of less well-known cnidarians (Cnidaria is the phylum to which sea anemones belong), the colonial octocorals (Octocorallia), and can be considered as the soft-seabed equivalent of rock-loving sea fans (Chapter 4). When present in large numbers, sea pens look like of a field of delicate ferns emerging from the mud. In shape they resemble old-fashioned feather quill pens, hence their name, but with a central stem and side branches lined with light-catching polyps, they also remind us of firework 'sparklers'. Structurally, each

LEFT: The Burrowing Anemone *Cerianthus lloydii* is a smaller but much more widespread relative of the Fireworks Anemone and, like that species, lives in a tube anchored in the seabed.

Coastal Seas

ABOVE: A Phosphorescent Sea Pen *Pennatula phosphorea*, with Tall Sea Pens *Funiculina quadrangularis* looming behind – characteristic and beautiful animals that inhabit soft muddy seabeds.

polyp is in effect a minute sea anemone, but with only eight tentacles (hence octocoral) and all connected together to form a functional colony. What one catches and eats can be shared by others. The commonest and most 'pen-like' species around the British Isles is the Slender Sea Pen *Virgularia mirabilis*, in which up to half its 60cm length lies hidden in the mud and the whole colony can shrink down below the surface. Whilst the best place to see them is again in the shelter of deep Scottish sea lochs, there are some well-known populations in diver-accessible harbours in the south, sheltered by breakwaters, such as Portland Harbour, Plymouth Sound, and Holyhead Harbour in Wales. The latter has the longest breakwater in the British Isles, nearly 3km long and well worth a visit in itself.

Two other sea pens are found in the British Isles, but it requires more determination to find them as they prefer deeper water. The Tall Sea Pen *Funiculina quadrangularis*, reaching 2m in length, has only been recorded live (around the British Isles) from muddy seabeds below about 30m in sea lochs on the west coast of Scotland, though it is sometimes dredged up from further offshore. The much stouter wider-bodied Phosphorescent Sea Pen *Pennatula phosphorea* also has a northern distribution. It is red to pink overall, but it can also glow with luminous waves of green/blue colour if disturbed by, for example, a diver's bubbles.

Burrowing cucumbers and brittlestars

Looming out of the murk, as Frances finned slowly along just above the seabed in another Scottish sea loch back in the 1990s, was a pink-spotted creature topped with 10 orange and white branched appendages, looking like a multi-legged alien that had dived headfirst into the mud. As this was a relatively deep dive, she thought that perhaps she was starting to suffer from nitrogen narcosis, a state similar to alcohol intoxication brought on by the anaesthetic effect of breathing compressed air at depth. However, the illusion was real, and this was a Pink-spotted Sea Cucumber *Psolus phantapus*. Burrowing sea cucumbers hold up finely branched, bushy tentacles (the equivalent to their starfish relatives' arms) to collect plankton and detritus, and there are at least nine species found living in muddy

ABOVE: The dramatically coloured Pink-spotted Sea Cucumber *Psolus phantapus*, whose shape reminds us of an African baobab tree.

habitats around the British Isles. The Pink-spotted variety is the most distinctive and dramatic, but the least likely to be encountered; it has mostly been recorded from sea lochs along the west coast of Scotland.

Sea cucumbers can be found in rocky areas as well, and are described in Chapter 9, but these elongated echinoderms are ideally suited to living 'upright' in sediment, where their soft bodies are well protected. They feed largely on suspended detritus and plankton, caught up in the finely divided branches of their tentacles. Each of these is periodically contracted and stuffed into the animal's mouth in toddler-like fashion to wipe off collected food.

Another group of echinoderms, the brittlestars, can also be found living and moving around over both rocks and sediments, and they are also described in Chapter 9. However, a few species specialise in burrowing into sediment, living with one or two arms projecting up into the water. *Amphiura filiformis* and *Acrocnida brachiata* are two such species, with exceptionally long arms in relation to their body size, compared to rock-living species. Both are found mostly below about 15m depth in fine, muddy sand around most of our coastline and can occur in large numbers, their raised arms looking like a field of bare plant stems, flexing in the water currents. Tube feet along the arms collect plankton from the water and pass it down to the mouth on the underside of the hidden animal's body.

Sea silk

With their infinite variety of shapes and colours, sea shells have long been a favourite collector's item. They featured prominently in Victorian 'cabinets of curiosity', examples of which can still be seen today in National Trust and English Heritage properties such as Wallington (Northumberland) and Anglesey Abbey (Cambridgeshire). Prominent within such collections is often the Fan Mussel *Atrina fragilis* (then called *Pinna fragilis*), the largest bivalve mollusc found around the British Isles. This unusual 30cm long bivalve lives with the pointed end of its elongate triangular shell deeply buried in mud or fine sand and anchored to stones and dead shells by long byssus threads, similar to those of Edible Mussel *Mytilus edulis* but much longer. These silky threads were once used to make fine stockings and ladies' gloves, testament to the fact that Fan Mussels must then have been fairly common. However, most historical records of 'sea silk' refer to the even larger Mediterranean species *Pinna nobilis*.

Today you would have to be very lucky indeed to find a cast-up Fan Mussel shell, and most divers will never see a live one unless taking part in a dedicated survey initiated by organisations such as Seasearch. A small number were found on just such a survey in Plymouth Sound in 2005, but the only large population so far known in UK waters is in deep water below 100m in the Sound of Canna, Small Isles, Inner Hebrides (Howson *et al*. 2012). The shell has thin and delicate edges, and most fan shells alive or dead have damaged tops. Such dodgy protection seems counterintuitive for an immobile and exposed bivalve that would make a good mouthful for a skate or large flatfish, but fan shells have an unmatched ability to repair the shell, and can make good at least a centimetre in a day. The shell is largely constructed of a flexible organic material (conchiolin), much more easily laid down than layers of calcium carbonate. Sadly this is no help when it comes to bottom-fishing gear such as heavy scallop dredges that dig down into the sediment, and today numbers of this long-lived and slow-growing species are badly depleted.

A live Fan Mussel *Atrina fragilis* embedded in mud, one of a small group photographed by Keith Hiscock in Plymouth Sound in 2005 during a survey, but not seen since.

Scampi and chips

Frances and Paul both remember digging seaside tunnels in the sand with their families, only for them to collapse as soon as they got interesting. Thick mud would have held together much better, as admirably demonstrated by a variety of crustacean mud architects, especially the Norway Lobster *Nephrops norvegicus*. This crustacean goes by a variety of names, including Scampi, Langoustine and Nephrops. It is also known as the Dublin Bay Prawn, for it was in Dublin, Ireland, that this commercially important species was first landed regularly, albeit at that time caught as bycatch and sold unofficially. 'Scampi and chips' really came into its own in the 1960s and 1970s, leading to breadcrumbed imitations. Frances used to regularly dissect her pub dinner to check if it was real.

For an animal only 20cm long, these miniature lobsters excavate particularly complex, mostly horizontal tunnel systems in muddy plains below about 25–30m depth. For those willing to dive into the gloom, such areas can be a mud paradise for watching crustacean behaviour. The animals are easy to spot because, unlike their larger Common Lobster *Homarus gammarus* relatives, which only turn orange on cooking, Norway Lobsters are bright orange alive or dead. During daylight hours divers most often see them resting head-out in the burrow entrance, as most only emerge under cover of darkness (except in deep dark water) to hunt smaller crustaceans, worms and molluscs. Other animals also take advantage of the shelter provided by Norway Lobster burrows, including Fries's Goby *Lesueurigobius friesii* (see *Cohabitation*, Chapter 11), and perhaps the strangest cohabiter is a tiny micro-animal named *Symbion pandora* that was discovered in 1995 by Danish scientists, attached to the mouthparts of a Norway Lobster they were examining. This microscopic speck was considered so different from other described animals that it was assigned to a new phylum, Cycliophora. Frances is now tempted to take a magnifying glass to pubs and restaurants.

Fishing for scampi is now a multi-million-pound industry, but the seabed trawls used to catch them can be extremely damaging to such muddy habitats and their inhabitants. Individual Norway Lobsters that escape being caught can build new burrows, but this requires considerable energy. Other mud-dwelling species, such as Tall Sea Pens (see *Fireworks and flamboyance*, page 140), cannot scuttle or retract down to safety and often come up in trawls as bycatch. In some areas, far less damaging creels and pots are being successfully used instead of

Loch Obisary: a special place

During a Nature Conservancy Council (NCC) survey in the late 1970s, Frances had the opportunity to dive several largely unexplored lochs in the island chain of the Outer Hebrides off the west coast of Scotland. Looking down from the top of Eaval (Eabhal), which at 347m is the highest hill in North Uist, Frances was able to get a real impression of just how watery this remote landscape is. Spread out below was a panorama of sea-loch arms, saline lagoons and freshwater lochs, large and small. To the west and north lay Loch Obisary (Obsaraigh), now considered a nationally and internationally important site for its saline lagoon habitat. At that time, little was known about the loch apart from long-ago visits by naturalist Edith Nicol in 1933–35, and it had never been dived. The loch's only connection to the sea is from the northern of its two basins through a shallow inlet channel running from the adjacent Loch Eport (Euphort) and it was suspected that there might be some interesting salinity stratification. The early NCC surveys that Frances was a part of showed that this was indeed the case, and that heavier (denser) tidally incoming, full-strength seawater sinks down as it enters the loch, resulting in an unusually persistent halocline (a sharp change in salinity) at around 4–5m depth in the northern basin.

Diving through such a halocline is a strange experience, the lighter, fresher water above it clear and still (though in this case stained pale brown by peat), then a hazy swirl in the halocline where the two water bodies mix like whisky and water, and finally through into the heavier saltier water beneath. The seabed of this loch is of very soft, undisturbed and rather featureless mud, inhabited by a few worms and the part-shelled sea hare *Akera bullata*, unusual amongst sea slugs in its ability to swim using a cape-like extension of the body. Nearby rocks are covered by Yellow-ringed Sea Squirt *Ciona intestinalis*, tolerant of the three-quarter-strength seawater, and an abundance of a common red seaweed, *Phyllophora pseudoceranoides*.

In complete contrast, mud communities in the 5m or so above the halocline have a distinctly freshwater appearance. Extensive beds of the salt-tolerant, grass-like Fennel Pondweed *Potamogeton pectinatus* root in the mud between rocks around the loch edges, along with species of predominantly freshwater algae.

A hilltop view of Loch Obisary in North Uist, Outer Hebrides. The fully saline Loch Eport lies behind it, with a single narrow entrance through which seawater flows into Loch Obisary at high tides.

trawls, often as part of fishery improvement projects. The type of trawl and the way they are used vary in their impact in different locations.

The Angular Crab *Goneplax rhomboides* also excavates complex burrows in the same sort of muddy habitats as Norway Lobster. With its angular carapace (back) and very long claws, this species would be a more difficult mouthful for predatory fishes than a Norway Lobster. The crab seems happy to scuttle around in daylight away from its burrow, and it reacts to a diver's presence in typical crab fashion by spreading its claws wide, making itself appear much larger – just as many land animals do when threatened by a potential predator.

With a little experience the various sizes, shapes and orientation of mud burrow entrances can be recognised in much the same way that fox, rabbit and badger holes can be distinguished. Mud burrows are also made by some fish species such as the Red Bandfish *Cepola macrophthalma*, described in Chapter 8, and side branches connecting their burrows to those of Angular Crabs or other burrowing crustaceans are not uncommon.

Sandy homes

At the other end of the sediment spectrum from soft mud are coarse shelly gravels, pebbles and sand, often found in areas where reasonably strong tidal currents have swept away finer material. However, gravel and pebbles are also found in shallow areas of some Scottish sea lochs with very weak tides and little wave action, because such lochs do not generally have a high input of silt. In contrast, the seabed in current-swept areas of some estuaries, such as the Severn, may still be very muddy because the water carries a high load of fine silt.

Worm tubes

As mentioned in the previous section, creating stable burrows and tunnels in sand, especially clean sand, can be problematic. One solution is to construct your own tube in which to live, and polychaete worms (Polychaeta) living a sedentary existence in sand (and muddy sand) are masters of this art. As its name suggests, the Sand Mason Worm *Lanice conchilega* is one of the leaders. It belongs to a family of worms called terebellids (Terebellidae), a group characterised by having an unruly mop of thin tentacles surrounding the mouth, used to collect food particles. Sand Masons employ these same mobile

Coastal Seas

BELOW: The Mediterranean Fan Worm *Sabella spallanzanii* (top) appears to be extending its range and has been recorded in several locations around the British Isles in the last few years, in sediment or among silty rocks (as here in Plymouth Sound).

This Eyelash Worm *Myxicola infundibulum* (bottom) had to be approached very carefully to capture its photograph, as they withdraw their fan of tentacles rapidly if disturbed.

appendages to collect individual sand grains and shell fragments and stick them together with mucus, building up a tube that projects well above the surface and in which the animal lives. This is topped with a fan of sand-grain sticks along which the tentacles are deployed. Much to the bemusement of her various diving buddies, Frances has been known to lie in front of one of these just watching the way the pink tentacles operate. However, this worm can more easily be viewed on lower-shore sandy beaches, where it is often very common, as well as in sandy patches on rocky shores.

Peacock Worms *Sabella pavonina* build similar tubes, but constructed of much finer material as this species prefers muddier conditions, such as those found in sheltered bays and estuaries. On a research boat in Southampton Water in 2011, Frances was impressed by the density of the worms, with one small dredge bringing up hundreds of 30cm-long tubes. However, it is more revealing to watch quietly underwater,

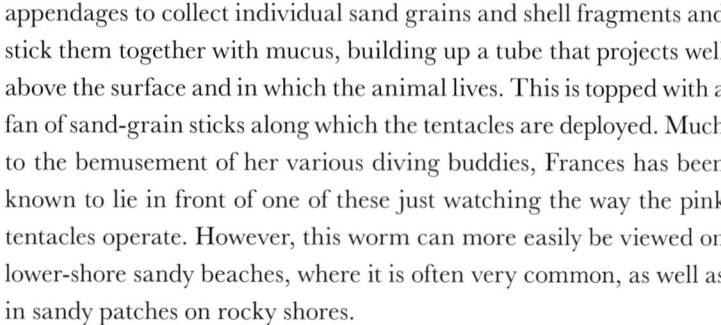

where 'forests' of rather dull grey tubes suddenly transform as each worm extends a peacock's tail of feathery, colourful tentacles from the top. The tentacle fan is used to trap plankton and detritus, duly passed down and into the worm's mouth. A small movement or exhalation by a diver is enough warning for an instant change, as every worm within reach retracts down into the safety of its tube. A second *Sabella* species, the Mediterranean Fan Worm *S. spallanzani*, has recently been recorded at a few sites from the Channel Islands north to Northern Ireland. It has also been spread to Australia and New Zealand, where it is considered invasive.

Another common fan or feather duster worm (Sabellidae), as this family is called, is the Eyelash Worm *Myxicola infundibulum*. In this species the tube is completely buried and all that can be seen is a funnel of black-tipped tentacles, resembling the funnel-shaped webs made by some garden spiders. Recent work by our friend and colleague Teresa Darbyshire in the National Museum of Wales has now shown that what was thought to be one species is actually two, the second one, *M. polychroma*,

ABOVE: A group of Peacock Worms *Sabella pavonina* with their distinctive fan of tentacles extended from the sandy tubes that they construct. The bottoms of their tubes are buried in the soft seabed.

lacking the black mascara markings on its 'eyelash' tips (Darbyshire 2024). This came about when sharp-eyed recreational divers spotted the differences in colouration and collaborated with our colleague to answer the question.

Living a sedentary existence in a protective tube and catching or trapping food particles from the water is obviously a successful life strategy for soft-bodied marine worms, as there are many different tubeworms found in both rocky and sediment habitats. Some species build impressive biogenic reefs (Chapter 4), with thousands of individuals packed closely together.

Crustacean creations

Another group of prolific tube-home builders are amphipods, small sideways-flattened crustaceans, familiar to many people as 'sand hoppers' jumping around when piles of cast-up seaweed are disturbed. Some species of these tiny animals, such as *Ampelisca* spp., can convert a muddy sand seabed into a landscape resembling a thick rug pile, their tiny tubes bunched close together. Others form similar mats in rocky areas.

The Masked Crab *Corystes cassivelaunus* may not build a permanent residence, but it is very much at home on sandy seabeds and superbly suited to that environment. Short legs give this highly distinctive animal an ungainly gait as it runs across the seabed, but they come into their own when digging rapidly into the sediment. Its carapace, in contrast to other crabs, is longer than it is broad and so the perfect shape for sliding quickly out of sight. Perhaps the neatest adaptation

Coastal Seas

ABOVE: Masked Crab *Corystes cassivelaunus*, showing off the long antennae that form a 'snorkel' through which it pulls down water for respiration when it is buried in the sand. The large claws show that this is a male.

for hiding under the sand is seen in the grooved antennae, which bind together with interlocking hairs to form a snorkel-like tube through which water can be drawn down for respiration. Masked Crabs can be particularly interesting to follow because, when they decide to hide in the sand, they seem to choose a spot occupied by another Masked Crab more often than one might expect by chance. While this behaviour may have the advantage of diverting a predator's attention towards the disturbed incumbent, it sometimes results in a stand-off between the two crabs. These are usually males, whose long claws make an eye-catching sight when two individuals raise them against each other in combat. Those long claws also give the male a very condescending appearance when he carries a female in preparation for mating, in stark contrast to the way a male swimming crab closely embraces his partner.

Another very different animal that uses a snorkel-like connection for breathing when buried in the sand is the Common Heart Urchin *Echinocardium cordatum*, sometimes called a 'Sea Potato'. In the urchin's case, the connection to the water above the sediment is formed by highly elongated tube feet, some of the special equipment unique to these animals that we describe in Chapter 9.

RIGHT: Unearthed from muddy sand in the Isles of Scilly, this Common Heart Urchin *Echinocardium cordatum* sports a tuft of extra-long spines that help support long tube feet up into the water for gas exchange. Hanging onto the spines at its rear is the small bivalve mollusc hitchhiker, *Tellimya ferruginosa*.

Sand, mud and maerl

Clean living

Whilst coarse sand and shell gravel, kept free from silt and debris by currents and waves, do not lend themselves to home-building, there are still some attractive species that prefer such sediments. As in sand dunes on land, it is in the less mobile sand that the greatest variety of life will be found. Typical of such habitats is the Gravel Sea Cucumber *Neopentadactyla mixta*, the ghostly-white front end of which protrudes from shell or stone gravel, or even live maerl beds (see page 156). It has a similar method of 'mouth-wipe' feeding to the mud-burrowing sea cucumbers described earlier in this chapter.

Coarse sand is not usually conducive to anemones, but the Clock Face Anemone *Peachia cylindrica*, one of Frances's favourite finds, is able to live in unstable sand and can even be found on semi-exposed sand beaches at low tide. It has a satisfyingly symmetrical face and 12 neat tentacles that lie flush with the sand surface, anchored firmly in place by a very long (30cm) column. Another favourite find is the Nodding Hydroid *Corymorpha nutans*, unusual not just for where it lives but also because it is solitary, not colonial like most hydroids. It resembles a small, long-tentacled anemone on a tall stalk. Just a few centimetres high, thin and translucent, it can be difficult to spot and even more difficult to photograph.

Such finds turn a potentially boring snorkel or dive into a very satisfying one – and, with little silt to cloud the water, a great photographic opportunity.

LEFT: The distinctive disc and 12 tentacles of the aptly named Clock Face Anemone *Peachia cylindrica* spread out just above coarse sand. The buried column supporting it can reach a length of 30cm.

Plain predators and scavengers

Like their grassland equivalents on land, sediment plains are stalked by scavengers and predators looking for a good meal. Top scavengers include a variety of crabs and starfish, some of which are large and obvious such as Spiny Spider Crabs *Maja brachydactyla*, travelling slowly and investigating anything edible as they go along. A dead fish, shellfish, or even a seal carcass lying out in the open will quickly attract them and others, much as Red Kites *Milvus milvus* are drawn to a dead deer on land. Smaller scavengers include Common Whelk *Buccinum undatum* and Netted Dog Whelk *Tritia reticulata*, both of which home in unerringly using their keen sense of smell, aided by a periscope-like siphon that draws in water and is raised up and out of the front end of the shell. Small hermit crabs can sometimes be seen sitting on the shell of a Common Whelk as it crawls along. While this may just be a result of the crabs' natural tendency to seek elevated positions for filter-feeding and evading predators, they are keen scavengers, so we suggest it could also give them the benefit of a free 'taxi ride' to their next meal. A variety of brittlestars and fish will also move in rapidly to clean up the debris left behind by a seabed trawl or thrown overboard as bycatch.

Whilst many predatory fishes employ speed in their pursuit of prey, the Spiny Starfish *Marthasterias glacialis* uses stealth. It is fascinating to watch a large specimen gliding towards a Great (or King) Scallop *Pecten maximus* lying part-buried in sand. These heavy bivalve molluscs are not known for their swimming ability, but if one detects the shadow of an approaching starfish, it will clack away backwards up into the water, like an animated set of false teeth. A strong, white adductor muscle (the bit you eat) opens and closes the shell, squirting out water to provide propulsion, but it soon tires and sinks back to the seabed. Smaller Queen Scallops *Aequipecten opercularis* react in a similar way but are lighter and more agile and sometimes even react to a hovering diver or snorkeller. There are some notable stealth-and-ambush predators amongst sediment-living fishes, and we describe the hunting tactics and fast reactions of the Angler *Lophius piscatorius* in Chapter 8.

The majority of small prey items such as worms and bivalve molluscs are found mostly well buried beneath the sediment surface, and so potential predators must follow them down. The Sand Star *Astropecten irregularis* has stiff, tapered arms, fringed and hardened by protective skeletal plates and long spines that help it move easily beneath the

ABOVE: Unlike most starfish, the Sand Star *Astropecten irregularis* lives on sediment and can bury itself within just a few minutes. Frances watched this one do so in just ankle-depth water, as shown in this sequence.

sand surface. They have a remarkable ability to disappear within half a minute or so in their search for prey, without any apparent effort.

Many sediment-dwelling worms are themselves predators. King Ragworms *Alitta virens* can reach a length of 8cm and have chitinous jaws capable of giving a nasty nip, as many people collecting them as bait know only too well. However, the most unusual predatory worm that we have encountered is the Sea Mouse *Aphrodita aculeata*. These stout, oval worms belong to a group called scaleworms (Phyllodocida) and are occasionally washed up on sandy shores looking like a bedraggled specimen of their namesake. Seen live underwater, they ripple with iridescent greens and blues, thanks to a covering of long bristles especially on the sides. Burrowing through sand and gravel, they hunt out other worms, including King Ragworms, longer than themselves, which they slowly swallow whole in a rather snake-like way. It seems strange, then, that this species is named after Aphrodite, the Greek goddess of love.

The Common Necklace Shell *Euspira catena* is another soft seabed resident with an attractive appearance and a hunter's disposition. The wide mantle or 'skirt' that spreads out as the animal glides along looks graceful, but is a very versatile item of predatory equipment. Its first function is to detect prey by feeling for where the siphons of small clams, buried out of sight, reach the sand's surface. Its next tasks are to help streamline the Necklace Shell as it burrows down to reach the clam and then to envelop it. This enables the predator to get to work boring a hole through the shell of its victim, using a technique similar to that of the Dog Whelk *Nucella lapillus* described in Chapter 2. As if that wasn't enough, the Necklace Shell's skirt is also valuable for defence because it can be extended up and around its owner to prevent a predatory starfish getting a good grip on the shell with its tube feet.

ABOVE: A Common Necklace Shell *Euspira catena* gliding across the sand seeking buried bivalves, which it will burrow down to envelop before boring through their shells to reach the flesh inside (see also photograph on page 56).

Maerl

Maerl is the collective name for some very unusual, free-living seaweeds that bear little resemblance to most people's idea of what a seaweed should look and feel like. For a start they grow unattached, lying freely on sediment rather than attached to rock or other hard substrata. Then there is their colour, Barbie-pink to purple, and their hard, coral-like feel and angular shape, which varies from delicate twiggy and spikey growths to overlapping, conjoined plates. Growth form differs both between and within species depending on environmental conditions. Their hard feel comes from a 'skeleton' created by the slow deposition of calcium carbonate within the cell walls. Whilst it might be quite underwhelming to find the odd piece or patch of maerl, it is a revelation to swim over a dense bed of it covering nearly every square inch of the sand on which it is lying. The three-dimensional and complex structure of such maerl

ABOVE: A particularly dense bed of maerl in the Fal Estuary, photographed with an ultra-wide-angle lens, hence the perceived curvature.

beds provides a home and attachment for many other species, transforming a 'boring' sand or shell gravel seabed into a biodiverse and photogenic community of attached seaweeds, hydroids and other sessile invertebrates, along with buried and tube-dwelling molluscs, worms and anemones. Bottom-living fishes such as dragonets and gobies search out amphipods and other small crustaceans living in the interstices between the maerl pieces. Other coralline seaweeds in the form of pink and red crusts and lumps can be seen covering rocks on shores and below.

Like other seaweeds, maerl needs light to photosynthesise, and maerl beds are therefore found mostly in shallow, well-lit water above 15–20m depth and where there is sufficient current to wash away smothering and light-reducing silt. Some occur as shallow as 5m or less and so can be appreciated by snorkelling, especially at sites sheltered from the strong wave action that can make life difficult for both seaweed and snorkeller. The tide-swept entrances to fully saline estuaries and sea lochs and the narrows within them provide ideal conditions, as do the meandering channels between archipelagos of small islands. Therefore it is no surprise that, with some notable exceptions, the majority of extensive maerl beds are concentrated along the Scottish west coast. On its website, the Scottish Wildlife Trust lists (in 2025) Arran, Wester Ross, Sound of Barra, South Skye, Wyre and Rousay Sounds in Orkney and Fetlar to Haroldswick in Shetland as some of the best areas. Along the English Channel,

ABOVE: Maerl provides a suitable habitat for suspension feeders such as the ghostly white Gravel Sea Cucumber *Neopentadactyla mixta* (top), adapted to living in coarse sediments, as well as for predators such as this Thornback Skate *Raja clavata*.

exceptionally ancient and extensive maerl beds are found in the Fal and Helford Estuaries. The bed at St Mawes in the Fal is probably the best example in England. Extensive beds are also found in Galway Bay and other sites along the west coast of Ireland.

Maerl can be difficult to identify accurately and is often recorded simply as maerl. However, the commonest species is Celtic Maerl *Phymatolithon calcareum*, found round most of the British Isles. In Scotland, Northern Maerl *Lithothamnion glaciale* is often found mixed in with Celtic Maerl, but generally occurs on its own in areas of variable salinity, which it can tolerate. Southern Maerl *Lithothamnion corallioides* has lighter and finer branches and, as its name implies, is mostly found in the south of England. In Ireland a much rarer species, Stone Rose Maerl *Lithophyllum dentatum*, takes the less usual form of cobble-sized nodules of flattened lobes and is found in various inlets in the southwest. Frances had a prized dried nodule of this species for many years, collected on an early, but never forgotten, dive in Roaringwater Bay, County Cork, but it was unfortunately lost when lent to a researcher.

Maerl is fragile and easily broken and damaged by seabed trawling for the edible Great Scallop and its smaller relatives. The Great Scallop lives with its lower dish-shaped shell valve snuggled into maerl, shell gravel or coarse sand and the upper flat shell valve flush with the surface. Boat anchors and chains and even the ropes of crab and other types of pots also cause mechanical damage. Maerl deposits, dead and alive, are also commercially dredged for use as soil improver, especially for acidic soils, and it is widely used in France for this purpose. However, maerl's slow growth means this is essentially a non-renewable resource, just as peat is on land, and the use of it either in gardening or farming is not sustainable in the long term. Individual maerl pieces can live for as long as a century, and some beds can be dated back at least 4,000 years, with a layer of living maerl topping deep layers of dead material.

It has recently been acknowledged that healthy, undisturbed maerl beds act as an important 'blue-carbon' store, with the ability to lock away organic carbon in the long term just as well as or better than other known marine carbon sinks such as seagrass beds (Chapter 6). This was one of the conclusions of Cornwall Council's Blue Natural Capital Project, completed in 2024, that surveyed and studied maerl, seagrass and mudflats within the Fal and Helford Estuary Special Area of Conservation. Just another reason why we should all get excited about this unusual seaweed.

Machair beaches

In the 1980s, Frances made a month-long visit to the Uists, part of the island chain of the Outer Hebrides, as part of an NCC team carrying out an extensive intertidal and sublittoral survey. After a long day's work, one of the joys in the evenings (apart from the local whisky) was a walk down to the white sands that fringe the west coasts of these islands. Here life flourishes from death in the form of flower-rich grassland growing on fine sand derived from the dead remains of seashells and offshore beds of maerl. This rare and beautiful habitat is known as machair, and it would not exist without the abundant calcium derived from this marine input.

Signs and signals

As already described, most of the animal activity that goes on in sand and mud areas is hidden from view beneath the sediment surface. However, an awareness of various signs and clues can lead to many interesting records, with hidden animals giving away their presence to an experienced diver naturalist. Some, such as hermit crabs, may leave identifiable tracks and trails as they move along, but most clues come from faecal deposits (the equivalent of scat on land), outlines of lightly buried fish, various protruding animal parts and deposited eggs. In contrast, washed-up 'beachcomber' clues are usually moulted skins and shells of crustaceans and molluscs and dead remains.

Flatfishes and skates lying on sediment often shuffle around in order to deposit a thin layer of sediment on their backs, hiding them from obvious view. However, their outline shape may remain visible to an alert diver or snorkeller, along with their high-set eyes. Nevertheless, we have both 'jumped' when a well-hidden fish has lost its nerve and burst from the sand beneath us. Paul will never forget the time he went for a dip in the sea at Brighton to cool off but, taking his diving mask as usual, started to pick up small hermit crabs from the sand as he was curious about which species they were. He was both thrilled and startled when what he thought was another hermit crab's shell was the breathing aperture of a juvenile skate. The fish, presumably as surprised as Paul but not as pleased, swam off at speed.

Buried bivalve molluscs retain a connection with the surface through a pair of feeding and respiratory siphons, sometimes several centimetres long, through which water is drawn in and out. These lie flush with or project just above the sediment surface, and the group they belong to, if not the species, can sometimes be told from their size and shape, with further hints from the type of sediment in which the animals are living. Some siphon tops appear as mere slits, others as wide-open tubes, with or without fringing projections to keep larger particles out. Dab *Limanda limanda*, a type of small flatfish, are experts at pouncing on worms as they emerge from their burrows but also specialise in biting off bivalve siphons. Luckily bivalves are good at repairing the tops and in some cases regrowing them, especially those species with long siphons. Where siphon tops reveal a bivalve's presence to predators such as the Necklace Shell (page 154), however, there is no such chance for recovery.

BELOW: Siphons of three bivalve molluscs showing at the surface of the seabed indicate their presence below.

The small, neat faecal casts of lugworms *Arenicola* spp. are a familiar sight on muddy sediment shores, but much larger mounds of sediment are produced by the aptly named Volcano Worm *Maxmuelleria lankesteri* in fine mud below the shoreline. Like lugworms they live in a U-shaped burrow with an opening at either end. Fluidised sediment is pushed up out of the burrow at one opening, forming the 'volcano', rather like a molehill on land. With patience, it is possible to see the animal extend a slithering green proboscis out of the second opening, which it uses to collect detritus from the mud surface. However, as it feeds at night this is much easier to observe in a laboratory aquarium, and neither of us has seen it first-hand. That said, Frances once came across the strange bifurcated, metre-long proboscis of a related species, the Green Spoon Worm *Bonellia viridis*; not knowing what it was, she touched it lightly, causing it to retract at a great rate. Both these species are echiurans, a group of apparently non-segmented worms once placed in a separate phylum (Echiura) but now considered to be a subclass of the segmented annelid worms (phylum Annelida).

On land, even after the owner has long departed, an empty bird's nest and eggshell fragments can indicate which species left these clues behind. Many marine gastropod molluscs (sea snails) leave similar indications, laying characteristically shaped egg cases that can persist attached to rocks long after the eggs have hatched. Living in sediment, the Necklace Shell does not have this option and instead binds its eggs into flat ribbons of sand grains, coiled up into a stiff collar shape. These are surprisingly tough, and can even be found cast up onto sandy shores.

The conclusion that we hope readers will draw from this chapter is that, far from being boring, sublittoral mud and sand habitats support colourful and fascinating communities of marine animals. We have not attempted to systematically cover all the various types and grades of sediment and their wildlife, nor do we deny that there are extensive 'deserts' of less productive mobile, current- and wave-scoured sand and ultra-sheltered anoxic muds. Instead our aim has been to encourage interest and awareness of the vital role sediment habitats play.

As far as we are concerned, mud is indeed glorious, as sung and enjoyed by generations of children. The importance of maintaining the integrity and quality of soil on land is being increasingly understood. 'No-till' agriculture, growing crops without ploughing, is gaining support. It is equally important that we stop indiscriminately churning up marine sediments through widespread bottom trawling. Then, like undisturbed soil, they can continue to store carbon and support productive communities (and thus fisheries) on a long-term basis.

Underwater meadows: seagrasses

chapter six

A 'sea of green' is a much-used expression that might conjure up anything from a hilltop view of a forest canopy, or acres of rolling countryside in spring, to a method of cultivation that uses green mesh netting to support plants. In the ocean a 'sea of green in the blue' would be a good description of a seagrass meadow, or seagrass bed as they are more often called. They were once widespread, with vast meadows growing in shallow, sunlit waters around the coastline of the British Isles, but we have lost a calculated 44 per cent, and possibly as much as 90 per cent, in the past 100 or so years through disease, pollution-driven loss of water clarity and physical damage.

With accelerating climate change and ocean warming, hidden seagrass beds are currently surfacing as a hot topic due to their ability to sequester impressive amounts of carbon. Estimating how 'good' they or other ecosystems, such as forests, are at this is notoriously difficult, but on a worldwide basis seagrass beds may be responsible for locking away as much as 10 per cent of the total carbon sequestered each year in the ocean. Aside from this, a well-established healthy seagrass meadow will support a high biodiversity of associated animals, plants and algae and is an important sediment stabiliser. Indeed, scuba diving or snorkelling over a seagrass meadow that is vibrant, both in terms of its bright green leaves catching the sunlight and the thriving marine life within and around it, is one of the most memorable underwater experiences to be had around our coastline.

Around the British Isles there are only two true seagrass species, both belonging to the genus *Zostera*, generally known as eelgrasses, and both can grow as extensive beds. Dwarf Eelgrass *Z. noltei* grows on

OPPOSITE PAGE:
A luxuriant seagrass meadow in clear water is a striking sight, especially when adorned by attractive animals like this small Snakelocks Anemone *Anemonia viridis*.

the shore, whilst Eelgrass *Z. marina* is a larger and more robust species that grows on the lower parts of shores but mainly in the sublittoral, typically down to about 4m but sometimes 10m, the depth depending mainly on water clarity. It also grows at middle and lower levels on the shore as a smaller variety, thought until recently to be a separate species known as Narrow-leaved Eelgrass *Z. angustifolia*. The current consensus, particularly from genetic studies, is that *Z. marina* and *Z. angustifolia* are synonyms (different names for the same species), with any physical differences a result of habitat, in other words phenotypic variants. However, in the UK the two are still sometimes recorded and considered separately.

Another aquatic plant in the same order (Alismatales) as *Zostera*, Beaked Tasselweed *Ruppia maritima*, is sometimes accepted as a seagrass because it can occur in full-strength seawater. However, *Ruppia* grows mostly in soft sediments fringing the brackish waters of estuaries, lagoons, creeks and saltmarshes, and this is predominantly a freshwater family and genus of plants.

Like most of the 60–70 or so true seagrasses found worldwide, *Zostera* has strap-like leaves that resemble those of familiar grasses found on land, hence the name seagrass. A few tropical species have distinctly un-grasslike oval, clustered or pinnate leaves. *Zostera* has an extensive root system and spreads by means of creeping rhizomes, from which clusters of leaves grow up directly at intervals. Rhizomes and roots anchor the plants and bind the sediment, resulting in stable beds even in soft sediments. However, calm and sheltered conditions are still a prerequisite, and seagrasses are found growing in sand and mud in sheltered bays, estuaries, sea lochs, channels and lagoons.

Are seagrasses true grasses?

The short answer is 'no', but it could also be 'yes and no', because they are related, albeit rather distantly. Like terrestrial grasses, seagrasses are true flowering plants (angiosperms). They are the only ones found in the ocean, and they produce flowers, pollen and seeds, just like their terrestrial cousins. In *Zostera* the inconspicuous male and female flowers are carried alternately on a flower spike that looks every bit like a delicate head of wheat. Most other seagrass genera are dioecious, a term that simply means they have separate male and female plants. Pollen is released as long strands rather than individual grains and dispersed underwater by currents and wave action, and in *Zostera* pollination

Underwater meadows: seagrasses

occurs underwater (hydrophilous pollination). The seedheads remain submerged, and seeds are released and again dispersed by water movement. They do not seem to travel very far, often metres rather than kilometres, and tend to remain within the parent bed. However, the seeds are fairly tough, and at least one study of *Z. marina* outside the British Isles has shown that they can survive passage through the guts of grazing ducks, geese, turtles and fish. *Zostera* can also spread to new areas via uprooted rhizomes and fragments.

The seagrass ecosystem

Seagrasses form the physical framework for the highly productive and biodiverse ecosystem of which they are a part. They provide a complex, three-dimensional habitat within, on and under which a wide variety of animals, seaweeds and microorganisms find food and shelter. Under favourable conditions, a seagrass bed builds

TOP ROW: This sublittoral seagrass bed in Little Colonsay, Scotland (left), and a grassland meadow in Cambridgeshire (right) rely on adequate hours of sunlight to form lush growths.

BOTTOM ROW: Seeds of Eelgrass *Zostera marina* before being released (left) and, for comparison, maturing seeds of a terrestrial meadow grass (right), with pollen-bearing male anthers still remaining.

up a thick layer of intertwining roots and rhizomes beneath the sediment surface, forming a stable mat. As long as conditions remain favourable, a well-established bed can maintain itself for many years and recover from periodic storm or human-induced damage. In the Mediterranean, records and research on *Posidonia* seagrass beds suggest some of these have been established for hundreds, potentially thousands, of years. There is little oxygen in the sediment beneath such dense, long-lived beds, and dead material accumulates beneath the live cover in a manner similar to a peat bog on land. This is why seagrass is so important for locking away and storing carbon.

Sublittoral *Zostera* beds consist of a single species of seagrass, *Z. marina*, but this does not mean they all look or are the same. *Zostera marina* is able to grow in a range of sediment types and under differing current, temperature and salinity regimes, with consequent differences in growth form and the habitat it provides for other organisms. Frances first dived on a *Zostera* bed in the Linne Mhuirich rapids area of Loch Sween, Scotland, in July 1982. In the clear water, a lush growth of long leaves was bent over like well-groomed hair, flowing in the direction of a fairly strong current. Tall seed-bearing stems were clearly evident, growing up from plants bedded into relatively coarse sandy mud. A later dive at a similar time of year in the Fal Estuary, Cornwall, revealed straggling, multi-directional

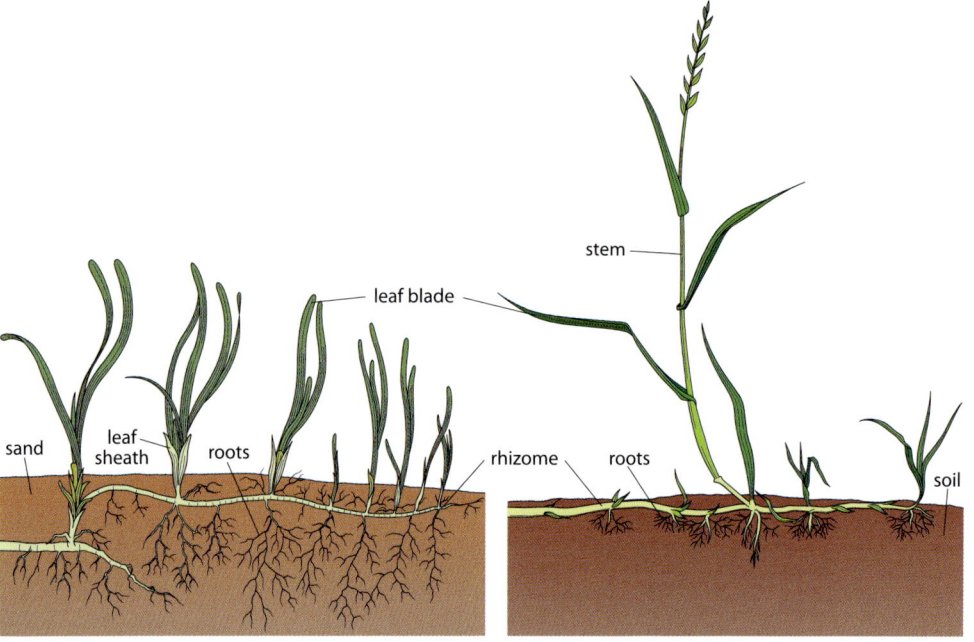

BELOW: Comparison of Eelgrass *Zostera marina* structure (left) with a typical terrestrial grass (right).

Underwater meadows: seagrasses

ABOVE: Whilst documenting and photographing the inhabitants of this dense seagrass bed, the diver stayed well above the seabed to minimise damage and disturbance of this fragile habitat.

leaves with a fair covering of silt, growing in fine, muddy sand. In the Isles of Scilly, *Zostera* beds growing in channels under current-exposed conditions take on a striated appearance, growing in wriggly lines visible in aerial photographs.

Seagrass meadows in the British Isles

Around Britain and Ireland, the cool climate allows seagrass to flourish intertidally as well as permanently submerged. In the heat of the tropics, intertidal seagrass is much rarer. Like terrestrial grass, seagrass can be found growing in small patches wherever conditions are suitable. However, its importance lies in its ability to form extensive meadows or beds that may cover hundreds of hectares. Both *Z. noltei* and *Z. marina* are found around most of the British Isles in suitable sheltered sediment habitats, but their distribution is patchy. The extent and location of significant seagrass beds is perhaps best known for *Z. noltei* in intertidal areas, as these are obviously easier to access than subtidal areas and more amenable to survey by aircraft or drone. Aerial survey of subtidal beds is only possible in clear waters such as those around the Isles of Scilly. Subtidal beds can be and are recorded and mapped by divers and snorkellers, including in citizen science projects, but this of course is very time-consuming. Remote surveying using techniques such as drop-down or towed video and ROVs (remotely operated vehicles) is also used but can be expensive.

ABOVE: Beds of the predominantly sublittoral Eelgrass *Zostera marina* are occasionally exposed on extreme spring tides – as seen here on the island of Ulva, Inner Hebrides, in September 2016.

Notable beds of intertidal *Z. noltei* are reported from the east coast of Scotland in the Cromarty and Moray Firths, and on the west coast in the Argyll and Clyde areas. Along the predominantly sedimentary English east coast, the extensive, muddy Wash estuary provides ideal habitat, and beds are also common in Essex estuaries and the Thames Estuary. The upper reaches of estuaries along the English south coast also provide suitable muddy intertidal habitat, as does Milford Haven in Wales.

Some of the best-developed and most extensive subtidal beds of *Z. marina* are found in Cornwall, particularly the Isles of Scilly and the Fal and Helford estuaries, with a notable recent discovery (in 2023) of a particularly large bed in St Austell Bay. Other important south-coast sites include Plymouth Sound, Torbay, the Exe Estuary, Studland Bay, the Fleet and various sites in the Solent. Perhaps the best-known subtidal *Z. marina* beds in Wales are those in North Haven at Skomer Island in the south and Tremadog Bay in the north. The clear waters of Ventry Bay in southwest Ireland provide exceptionally good conditions, with well-developed beds down to 10–13m depth.

There are of course many other important and localised seagrass beds that we have not noted, but we describe three of the beds mentioned here in more detail under *Selected southern seagrass meadows*, page 178.

Finding seagrass

Around the world there is a general lack of awareness and appreciation of the ecological, social and economic importance of seagrasses. Given their recently acknowledged role as a carbon sink, we need to know in much more detail just where seagrass and seagrass beds are located in order to put conservation measures in place where appropriate. This is so easy to say, but in truth so difficult to do …

To this end, the UK registered charity Project Seagrass, in association with Swansea and Cardiff Universities, has developed an app called SeagrassSpotter to encourage divers, snorkellers, anglers and holiday-maker citizen scientists to further study and record seagrasses. Even better, and unlike many citizen science projects, the results are all uploaded and available on the SeagrassSpotter website. So far, from the start of the project in 2016 to date (2025), over 2,900 records of *Zostera marina* have been sent in from around the UK. To find local areas in the British Isles where seagrass has been recorded is a simple matter of zooming in on a worldwide map. The global version of the app was only launched in 2018 and of course past records are not included, but as the project gains momentum it should give a much more detailed picture of the distribution and abundance of both *Z. noltei* and *Z. marina* around our coasts, since they often occur in localised patches as well as extensive beds.

The seagrass detritus cycle

Seagrasses are 'evergreen' perennials, but in the temperate waters around the British Isles *Zostera* grows most strongly during the long and sunlit days of spring and summer. Although it does not shed its leaves all in one go, it does die back in winter. Long summer leaves are lost particularly during storms and are replaced by shorter leaves that grow much more slowly. More new leaves appear in spring. It also loses old and damaged leaves throughout the year and, in addition, the ends of growing leaves fray as they are whipped to and fro by water movements. This continual rain of detritus provides food for a wide variety of invertebrates living on and in the sediment. Polychaete worms, amphipods, shrimps, crabs and sea cucumbers all benefit, and they in turn are eaten by larger predators and scavengers.

Zostera noltei beds on intertidal flats can often be seen expanding in spring as the rhizomes grow and spread and new leaves develop. However, annual changes are much

BELOW: A bonus to the seagrass detritus cycle: a dead fish is providing a variety of crabs (at least four species) with a good meal.

Natural beach cleaners

Walking along the edge of the sea on a sandy shore in southern Greece in 2015, searching for interesting seashells and egg cases, Frances found herself sinking into spongy, knee-deep heaps of washed-up seagrass. Staggering out of this to walk along the clearer sand near the top of the beach, she was surprised to see a scattering of small, palm-sized, fibrous balls. These turned out to be seagrass debris, formed from fibrous material turned over and over by wave and current action and eventually cast ashore. In this case these originated from the extensive beds of Neptune Grass *Posidonia oceanica* that predominate in some areas of the Mediterranean. They are known scientifically as aegagropilae, but colloquially as 'Neptune balls' or, more dubiously, 'Neptune's balls'.

These balls often have man-made debris trapped in them, particularly pieces of plastic. New research from Mallorca has shown that the formation of these balls is acting as a natural seabed cleaner, collecting up small pieces of plastic and particularly 'negatively buoyant polymer filaments and fibres' (Sanchez-Vidal *et al.* 2021). When the balls wash up on the beach, the plastic has effectively been removed from the ocean. On tourist beaches that are regularly cleaned, this could have a significant effect – though such beach cleaning can be damaging in itself. Sadly this natural cleaning effect is unlikely to be helpful around the British Isles due to the smaller size and lesser extent of *Zostera* seagrass beds. Neither of us has so far found similar balls around the British Isles.

Washed-up *Posidonia* seagrass, Neptune balls and land-plant debris on a beach in southern Greece.

more pronounced in some seagrass beds than in others. In the shallow waters of the Fleet Lagoon in Dorset, most areas of both *Z. noltei* and *Z. marina* show leaf dieback as winter approaches and regrowth as the water warms in spring and summer. In seagrass populations growing in more exposed areas, leaves can be ripped off and whole plants uprooted by storms. In some areas autumn gales result in great drifts washed up onto the strandline, testament to the great productivity of these underwater meadows. Here their remains continue to provide a food source for detritivores such as amphipods and therefore, in turn, large numbers of shorebirds.

Seagrass grazers

Walking over the wonderfully varied grass and flower turf of the South Downs or other chalk grasslands, it would be hard to miss the grazers responsible for keeping the vegetation down. Rabbits, deer and sheep are all a familiar sight both there and in any farmer's field, along with hares and other grass-dependent animals. In contrast, seagrass beds in Europe and other temperate waters support very few large grazers. Instead, their productivity depends mainly on detritus produced from dead leaves, broken-off leaf ends and uprooted plants, as described above. The few grazers that do feed directly on *Zostera* are mainly small gastropod molluscs, such as Edible Periwinkles *Littorina littorea*, Banded Chink Shells *Lacuna vincta* and species of *Hydrobia* and *Rissoa*, plus small amphipods, isopods, mysid shrimps and the much larger Green Sea Urchin *Psammechinus miliaris*. However, these grazers are

BELOW LEFT: Tiny Banded Chink Shells *Lacuna vincta* graze directly on both seagrass and seaweed.

BELOW RIGHT: The Sea Hare *Aplysia punctata* is a herbivore and is often found grazing on the seagrass itself.

ABOVE: Brent Geese *Branta bernicla* grazing on algae growing on mudflats in the Thames Estuary, Essex. Intertidal seagrass restoration efforts here by the Zoological Society of London could provide increased grazing for them in the future.

just as likely to be feeding on epiphytic growths of bryozoans and hydroids growing on the seagrass leaves as on the vegetation itself. Around the British Isles, the exception to this are birds grazing on intertidal beds of *Zostera*, which provide essential food for species such as Brent Geese *Branta bernicla* and Wigeon *Mareca penelope*.

During autumn, over 90,000 of the dark-bellied subspecies of Brent Geese *B. b. bernicla* migrate from their breeding grounds in Siberia to estuaries, saltmarshes and coastal fields on the east and south coasts of England. Here these small, duck-sized geese feed on coastal plants, but especially on mudflats covered in *Zostera* and fine seaweeds, following the tide down as the beds are exposed. Coastal mud and marshes on a cold winter's day may not be everyone's idea of a day out to the coast, but pick the right spot, almost anywhere from the Yorkshire side of the Humber Estuary south to Lincolnshire, Norfolk, Suffolk and Essex, around to Sussex and as far west as Hampshire, and you will have a good chance of seeing this, the smallest of our native geese.

In warmer tropical and subtropical waters, seagrasses grow more prolifically and can support a variety of larger grazers, including herbivorous fishes, turtles and sirenians (manatees and the Dugong *Dugong dugon*). Sirenians are sometimes known as sea cows – and, snorkelling off Western Australia, Frances was lucky enough to see a Dugong living up to its 'cow' name by munching happily on seagrass in Shark Bay. Green Turtles graze largely on seagrass and algae, though young ones are omnivorous, and Frances has often observed them eating sponges on coral reefs in Sabah, Malaysia.

Home sweet home: hangers on, lodgers, visitors and resident fishes

Hangers on: epiphytes and zoophytes

In the terrestrial environment, monocultures of agricultural crops, grazing grass or trees are generally considered to be 'bad' in terms of supporting biodiversity. In contrast, a natural ancient meadow or a newly planted wildflower meadow will be made up of many different plant species, and these in turn will support a myriad of insects and other invertebrates. Interestingly, seagrass beds around the British Isles are effectively natural plant monocultures, sometimes spiced up with a few seaweeds that are able to grow in sediment areas, attached to small stones, shells and other debris. Yet seagrass beds support a high biodiversity. This is in large part due to their high productivity and efficient recycling of nutrients, akin to that in a tropical rainforest, but also to the structural, three-dimensional habitat they provide which, amongst other things, allows filamentous algae and sessile animals to attach and live epiphytically. Held aloft on the swaying seagrass leaves, hydroids, bryozoans, sea anemones and sea squirts are in an ideal position to filter or comb the water for their plankton food.

By the end of the summer, many once squeaky-clean seagrass leaves are covered in a 'fuzz' of often rather dingy small growths, along with films of microorganisms, particularly diatoms and bacteria. Exactly what grows on the leaves varies both geographically and seasonally, as it is dependent on planktonic, drifting larvae settling out from the water to grow on the leaves. Seagrass leaves do not provide the stable, permanent attachment platform needed by larger, longer-lived sessile species such as sponges because the leaves die back or break off regularly, along with their epiphytic load. However, what they do provide is a way for smaller annual or short-lived species to extend their habitat range away from rocky places and out into sediment areas. With a few exceptions, the most common of which are shown in the table on page 172, most of these epiphytic species can also be found growing on rocks and other hard substrata. Sediment itself provides few footholds for algae and sessile animals.

BELOW: Tiny stalked jellyfish such as *Calvadosia campanulata* are often found clinging onto seagrass leaves.

Common epiphytic algae and hydroids recorded only from *Zostera* spp. in the British Isles

Red algae	*Rhodophysema georgii*
Brown algae	*Halothrix lumbricalis*
	Leblondiella densa
	Myrionema magnusii
	Cladosiphon zosterae
	Punctaria crispata
Hydroids	*Laomedea angulata*

Lodgers

As described on page 169, relatively few animals graze directly on the seagrass. However, the epiphytic hydroid and bryozoan growths are munched avidly by nudibranchs or sea slugs. Nudibranchs (Chapter 9) are fussy feeders and, like many terrestrial caterpillars, most will feed only on one or a few species. For example, *Polycera quadrilineata*, a common white and yellow sea slug, is frequently found feeding on Sea Mat *Membranipora membranacea*, which often grows on *Zostera* as well as on kelp and rocks.

The small size of sea slugs makes them difficult to spot, but their presence is often given away by the variously shaped strands of eggs that they lay. Many nudibranchs can be identified simply from these. The variety of egg masses laid by different animals on seagrass is a visible testament to the habitat's importance as a nursery area. Many of the most obvious masses are from molluscs. They range from the white coils and threads resembling miniature strings of pearls, laid by various nudibranchs, to the aptly named black 'sea grapes' that are tied onto the seagrass individually by female cuttlefish, usually under the watchful eye of an attendant male who is ensuring his paternity. Each 'grape' houses a single developing cuttlefish that, remarkably, has been shown to

BELOW: Bunches of cuttlefish eggs on seagrass.

ABOVE: Deep in the seagrass, and largely obscured by the boldly striped male, a female Common Cuttlefish *Sepia officinalis* lays her eggs. One of her brown arms is wrapped round the seagrass as she ties on each egg individually.

learn about the world outside while it is still in the egg (see *Cuttlefish breeding*, Chapter 10).

The spaghetti-like, usually pink, egg string of the Sea Hare *Aplysia punctata* is one of the most distinctive, forming a tangle that joins several seagrass leaves together. Close examination of the string reveals that it contains thousands of tiny spherical eggs. This is true of many mollusc egg strings, but the relatively large Sea Hare eggs make it more obvious. The Sea Hare is generally treated as one of the sea slugs, but it has a vestigial shell within its tissues and is not a nudibranch, which lack a shell entirely (see Chapter 9). Another difference is that unlike the generally predatory and specialist nudibranchs, Sea Hares are versatile herbivorous grazers (see photograph on page 169). Sea Hares are therefore found in a range of habitats, including on rocky shores, but seagrass meadows are a good place to observe groups of them in action. They can be seen browsing on the seagrass itself, mating, or – in a display of enviable versatility – doing both at the same time.

Like all sea slugs, the Sea Hare is a hermaphrodite, with every individual able to function as both male and female simultaneously. Most sea slugs mate in pairs with reciprocal fertilisation, but the Sea Hare's arrangements can be more complex and dramatic. They congregate in chains, with each one acting as a male to the one in front of it and a female to the one behind. Such chains typically comprise three or four individuals, but sometimes over a dozen Sea Hares form a complete ring, thus ensuring that they all enjoy the full experience.

Visitors

Many mobile animals commonly found in open sediment areas take advantage of the increased shelter and feeding opportunities provided by seagrass beds. They come and go, and whilst they may be common within the seagrass, they are not restricted to it. Paul often sees Flying Crabs *Polybius holsatus* amongst *Zostera* in Torbay, Devon. These are one of the swimming crabs, with flattened rear legs that act like paddles. The Wrinkled Swimming Crab *P. corrugatus* is another, looking prematurely aged due to the 'wrinkles' that run across its shell. They are commonly found on coarse sand, gravel and maerl, and Frances has also seen them scuttling amongst seagrass growing in coarse maerl gravel off the island of Ulva, Inner Hebrides, with an adjacent bed of live maerl nearby. Paul recently had a very unusual encounter with a Wrinkled Swimming Crab in Plymouth Sound, the first one he'd ever seen there; he didn't spot it underwater but the crab crawled out of his weight harness in the car park after the dive, presumably a side-effect of an underwater photographer staying in one spot for a long time. He returned it to the sea as quickly as possible.

The Spiny Spider Crab *Maja brachydactyla* is a common sight in seagrass meadows, their large size and gangly gait making them particularly obvious as they force their way through the dense growth. In the summer, a relatively large proportion of these crabs may be couples in pre-mate embrace, the seagrass perhaps providing welcome cover for more relaxed romance.

RIGHT: Large Spiny Spider Crabs *Maja brachydactyla* found among seagrass in the summer often include pairs just before or after mating.

LEFT: A swarm of juvenile bubble shells *Haminoea navicula* ploughing through soft mud at Valentia Island, Ireland. This species is common in seagrass beds on muddy sediments.

Ploughing through the sediment itself may be a brown bubble shell, *Haminoea navicula*, and it can be a slightly unnerving experience to see a dense swarm of these making their way purposely along between the seagrass stems. These too are usually included with the sea slugs, but they carry a thin, rudimentary, bubble-like shell hidden beneath two large body flaps called parapodial lobes. The best way to spot them is a nighttime snorkel or dive in sheltered muddy areas with or without seagrass, as they spend much of the day buried in the sediment. This species also lays its egg masses on seagrass and algae.

BELOW: A seagrass bed near St Mawes, Cornwall, with a particularly rich fauna including Daisy Anemones *Cereus pedunculatus* and Peacock Worms *Sabella pavonina*.

Tube-dwelling sea anemones find a home seated snuggly in the sediment below seagrass, with only their tentacles showing up as colourful rings. The Burrowing Anemone *Cerianthus lloydii* is one of the commonest, with an effective defence against having its head bitten off (literally): a vibration or shadow causes it to withdraw rapidly down into its soft protective tube. This species can be found in almost any soft, subtidal sand and mud habitat around the British Isles (see photo on page 141). The Daisy Anemone *Cereus pedunculatus*, a large species up to 15cm across the disc, sometimes occurs in significant numbers beneath seagrass, but it needs a buried object such as a stone or shell on which to attach the base of its body column. It has no protective tube but can curl in its tentacles and fold over the edges of its disc.

Resident fishes

Many species of fish benefit from the shelter of seagrass meadows, while a few are seagrass specialists. One of the latter is *Syngnathus typhle*, sometimes known as the Seagrass Pipefish. Its more usual common name, Deep-snouted Pipefish, is also seagrass-related, because the distinctive deep and laterally compressed snout, combined with the lack of 'forehead', gives it the same shape as a blade of seagrass and provides excellent camouflage. Whenever Paul spots one of these pipefish in a seagrass meadow, its presence given away by the glint of an eye or the flutter of a fin, he wonders how many he has swum past without realising. As in all pipefishes, it is the male that broods the eggs in a special belly pouch until they hatch into miniature versions of the adults. Youngsters of this species have even been observed swimming back into 'Dad's' pouch when danger threatens.

Research by Goncalves *et al.* (2010) on *S. typhle* has revealed further intriguing aspects of its breeding behaviour. As you would expect, females are choosy about the male to which they entrust their precious offspring. It is also not surprising that they favour bigger males, size being a positive factor in mate selection in many animals because it indicates that they have more resources for parental duties and a greater overall 'fitness'. What is most impressive about this pipefish, however, is that if females have reduced choice and 'make do' with a relatively small male, they compensate for his shortcomings by laying eggs with a higher protein content. Male *S. typhle* put a lot of effort into their fatherly duties, so it pays them to be choosy about

A dry seagrass dive

Snorkelling or diving over a seagrass bed is the best way to see, experience and photograph the wildlife on these underwater 'grassy plains'. However, in the clear, Atlantic waters of the Scottish west coast Frances found another way. When taking part in a Porcupine Marine Natural History Society survey of the Staffa Archipelago in 2016, she found that she could simply stand still, knee-deep in the clear water on a low spring tide, and watch what was happening – admittedly with a wetsuit on, as Hebridean waters are decidedly chilly even in summer. This was in a shallow subtidal *Zostera marina* bed off the island of Ulva. Taking photographs was a matter of bending down and slowly positioning her small waterproof camera amongst the seagrass. Green Snakelocks Anemones *Anemonia viridis* swayed gently, clinging to the seagrass leaves, in an ideal position to catch passing zooplankton with their purple-tipped tentacles. The lurid green colour comes from symbiotic algae in the tissues. The plain brown variety of this anemone occurs mostly in shaded areas or deeper water, where their single-celled lodgers would not be able to photosynthesise. However, both varieties were apparent in this particular spot.

On the coarse sediment seabed a Harbour Crab *Polybius depurator*, busy stalking the many small gobies that flitted through the seagrass, raised its formidable claws defensively as the camera approached. A Great Scallop lay partially buried with its shell agape, apparently eyeing up this human intruder with its fringe of simple eyes. Had Frances cast her shadow over it, it would have instantly shut up shop, or a step too near and it would have shot off, clapping its two shell halves clumsily together to create backward squirts of water. Scallop eyes cannot form images but are very sensitive to changes in light level such as the shadow cast by a would-be predator, or an inquisitive naturalist.

While remaining warm and dry, Frances was able to photograph both varieties of Snakelocks Anemone *Anemonia viridis* in this shallow, sublittoral seagrass bed off the island of Ulva, Inner Hebrides. The anemones' elevated position provides increased opportunity for plankton capture.

ABOVE: Spot the fish: the Deep-snouted Pipefish *Syngnathus typhle* is a specialist in seagrass living, where its colour and shape can make it very difficult to see.

whom they mate with too; they prefer larger females and also avoid those carrying a flatworm parasite that shows as small black spots. When researchers mimicked this effect with tiny marks of tattoo ink on some females, the males shunned them as well (Rosenqvist and Johansson 1995). This is just another small example of how the more we find out about fish, the more we admire their amazing abilities, a theme we explore much further in Chapter 8.

Selected southern seagrass meadows

Extensive beds of sublittoral seagrass *Z. marina* are best developed along the south and southwest coasts of England, and to a lesser extent along the west coasts of Britain and Ireland. Here we describe three of the most important and well-documented southern meadows.

Isles of Scilly

The sandy, sheltered channels and clear waters of this archipelago provide ideal growing conditions for sublittoral *Z. marina*, with beds covering an estimated 3km^2 of seabed. These beds are not only extensive and important in a national context, but also support an unusually diverse range of species including seaweeds, burrowing invertebrates and fishes. In summer, the calm, very clear water means that aerial surveys are possible, and the beds were well documented some years ago in a Natural England report (Jackson *et al.* 2011).

It also means that this is a place where sublittoral seagrass can be seen just by leaning over the side of a boat or canoe, and of course by snorkelling and diving, though mostly it is too deep for paddling.

The Fleet, Dorset

The Fleet is an extensive saline lagoon, isolated from the sea by the ancient shingle barrier of Chesil Beach. It has one narrow connection with the sea, water flowing in and out of Portland Harbour at the eastern end, and consequently the tidal range is only about 1.5m. With a predominantly sediment seabed and extreme shelter from wave action, it supports extensive areas of intertidal and shallow water *Z. noltei* and the narrow-leaved form of *Z. marina* (var. *angustifolia*). These beds form important forage areas for large numbers of Wigeon. Walking the length of the Fleet along the shingle of Chesil Beach is tough going (as is trying to launch an inflatable boat across the shingle, as Frances found out on an early diving survey). It's much better to follow the southwest coastal path, which runs behind the Fleet at sea level along the eastern half. The most extensive seagrass areas are just west of The Narrows and towards Clouds Hill (west of Rodden Hive). The seagrass here is at its best in spring and summer and dies back with the approach of winter. One of the most accessible ways to see the seagrass and wildlife of the lower reaches of the lagoon is to take a trip on a shallow-draft boat such as that run by the Dorset Wildlife Trust.

BELOW: The Fleet Lagoon (the small body of water to the left, in the far distance) lies behind Chesil Beach and opens into Portland Harbour. It is home to extensive and important seagrass beds in shallow water.

Coastal Seas

Sadly, an assessment of the Fleet Lagoon in 2018 as a marine Special Area of Conservation (SAC) reported much of it to be in 'unfavourable condition', largely in terms of reduced abundance and distribution of *Zostera*, the evidence suggesting that a decline in water quality and eutrophication were to blame. This is a continuing problem, and one that remains difficult to solve.

Studland Bay, Dorset

Studland Bay is an oasis of calm lying just south of the entrance to busy Poole Harbour. It stretches between Shell Bay in the north and Old Harry Rocks in the south and is a magnet for yachts and other recreational boats. In summer the beaches are awash with holiday-makers. It is also home to an extensive meadow of *Z. marina*, considered one of the best along the English south coast. In turn the seagrass provides an ideal habitat for both the Long-snouted (or Spiny) Seahorse *Hippocampus guttulatus* and the Short-snouted Seahorse *H. hippocampus*. Seahorses are poor swimmers and have the endearing habit of curling their prehensile tails around blades of seagrass (or seaweed) in order to stay in one place. This makes them popular subjects for underwater photographers, but both species now have only a tentative hold as native species in the British Isles and are protected by law. Under the Wildlife and Countryside Act it is illegal to knowingly disturb them. Such disturbance includes snorkellers

BELOW: Studland Bay, Dorset, home to seagrass and seahorses and playground for holiday-makers. A no-anchor zone and summer-deployed eco-mooring buoys help prevent damage from anchor chains.

Underwater meadows: seagrasses

ABOVE LEFT: A bed of tall Eelgrass *Zostera marina* in Studland Bay, with plants up to a metre high.

ABOVE RIGHT: Seagrass is a favourite habitat for the Long-snouted Seahorse *Hippocampus guttulatus*, a charismatic, protected and rarely seen species.

and divers deliberately seeking them out to photograph or using any artificial light to obtain images.

The Studland Bay seagrass bed is the only well-known breeding site in the British Isles for *H. guttulatus*. Intriguingly, it is the male that becomes 'pregnant', as in the closely related pipefish. Following courtship, a couple mate with their tails entwined and in a face-to-face position so the female can deposit her eggs into the male's brood pouch with her ovipositor. Following mating, the pair feed separately near each other and meet up each day for a pair-bonding ritual. In Steve Trewhella and Julie Hatcher's book *In the Company of Seahorses* (2017), there is a delightful account of witnessing this very rarely observed behaviour at Studland. They describe it as 'an elaborate ballet' lasting around 15 minutes during which the Long-snouted Seahorse couple 'entwine their tails and pirouette, sometimes facing each other and sometimes facing away, with an equine tossing of their heads.' Paul has seen a similar, but seemingly simpler, interaction between a pair of Short-snouted Seahorses among seaweed on a muddy seabed in Torbay. The 'pregnant' male remained with his tail anchored to the weed while the female approached, appeared to inspect him as if checking he was caring properly for her precious young, and then rested against him for a few minutes.

Studland Bay was designated as a Marine Conservation Zone (MCZ) in 2019, specifically to protect the seagrass habitat and the seahorses. There is currently (2025) a voluntary no-anchor zone, marked with buoys during the summer months, covering the majority of the seagrass bed off South Beach. Over the years, anchoring has caused significant damage to the seagrass and consequently to its resident seahorses. Interestingly the Seahorse Trust recorded 16 Long-snouted Seahorses on a single survey dive following the lockdown in 2020, imposed to help control the spread of COVID-19 during the pandemic. Only two had been recorded since 2015, and numbers had been declining since the first annual survey in 2008, when 40 were counted. The suggestion is that the increase after 2020 can be attributed to almost no disturbance during the lockdown period when boating, diving and other recreational activities were almost entirely absent. The Trust, in partnership with local boating services, has subsequently installed 10 eco-moorings (see diagram opposite), the start of a project that should help to prevent further anchor damage, whilst still allowing continued recreational use of the area.

Conservation and restoration

In the 1930s a marine pandemic of a wasting disease severely reduced the extent of (primarily) *Zostera marina* beds in the North Atlantic. At that time, this was largely a hidden problem since scuba diving and remote cameras were not in use. Estimates suggest that as much as 90 per cent was killed throughout the North Atlantic. This is unlikely to be an accurate figure since seagrass surveys were only just starting at that time. The slime mould *Labyrinthula zosterae* (only described in 1991) is the suggested culprit, and the disease still lurks at a low level today, though it is not considered a current threat. Seagrass beds have the capacity to recover from such diseases, and there has been significant recovery, but the question remains as to why beds around the British Isles (and Europe) have never got anywhere near to attaining their former glory. Continued declines in coastal water clarity due to infrastructure development, sewage and industrial waste input is a likely candidate, combined with increases in fishing and recreational boating. An analysis of published data and 'grey' literature on seagrass has shown that within the UK at least 44 per cent of seagrass has been lost since 1936, and that much of this loss has occurred since the 1980s (Unsworth *et al.* 2021). The losses were probably much greater than this, with many seagrass beds quietly disappearing without being documented. The same researchers indicate that mapped seagrass remaining in UK waters currently amounts to around 8,500 hectares (21,000 acres).

Underwater meadows: seagrasses

Physical damage

The trouble with boats is that you cannot effectively 'park' them without using an anchor – as Frances learned the hard way when, as a novice marine biologist, she once gaily chucked out the anchor from an NCC inflatable as instructed, only to find that the anchor rope was not attached to the boat. To anchor a yacht safely, a length of chain twice the depth of the water must be deployed, and as the wind and tides change, the boat may swing and drag the chain in an arc over the seabed. Within a seagrass bed, chain and anchor can lift and uproot the matted base layer, destroying its stability, especially when the anchor is lifted. Seagrass and recreational sailors share a liking for sheltered bays, and where popular boating sites and important seagrass beds coincide, anchor damage can be a significant problem, albeit mostly caused unwittingly. Along the south coast of England in particular, various solutions to this problem are undergoing trials.

In Cawsand Bay near Plymouth and at other south-coast sites, Advanced Mooring Systems (AMS) are now in use, installed in 2019 in Cawsand through the ReMEDIES project (Reducing and Mitigating Erosion and Disturbance Impacts affecting the Seabed). This allows recreational boats to moor up above the seagrass (or other sensitive habitats) without using either anchors or traditional mooring buoys, which both rely on chains that can damage the seabed. An AMS is designed to keep the tether well above the seabed at all states of the tide using an elastic rode or mid-water floats.

BELOW: A comparison between traditional swing moorings with a potentially damaging chain (left) and two versions of Advanced Mooring Systems (AMS; middle and right) that minimise contact with the seabed.

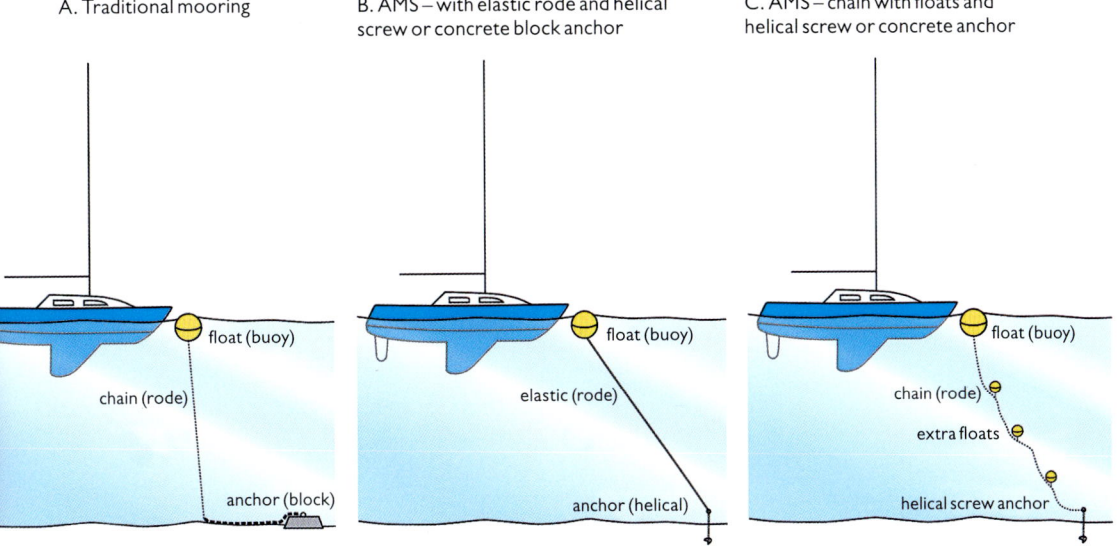

What is the connection between a beer mat and seagrass? Visit a pub in the vicinity of Falmouth Harbour and you might find the answer. The beer mats are an innovative way of informing the public, especially boat users, of the existence of voluntary no-anchor zones in the harbour, set up over important seagrass and maerl beds and marked by special buoys. Similar zones have been set up in Studland Bay, Dorset, as mentioned on page 180 and elsewhere. Such schemes are of no use unless the intended audience knows about them – hence the beer mats. In the future, if such areas are marked up on the electronic navigation charts in use on many recreational boats, this will be a big step forward.

Physical damage to intertidal *Z. noltei* beds is mostly caused by trampling and digging, from activities such as shellfish and live-bait harvesting and recreational walking and exploration. The impact this has depends largely on the intensity and frequency of the activity and the type of sediment in which the seagrass is growing.

Restoration projects

Whilst initiatives such as no-anchor zones can prevent further damage and allow natural regeneration, so much has been lost that serious attempts are being made to establish new seagrass beds in suitable areas, and to extend and restore existing ones. On land, creating new wildflower meadows to replace some of the 95 per cent or so lost throughout the British Isles over the past 100 years has now become a well-established practice. Even King's College in Cambridge, not far from home for Frances, has, since 2020, transformed its back lawn, which is now well on its way to becoming a traditional biodiverse East Anglian hay meadow. The survival of the wild remnants of this precious and still precarious habitat is by no means assured, but the methodologies for creating new habitat are there. So can the same thing be done underwater to restore and extend seagrass meadows around our coasts?

There are obviously huge practical and financial challenges, but there is now an increasing number of experimental initiatives around the British Isles aimed at doing just that. There is even a *Seagrass Restoration Handbook* of techniques applicable to the UK and Ireland (Gamble *et al.* 2021). The scientific literature too is full of experiments and trials. At the local level, finding suitable sites and securing permission for wild seed collection is always the first step, followed by development of techniques for storage (underwater or in aquaria) and

Selected examples of seagrass replanting initiatives

Lead organisation	Site	Date of planting	Methods and extent
Swansea University	Dale Bay, Pembrokeshire	2019 2020	One million *Z. marina* seeds in hessian sacks. Subtidal
Natural England, ReMEDIES project	Plymouth Sound and Solent Maritime SACs	2021	*Z. marina* in hessian sacks *Z. marina* seedlings on coir mats
Hampshire & Isle of Wight Wildlife Trust	Langstone Harbour and Seaview (Isle of Wight)	2021 onwards	*Z. noltei* and *Z. marina* in hessian seed bags/pouches. Intertidal
Cornwall Wildlife Trust	Fal Ruan NR, Fal Estuary	2022	*Z. noltei* in hessian bags and transplanted seedlings. Intertidal
North Wales Wildlife Trust	Llŷn Peninsula and Anglesey	2023 onwards	*Z. marina* seed planting; various methods
Restoration Forth	Firth of Forth, Scotland	2023 onwards	*Z. marina* and *Z. noltei* seed planting

deployment of seeds, and for growing seedlings and planting them out. So far two main approaches have been tried in the UK – the first is to enclose collected seeds in biodegradable bags or sacks, with deployment usually from boats (or on foot for intertidal sites); the second is to grow seedlings on biodegradable mats in onshore facilities and then plant them out, usually using divers. The collection and bagging up of seed often involves local community volunteers. The obvious terrestrial equivalent of simply broadcasting seeds over suitable seabed seems to have been unsuccessful in trials in other countries, and none of the initiatives described here have tried this technique.

Some major initiatives (shown in the table above) include the deployment of upwards of a million *Z. marina* seeds in Dale Bay, Pembrokeshire, by Swansea University (working with Sky Ocean Rescue and WWF). The ReMEDIES project, led by Natural England with several other key partners, had a five-year remit to develop and deploy methods to protect seagrass beds in five Marine Protected Areas (MPAs) along the English south coast and where necessary replant an estimated 8ha by the end of 2023. An important part of the protection element was delivered by the Royal Yachting Association (RYA)'s Green Blue initiative, in engaging and changing the behaviour of recreational boat users. The planting was achieved by a variety of organisations and with various degrees of success. The initial ReMEDIES planting work in Plymouth Sound SAC and Solent Maritime SAC, deploying *Z. marina* seeds encased in a suitable medium in hessian bags, was very successful in terms of methodology and involvement of local volunteers, but less so in achieving good germination and establishment of seedlings. It may though prove a suitable technique for intertidal restoration. Divers planting out seedlings grown in the National Marine Aquarium, Plymouth, on pillows of coir matting, achieved much better (though small-scale) results (February 2023) with colonisation of bare sand, surprisingly mostly between and around the mats. Growing the seedlings and planting them out is, however, both time-consuming and expensive.

The answer to whether seeds in hessian bags will work for intertidal *Z. noltei* may in part be answered by the Cornwall Wildlife Trust (CWT). In 2022 CWT initiated trials (in partnership with a local clothing company, Seasalt Cornwall) to identify the best methods for restoring and expanding the size of *Z. noltei* beds in their Fal Ruan nature reserve, which lies within the Fal and Helford SAC. The creek chosen for the trial is in the upper reaches of the estuary and is remote and difficult to access, so the area is unlikely to be affected by human activities such as dog walking. Additionally, it has no direct sewage or other pollution input. Trials include *in situ* storage of seeds in containers such as lobster hatchery boxes, deployment of seeds in hessian bags (as for the ReMEDIES sublittoral sites described above) and transplanted seedlings held down by bamboo strips. The use of body boards helps to ease access onto the mudflats and minimises disturbance when planting out the hessian bags.

Small-scale restoration of seagrass in the UK is an exciting first step, but what is needed is large-scale restoration. The seagrass ecosystem research team at Swansea University is working on ways to upscale seagrass restoration methods, for example by developing ways of automating the process. However, it should also be remembered that if favourable conditions return (or are returned) then existing seagrass beds can expand and recover, as they have in the past, especially in intertidal areas.

Seagrass harvests

Although little used today, the long strap-like leaves of seagrasses, especially the larger warm-water and tropical species, have in the past provided traditional material for thatching and for weaving into baskets and mats. Indigenous peoples living along the northwest coast of North America used to harvest spring rhizomes of eelgrass for food. With classic ingenuity, researchers have come up with a potential new use for eelgrass, using washed-up material. We started this chapter by describing just how important healthy beds of seagrass are in locking away carbon on a long-term basis and therefore helping mitigate climate change. Now it seems that seagrass can potentially help further by keeping our homes warm and at the same time saving local authorities money. As described above, dead and storm-broken seagrass can wash ashore and cover huge swathes of beach in soggy heaps. In Europe this material is often removed at some cost to clean up popular tourist beaches. However, a way of using this waste material has now been found, in that it can potentially be turned into insulation boards for use in the housing sector; wood fibre is used in a similar way. Most of the research on this has been done using the larger Neptune Grass, the species prevalent in the Mediterranean. However, two wood biology scientists from Germany have recently produced flexible insulation mats using Eelgrass *Z. marina* (Kuqo and Mai 2022). These experimental mats have low thermal conductivity and good fire resistance. Currently in the throes of trying to insulate a cold 17th-century house, Frances was especially interested to read this. The technology may be new, but around the year 1900, dried Eelgrass, sewn between thick paper sheets and known as Cabot's Quilt, was marketed as a house insulation material in the US and Canada.

Having now finished exploring seagrass meadows, it is interesting to look back to kelp forests (Chapter 3) and maerl beds (Chapter 5). A distinct similarity between these three ecosystems becomes apparent. Although belonging to very different marine 'plant' groups (flowering plants, brown seaweeds and red seaweeds, respectively), they all provide an essential living framework, on which the whole ecosystem and its biodiversity depends. Each of these three ecosystems relies on just a few key species (one, in the case of sublittoral seagrass beds), something that can only increase their vulnerability to human interference and exploitation. The good news is that the public, through organisations such as the Royal Yachting Association (RYA), are becoming increasingly aware of the importance and fragility of seagrass beds, maerl and kelp and are taking action and voicing their concerns. Small steps that are making the future look a little brighter. We now move on in the next chapter to explore the open sea – where the habitat is provided purely by the water body itself.

The open sea

chapter seven

At the height of summer, the water off Clacton-on-Sea in Essex can reach a heady 18°C, reportedly the warmest place for a sea dip around the British Isles. Even at this temperature a wetsuit or drysuit allows a longer and more comfortable stay in the water, but some people prefer to do without the restriction of movement these impose. Whatever the choice, snorkelling is the best way to get closely immersed in the mesmerising beauty of drifting jellyfish and other gelatinous plankton in open water, though being partially uncovered does increase the risk of getting stung. We think it is a small price to pay for meeting these intriguing open-water denizens.

Jellyfish are among the larger and more spectacular visible elements of plankton, those organisms that live suspended and drifting in the water column at the mercy of tidal currents and winds. Most plankton is microscopic in size, and as snorkellers and divers we fin blithely along unaware of its presence. Almost all life in the ocean is ultimately dependent on the smallest organisms, the photosynthetic phytoplankton, vital producers of oxygen. In this chapter we restrict ourselves to descriptions of visible plankton, but also include phosphorescence and red tides, two phenomena where invisible plankton becomes temporarily visible. We also describe our encounters with coastal mammals, birds and open-water fishes, often grouped together ecologically as nekton, those active, swimming animals encountered living and feeding in the water column rather than on the seabed. Such is the variety and importance of fish and their varied behaviour, that we have devoted the whole of the next chapter (Chapter 8) to those found on or near the seabed.

OPPOSITE PAGE:
Barrel (or Dustbin Lid) Jellyfish *Rhizostoma octopus* are so large that they are easily spotted from above the surface in calm seas.

Blue-water diving

Many of our encounters with jellyfish and other gelatinous plankton are serendipitous meetings during a dive or snorkel. However, there are opportunities to watch for plankton, fish and other nekton at the end of most dives. It is standard procedure to make a 'safety stop' when coming up from any dive below 10 metres, even when the depth and length of that dive do not require specific decompression stops. Divers are recommended to pause for around 3–5 minutes at a depth of 5–6 metres to allow accumulated gases in tissues and bloodstream to dissipate. This is a great opportunity to look out and around for open-water wildlife, either while hanging onto your surface marker buoy or with a hand on a weighted 'shot line' deployed at the start of a dive to mark a shipwreck or other interesting site.

A few intrepid plankton scientists and other divers undertake 'bluewater' dives well away from any coastline, with the seabed hundreds or thousands of metres below them. This technique allows researchers to photograph, study and collect jellyfish and other delicate zooplankton without recourse to damaging nets. It is a strange and slightly disorientating feeling to be able to see neither surface nor seabed in clear water, and safety lines and procedures are vital.

Lighting up the sea

As a teenager, Frances lived in a remote rural area of Sussex, and on still, warm summer evenings the lane verges behind her house were punctuated by bright pools of greenish light from Glowworm beetles *Lampyris noctiluca*. These are the wingless females, using bioluminescence signals to attract a flying male in from the surrounding darkness. Later encounters with tropical fireflies and cave-dwelling 'fungus gnats' were equally enchanting, but it is in the ocean that bioluminescence really comes into its own. It is used in communication by a wide range of marine taxa (groups), particularly those living in the perpetual darkness of the deep-sea realm, and is found in at least 11 marine phyla.

During the warmth of summer months, coastal plankton around our coastline can produce spectacular light shows once the sun has set and darkness descends. In June 2022 the quietly lapping water along the shoreline at Romney Marsh in Kent, a favourite and familiar shoreline to Frances, was lit up by a ribbon of ethereal blue with blue-topped wavelets. Under calm conditions and with nutrients washed out from the marsh, planktonic algae called dinoflagellates had divided rapidly to form a bloom. These, and in particular the relatively large (up to 2mm) dinoflagellate *Noctiluca scintillans*, were emitting bioluminescent light, set off by the movement of the water. In *Noctiluca*, water vibrations deform the membrane around this single-celled organism, resulting in a sudden flash of light. A person in the water also creates vibrations, and we must both admit to child-like waving during night dives under such conditions, in order to create starbursts of light; we also enjoy following the bright vortex of light created by our buddies' fins. Another easy way to enjoy the spectacle is to give a few tugs on the line of your surface marker (which is always used at night) and watch it set off little fountains of sparks between you and the surface.

Some larger plankton including comb jellies (Ctenophora), arrow worms (Chaetognatha) and jellyfish (Scyphozoa) also emit bioluminescence. The Mauve Stinger *Pelagia noctiluca* is a bioluminescent jellyfish occasionally (but increasingly) encountered around the British Isles. With a 10cm diameter body and thin tentacles trailing up to 3m, it has a virulent sting (as Frances can attest), but, dressed and spotted in shades of pink, purple and mauve, it is a beautiful sight by day or night.

BELOW: Mauve Stinger Jellyfish *Pelagia noctiluca*, its umbrella covered in 'warts' that contain a high concentration of stinging cells. Usually uncommon, this was one of large numbers seen around Cornwall and the Channel Islands in 2024. Colourful by day, it also lights up with bioluminescence at night.

Bioluminescent plankton are thought to use their light mainly to confuse and deter potential predators. Whatever the organism, the mechanism is chemical, with light produced when enzymes called luciferases activate compounds called luciferins.

Red tides

Whilst *Noctiluca* light up the darkness and many blooms of phytoplankton are a valuable and important part of the natural cycle, some dinoflagellates and microalgae form blooms of a less welcome nature. These blooms often colour the water red and so are very noticeable – hence their popular name of 'red tides' – but there are also other variously pigmented species that streak the water yellow or green. We see wind-blown lines and patches of these on the water when working on shores in sheltered bays and from boats when out diving.

Although this can be a natural phenomenon, the size and frequency of such blooms is increasing due to concentrated inputs of nutrients from sources such as sewage and agricultural run-off that fuel a rapid increase in microalgae. This is a potential problem because some species release toxins as they die or are ingested by fish and shellfish. Whilst wild fish will generally avoid these areas, captive farmed species such as salmon are not so lucky, and there have been many instances where a red tide has killed large numbers. A further problem is that whilst shellfish such as mussels may be unaffected themselves, they can bioaccumulate toxins; they should therefore never be collected for food from the wild in affected areas.

Double lives

Like secret agents, many jellyfish live double lives, and it can be hard to match one form with another. True jellyfish belong to a class of Cnidarians (the phylum that also includes anemones and corals) called scyphozoans (Scyphozoa). In all of them the main phase, termed the medusa, is the free-floating familiar jellyfish with a bell- or saucer-shaped body and peripheral trailing tentacles. The most commonly encountered and ubiquitous species around the British Isles is the Common or Moon Jellyfish *Aurelia aurita*. It can be so abundant that it clogs up the cooling-water intakes of coastal power stations. This harmless (to most people) species is easily recognised by its round translucent bell, through which can be seen four horseshoe-

ABOVE: Compass Jellyfish *Chrysaora hysoscella* (left) and Moon Jellyfish *Aurelia aurita* (right) are both common and easily identified species.

or ring-shaped white, pink or purple reproductive gonads. If you have never seen one washed up on the shore or in the water, then try a local aquarium, as it is one of very few jellyfish that is able to thrive in captivity (at least short term) in specifically designed, columnar tanks. This species is also very photogenic and adorns the front of Frances's book *The Marine World* (Dipper 2016).

The alternative life form of *Aurelia* and many (but not all) true jellyfish is a tiny columnar polyp called a scyphistoma, attached to the seabed and superficially resembling an upside-down anemone. The scyphistoma grows from a free-swimming larva known as a planula that settles out from the plankton, the larva resulting from eggs and sperm released into the water by male and female medusae. The polyps can cover large areas of rock or other hard surfaces, and we have even seen them attached to the tough outer covering of large, solitary sea squirts such as *Ascidia mentula*. The polyps increase in numbers and spread by asexually budding off new polyps. At some point each polyp starts to split horizontally, a process called strobilation, forming a 'stack' of mini plate-like jellyfish. Individual 'baby' jellyfish are released from the top of the stack. To our mind this process is at least as fascinating as a ground-based caterpillar turning into a free-flying butterfly.

Coastal Seas

TOP ROW: Compass Jellyfish *Chrysaora hysoscella* (left), with distinctive markings on its umbrella and long trailing tentacles which are extended when feeding. The Lion's Mane Jellyfish *Cyanea capillata* (right) has a powerful sting from its impressive spread of tentacles used for ensnaring prey (including smaller jellyfish).

BOTTOM ROW: The Blue Jellyfish *Cyanea lamarckii* (left) is similar in shape to the much larger Lion's Mane but is usually a bluish to purple colour and has a weaker sting. Barrel Jellyfish *Rhizostoma octopus* (right), with a diver enjoying a close-up view.

There are four other true jellyfish species commonly encountered around the British Isles, along with the less common Mauve Stinger already mentioned. They include the beautiful Compass Jellyfish *Chrysaora hysoscella*, named for the radiating brown lines running down its bell, and the large Lion's Mane Jellyfish *Cyanea capillata* that is mostly present in our waters between June and September. The Lion's Mane has a mass of long trailing tentacles that carry a severe sting, which persists on detached fragments of tentacles. Like many divers, Paul has had the uncomfortable feeling of 'second-hand' stings when wiping his face with gloved hands that had held a rope past which the jellyfish had drifted. The quartet is completed by the similar but smaller and more ubiquitous Blue Jellyfish *C. lamarckii* and the Barrel or Dustbin Lid Jellyfish *Rhizostoma octopus*, with a huge, blubbery white bell that can reach nearly a metre in diameter. Luckily this last one does not sting, but it is certainly an impressive animal and unusually solid for a jellyfish, as Paul can testify from the thud when one collided with the back of his head while he was taking photographs in a strong current. Records of all jellyfish can be sent to the Marine Conservation Society to add to their large database. Sustained changes in the number and distribution of jellyfish can be indicative of changing water temperatures, fishing activity and alterations in seabed ecosystems.

When is a jellyfish not a jellyfish? On snorkels and dives around Great Britain we encounter many other 'jellies' easily mistaken for true jellyfish. Like jellyfish, the hydroids or sea firs have two different life stages, but in their case the main growth form is the sessile one, with colonies forming variously shaped, plant-like growths attached firmly to the seabed. The 'jellyfish' stage is usually short-lived, and hydroid medusae are generally small (less than a centimetre) and inconspicuous. As with true jellyfish, the medusae release eggs and sperm, the resulting larvae settling and growing into the sessile stage. Of course, there are variations and exceptions, and some hydroids such as *Aequorea* have a large medusa.

BELOW: In their medusa stage, hydroids look like tiny, millimetres-wide 'true jellyfish' and are called hydromedusae. Most are difficult to identify and belong to a group called Leptomedusae (left). At up to 18cm diameter, *Aequorea* species (right) are exceptionally large examples.

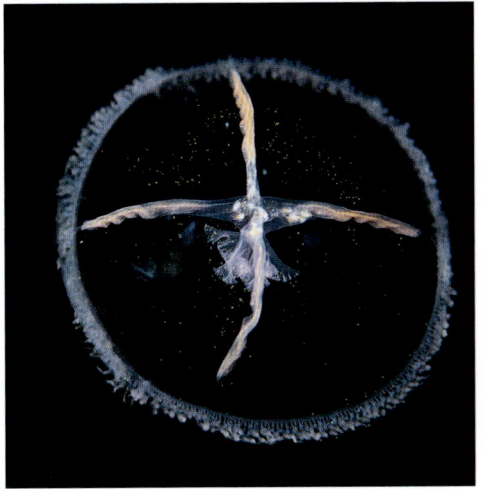

Coastal Seas

ABOVE: Tiny stalked Kaleidoscope Jellyfish *Haliclystus auricula* on a blade of seagrass.

Stalked jellyfish

Another atypical jellyfish might be revealed by a patient search through seaweed growths in a rock pool, or in seagrass beds when snorkelling or diving. If you are lucky, you might find tiny organisms hanging upside-down attached to the vegetation by a stalk. Shaped like a handbell, urn or goblet, these intriguing animals look like miniature jellyfish, but instead of floating free, they stay in one place and use eight stout arms, each tipped with a knob of short tentacles, to catch planktonic food. Some species have 'anchors' on the bell web between the arms that allow them to somersault to a new position by bending over, attaching the bell, and then releasing their stalk attachment to swing over and find a new foothold.

Combs and gooseberries

Comb jellies are another group, in this case a phylum (Ctenophora), of easily visible planktonic animals that light up. They can sometimes be found washed ashore in summer looking like soft marbles. The reward for putting them back into a pool or a bucket of water is to see the mesmerising ripples of iridescence that run down their sides as they revive and swim. Living up to their common name, comb jellies propel themselves along by beating vertical rows of hair-like

RIGHT: Sea gooseberry *Pleurobrachia* sp. with long tentacles for catching food. The general name for these animals, 'comb jellies', comes from the rows of cilia on the body that beat rhythmically to provide propulsion, producing the beautiful iridescence seen here.

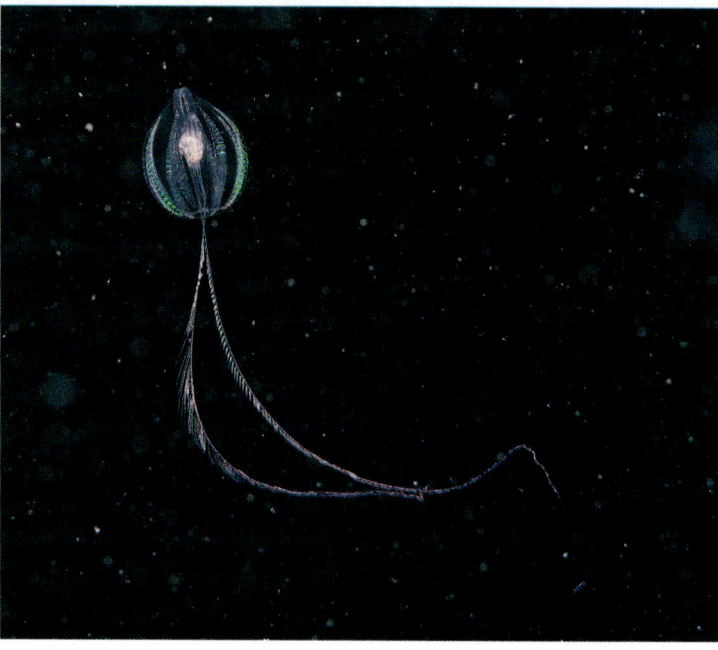

cilia arranged in comb blocks, and it is these movements that produce the transient rainbow colours. The Sea Gooseberry *Pleurobrachia pileus* is a common species about the same size and shape as its namesake, but others such as Common Northern Sea Gooseberry *Bolinopsis infundibulum* are more sausage-shaped and can be larger.

Surface drifters

Sadly, one of our most common encounters with surface drifters today comes in the form of plastic rubbish. During surveys in the Semporna Islands, Malaysia, a decade or so ago, the dive boat that Frances was in had to stop constantly to unwind plastic bags caught around the propeller (the Malaysian government is now moving towards a nationwide ban on single-use plastic bags for retail by 2026). Long-lasting plastic jetsam is even associated with the wider spread of some non-native species. Natural drifting platforms such as tree branches disintegrate faster, restricting how far associated organisms can travel. Marine animals such as seals and cetaceans have an innate curiosity and often become entangled in plastic debris whilst others try to eat it.

There are, however, some much more interesting drifters to be seen from beaches, boats, pontoons and jetties. The Portuguese Man-of-war *Physalia physalis* and the By-the-wind Sailor *Velella velella* live a permanent floating existence at the sea surface, sailing along with the wind like miniature yachts. Animals with this way of life are collectively known as pleuston. These two complex organisms are specialised hydroid nomads, adapted to a roaming existence, in contrast to their immobile seabed relatives. The individual polyps of each colony hang down in long strings beneath a gas-filled float with an upright 'sail'. Around Great Britain these ocean wanderers

ABOVE: By-the-wind Sailor *Velella velella*, a colonial hydroid, blown inshore and trapped in a rock pool. The distinctive 'sail' on top of its float is clearly visible.

BELOW: A drifting Portuguese Man-of-war *Physalia physalis*. The wind-catching 'sail' topping the colourful gas-filled float can be deflated if danger threatens. The long trailing tentacles of this colonial hydroid, here hidden beneath the water, carry a powerful sting.

are usually encountered washed up on the shore, mostly in ones or twos, but sometimes in large numbers, particularly after storms. In May 2024 various beaches in Cornwall and Devon, and on Guernsey in the Channel Islands, were covered in hundreds of *Velella*, a smelly feast for gulls and invertebrate scavengers. *Physalia* is predominantly a warm-water species but appears on southwestern coasts of Britain and Ireland driven in by prevailing winds. Its scarcity here is probably just as well, because whilst beautiful, the long feeding tentacles are packed with polyps that have a debilitating sting. Frances saw this first-hand whilst swimming with her father-in-law off the west coast of Australia. Just a single trailing tentacle was enough to leave him with a painful, raised weal from shoulder to waist. These jellies should never be picked up from the beach with bare hands.

Surface giants

Jellyfish are the principal food for giants such as Leatherback Turtles *Dermochelys coriacea*, the only sea turtle native to our waters, and Ocean Sunfish *Mola mola*. Small jellies that bumble down near the seabed can also become dinner for large anemones, and even crabs will catch one given the chance (see photo on page 88). *Mola mola* is the heaviest bony fish native to the British Isles, its two tonne weight

BELOW: Most Ocean Sunfish *Mola mola* sightings are made from boats, but this beautiful portrait was taken by a photographer underwater, off Donegal in Ireland.

surpassed only by the Bumphead Sunfish *M. alexandrini*, another ocean wanderer found mainly in the southern hemisphere. Sunfishes have the habit of lounging around at the surface lying on their sides apparently sunbathing, hence the name. The reasons for this behaviour have long been debated, and suggestions from observations include allowing seabirds to stomp around and peck parasites off their sides. Whilst divers very occasionally encounter one underwater, most sightings are made from boats. In fine weather and calm seas, sightings are relatively frequent from the deck of ferries sailing out to places such as the Isles of Scilly.

Basking Sharks

The Basking Shark *Cetorhinus maximus* is our largest native fish species, attaining lengths of at least 10–12m (accurate measurements of live ones are difficult). When one is feeding at the surface, filtering out plankton through its gill rakers, the tall dorsal fin and upper tip of the tail often show above the water – a majestic sight as they swim purposefully past. Most people who see them are aware of their feeding habits so are awe-inspired rather than frightened, but a press report some years ago memorably described a Devon kayaker who was not in the know as 'running up the beach in some distress' after an encounter. If you are lucky enough to see a basking shark while snorkelling, a view of the enormous mouth agape underwater is even more impressive. After years of trying, Paul finally managed one such brief encounter and a few photographs in 2004, but most of his views were like the one remembered by Frances from the late 1970s, of a tail disappearing rapidly into the gloom.

Whether observing these sharks from the surface or underwater, and whether the meeting is unplanned or through an organised wildlife-viewing boat trip, it is essential that we take care not to stress or harass them. To this end, the Shark Trust has produced a practical Basking Shark Code of Conduct. It is also illegal to intentionally disturb one, such as by close circling with a boat.

Most sightings are in the summer off western coasts of Britain and Ireland, with known hotspots around Cornwall, the Isle of Man and the Hebrides. In 2020 a Marine Protected Area called the Sea of the Hebrides was declared, largely on the basis of the number of Basking Sharks using this area, along with regular visits from Minke Whales *Balaenoptera acutorostrata*. Coming close inshore during the summer

RIGHT: Basking Shark *Cetorhinus maximus* swimming with its huge mouth wide open to engulf and filter out the tiny planktonic animals (mainly crustaceans) on which it feeds.

months, the sharks can also be spotted and counted from clifftops and other vantage points.

There is still much to learn about the lives of these enigmatic giants but, through a variety of citizen science projects, based on detailed records of sightings, and an increasing number of scientific studies using advanced tagging, telemetry and satellite technology, our knowledge is gradually increasing. Research has been carried out into Basking Shark biology and ecology at the Marine Biological Association (MBA) in Plymouth since the 1960s, for example. Findings have shown how the sharks can occasionally migrate at depth between northern and southern hemispheres, and across oceans in the northern hemisphere. They move horizontally and vertically on both a daily and seasonal basis to maximise feeding opportunities, and return within and between years to specific locations. Particularly striking is the way they assiduously follow ocean fronts (the boundaries between water masses) where the density of specific types of zooplankton is greatest. We should probably, therefore, think of them as skilful hunters of tiny prey rather than haphazard filter-feeders.

We are still ignorant of where and when or even if they breed around the British Isles, and no one has ever observed them mating. However, an answer to these questions recently moved a step nearer. In 2020 and 2021 the Irish Basking Shark Group (IBSG) documented large Basking Shark aggregations off County Clare in which the animals were not feeding, but swimming around following one another in a purposeful, tight circle. It is exhilarating enough to see one shark, let alone many tens of them, so there must have been considerable excitement amongst the observers. This late-summer behaviour, dubbed a 'torus' (a geometrical term used to describe a circle revolving around an axis), has also been observed in the Hebrides and is believed to be a form of courtship, wonderfully described by one of the scientists as 'slow-motion shark speed-dating'. Although instances had been seen in other years, the County Clare aggregations were the first to be filmed, allowing detailed analysis (the behaviour can be watched on social media channels such as YouTube). Interactions between sharks whilst circling strongly suggests a courtship function for the toruses, as explained in an open-access paper authored by David Sims from the MBA and colleagues from several other organisations (Sims *et al.* 2022). That conclusion is further supported by observations of circling sharks breaching – spectacularly propelling their body out of the water – which has previously been linked to courtship. Basking Shark records can be sent to the Shark Trust, the Manx Whale and Dolphin Watch or the IBSG. This species is now protected around the whole of the British Isles.

Fish at school

Watching the Swifts *Apus apus* wheeling and screaming around her house each summer, Frances always finds it amazing to think that these welcome visitors have almost certainly not touched ground since their previous year's visit to the nest boxes provided in the church tower (and monitored with cameras). Swifts are unique amongst birds in this respect, but there are many fish species that spend their entire lives up in the water column. As described in Chapter 1, water provides sufficient support to make this pelagic existence a tenable way of life, and the water column itself is an immense living space. Atlantic Herring *Clupea harengus*, Atlantic Sprat *Sprattus sprattus*, Atlantic Mackerel *Scomber scombrus* and Atlantic Horse Mackerel *Trachurus trachurus* are amongst the most familiar and important commercial

Coastal Seas

ABOVE: Saithe *Pollachius virens* swimming by a shipwreck (the *Glanmire*, near St Abbs) display the beautifully precise arrangement of a closely packed fish school.

species around the British Isles. What all these pelagic species have in common is their habit of living and feeding together in shoals, some small but others numbering hundreds or thousands of individuals. Out in open water there is nowhere to hide, except amongst your own peers. Shoaling provides safety in numbers, confusing predators in the same way as flocks of Starlings *Sturnus vulgaris*, wading birds or herds of antelope. There are also more eyes to spot predators.

That the strategy sometimes backfires was demonstrated to Frances and colleagues on a 2016 field trip to a seashore in Aberystwyth, Wales. Along the rocky shoreline were scattered heaps and lines of dead and dying Sprat, flashing silver in the sunlight. In 2020, as well, thousands of Sprat (and possibly young Herring – it's very difficult to tell the difference) were stranded on several sandy shores in Gwynedd. In calm weather, shoals of Sprat are chased close inshore by Atlantic Mackerel, as well as larger predatory fish and seals, and in their efforts to escape they become trapped. When out in boats we sometimes see cascades of small silvery fish just ahead and to the side of us. Mistaking the boat vibrations for a predator approaching from below, the fish push to the surface, their panic making them momentarily airborne. Shoaling fish are also vulnerable to modern fishing technologies: pinpointed, tracked and caught with precision.

School rules and lines

Some shoaling fish such as the smartly striped Bib *Trisopterus luscus* or pencil-thin sandeels (Ammodytidae) are relatively tolerant of being approached by divers, so we can watch their group behaviour. For much of the time, each individual goes about its own business investigating potential bites to eat, but the whole group stays together. On other occasions such shoals will pass purposefully by, heads all pointing in the same direction, tails beating to keep them moving at an even speed. Such disciplined shoals, with individuals all following unseen rules of spacing, are technically called schools, though the two terms are often used interchangeably. These are fish that are going somewhere, and their tidy formation swimming helps save energy, particularly on medium and long migrations, such as those made between feeding and breeding grounds. Atlantic Mackerel and other migratory species living in the chilly waters around the British Isles also migrate to avoid adverse temperatures, appearing seasonally along our coastline from warmer and deeper winter quarters.

ABOVE: School of small sandeels (Ammodytidae) moving purposefully in the same direction. They are a vital food source for many animals, including seabirds and cetaceans.

INSET: Sand Smelt *Atherina presbyter* shoals often appear relatively 'disorganised' until approached by a predator.

Schooling fish respond to a predator by making spectacular synchronised swoops, turns and splits, at times as mesmerising as the murmurations of Starlings coming in to roost from wide winter skies. So how do they do this? One of the ways we distinguish lookalike fish such as Pollack (or Lythe) *Pollachius pollachius* and Saithe (or Coley) *P. virens* during a dive (or from photographs afterwards) is to look at the lateral line, a distinctive row of scales that runs along the flanks of most bony fishes. In Pollack the line makes a graceful curve near the head, whilst in Saithe it runs straight. From the fishes' point of view this is purely incidental, and the line has a far more useful function. Beneath the scales runs a fluid-filled channel, lined with sensory cells that detect water vibrations in a manner similar to the way our inner ear cells detect sound vibrations. Signals sent to the brain are interpreted to provide information on the whereabouts of moving prey, predator, friend and foe. Within a fish school, the information allows maintenance of a standard 'nearest neighbour' distance. When fish on the outside of the school change direction and speed in response to a potential predator (or perhaps an obstruction), their neighbours detect and follow the change and the whole mass of fish moves almost in unison. Check out the lateral line next time you see a whole fish at a fishmongers.

Coastal mammals and birds

Marine mammals

Coastal waters around the British Isles are home to a surprising number of marine mammals, defined as those that spend most or all of their lives in the sea and depend on it for food. This obviously applies to whales and dolphins (cetaceans), of which 28 species might be termed resident or at least visit fairly regularly. Bottlenose Dolphins *Tursiops truncatus*, Common Dolphins *Delphinus delphis* and Harbour Porpoises *Phocoena phocoena* are the three most commonly recorded cetaceans around the British Isles. The Bottlenose habit of 'bow riding' in front of boats, seemingly for the pure pleasure of doing so, is something we have both been lucky enough to enjoy when on the way to or returning from dive sites in calm weather. The Moray Firth on Scotland's east coast and Cardigan Bay in Wales both have resident pods of Bottlenose Dolphins. In contrast, the much smaller Harbour Porpoises rarely show more than a glimpse of their backs before they are gone.

ABOVE: Common Dolphins *Delphinus delphis* can be seen all round the British Isles, both inshore and far out to sea, making energetic leaps and breaches as well as being enthusiastic boat bow-riders like Bottlenose Dolphins *Tursiops truncatus*.

At the other end of the cetacean size spectrum are the plankton-feeding Minke Whales sighted particularly often in the North Sea and off western Scotland. Orca or Killer Whale *Orcinus orca* sightings cause great interest and excitement, with Shetland a 'hotspot' as evidenced by the Facebook group 'Shetland Orca Sightings' which has over 48,000 members, and most records come from around north and west Scotland. A small (eight or nine individuals) 'resident' pod of Orca can be seen in summer off the west coast of Scotland, particularly around the Small Isles and Skye (Inner Hebrides). An increasing number of Humpback Whale *Megaptera novaeangliae* sightings in recent years, particularly around Cornwall in the winter months, suggests our waters are an important feeding habitat for these spectacular animals. Photo-identification studies are starting to show that some individuals return here year after year.

Grey Seals *Halichoerus grypus* and Common or Harbour Seals *Phoca vitulina* are year-round residents, most commonly encountered during the brief periods when they haul out on shore to rest and particularly to give birth. These are the only two species of pinnipeds (seals, sea lions and Walrus *Odobenus rosmarus*) native to the British Isles, although the very occasional vagrant Walrus makes headlines after straying south from the Arctic, a pinniped stronghold. Other occasional strays from there include Ringed Seal *Pusa hispida*, Bearded Seal *Erignathus barbatus*, Harp Seal *Pagophilus groenlandicus* and Hooded Seal *Cystophora cristata*.

Otters *Lutra lutra* are an essentially freshwater species, but in north and west Scotland and Ireland the majority live on the coast and hunt their prey in sheltered coastal waters. They are often called sea otters, but the true Sea Otter *Enhydra lutris* is a charming inhabitant of Californian and Alaskan kelp forests that only ever comes ashore if driven to do so by violent storms. Worldwide, the marine mammal count is around 130 species.

As divers we rarely encounter a marine mammal underwater, and most sightings are made from the shore or when out in a boat. However, at some popular and protected dive sites such as Lundy in the Bristol Channel, the resident seals have become used to bumbling, bubble-blowing visitors and, with an innate curiosity, will come and investigate. At the Farne Islands off Northumberland, some of the seals gather and watch divers enter the water from their

---

Lone dolphins

During her time at the Port Erin Marine Laboratory, Isle of Man, in the 1970s (see box on page 78), Frances and her colleagues were often entertained by the antics of a friendly Bottlenose Dolphin named Donald. Lone dolphins, usually young males, separated or ousted from their family pod, sometimes choose to associate with humans. Donald mostly roved between Port St Mary, Port Erin and Douglas harbours, having learnt he would be thrown fish and might find company in the form of divers and swimmers. He was particularly enamoured of a lady called Maura Mitchell (who taught Frances to dive) but seemed at times to become rather too amorous. He was very playful and enjoyed shoving boats around so that they swung on their moorings. Such animals are often known as 'ambassador' dolphins (there are also ambassador seals), presumably because they improve the image of their species in the minds of the public. However, Donald was shot at and wounded in 1976, as not everyone involved in the fishing industry appreciated his liking for fish. At some point he moved south to Wales and Cornwall, and his story is told by Dr Horace Dobbs in a book called *Follow a Wild Dolphin* (1977).

Other Bottlenose Dolphins that have caught the public imagination include Fungie, resident in Dingle, Ireland, from 1983 to 2020 (when he died), and Clet, named in France in 2008, who subsequently travelled widely around the British Isles, the last sighting being in 2015 (as far as we can ascertain). An interesting science-based read on solitary cetaceans can be downloaded from the Manx Whale and Dolphin Watch (MWDW) website.

LEFT: A graceful Grey Seal *Halichoerus grypus* caught in the sun's rays at Lundy in the Bristol Channel.

boats, apparently waiting for an opportunity to approach and swim with them. Divers at both locations have had memorable face-to-face encounters and even nibbled fins, but for a diver's safety and the wellbeing of the animals, maintaining a sensible distance is important (though not always possible).

Seals on land and therefore out of their natural element are far more wary, especially Grey Seals with pups, and it is essential to keep your distance and avoid stampeding them back into the water. This not only wastes their precious energy but can lead to seals being injured as they rush across a rocky beach in fright. Organisations such as the Cornwall Seal Group Research Trust work hard to spread awareness of how to watch seals without affecting their safety and welfare, a very important role given the number of people that visit the southwest coasts to spend time with nature, but who may not always appreciate the vulnerability of some of their favourite animals.

African safaris to see lions, elephants and other wildlife at close range often rely on the fact that the animals do not seem to connect vehicles with people. The same applies to seals at places such as Blakeney Point in Norfolk. Here, locally operated boats provide close-up views of seals hauled out on sand banks, the seals seemingly recognising the regular boats and taking very little notice of them. Over the past 20 years or so this colony has grown hugely in size, and it is now one of the largest in England with more than 10,000 individuals.

Sadly, for many people their most common or only encounters with dolphins and whales are strandings of dead or live animals. Fortunately, there are dedicated volunteers supporting Marine Strandings Networks that record and collate these events. The data they collect can then drive improvements in fishing practice to minimise damaging impacts, such as the use of acoustic devices on fishing gear and a ban on 'pair trawling' (where vast nets are dragged between fishing vessels) in UK territorial waters. The UK Cetacean Strandings Investigation Programme (CSIP) latest report (UK CSIP Annual Report 2017) shows that the number of strandings in 2017 was over 50 per cent higher than the average of the previous five years and the highest since the start of records in 1990. Harbour Porpoise and Common Dolphin are the commonest species reported in most years. High on the list of causes of death for these two species are starvation, accidental entanglement in fishing gear (bycatch) and disease. Interestingly, in 2017 the highest post-mortem-revealed cause of death for Harbour Porpoise was attack by Bottlenose Dolphins. It has been suggested that this may be the dolphins' response to current low fish stocks and hence aggressive competition for this resource.

Seabirds

A wide variety of birds live and feed along the coastline, making use of cliffs, shores, marshes and estuaries, in fact all habitats that fringe the sea. Oystercatchers *Haematopus ostralegus* probe sediments for invertebrates, flying noisily away if approached, whilst dainty Ringed Plover *Charadrius hiaticula* run in stop-start fashion, eyeing up any intruder warily. Like other waders, they restrict themselves to the edges of the sea, along with Rock Pipit *Anthus petrosus*, a passerine bird that makes good use of strandline and sea-cliff invertebrates. Ducks and geese (collectively wildfowl) flock seasonally to estuaries and sheltered bays to feed on the rich pickings from mudflats.

ABOVE AND LEFT: Gannets *Morus bassanus* are spectacular birds, whether seen above or below water.

LEFT: Like other true seabirds, Fulmars *Fulmarus glacialis* spend most of their lives out at sea, picking food from the sea surface. They often eat carrion, and regularly follow in the wake of fishing boats.

In contrast to all these land-attached coastal birds, true seabirds spend the majority of their lives out at sea, weathering winter storms and summer heat. Special adaptations allow them to drink seawater and cope with the salt from their fish diet. Many of these open-ocean dwellers only spend time ashore during the summer breeding season. This is when cliff-face cities of seabirds become tourist attractions at places such as Bempton, Yorkshire, where around half a million Northern Gannets *Morus bassanus*, Kittiwakes *Rissa tridactyla* and Guillemots *Uria aalge* come to nest. Compared to its size, the British Isles has a disproportionately large number of the world's most spectacular and important seabird breeding colonies. Bass Rock off the east coast of Scotland turns white during the breeding season, as it is home to the largest colony of Northern Gannets in the world, cramming in 150,000 birds at peak breeding times. However, numbers here and at other sites have recently been affected by avian flu outbreaks. Watching their frequently clumsy landings only emphasises how these various nomadic seabirds are structured for a life in the air and on the water, with a long, streamlined body and short legs set well back. Manx Shearwaters *Puffinus puffinus* can only scuttle uneasily when on the ground, and Frances well remembers their eerie night cries emanating from underground nest burrows on Lundy, as she stumbled from the (then) basic accommodation to the outside conveniences.

Seabirds have always provided us with endless distraction during the inevitable waits between dives on a dive boat. A Fulmar *Fulmarus glacialis* skimming the waves with stiff-winged precision, a Gannet plunging for fish with its wings folded back, or a raft of floating Guillemots certainly make such times enjoyable. Looking out for seabirds is also an excellent way to make a ferry crossing pass more quickly. The Joint Nature Conservation Committee (JNCC) runs Volunteer Seabirds at Sea (VSAS), a citizen science programme that trains volunteers to record seabird sightings made from ferries ('vessels of opportunity') using standardised methods. First set up in 2018 in collaboration with the Scottish ferry company CalMac, the initiative now also operates in English waters, working with the charity MARINElife.

In 2024, Frances was lucky enough to sail in the remote Lofoten Islands, Norway, where White-tailed Eagles *Haliaeetus albicilla* perch unconcerned on rocky outcrops, waiting for daily visits from fish-throwing tourist boats. Her highest count in one view was eight.

These raptors are not seabirds, nor is their diet restricted to fish, but as the largest bird in the British Isles they are a magnificent, if rare, sight. The species was reintroduced into Rum, one of the Small Isles in the Inner Hebrides, in 1975 with birds sourced from Norway after they had become extinct in the British Isles. There have been further introductions, and an estimated 150 or so pairs are now found in Scotland. If recent reintroductions to the Isle of Wight (2019) and Wales (feasibility still being explored at the time of writing) are successful (practically and politically), then the sight of one snatching a fish from the water with its huge talons may become a reality there as well.

The majority of this book is devoted to the seabed habitats, communities and species found at the bottom of the ocean, below varying depths of water. We have only devoted this one chapter to what lives in the open sea – the water above the seabed. There are good reasons for this, in spite of the fact that the vast majority of the ocean ecosystem is actually open water, the principle one being that the majority of open-sea inhabitants are planktonic and mostly invisible to us in the wild. So we have limited our descriptions to easily visible jellyfish and other gelatinous organisms, plus fish, sea mammals and seabirds. We have mostly treated this open-water living space as one habitat, because that is what it seems like to us. However, to at least the smaller organisms at home in open water, this is not the case. Differences in water temperature, detailed chemical composition, density, light, depth (pressure) and water movements delineate and define discrete water bodies even within a relatively small geographic area such as the British Isles.

Sadly these subtle differences provide little in the way of barriers to pollution originating from human activities. The drift of an oil spill, like the 'red tides' we describe here, is largely controlled by wind and tide. More positively, neither are they a barrier to those fish, marine mammals and birds that undertake extensive migrations, both within and well outside the marine jurisdictions of Britain and Ireland. As a result, conservation, research and recording efforts directed at animals such as Basking Sharks, Blue Sharks *Prionace glauca* and drifting jellyfish need international cooperation in order to succeed, and there are hopeful signs that this is indeed starting to happen.

Part Three
Species

Fish tales

chapter eight

Depending on our interests we catch fish, study them, count them, measure them, age them, track them and of course eat them. However, as with terrestrial animals, only patient watching, photographing and filming will reveal the details of their lives and relationships. Fish often get a bad press and are usually considered as rather dim and dull alongside vertebrate relatives such as mammals and birds. However, a growing body of literature and increasing numbers of direct underwater and laboratory observations show that this is far from the truth. Many fish species exhibit wonderfully complex behaviour, and in such a rich and diverse habitat as the shallow seas around the British Isles, there is plenty of it on show.

Fish form an integral and vital part of the shallow-water communities described in the preceding chapters, and could even be described as their 'backbone'. They act as grazers, predators and prey at various levels of the food web. Shallow inshore waters provide a wide variety of habitats and microhabitats, due to different rock and sediment types and physical conditions such as wave exposure and tidal currents, and therefore, in terms of fish species, biodiversity can be high. Adaptation to these different environmental parameters has led to an astonishing array of body shapes, behaviour and fascinating 'accessories' such as head tentacles, chin barbels and flamboyant fins. Inshore waters sport species that vary from typically 'fish-shaped' fishes, such as the variously named Pollack or Lythe *Pollachius pollachius* that may be seen cruising through a kelp forest, to the delicate Long-snouted Seahorse *Hippocampus guttulatus*, its tail curled around the stem of a seagrass, that is hardly recognisable as a fish at all.

Most of the species in the shallows belong to a class technically termed ray-finned fishes (Actinopterygii), commonly known as bony fishes. However, there are also sharks, albeit small ones, such as the

PREVIOUS PAGES: Gotcha! The Long-spined Sea Scorpion *Taurulus bubalis* is an ambush hunter, and its expandable mouth enables it to deal with surprisingly large prey such as this dragonet *Callionymus* sp.

OPPOSITE PAGE: This male Tompot Blenny *Parablennius gattorugine* is a recognised individual from a study that Paul carries out in a small patch of Devon reef. Named 'Bradley', he was a record-breaker in that he held the same crevice territory continuously for seven years.

Small-spotted Catshark *Scyliorhinus canicula*, less accurately known to many as a 'dogfish', as well as their flattened relatives, the skates and rays. Sharks, skates and rays belong to a completely different class, the cartilaginous fishes (Elasmobranchii). Familiar fish identification guides covering waters around the British Isles usually include upwards of 300 species, the number varying depending on the target audience, usually anglers, divers, naturalists or scientists.

Fish as individuals

For both of us, and for many recreational scuba divers, snorkellers and anglers, identifying and recording different species of fish underwater is a passion similar to birdwatching, but without the binoculars. It is immensely enjoyable as well as a way of collecting data essential for following trends in fish populations and combating new threats such as the collection of wrasses and Lumpsuckers *Cyclopterus lumpus* for parasite control in fish farms. Whilst not yet on a scale to compete with projects such as the RSPB Big Garden Birdwatch, there are nevertheless many citizen scientists out there willing to take part in national recording schemes.

In recent years, Paul and a number of other dedicated divers have realised that fish identification can be taken a step further. Many hours of long-term, patient observation and photography at particular sites have shown that, without doubt, one fish is not necessarily just like another. As well as recognising different species, we can now recognise individual fish within one species. This works mainly for fishes that maintain territories or have limited home ranges, spend a lot of time just lying around on the seabed, are relatively long-lived and vary slightly in their colour patterns between individuals. Humans are very good at pattern recognition. Paul's work on Tompot Blenny *Parablennius gattorugine* individual recognition, and the work of others, such as Martin and Sheilah Openshaw on Undulate Skates *Raja undulata*, are starting to reveal just what complex lives and relationships some fishes have (see further details of these two studies below). Once individuals within a species can be recognised, then the complexities of their everyday lives and interactions can be unravelled. Long-term homes, partners, 'friends' and rivals are all part of the mix. Digital underwater photography is a key tool in this research.

In terms of population ecology, the digital photography technique can also work well for large, slow-moving open-water fishes. One of

ABOVE: The Small-spotted Catshark *Scyliorhinus canicula* is another example of a species where individuals can be recognised from their skin patterns.

the first and most successful worldwide photo-identification databases is of Whale Sharks *Rhincodon typus*, the largest fish in the ocean. Each individual has its own pattern of white spots, and Whale Shark watching is increasingly popular with recreational divers, who are almost always keen to take photographs. By submitting these to the database, divers have provided the means to follow the ocean-wide movements of these giants. Our coastline is the regular summer haunt of the second-largest fish, Basking Shark *Cetorhinus maximus*. Whilst the fish is plain coloured, the tall first dorsal and tail fins project clear of the water when the fish is feeding on plankton near the surface. As with some whales, nicks and cuts in these provide the potential for individual recognition.

As described above, being able to recognise individual fish within a species is a useful research tool. However, individual fish recognition only works for a limited number of species. For example, it would be very difficult with species such as Long-spined Sea Scorpion *Taurulus bubalis*, which whilst highly territorial and with very colourful patterns, can change their colour patterns radically, adopting different hues according to the habitat. A question yet to be fully answered is whether colour and pattern recognition is used by the fish themselves to recognise another member of the same species. Colour and pattern are certainly used by a number of fish species to recognise male versus female, age and maturity of individuals, and even mood. However, the extent to which they can recognise each other and how they might do it requires much further research. As well as colour patterns, smell and subtle behavioural movements are also likely to be involved. That some fish probably can recognise other individuals of their species is indicated by records where two or more documented individuals have been recorded together in different places (see the account of Undulate Skates, page 223). Research on coral-reef 'cleaner fish' shows that some individuals get bad reputations for being 'dishonest' cleaners who nip pieces from their hosts. These cheating cleaners are recognised by the fish they previously cleaned and shunned when the affected fish return for their next cleanup. This then indicates that at least in this instance, one fish species appears able to distinguish between individuals of a second species.

Life and times of the Tompot Blenny

Around the British Isles the Tompot Blenny is a famous fish for divers, snorkellers and especially underwater photographers. The distinctive face, topped with a splendid pair of head tentacles and typically spotted looking out from a hole in a reef or shipwreck, is an appealing subject and one that can often be seen on successive visits to the same location. Paul's own photographer's affection for these small but charismatic fish quickly became a biologist's passion when he realised that the patterns of unique skin markings on their heads could be used to identify individual fish reliably. Once individuals could be readily recognised, discoveries about their lives came thick and fast – because, as is often the case with non-commercial fish, surprisingly little is known about the biology even of a common and widespread species.

Paul has always enjoyed diving and snorkelling repeatedly in the same spots. This 'unadventurous' habit amuses his colleagues and friends but he would thoroughly recommend it for getting an insight into the habitats and natural history of the marine world, and it suited his Tompot Blenny studies perfectly. For more than 10 years and over several hundred dives on two small patches of shallow rocky reef in South Devon, he has 'kept tabs' on dozens of individuals. Watching their behaviour as they defended their patches against marauding crabs and each other was fascinating enough, but tracking individuals by examining and cataloguing their 'mug-shots' took the intrigue to another level.

ABOVE: A feisty Tompot Blenny *Parablennius gattorugine*, recognised as 'Bruce' by his head markings, won this contest with a Velvet Swimming Crab *Necora puber* that entered his territory.

An early and striking finding, and something not previously known, was that a male Tompot Blenny can keep the same crevice territory continuously and not just in the spring-to-summer breeding season. Two to three years of territory retention at the study sites was standard, but it was sometimes more, and one star individual, 'Bradley' (see photo at the start of this chapter), also known more prosaically as WBM05 for the scientific reports, kept his home for seven years. Competition between males for the best territories appears to be intense. In addition to seeing frequent 'stand-offs' and occasional fights, Paul often observes males with fighting injuries around the mouth and fins at about the same time that there are changes in occupation. It seems that the most sought-after crevices combine a very narrow section, where a male Tompot Blenny can squeeze in to evade roaming predators (such as Conger Eels *Conger conger*), with an open front section where he can advertise his presence and entice females to lay their eggs on the rock surfaces that he has cleaned in preparation for their visits. As a group of fishes, blennies typically have a mating system where both sexes are promiscuous, so a single female visits several males in a breeding season to lay her eggs and a male hosts several females. Paul's observations clearly showed this was indeed the case for Tompot Blennies, with a remarkable number of visitations seen during the small fraction of total time (despite many dives) that he was at the reef. When the BBC came to film the blennies for *The One Show*, they described it as 'an underwater soap opera' – which was spot-on!

Promiscuous, however, does not mean indiscriminate, and there is every indication among blennies in general, and the Tompots in Paul's study, that they are very choosy about their partners. Females will benefit from laying more of their valuable eggs with the 'best' males, and males will benefit from expending their prodigious efforts guarding eggs from the 'best' females. When both sexes are promiscuous *and* choosy, you have the ingredients for complex social lives – and this is certainly borne out by the behaviour of Tompots in the studied areas of reef and beyond. There are numerous interactions in and out of the breeding season and within and between the sexes that suggest an intricate system of pecking orders. Paul has spent many happy hours watching in fascination as an individual that appears to be just gaining the upper hand (fin?) in an argument with a colleague is suddenly approached by another even more dominant individual who quickly puts them in their place.

A further notable discovery from the Devon reefs was that some young male Tompot Blennies are 'sneakers' who enter the crevices of territory-holding or 'bourgeois' (the correct technical term) males during a female's visit and surreptitiously fertilise some of the eggs that she has just laid. Although a new finding for Tompot Blennies,

BELOW: 'Bobby' (left), a territory-holding male Tompot Blenny, with a female, 'Bathsheba' (right), visiting him to lay eggs. 'Bobby' was observed as a 'sneaker' male in 2017 before being recorded as a respectable 'bourgeois' resident from 2019 to 2022 (when seen here) in Paul's Devon reef study.

LEFT: One of the thriving population of Tompot Blennies that lives among the mussels under Brighton Pier. Another fascinating aspect of these fish is the way that the size of their head tentacles appears to vary between different locations; they are longer here than on the Devon reefs.

such tactics are common in other blenny species, and the benefit to the sneaker of passing on his genes without doing the hard graft of egg-guarding is obvious. Of even more interest was that all the observed male sneaker Tompots gained respectability with age and became bourgeois territory-holders in later years. Demonstrating the sequential application of different reproductive tactics in individual fish is relatively rare and scientifically intriguing, and came purely from the ability to recognise individual animals. What drives the changes is not yet known.

A particular advantage of recognising individuals from their inherent markings, rather than with an artificial label or tag, is that they can be picked out retrospectively from old photographs. A well-established territory-holding male, for example, can be recognised as a timid youngster in previous years, rather like the way people have fun spotting politicians or celebrities in their old school photographs.

The more Paul watches Tompot Blennies, the more fascinating they become, including when he encounters them in different locations. The thriving population under Brighton Pier is a prime example. When he dives around the structure at the far end of the pier, he sees Tompots swimming across the seabed, peering out from their hidey-holes and interacting with one another wherever he looks. He used to wonder if the large numbers of these versatile omnivores were exploiting the Edible Mussels *Mytilus edulis* that cover the legs of the pier and other metalwork as a food source, but couldn't work out how these small fish could break into the molluscs' strong shells. Observations eventually showed the answer was simple – wait for a crab to break a mussel open with its strong claws and extract a piece of the soft flesh, then steal it.

Speaking of crabs ... if, like many, you view the Velvet Swimming Crab *Necora puber* as the fierce 'hard-nut' of shallow seas, wait until you see one confronted by a Tompot Blenny that is either seeking to steal a meal or protecting precious eggs. The crab doesn't stand a chance, and typically folds its claws across those distinctive angry-looking red eyes and retreats to a safe distance.

Assisted by others, such as the Wildlife Trusts, and by the appealing nature of the Tompot Blennies themselves, Paul's research has piqued media interest on several occasions, such as with *The One Show* mentioned earlier. All the resulting media pieces have noted the 'surprising' vibrancy of undersea life around the coasts of the British Isles, so Paul and his partner Teresa like to think of the Tompot Blenny as an ambassador for our marine environment. A blenny known as 'Benny' was therefore the ideal subject and narrator for a children's book on marine life by Teresa, and the book's launch demonstrated this amazing animal's character to perfection. Paul and Teresa took a copy underwater to the study site where 'Benny' lived, with the rather fanciful idea of taking photographs of him alongside the book. The results exceeded all expectations as he swam out from his home to have a good look at a publication that really was 'all about him'.

LEFT: Teresa visiting 'Benny the Blenny', the first recognised individual in the Devon reef study. When Teresa wrote a children's book about Benny's life and showed him a copy (inset), he came out for a closer look.

Undulate Ray (Skate) project

The Undulate Ray Project is a wonderful example of what can be achieved by dedicated people with diverse skills across the disciplines of diving logistics, underwater photography, biology and computing. As with Paul's Tompot Blenny study it arose from the realisation that individuals of some fish species can be recognised by their unique markings. In this case, it was *Raja undulata*, commonly called the Undulate (or Painted) Ray. In biological terms and like most of the so-called 'rays' found around the British Isles, it is actually a skate because females lay eggs ('mermaid's purses') rather than bearing live young, so we call it a 'skate' here (see *Skate or ray?*, page 231).

Undulate Skates are decorated with obvious dark wavy lines that are edged with white spots and interspersed with larger white blotches to produce a strikingly attractive pattern. Our colleagues Martin and Sheilah Openshaw appreciated that the markings on each skate made up a unique 'signature'. They then developed a methodology for photographing the skates and for using image analysis software (originally designed for identifying giraffes from their hide patterns) to recognise individual skates seen on different occasions up to seven years apart. Matches are confirmed by eye as well as by software, and DNA analyses of mucus samples collected from a small number of skates have confirmed the reliability of the image recognition technique. The project, which is still ongoing, has focused on two small areas off the Dorset coast where Undulate Skates are seen relatively frequently, but it has also invited divers and anglers over a wider area of the south coast of England to contribute photographs, allowing an impression of how far the animals move.

In all, Martin and Sheilah's project has identified around 1,000 individual Undulate Skates, with repeat sightings indicating a population of 300–500 in the most studied location. It suggests that the skates typically stay within a relatively small area with, for example, only two of the repeat sightings within the whole study occurring more than 30km apart. It also shows that a particular group can be tight-knit, having little exchange with another cluster nearby. Such findings on populations are important in terms of protecting these wonderful animals. Undulate Skates are thought to have declined around our coasts as a result of fishing pressure and are now classed on the IUCN *Red List of Threatened Species* as Near Threatened in European waters and Endangered worldwide. As with all sharks, skates and rays, they are very vulnerable to overexploitation because they grow slowly,

Coastal Seas

ABOVE: Two Undulate Skates *Raja undulata*, showing the attractive markings that make individuals recognisable.

mature late and produce few young, so any fishery should be very carefully managed – but this is by no means always the case.

In terms of fascinating and intricate fish behaviour, the Undulate Ray Project's most eye-catching observation is that these fish have 'friends'. Particular pairs (sometimes of the same sex), threesomes and even a foursome of individuals have turned up together at the same place on different occasions years apart. Statistical analysis of the observed co-occurrences shows that the chance of this happening randomly can be as low as one in several hundred thousand, so it appears safe to conclude that individual skates choose to move around together or, perhaps even more mysteriously, choose to 'meet up'. This is consistent with research on Grey Reef Sharks *Carcharhinus amblyrhynchos* in the Pacific by Papastamatiou *et al.* (2020) that, as summarised in *New Scientist*, 'hang out with the same friends year after year'. It is intriguing to postulate on what fish may gain from their 'friendships', and it is often suggested that one benefit may be the exchange of information on topics such as feeding opportunities.

Groups of female Small-spotted Catsharks (previously known as Lesser Spotted Dogfish) can sometimes be seen in seabed gulleys or caves around the British Isles, and a specific reason for their congregation in these refuges is proposed by Sims (2005). Unless it is the appropriate time for conception, they are protecting themselves from the unwanted attentions of males, who mate very aggressively. Females also follow a different diurnal migration pattern to the males to stay out of their way as much as possible. Other work on this species by Jacoby *et al.* (2014) shows how some individuals are inherently more sociable than others and that these differences persist with time, the very definition of personality.

Staying in bed: benthic fishes

Anyone who has ever had the misfortune to tread on a Lesser Weeverfish *Echiichthys vipera* whilst wading through sandy shallows for a paddle or a swim will appreciate that some fishes spend their lives lurking unseen on the seabed. Of the 200 or so fishes that are found within normal diving depths around the British Isles, more than half have this way of life. These are referred to as benthic or bottom-living fishes, as opposed to nektonic or free-swimming species; we describe the latter in Chapter 7. The Lesser Weever is one of only a very few venomous fishes found around the British Isles, and whilst its sting is not usually dangerous, it is very painful (see *Stingers*, page 227).

Without the necessity to keep swimming, benthic fishes have evolved a multitude of different and often rather un-fishlike body shapes and behaviours, suited to a wide range of different seabed habitats. Many

BELOW: The Common Dragonet *Callionymus lyra* is one of many benthic fish species. This one on a maerl and mud seabed can be seen expelling a cloud of sediment from its gills after ingesting buried invertebrates. Two Painted Gobies *Pomatoschistus pictus* have come to see what titbits the dragonet has uncovered.

of them lack a swim bladder, the usual bony fish's buoyancy organ but just an encumbrance for seabed living. Benthic fishes live in both sediment and rocky areas, but around our shores there are more species in the latter, which provide a wide range of habitats in the form of reefs, steep cliffs, boulder and bedrock slopes, cobbles and more. Here there are plenty of suitable cracks, crevices and holes for homes and refuges and, at sunlit depths, often plenty of seaweeds for cover. Whilst sediment areas in shallow water are not entirely featureless, because they are sculpted by tidal currents, wave action and the burrowing activities of many different invertebrate animals, nevertheless they provide greater challenges as a place for fish to live.

Flat living

Out in the open on sandy and muddy flats, camouflage and other defence tactics are vital if benthic fishes are to avoid the attention of predators – including other fish. For this reason, many have a distinctly flattened shape, are coloured to suit their background, and have the habit of staying still unless approached too closely. This was demonstrated to Frances on one occasion in her early diving days in the Isle of Man, when she was learning to control her buoyancy underwater. She found herself suddenly enveloped in a cloud of sediment as a Plaice *Pleuronectes platessa* exploded away from beneath her rapidly approaching knees. She was reminded of this recently when walking through chest-high bracken in the New Forest and jumping sky-high as a deer fawn demonstrated the same sort of protective camouflage and behaviour by shooting away in fright from right beneath her feet.

Two main groups of flattened fishes live on sediments around the British Isles – flatfishes (Pleuronectiformes) and skates plus rays (Batoidea). Flatfishes are ray-finned or bony fishes, whilst skates and rays are cartilaginous fishes related to sharks. The two groups differ fundamentally and to a similar extent to other classes of familiar vertebrates such as reptiles and birds. Consequently they have gone about the flattening process in two quite different ways. Skates are simply flattened dorsoventrally, that is they are compressed from the back down towards the belly and resemble squashed sharks with 'wings' – in reality expanded pectoral fins. Flatfishes on the other hand are flattened laterally (from side to side) and end up lying on the seabed on either their right or their left side depending on the

Stingers

Many of the familiar benthic fishes we are likely to encounter around the British Isles have at least one or two, if not many, sharp spines in their fins or on their gill covers, and catching, handling or stepping on them can be a painful experience. Children often learn this for the first time when netting for famously prickly sticklebacks in streams, ponds or rock pools. However, only a very few have spines capable of stinging us in the true sense of the word, by injecting a venom. Of these few, the Lesser Weeverfish is the only one most people are ever likely to encounter around our coasts. Most stings from this fish occur when bare-footed bathers are wading out into deeper water through the warm, sandy shallows that this fish likes. The short, first dorsal fin can be raised when the fish feels threatened and consists of several tough spines armed with venom sacs. Frances and colleagues have encountered them when sorting through seaweed and hydroid material dredged up during research surveys.

The venom is a complex protein-based mixture of compounds and can cause intense pain. This can be relieved by immersing the affected part in water that is as hot as is comfortable, topping it up as it cools, until the pain subsides. The water effectively 'cooks' the protein, and lifeguard stations around our coasts often deal with weever stings in this way. Following hot-water treatment, first aid should always be sought in case of infection or other complications. Stingray stings can be similarly treated.

There is some speculation that harmless flatfishes such as Eckström's Topknot *Zeugopterus regius*, Sole *Solea solea* and Dab *Limanda limanda* might mimic weevers by raising the small pectoral fin on their upward-facing side. We have never personally observed this, and there seems little point in mimicking such a well-disguised fish, but there are plenty of precedents in the insect world where harmless species closely resemble venomous ones such as wasps (Batesian mimicry).

Lesser Weever *Echiichthys vipera* partially buried in the sandy seabed. Its dorsal fin, which has venomous spines, is folded down here but can be raised rapidly when the fish is threatened.

Can you tell your left from right flatfish?

Plaice, Flounder *Platichthys flesus*, Dab, soles and a number of other less familiar flatfishes have both eyes on what was their right side and so are categorised as right-eyed flatfish. Turbot *Scophthalmus maximus*, Brill *S. rhombus* and topknots *Zeugopterus* spp. are left-eyed. Next time you catch or buy a whole flatfish, or photograph one underwater, look carefully to see if you can tell which side the eyes are on.

First look for the lateral line, running from just behind the head, along to the tail base. This is a sense organ used to detect vibrations in the water, and it shows up because it is covered by a line of modified scales. The line runs closer to the original back of the fish than it does to the original belly, and the fish's small pectoral (side) fin, situated just behind the head, is always below it. This then allows you to visualise (or hold) the fish in its original upright position and so tell which side the eyes are on. However, just to confuse the issue, some species, including Plaice, Dab and Flounder, have occasional so-called 'sports' with reverse-sided individuals. This is particularly common with Flounder. Interestingly, reverse-sided individuals are rare in left-eyed species.

The Plaice *Pleuronectes platessa* has characteristic orange spots and is a 'right-eyed' flatfish. The lateral line is visible as a faint pale line running from just above the pectoral fin to the base of the tail.

The Topknot *Zeugopterus punctatus* is a 'left-eyed' flatfish. Unusually for a flatfish, it lives in rocky terrain, where its thin body enables it to glide into crevices in search of prey or to escape predators.

species. The planktonic larval stage of a flatfish has a normal upright shape and stance, but when just a few centimetres long starts to flatten out ready to settle on the seabed. Once there it undergoes a remarkable metamorphosis. The eye on what is now the underside moves up to join that on the upward-facing side through a process of tissue growth and destruction. The mouth also twists round to a more useful position just below the pair of eyes.

Around the British Isles, 17 species of flatfishes live in or extend into shallow water (within normal diving depths), with about eight other species confined to greater depths. For many of these fishes, the shallow, warm waters of the numerous bays, inlets, lochs and estuaries that help make up the complex 18,000km or so of Britain's coastline are essential nursery grounds. Such areas provide shelter from waves and currents as well as protection from larger, offshore predatory fishes that rarely visit. Juvenile flatfish and other small sediment-living fishes such as gobies can often be caught within wading depths using a simple push net. Armed with a wide wooden-framed net in less than knee-high water just beyond the low tide mark, Frances was delighted to find perfect, miniature-sized Turbot and Plaice during a survey in North Cornwall in 2012, as well as a perhaps less welcome Lesser Weeverfish.

The migration of Plaice from their shallow summer feeding grounds into deeper water to spawn in the winter is another example of how there is more to the lives of fish than we might at first assume. Research with tagged Plaice has shown how they move up into mid-water when strong tides are running in the direction they are travelling but stay on the seabed when the current is against them. This clever 'tide-riding' technique allows the flatfish, not usually regarded as the strongest of swimmers, to move up to 30km in a day and several hundred kilometres in a few weeks. Plaice on their way to spawn and others returning from spawning may pass in opposite directions over the same area by utilising different parts of the tidal cycle. Individuals have also been shown to return to the same spawning location in successive years, following the same migration route.

Skates (Rajiformes) are rarely seen or caught as close to shore as flatfish, either as adults or juveniles, but eight species may be encountered in shallow coastal waters around Britain and Ireland, with at least the same number again in deeper offshore water. The most common skate recorded by divers is the Thornback Skate *Raja clavata*, whilst one of the most attractively patterned is the Undulate Skate (see page 224). These and deeper-water species are also frequently caught by anglers. The Thornback is named after the very large wide-based spines, resembling rose or bramble thorns, that run the length of its back. This stripey-tailed skate seems to thrive in captivity, and a well-run aquarium is an excellent place to appreciate their wide pectoral fins with which they 'fly' through the water, using their long stick-like tail as a rudder. Contrary to popular belief, skate tails are not armed with venomous spines, though a skate's sharp thorns and rough skin can cause abrasions. Stingray (Dasyatidae) tails on the other hand are so armed. Only one species of stingray, the Common Stingray *Dasyatis pastinaca*, frequents coastal waters around the British Isles, and it is a relatively rare summer visitor from further south. That will probably come as a relief to many, as treading on a stingray can be a very painful experience.

The largest of all European skates, and sadly now the rarest, is the Flapper Skate *Dipturus intermedius*, which reaches an impressive 2.5m in total length (including the tail). Prior to 2009 all such large skates were thought to be the Blue Skate *D. batis* (sometimes called Common Skate), a slightly smaller but similar species. This in spite of scientific murmurings going back to the 19th century to the effect that there were probably two different species of these large skates around the British Isles. Genetic research finally resolved the problem, and this is now backed up by photographs from divers and anglers that show subtle differences in pattern and colouration. Both species are Critically Endangered on a worldwide basis and are designated as 'prohibited species' for commercial fisheries over a wide area around the British Isles and in the EU, including the Mediterranean (the exact areas are specified by reference to a standardised division of European waters known as ICES sea areas). This means they must not be targeted and any that are caught must be released immediately.

BELOW: The Thornback Skate *Raja clavata* (often called a 'Ray') is the skate species generally seen most often by divers. The spines from which its common name arises are clearly visible along its back.

Skate or ray?

Around the British Isles the terms 'skate' and 'ray' tend to be used rather indiscriminately. Thus in a fish market or a restaurant, you might be offered skate wings but never ray wings. Yet the fish they came from, though actually a skate, would most likely have been called a ray. In one common convention, skate species have long snouts – and the decidedly long-nosed Blue Skate has traditionally been called that. Those with short snouts are commonly known as rays, hence Thornback Ray, Cuckoo Ray *Leucoraja naevus* and so on.

There is, however, a scientific basis by which skates and rays can be separated. Skates reproduce by laying individual eggs, each protected by a tough egg case known colloquially as a 'mermaid's purse'. Rays on the other hand give birth to live young, as do many (though not all) sharks. Almost all the so-called rays around Britain and Ireland, whether living deep or in the shallows, are in fact skates and belong to the same family, the hardnose skates or Rajidae. As for rays, our waters boast only a single species of stingray, as described opposite, two species of electric rays *Torpedo marmorata* and *Tetronarce nobiliana* and a single eagle ray *Myliobatis aquila*, all of which are rarely recorded and mostly distributed in warmer southern seas.

Does it matter whether we call them skates or rays? We prefer to be as scientifically accurate as possible and we therefore use the scientific basis for separating skate from ray, but the long and the short of it is that it doesn't really matter as long as you know which species you are dealing with. That of course is why using the scientific name as well as the vernacular can be so important.

It seems amazing now, but fishing records from around Plymouth more than a century ago show more very large skates, presumably *Dipturus*, being caught than the now much more common Thornback Skate. While Thornbacks are still regularly seen in those same waters, large skates are extinct from most British and Irish coastal waters, a sad reflection of human impact on these magnificent animals.

Finding food

Small pelagic fish living up in the water column are always at risk from larger predatory fish, but for fish that live and swim just above the seabed, there is also a risk of attack from a benthic predator. Some benthic fishes such as the rock-living, well-camouflaged Long-spined Sea Scorpion are ambush hunters and spend much of their time waiting unseen on the seabed for small fish to swim past or crabs to wander close before lunging a short distance to engulf them in their large mouth. The Angler *Lophius piscatorius* takes this further with special adaptations and is the epitome of an ambush predator. Familiar to many people as 'monkfish' served up in a restaurant and now increasingly rare due to overfishing, this patient predator has

ABOVE: In order to both ambush its prey and avoid predators, the Long-spined Sea Scorpion *Taurulus bubalis* can change colour to match its surroundings, which here includes pink encrusting algae.

a mouth as wide as its flattened body, filled with razor-sharp teeth. Whether lying on rock or sediment, it is well camouflaged with leafy skin tassels and matching colouration. Unsuspecting smaller fish are enticed within reach by a tassel-tipped, mobile fishing lure or illicium, a modified dorsal fin ray on top of the head. A lightning-fast lunge and the prey disappears into its capacious mouth.

Frances encountered another impressively toothed fish when diving at St Abbs in southeast Scotland. This popular dive site is known for its shallow-water resident Wolf Fish *Anarhichas lupus*. Well-named for their canine-like protruding teeth and large, craggy heads, these grey fish normally live in deeper water. Unsuspecting, Frances was led by her two local dive buddies down a steep underwater cliff to a particularly large crevice. She had been teasingly briefed to expect to photograph small Leopard-spotted Gobies *Thorogobius ephippiatus* and consequently had a close-up lens on her Nikonos camera. The sudden and dramatic appearance of two huge grey heads at the crevice entrance was unnerving to say the least. In reality, these two were habituated to divers and perfectly docile.

Other small benthic fishes and many that live near the seabed, such as wrasses, search for invertebrates, foraging for the likes of worms, gastropod molluscs, amphipods and crabs, as well as smaller fish. They search by sight and smell amongst seaweeds and between rocks, but more refined techniques are needed for prey hidden beneath sediment. Equipped with two long, mobile chin barbels sensitive to touch and taste, Red Mullet *Mullus surmuletus* probe for

ABOVE: Two large Wolf Fish *Anarhichas lupus* in their lair; a sight similar to the one that surprised Frances when she had been briefed to photograph small, shy gobies.

hidden snacks. The resulting cloud of fine sediment as they find and dig out their dinner often attracts small gobies looking for a free meal. This behaviour always reminds us of Robins *Erithacus rubecula* following a busy gardener. Whilst her dive buddy was engrossed in recording or taking photographs, Frances has often mimicked this behaviour, kneeling in a sediment patch and digging gently with her fingers. The local gobies have rarely disappointed. Red Mullet are 'southerners', most commonly found around the southwest of Britain and Ireland and in the Irish Sea, although there are scattered records from as far north as Scotland. This species belongs to the

LEFT: Two Red Mullet *Mullus surmuletus*, the one in the foreground searching for food (small invertebrates) within the sediment with its two long white barbels.

goatfish family (Mullidae), most of which are found in warmer Mediterranean and tropical waters where they can be seen feeding in the same way.

Gurnards (Triglidae), another family of sediment-living fishes, also detect buried food items, but in this case using modified pectoral fin rays. With their wide, sloping, bony heads and armour-encased bodies, these fish resemble miniature bulldozers but move with remarkable delicacy, seemingly 'walking' along on three separated and thickened fin rays. In reality, their rays are used to taste and feel for food items. They also grunt to each other as they move along, so that they can retain contact with other members of their group. In between exhaling noisy bubbles, it is well worthwhile for any diver to stop and listen for natural underwater sounds. In spite of the quiet implied by Jacques Cousteau's fascinating early book *The Silent World* (1953), the sea is a noisy place. Gurnards produce their grunts from a gas-filled swim bladder, vibrating it using special muscles so that it resonates like a drum.

Dab are a dab-hand at spotting the tips of bivalve mollusc siphons that stick up from the sediment and nipping them off with their sharp teeth. Siphons are tubes used by such molluscs to draw plankton and oxygen-containing water through their bodies and out again, and some at least seem capable of regrowing them.

Recreational scuba divers rarely venture out onto rather monotonous soft-mud underwater plains, but those that do so might be rewarded by an encounter with the Red Bandfish *Cepola macrophthalma*, a most unusual benthic species. Bright red in colour and shaped like a snake edged with wide ribbon-like fins, this fish excavates a metre-deep vertical burrow using its capacious mouth to shift the sediment. This is where it lives, reaching up into the water column to feed on planktonic animals, but very rarely leaving the safety of its home completely. Like the better-known garden eels found in sandy areas of tropical reefs, this planktivore has a wide upturned mouth, well suited to picking passing morsels from the water. It exploits a wide range of zooplankton, including arrow worms, small hydroid medusae and especially copepods, a distinct contrast to the foraging and predatory feeding habits of most benthic fishes, some of which we have just described. Plankton is more usually utilised by small pelagic fishes such as Herring *Clupea harengus* rather than by benthic species. However, not all pelagic plankton-eating fishes are small, as shown by the giant Basking Shark (see Chapter 7).

LEFT: A Red Bandfish *Cepola macrophthalma* at the entrance to its burrow in Plymouth Sound, one of a small colony living in unusually shallow water.

Whilst moderately common in soft sediments offshore, Red Bandfish are rarely encountered in shallow water or caught by anglers. However, for those in the know, there are a few spots around Britain and Ireland where colonies occur within diving depths, especially along the south coast of England. Paul enjoyed watching a small colony in Plymouth Sound some years ago and saw individuals occasionally lunge out from their burrows at passing gobies, suggesting that their needle-like teeth may be able to cope with larger prey. Frances first encountered this enigmatic fish on a visit to Lundy in the Bristol Channel with her PhD supervisor Roger Pullin and Jim Atkinson from the Millport Marine Station. Jim was researching the habits of the fish and the construction of its burrows. Hovering in the background and trying not to fin up clouds of obscuring silt, Frances was fascinated to see the rapid exit of a large Red Bandfish as Jim poured liquid polyester resin down its burrow. The burrow acts as a mould, the resin sets, and the resulting cast can be extracted and taken back to dry land, leaving the fish to resolutely excavate a new burrow. This work, described in papers by Atkinson *et al.* (1977) and Atkinson and Pullin (1996), revealed many side branches joined to the main burrow, belonging to a variety of associated burrowing crustaceans. The original and subsequent *Cepola* casts (together with around 700 casts from other species) are lodged in the Hunterian Museum of the University of Glasgow. Photographs of the intricately shaped casts can be seen on the Hunterian Museum website.

The Lundy population numbered many thousands in the 1970s, but a decade later they had almost all disappeared. Colonies can be and are damaged by trawling and netting, but this colony was within an area protected from such activities and so the causes of its demise are unclear. The species is not commercially targeted in the UK, but boxes of it can be seen for sale in some Italian fish markets. A recipe for Red Bandfish, written by a 5th-century BC Sicilian cook called Mithaecus or Mithaikos, survives to this day in a 3rd-century AD Greek work called *Deipnosophistae*.

Nests, eggs, courtship and cleaning

The territorial habits of familiar garden birds give a great deal of pleasure to the many people who enjoy their often elaborate songs. Holding a territory in this way provides birds with both nesting sites and good feeding areas. There are many parallels to this amongst those shallow-water fishes that live on and near to the seabed. Fish may not sing (although some grunt), but many build nests, guard their eggs, and are adept at seeing off intruders that stray into their home patch. Territorial fishes form an important element of the fish fauna around the British Isles, especially in rocky areas. Some even modify the seabed habitat through their nesting and courting activities, for example Black Seabream *Spondyliosoma cantharus*, as we describe on page 242.

In contrast, sharks pay no attention to their eggs and young and do not hold individual breeding territories. However, as a group, sharks, skates and rays all have internal fertilisation and subsequently either lay large eggs in tough egg cases ('mermaid's purses') deposited on the seabed or give birth to live young. So they must meet up to mate, and this can include complex courtship behaviour. During nest-building, courtship and egg-laying many fish become less wary, and some of our most fascinating encounters are explored below.

Colourful wrasse courtship

Amongst the most skilful of nest-builders are some of our most colourful resident fishes, the wrasses (Labridae), of which we have five common species, all found in shallow coastal waters. Ballan Wrasse *Labrus bergylta*, Cuckoo Wrasse *L. mixtus*, Corkwing Wrasse *Symphodus melops* and Rock Cook *Centrolabrus exoletus* all defend egg-laying territories, whilst Goldsinny Wrasse *Ctenolabrus rupestris* is a broadcast spawner, simply releasing eggs and sperm to drift in the water column.

Wrasses in general have very complex life histories, with the common aim of maximising their reproductive potential. Widespread rocky reef and submerged cliff habitats in the rugged southwest and west of Britain and Ireland provide many opportunities for male Cuckoo Wrasse to establish breeding territories. A single male often maintains a loose 'harem' of several females, and in any one population there are many more females than males. All young Cuckoo Wrasse start life with the pink female colouration, and most go on to develop into mature females. Then, when they are several years old (mostly 7–13) and probably depending on the availability of suitable territories, some of the larger females gradually take on male blue and orange colours, change sex and become fully functional 'secondary' males. These are the ones that set up territories. However, some pink juveniles retain the female colour but develop into apparently functional 'primary' males. These may act as 'sneaker' males (see page 240), but there is still much to learn about this. The large Ballan Wrasse also has a similar sex-changing lifestyle but does not 'advertise' the development with any obvious colour change.

ABOVE: Female (top) and male (bottom) Cuckoo Wrasse *Labrus mixtus*, showing their markedly different colouration. All individuals start life as females, with some subsequently becoming males.

Male wrasses certainly 'strut their stuff' during courtship. Standing in front of an aquarium tank in Port Erin marine biological station in the early 1970s, watching a spectacularly coloured blue and orange male Cuckoo Wrasse, Frances was surprised to see the fish's whole head blanch pure white in a matter of seconds – the male equivalent, perhaps, of a blushing bride. At the same time the fish was using his tail to excavate a depression in the sand at the bottom of the tank. Sadly, the several rosy pink females present viewed all this courtship with sublime indifference. Although this blanching behaviour has also been observed in the wild, details of Cuckoo Wrasse nest-building remain remarkably sketchy.

Brave defenders

On one memorable diving trip around Devon in the 1990s, Paul and his colleagues had been watching a particular male Cuckoo Wrasse exhibit typical territorial behaviour. He clearly got tired of the bubbling intruders with their cameras and finally took a nibble at the lip of one of the photographers. Perhaps it looked rather tasty stretched around the scuba mouthpiece, but more likely he saw his reflection in the diver's mask and wanted to see off this potential rival. Minimal damage was inflicted but, with seawater washing his cut, the diver came up the dive-ladder unaware that his face was streaming with blood. The initial consternation of his colleagues quickly turned to admiration for the feisty harem-defending wrasse.

Egg-guarding fish protect their precious future with vigour, perhaps none more assiduously than the male Lumpsucker *Cyclopterus lumpus*. Clinging to surf-tossed rocks with a strong pelvic sucker, he resists all approaches from hungry fish and crabs intent on making a meal of the eggs blithely left in his care by the female.

When defending his territory, this male Cuckoo Wrasse *Labrus mixtus* took a bite at a photographer's lip.

Corkwing nests

If you visit any rocky beach or cove around the southwest of Britain in June, don a mask and snorkel, and venture out across the shallows, the first fish you encounter will often be a Corkwing Wrasse, swimming among the rich forests of seaweed. Wrasses as a family are renowned for their inquisitive nature, and whilst some are more aloof than others, a careful approach may allow a close look. With a Corkwing this will reveal whether it is a female, with pretty but relatively drab green and brown colouration, or a male, with more resplendent stripes of blue, orange and red. Aside from his attractive breeding livery, a male Corkwing is worth a second look to see if he is carrying a mouthful of seaweed. If he is, then it means this 'colourful craftsman' is hard at work, collecting materials for making or maintaining a nest. In the world of fish, it is most often the male that builds nests and guards eggs.

Corkwing nests are quite often built in rather prominent positions on the tops of rocky reefs, though based within crevices into which the wrasse may dart for cover. This is important, because the nests' prominent position, combined with the males' preoccupation with construction and plucky guarding behaviour, makes the males particularly vulnerable to predators, such as diving birds. Indeed, coastal birdwatchers spying on the nests of Shags *Gulosus aristotelis* and other seabirds report frequent flashes of bright colours in the material that the parent birds regurgitate for their hungry young in the summer, testament to the fate of many brave but unfortunate Corkwings. No doubt due partly to this, but also because males may leave an established nest and start another elsewhere, it is quite common to find Corkwing nests with no fish in attendance, even in the middle of the breeding season. This is in striking contrast to the tenaciously occupied crevice homes of Tompot Blennies that we have already described.

As for the nest itself, what might appear at first glance simply to be a mass of seaweed rammed into a rocky fissure in fact has 'a complex structure analogous to that found in some birds', created by behaviour that 'reaches an elaborate degree of sophistication'. These are the words of Geoff Potts, a scientist then working at the Marine

BELOW: A male Corkwing Wrasse *Symphodus melops* guards his nest under Swanage Pier. With a lack of seaweed growth in the shade under the pier, the red seaweed he has collected to build his nest is much easier to see. This wrasse has a damaged lip, possibly from fighting with a rival or from an angler's hook.

Biological Association in Plymouth, who carried out a detailed study of the Corkwing Wrasse's nest-building activities in nearby Wembury Bay (Potts 1985). His study showed that these industrious fish use soft seaweed with a texture that permits good water flow for the centre of the nest where the eggs are laid, and coralline (calcified) seaweed for the outside of the nest to give structure and a protective covering. Perhaps most impressive is that the selected algal species are capable of continued survival and growth after detachment. Not only does this mean the nest material is unlikely to decompose but also, particularly with the coralline algae in the outer shell, it grows *in situ* and knits the nest together. This makes the nest resistant to wave action, so important in these shallow areas, and protects it against egg predators including marauding fish and wandering crabs.

The male Corkwing Wrasse makes journeys of up to 50m from the nest to collect material, a long way for a fish only 20cm long. In addition to using different materials at different depths in the crevice, he also builds laterally along the crevice, so that subsequent parts of the nest are ready for receiving the eggs from a succession of females visiting at different times. This helps to maximise his reproductive success. Perhaps surprisingly, Potts found that some of the Wembury Bay nests were built above low tide level, leaving them prone to overheating and drying out when the tide receded. However, he also discovered that their interiors were protected from this fate by their moisture-retaining construction and because they were always built facing north. It is fascinating to stroll across the Wembury reef at low tide and see what the busy Corkwings have been doing whilst the tide was in. The air-exposed nests are, however, quite difficult to spot because the distinctive pale pink of the coralline seaweed gets bleached in the sun.

As if the hard work of nest construction combined with exposure to predation is not enough for our skilled builder to contend with, the male Corkwing also faces potential deception from his own kind. While most male Corkwing Wrasse are conscientious homebuilders, a small percentage try to cash in as sneaker males. Dressed entirely in female colours, a disguised male is welcomed by the nest owner, who is then cuckolded as the sneaker releases sperm in the hope of fertilising previously laid eggs. Tompot Blennies try the same trick (see *Life and Times of the Tompot Blenny*, page 218) and there are plenty of parallels to this behaviour in terrestrial animals, in groups as diverse as beetles and mammals, so it must be a successful strategy.

Wrasse cleaners

Another interesting aspect of wrasse domestic behaviour that has been observed in the wild is that of acting as 'cleaner fish'. As part of their normal and varied feeding activities, Ballan, Corkwing, Goldsinny and Rock Cook wrasses remove crustacean parasites from larger fish, including each other. Some locations on British reefs seem to act as 'cleaning stations' akin to those on tropical coral reefs, and although there is little published work on whether wrasses maintain their territories from year to year and on how permanent their residency is on particular reefs, Paul has observed (by analysing photographs) the same large individual Ballan Wrasse on the same Devon reef for at least eight years. These are slow-growing and long-lived fish (at least 30 years) and this raises considerable concerns over the effect of wild capture of this and other wrasse species for the salmon farming industry. In recent years various fisheries have developed to supply live wrasses for salmon farmers to use for parasite removal in place of chemicals. However, the consequences of removing significant numbers of these fish from local reefs have not yet been fully ascertained.

Sex changes, nest-building, sneaking and parasite cleaning are probably just the tip of the iceberg in terms of the complex behaviour of our five common species of wrasse. There is, for example, an interesting aspect of cooperation that occurs between large Ballan

LEFT: A group of small Rock Cooks *Centrolabrus exoletus* following a Ballan Wrasse *Labrus bergylta*. It is an intriguing relationship, in which the Rock Cook appear to gain extra food from the larger fish as well as helping to remove its parasites.

Wrasse and the group of Rock Cook wrasse that often follows them closely as they cruise our rocky reefs. Paul has observed that a large Ballan may sometimes grab a loose piece of kelp from the seabed in its mouth and swim up a metre or two before releasing it. These rotting seaweed fragments invariably harbour numerous small crustaceans, which are dislodged and become prey for the eager Rock Cooks that dash in to claim an easy meal. The Ballan Wrasse does not appear to join the feast, so what does it gain? Our assumption is that keeping the smaller Rock Cooks nearby benefits the Ballan by ensuring it has a readily available parasite removal service and an earlier warning of a predator's approach.

Black Seabream nests

Around Eastertime, between Kimmeridge and Poole Bay, Dorset, the stone, sand and gravel-strewn bedrock seabed is transformed into a lunar landscape by the nesting activities of Black Seabream *Spondyliosoma cantharus*. Recreational anglers have been heading out here for years to try for a seasonal catch of this prized fish, which arrives in its thousands from warmer waters further south. The herculean nesting efforts of these shy animals, normally intolerant of divers, are difficult to study, but have now been captured on film by two independent underwater naturalists and photographers, Matt Doggett and Martin Openshaw, using strategically placed video cameras and a great deal of patience over nearly 10 years. The footage demonstrates that the aim of each male is to clear a roughly circular area of all material, revealing clean bedrock, and then rimming the area with cleared material – up to 70kg of it. Females are enticed in to lay their sticky eggs onto the bedrock, and the males protect and fan the eggs until they hatch. Not all nests at this location are exactly the same, and in some other places eggs may be laid in deep gravel or shell-gravel holes. Egg predators such as Goldsinny Wrasse, Bib *Trisopterus luscus*, gobies, blennies and various whelks take advantage of even the briefest absence of a male nest-holder.

Such projects collect vital data for effective management and conservation of this prized fish. This allows important spawning areas to be protected, at least at certain times. One of the largest known south-coast spawning areas was identified off West Sussex and now lies within the Kingmere Marine Conservation Zone (MCZ) with protection provided by Sussex IFCA (Inshore Fisheries and

Conservation Authority) byelaws. Activities that would be damaging to the features for which the MCZ was designated (which includes Black Seabream spawning) are prohibited in certain zones at certain times of the year. For example, towed fishing gear is prohibited all year round in three out of four zones within the MCZ, whilst angling for Black Seabream is allowed (with catch limits) except in Zone One. Dredging for aggregates is not allowed in the main spawning areas between the beginning of May and the end of July.

There are now reports of large nesting grounds elsewhere around Britain and also increasing evidence that many of the Black Seabream congregating seasonally at spawning sites on British coasts have overwintered in sheltered waters here rather than arriving from further south.

Sticklebacks' complex nests

Many readers will be familiar with the (mainly) freshwater Three-spined Stickleback *Gasterosteus aculeatus* and its elaborate and fascinating courtship and nest-building. These feisty little fish also live in estuaries and sometimes in rock pools on the shore. In spring the male develops bright red breeding colours and builds a nest, usually in fresh water, by piling up aquatic plant material and

BELOW: A male Fifteen-spined Stickleback *Spinachia spinachia* with his nest of seaweed bound together with fine white threads. The threads are most obvious in the top-right of the photograph and just by the fish's mouth.

binding it together with sticky secretions produced by his kidneys. He then entices successive females to lay eggs in the tunnel he has bored through it. He is an exemplary guardian of both eggs and fry. The fully marine Fifteen-spined Stickleback *Spinachia spinachia* does much the same thing, but in shallow coastal waters. Preferring high-rise living, away from marauding crabs, the male of this species often builds his nest well above the seabed, binding together the swaying fronds of taller seaweeds and adding in more material all held together by white protein threads, which look remarkably like fine fishing line, secreted from his kidneys. So, if you are hardy enough to be out snorkelling in March, peer closely at anything that looks like a tangle of fine fishing line and live seaweed as it may be a stickleback nest with its nervous male owner hovering nearby.

Male mums

As we have seen with Black Seabream, wrasses and sticklebacks, it is often the male that does all the hard work of nest-building and egg-guarding. Laying a relatively small number of eggs in nests or stuck to protective rocks and shells and providing some parental care is common amongst small fishes such as gobies and blennies that live on the seabed and face myriad dangers. The female invests her energy into producing a relatively few large eggs that the male subsequently looks after, at least until the well-developed young hatch.

BELOW: This Steven's Goby *Gobius gasteveni* is guarding eggs, inside which the eyes of developing larvae can be seen. We think the small number of opaque white eggs were possibly unfertilised, or have otherwise failed to develop.

Seahorses and their straightened-out relatives the pipefishes take things one step further. Seahorses are often thought of as warm-water fish, but the cool waters around the British Isles are home to two species, the Short-snouted *Hippocampus hippocampus* and Long-snouted *H. guttulatus*, as well as five pipefish species. In both groups the eggs are laid by the female into a brood pouch on the male's belly. Paired-up seahorses perform a quietly graceful 'dance' around each other beforehand, and we describe their courtship in more detail in Chapter 6. The eggs hatch inside the pouch into perfect miniature replicas of their parents, and are finally forcibly ejected by contractions of the male's swollen belly.

ABOVE: Nursehound *Scyliorhinus stellaris* egg cases laid by the mother in very shallow water and attached to seaweed with long tendrils. These egg cases (inset) have been labelled with a plastic tag to enable their development to be monitored on regular visits.

Skate and shark egg cases

We have already mentioned that all skates and some small sharks lay individual eggs protected by a tough egg case within which the young develop. These are colloquially known as mermaid's purses and are regularly washed up on the shore, where anyone who walks along a beach and looks inquisitively at the strandline may spot them. As well as being good beachcombing finds, they can give us valuable information about the enigmatic animals that produce them. The egg cases differ in size and shape between species and provide clues to the presence and abundance of skates (and sharks) in different areas. The Great Eggcase Hunt is a citizen science project started by the Shark Trust in 2003 that encourages all reports of shark and skate egg cases and provides guides for identifying the species that laid them (see Chapter 2). The project hit the 100,000 mark for egg-case records by 2016 and more than 375,000 by their 20-year anniversary in 2023, and has collected large amounts of information on the distribution and breeding grounds of sharks and skates around the British Isles.

There are still many mysteries about the egg-case laying and development processes that cannot be resolved so easily, but one species helps us out by coming into surprisingly shallow water to lay its eggs. John Hepburn, a particularly enterprising citizen scientist, discovered a rocky channel close to the shore at Wembury, Devon, where the egg cases of Nursehounds *Scyliorhinus stellaris* were often deposited. Then, in association with the Shark Trust, he set up a project to monitor them. He visits the egg-laying area by snorkelling with other volunteers at least monthly, exploiting the lowest spring tides. He has now tracked the presence and development of the egg cases in this spot since 2014, by photographing them *in situ* and attaching a small, coded tag to each one when it is first found. The Nursehounds attach their egg cases to undergrowth by means of long, curly cord-like tendrils at each corner, with a preference for the attractive and aptly named Rainbow Wrack seaweed *Ericaria selaginoides* that grows prolifically in the shallow and sheltered channel. John's study has found new egg cases laid in every month of the year, with most in April, May and July, and he has observed that their development time from laying until a miniature shark emerges is around 7–9 months. Intriguingly, there is a mention of a Nursehound egg-laying site in Wembury Bay in a marine biological journal from around 100 years ago, and it is wonderful to imagine these diligent mothers seeking out this safe location to leave their precious future generations over the centuries.

As described on page 230, the largest and rarest of all skates in our waters is the Flapper Skate. Its egg cases, up to 28cm long, are correspondingly huge when compared to those of most other skates in British and Irish waters. They are most commonly found washed up on shores in the northwest of Scotland and in Orkney, reinforcing evidence for the northerly distribution of this species. In contrast, the similarly rare Blue Skate is a predominantly southern species, with most records from English, Welsh and southern Irish coastlines. However, egg cases can drift with ocean currents and underwater finds of live egg cases make for more accurate distributional records. In 2019, divers reported seeing numerous live egg cases of Flapper Skate in the sheltered, shallow waters of the Inner Sound of Skye. The number and density of these indicated an important nursery area, and the site was subsequently designated by the government in 2021 as the Red Rocks and Longay urgent MPA (Marine Protected Area), with full designation in 2023. Whilst the traditional egg-laying and nursery grounds of most important commercial fish species around the British Isles are well known and well documented, the same cannot yet be said of skates. Protecting such sites is vital.

New fish residents and summer visitors

Cold, grey winters are a fact of life in the British Isles, especially in northern areas, and whilst we both embrace the variety of weather that our seasons bring, many other people have made the decision to move to warmer Mediterranean climes. However, it is now an indisputable fact that our oceans are warming due to global climate change, and this is allowing wildlife from southern areas to expand their ranges northward. Records indicate that water temperature in the seas around the British Isles are now around 1°C warmer than they were when we both started diving in the 1970s to 1980s. It should therefore not come as a complete surprise that sharp-eyed naturalists, divers, anglers and those in the fishing industry are recording species of fish new to our waters. Fish are after all pretty mobile. A recent example of this is the Variable or Ringneck Blenny *Parablennius pilicornis*. This southern and Mediterranean species was first noticed and recorded by Seasearch divers in South Devon in 2007. Subsequent sequential records indicate that it has since spread to just east of Portland Bill and it is now known to inhabit shallow rocky areas from Cornwall along to Dorset. Males assiduously guarding patches of eggs attached to rocks have been photographed, confirming that it is now an established breeding fish in our waters, not just a summer visitor.

Species like the Variable Blenny have presumably moved of their own accord by expanding their known ranges, rather than being introduced by human activities. Introduced non-native species can cause considerable problems for local wildlife and for people, as discussed in Chapter 12. So far there have been no reported adverse effects from range expansion of marine fishes to the British Isles.

Several fishes including Common Pandora *Pagellus erythrinus* and Couch's Seabream *Pagrus pagrus* are well-known summer visitors, the majority of individuals moving into our waters during the summer and moving back south, or dying, as winter approaches. Grey Triggerfish *Balistes capriscus* are probably carried north on currents from the Mediterranean area and from North America across to the eastern Atlantic on the Gulf Stream. They are relatively poor swimmers and are unlikely to be able to return south to warmer waters as winter approaches. Dead stranded individuals are most often recorded in winter, the fish unable to survive low water temperatures. Occasional Grey Triggerfish have been caught around the British Isles at least as far back as the mid-19th century, but

Varied Variable Blennies

The two usual vernacular names for *Parablennius pilicornis* reflect its colour and pattern: 'Ringneck' for two dark bands under the chin, and 'Variable' for the fact that it occurs in several different colour patterns. In the Mediterranean, four distinct patterns have been recorded, and so far individuals with three of these very different colour patterns have been found regularly in our waters. The basic colouring of both males and females is a mixture of reddish brown and cream blotches. In the first variant there is a series of dark, smudged H-shapes running along the midline on each side. In the second this is replaced with a continuous stripe from head to tail. The third variant is almost black all over and is only shown by breeding males when they are guarding eggs. A fourth variant – an all-over orange/yellow colour – has only rarely been recorded here. In the Mediterranean its occurrence and abundance seem to vary between localities.

Interpreting the roles of different colour variants of Variable Blennies is further complicated by our recent observations that indicate an individual can switch quickly between patterns. Paul spent most of a (mystifying but enjoyable) dive in Plymouth Sound in 2022 closely watching a particular Variable Blenny. Every few minutes it emerged from its hiding place under a small boulder to make a quick 'tour' of the seabed nearby and, when doing this, it was pale with a prominent longitudinal dark stripe. When back in its shelter, the blenny took on a more consistent brown colouration. To add further mystery, this was in mid-October, so outside the expected breeding season. In 2020, Paul had witnessed an individual with a bold stripe dash into a crevice to join what appeared to be a mating pair of Variable Blennies – an even, reddish-brown (female) visitor with a very dark resident (male). Guests at a talk given by Paul soon after this asked him about his recent underwater encounters, and some looked slightly shocked when he described seeing a 'three-in-a-bed blenny scenario'.

A Variable Blenny *Parablennius pilicornis* male (black) with two visitors to his crevice territory, probably egg-laying females, although one could possibly be a sneaker male.

A boldly striped Variable Blenny out in the open. Interpretation of colour patterns in this species is difficult, especially as some individuals seem able to change colour within minutes.

records have increased significantly in the past 30 years or so and divers now see them regularly all along the south coast of England. There are also records from as far north as Scotland, but very few in the North Sea. This is a species that seems on course to become a breeding resident. Whilst there are currently no diver records of nesting and courtship behaviour, since about 1990 there have been a few autumn and winter records of juveniles. Most of the rest of the family to which the intriguing Grey Triggerfish belongs are tropical or subtropical species.

Triggerfishes excavate nest depressions in sediment, and the parents are aggressive defenders of their nests. They are masters of defensive tactics and can wedge themselves tightly into rock and wreck crevices. Once in a crevice, a stout spine (the 'trigger') at the front of the three-spined first dorsal fin can be erected and then locked in place by the following much shorter spine. Neither rough water nor a predator is likely to be able to dislodge a wedged triggerfish, and their strong front teeth are an equal deterrent when they are nesting out in the open. Whilst working in a coral reef area in Malaysia some years ago, Frances made a strategic retreat when a nest-protecting Titan Triggerfish *Balistoides viridescens* made repeated approaches. Unwary divers have been bitten by these feisty fish.

Diving is not the only way to track visiting fishes and new arrivals. Commercial catches of open-water fish provide another ready source of information. A visit to a local fish market and encouraging local anglers to report their catches can both turn up unusual species. With most fish visitors coming from south of the British Isles, these methods have proved particularly effective in keeping track of many rare visitors along the English Channel coast. Whilst some are simply off-course strays, upward trends in the number of records of a particular species may indicate expanding ranges.

Overlooked species

Confirming that a fish is indeed newly resident in our waters is not always straightforward. Some small but easily identified shallow-water fish species have been overlooked in our waters for many years because they live in places that are awkward to sample remotely or difficult to dive. A classic example is the Red or Portuguese Blenny *Parablennius ruber*. This species was known to occur along the coast of Portugal (hence the vernacular name), the Azores, Madeira and

Red-mouthed Goby: a rare outlier

'Ready? Go.' The divers, including Frances, obediently rolled backwards off the inflatable, and as they descended into the clear water they were picked up by the current and whisked smartly along through the wildly swaying fronds of an elegant kelp forest. After just a few exhilarating minutes the current spat them out into the body of Loch Hyne, County Cork, and they were left to fin at a more leisurely speed down to the deeper rocky reefs below. This was a site that Frances had long wanted to visit, to see for herself the elusive Red-mouthed Goby *Gobius cruentatus* – and she got her wish that day. A number of these gobies were lying quietly on hydroid-covered rocks, dorsal fins raised and their lips seemingly covered in badly applied bright-red lipstick.

Known in the British Isles from only a very few sites in west and southwest Ireland, the Loch Hyne and nearby populations appear to be outliers from this goby's main distribution, which extends from northwest Spain south to Senegal and into the Mediterranean. How long this little fish has been present in Ireland will probably never be known, but they were first 'discovered' in 1968 by Alwyne Wheeler, a renowned ichthyologist working at the Natural History Museum (NHM) in London. He re-examined three of the museum's preserved goby specimens from Ireland, two collected in the 1930s and one in 1960 and all labelled as Black Gobies *Gobius niger*. All turned out to be the Red-mouthed Goby. The population in Loch Hyne remains the largest and most well established.

A Red-mouthed Goby *Gobius cruentatus* shows off its scarlet lips perched on a rocky outcrop in Kenmare Bay, County Kerry.

as far north as western France (where it was originally described in 1836). However, around the British Isles it was not reported until 2003, from Galway on the west coast of Ireland. Once the species had been recognised, earlier diver photographs of it were unearthed, taken in the same area in 1982. The problem is that its preferred habitat of very exposed rocky reefs does not make for easy diving. In addition, at first glance it is easy to confuse it with the similar Tompot Blenny, although this widespread species generally (but not always) prefers less exposed sites. Knowing where to look and what to look for (in terms of habitat) has resulted in diver records from west- and south-coast Ireland, the Isles of Scilly, Cornwall and the west coast of Scotland right round to Orkney. So, it is highly likely that it has been here all along, or at least for a considerable time.

The Leopard-spotted Goby is widespread in shallow water around the British Isles, and because of its all-over leopard-like spots it is perhaps the easiest of all our resident gobies to identify. However, it was only officially recognised as part of the British Isles fauna in the 1950s. This was when scuba diving started to become readily accessible to scientists and recreational divers. The goby's small size and habitat preference for silt-covered ledges, adjacent to crevices, meant that it had always evaded capture in fishing nets or on lines.

ABOVE: Unlike some gobies, which can be difficult to identify, the Leopard-spotted Goby *Thorogobius ephippiatus* has extremely distinctive markings. This unusually bold and photogenic individual was probably a male defending his territory.

For those readers not previously familiar with the wonderful fish life of our coastal seas, we hope this chapter has left plenty of positive impressions. One thing that may come as a surprise is that a good proportion of them are very far from the silvery-grey, torpedo-shaped archetypes of popular perception, and that they display an amazing variety of appearance and form. Another is that while many are 'colourful' in the visual sense, that term applies even more emphatically to their behaviour. As well as feeding and reproducing in a great variety of ways, different species can guard territories for several years, build intricate nests, have 'friendships' with other individuals, clean each other and even change sex when the situation demands. Because our coastal fish live in a relatively 'secret' world, it is also evident that careful observations of them going about their lives can quickly reveal hitherto undiscovered aspects of their behaviour.

To reinforce that point, and if readers want a wider appreciation of fish capabilities and intelligence (or harbour doubts about them), we recommend a delightful but science-based book called *What A Fish Knows* (Balcombe 2016).

Invertebrate variety

chapter nine

As vertebrates ourselves, we may feel a certain kinship with sea mammals, and perhaps also with fish. The way they look, and how they lead their lives, are at least to some extent familiar. Dressed from head to toe in neoprene and with fins on, a diver might even make a reasonable impression of a seal. But invertebrates are a different matter. Whether terrestrial or marine, there are many that, if you had not heard of them before, would seem like something doodled on a science-fiction author's notepad. Encounters with unfamiliar species face to face (though not all have a head, let alone a face) have been among the most memorable of our marine explorations.

In Chapter 1 we introduced the concept of how, in contrast to terrestrial invertebrates, many marine species are able to live out their lives 'rooted to the spot', firmly fixed in one place. We described many of these prominent sessile invertebrates, such as sponges and sea anemones, in Chapter 4 because they are an obvious and integral part of rocky-reef communities. Others such as sea pens and some sea cucumbers and tubeworms live an immobile life part-buried within sediments and are included in Chapter 5. However, there are also many marine invertebrates that have a more familiar, mobile (though often slow) lifestyle, including starfish and other echinoderms, crustaceans, sea snails and sea slugs – and it is these that we concentrate on in this chapter. At the risk of bias, the obvious intelligence of those most rapid of invertebrates, the cephalopods, makes them so utterly unique that they get their own chapter (Chapter 10). The book on *Rocky Shores* in this series provides further information about the members of these groups found on rocky shores, along with others such as polychaete worms that we barely touch on (Archer-Thomson and Cremona 2019).

OPPOSITE PAGE:
Two large predatory Common Sunstars *Crossaster papposus* and a group of filter-feeding featherstars on rock below a kelp forest, just some of the many colourful marine invertebrates around the British Isles.

Echinoderms: prickly (and very strange) customers

Have you ever considered what unusual creatures starfish and sea urchins are? Would you recognise a brittlestar, featherstar or sea cucumber, each representing one of the other three echinoderm groups? Most marine animals have a land-based equivalent for comparison; for example, small crustaceans such as shrimps and the like could be considered the 'insects of the sea' and both crustaceans and insects belong to the same phylum, the arthropods (Arthropoda). There is no such conceptual 'bridge-builder' amongst echinoderms (phylum Echinodermata), which are one of only a few phyla that are uniquely marine. Peter Holland, in his wonderfully concise book *The Animal Kingdom: a Very Short Introduction* (2011), which we heartily recommend to anyone confused or curious about different phyla, notes how echinoderms have been described as 'the strangest animals on Earth' and 'especially designed to puzzle the zoologist'. Echinoderm means 'spiny skin' and refers to the calcareous plates or ossicles and spines found to a varying extent in the body wall of all echinoderms, and which dictate the various peculiar ways that they go about their lives.

Look at a starfish and try to find its head and you will struggle. Most animals that move freely across the seabed or the ground have a front and a back end, but starfish have an unusual radial symmetry and can set off with any arm in the lead. Radial symmetry is common

BELOW: Any which way? Common Starfish *Asterias rubens* can move with any of their five arms leading. Here they are feeding on barnacles beneath a rocky overhang.

to adults of all five echinoderm groups, though the elongated, cylindrical shape of sea cucumbers gives them a superficially bilateral appearance. The symmetry of adult echinoderms is five-fold or pentamerous, as shown by the five arms of typical starfish and brittlestars, so it seems appropriate, although totally coincidental, that their phylum divides neatly into five classes: starfish, brittlestars, sea urchins, sea cucumbers and featherstars.

Versatile feet

The gliding motion of a starfish appears effortless and unearthly, although it is readily explained by the thousands of tiny 'tube feet' that most echinoderms use for locomotion. A terrestrial millipede has to control hundreds of feet (in spite of the name, only one species with more than a thousand is known), but a starfish or sea urchin must coordinate thousands of tube feet. In a starfish, these project from the undersides of the arms, whilst in the much clumsier sea urchins they project all over the body. Each tube foot can be extended by fluid pressure from a muscular sac that acts like the bulb of a pipette, with the fluid in it fed by a hydraulic system unique to echinoderms. The tube foot can then be contracted by its own muscles. By alternately extending and contracting, the armies of tube feet can march a starfish along at a reasonably brisk pace. Tube feet are generally tipped with suckers to grip the seabed, and their power can be seen by watching an urchin climb up the glass walls of an aquarium. However, from a mussel's or clam's perspective, the impressive force exhibited by the tube feet of a starfish has another, far more sinister, function.

BELOW: Common Sea Urchins *Echinus esculentus* have long tube feet to reach out beyond their spines, which can be used for 'walking', climbing and clinging on.

Many starfish hunt bivalve molluscs, and when they encounter one they will arch over it with their arms wrapped around both halves of the shell. This position ensures that the maximum number of tube feet are put into action and that the starfish's mouth on its underside is positioned strategically close to a potential opening. With a combination of steady pulling and using the tube feet in relays, the starfish eventually overcomes the powerful muscles that usually keep a bivalve's shell tightly closed. Only the tiniest gap in the shell is needed, then the starfish turns the lower

RIGHT: A Common Starfish *Asterias rubens* arching over mussels and applying its tube feet to pull a shell open. This enables it to slip its everted stomach inside the shell.

part of its stomach inside out, extends it out through its mouth and into the bivalve's interior. With the stomach inside its victim, enzymes are poured in, and the mollusc is digested without being first swallowed. Digested material is transported by cilia back through the upper part of the starfish's stomach to digestive glands in its arms. Small clams and snails are sometimes taken whole into the starfish's stomach, with their shells eventually ejected back out through its mouth.

Another and perhaps surprising aspect of echinoderm tube feet is that as well as their obvious use in locomotion, they can variously have a role in light sensitivity, respiration and chemoreception. In other words, some echinoderms can 'see', 'breathe' and 'smell' through their feet. For example, researchers at the University of New Hampshire, US, found tiny ossicles forming concave light collectors in the tips of the tube feet of a local sea urchin species, allowing them to detect subtle changes in light intensity (Lesser *et al.* 2011).

No hitchhikers

Another unique adaptation of echinoderms is the way that these rather slow-moving creatures remain unencumbered by unwanted debris, seaweed and settling sessile animal larvae. This is achieved by structures called pedicellariae, which consist of a set of jaws mounted on a long stem with a flexible neck and are very reminiscent of miniature pairs of pliers. A sea urchin, for example, has different types of these tiny pincer-like structures all over its outer surface, and these variously clear detritus and kill and discard small animals, such as barnacles, that would otherwise settle on it. The number and variety of pedicellariae seems to be correlated with the vulnerability of the animal to freeloaders. Urchins need plenty, but they are present only in a simpler form on faster-moving starfish, and the speedy brittlestars do without them entirely. There is an interesting anomaly with Green Sea Urchins *Psammechinus miliaris*, as these regularly place and carry a 'hat' of quite large pieces of shell and seaweed on their spines, seemingly as deliberate camouflage. Frances has seen similar behaviour in various species of tropical sea urchin, some of which also have venomous pedicellariae.

Starfish: variations on a theme

Starfish are perhaps the most familiar of all echinoderms, and the Common Starfish *Asterias rubens* is generally the one that people encounter around the British Isles, either live or tossed up dead on the strandline, although it is not necessarily the most frequently seen starfish everywhere. We are fortunate in having a good variety of these remarkable creatures in our coastal waters. In the southwest the most obvious species is the large Spiny Starfish *Marthasterias glacialis*, typically a distinctive pale blue and armed with rows of impressive spines. It is a versatile predator and, in common with other starfish, has a neat excavation technique for attacking buried prey. Its tube

BELOW: Leaving the scene of the 'crime', a Spiny Starfish *Marthasterias glacialis* crawls away from the distinctively shaped pit it has excavated in the maerl seabed to prey on buried clams.

ABOVE: While five arms is the norm for most starfish, the number can vary due to their ability to regenerate lost limbs. This Spiny Starfish (left) is regrowing an arm, while another (right) has overdone it and now has eight arms.

feet move seabed sediment outwards along its arms, rather like a conveyor belt, so that the centre of its body is gradually lowered down towards its victim.

Around Scotland and, to a lesser extent, the north of England, a wider variety of large starfish species are common. These include the imposingly voracious multi-armed sunstars. The Common Sunstar *Crossaster papposus* is covered in brush-like spines and often has an attractive 'target' type of pattern with alternating deep red and paler banding. Large individuals can even attack and envelop that scourge of bivalves, the Common Starfish, which then meets its own nemesis. The less frequently seen Purple Sunstar *Solaster endeca*

RIGHT: The Common Sunstar *Crossaster papposus* is naturally multi-armed and can have up to 14 arms.

(not always purple but distinctively smoother) specialises in devouring sea cucumbers. Both sunstar species will also readily prey on brittlestars (see page 260), but these spindly starfish relatives can evade their grasp with a surprising turn of speed. This often leads to a sunstar surrounded by abundant brittlestars, but with an empty space immediately around it as the brittlestars have sensed its approach and crawled out of the danger zone. However, the brittlestar hunter supreme is the Seven-armed Starfish *Luidia ciliaris*, which has tube feet tipped with little knobs instead of the usual suckers so they act like running spikes and move the starfish surprisingly rapidly across the seabed in pursuit of its quarry. In sheltered habitats such as sea lochs, the array of starfish may also include Spiny Starfish (mentioned on page 257), which can reach an especially large size here, up to nearly a metre in diameter.

Cushion stars are starfish with short, stout arms, and it is presumably no coincidence that their diets do not call for rapid movement. The small and abundant, but unobtrusive, detritus-browsing Cushion Star *Asterina gibbosa* of rocky shores and shallow water is unlikely to conjure up a vision of a soft seat, but the larger Red Cushion Star *Porania pulvillus* has the distinct look of a luxuriant velvet cushion. Usually vibrant red in colour, it feeds on encrusting animals such as sponges, soft corals and sea squirts and is most frequently seen around the north of the British Isles.

Gatherings and strandings

When diving, we encounter starfish mostly as scattered individuals, but it can be a different story on mussel beds, where we have seen Common Starfish aggregated in huge numbers feasting on these bivalves. A less pleasant sight are so-called 'wrecks' of starfish (or other invertebrates), where huge numbers of animals can sometimes be washed up, moribund, on beaches, mainly during stormy or exceptionally cold weather. For Common Starfish a possible contributing factor to these mass strandings came to light when scientists using remote cameras to monitor the seabed observed large numbers of starfish doing what they aptly termed 'starballing'. The camera footage showed that many of the starfish had folded their arms up into a ball shape and were being moved rapidly across the seabed by the current (Sheehan and Cousens 2017). While a way of 'riding' water flow in this way might be useful if it transported the starfish to new feeding grounds much more rapidly than they could crawl, the authors suggest that, in some circumstances, it could also leave them at the mercy of swells in shallow water and vulnerable to stranding.

Brittlestars: arms aloft

Brittlestars have their own story. At first glance they might just seem to be small, emaciated starfish – but, although closely related, they are quite different in form and lifestyle. They have thin, flexible arms that meet the central disc abruptly, unlike the tapering arms of starfish, and these move with a snake-like motion to 'row' the animal across the seabed. Brittlestar tube feet provide traction for the arms rather than doing the 'walking' themselves, and this technique allows for more rapid locomotion. The tube feet can also pick up small food particles or, when the arms are held up, catch them in the passing current; some even secrete mucus that acts as a net to improve their capture rate.

Many brittlestars, tucked away in crevices or beneath boulders, lead a low-profile existence, albeit an ecologically important one, recycling nutrients from seabed debris. Others live largely buried in soft sand or mud with just a few centimetres of their arms protruding above the sediment's surface. Such slender wisps often belong to sand brittlestars *Ophiura* spp., but it is difficult to determine their identity. Some brittlestars are more prominent, especially when present in large numbers. Common Brittlestars *Ophiothrix fragilis* can occur in massive aggregations, up to 10,000 individuals per square metre, where the dense forest of their stripy arms in a variety of colours, held up to catch plankton food, makes a wonderful spectacle. Individuals use one or more arms to link to their neighbours to prevent themselves getting washed away if the current is strong. Black brittlestars *Ophiocomina nigra* form less dense groupings but can be attractive individually, especially when coloured a deep red rather than their 'traditional' black.

Sea urchins: powerful grazers

Sea urchins appear very different from starfish and brittlestars, but a close-up look reveals the distinctive echinoderm features. They have long spines and even longer tube feet reaching beyond them. The radial symmetry is there too, but the bony plates that are loosely arranged in a starfish's tissues are fused to form the urchin's rigid,

ABOVE: Common Brittlestars *Ophiothrix fragilis* holding some of their arms aloft to catch food, whilst other arms grip the seabed or link with fellow brittlestars to avoid being swept away. Two small Green Sea Urchins *Psammechinus miliaris* are in the foreground.

globe-shaped skeleton known as a 'test'. Their feeding apparatus is unique amongst the echinoderm groups. Five strong chisel-like teeth are positioned around the mouth on the urchin's underside, as described in Chapter 3. Reef-dwelling urchins such as the large Common Sea Urchin *Echinus esculentus* and the smaller Green Sea Urchin use this apparatus, known as Aristotle's lantern, to scrape off and chew up seaweed and any encrusting algae or small animals as they slowly crawl along. Their powerful grazing, which can clear a rock face of all cover including seaweeds and even animals as well-defended as barnacles, makes urchins very influential members of a seabed community. It also means that any impact we have on urchins or their predators, such as wrasses, can have dramatic effects on kelp forest and other habitats.

Sea cucumbers

With their elongated bodies and tentacle-fringed mouths, sea cucumbers are ideally suited to living upright in sediment, where their soft bodies are protected. Unlike sea urchins and starfish, sea cucumbers do not have much of a hard skeleton, though they do have microscopic calcareous spicules in their body wall. Sediment-living sea cucumbers are described in Chapter 5, but there are similar species that instead make use of cracks and crevices in rocky areas. Two such

Coastal Seas

are the crevice sea cucumbers *Aslia lefevrei* and *Pawsonia saxicola*, their extended tentacles sometimes mistaken for anemones. In the British Isles, only one species of sea cucumber, the Cotton Spinner *Holothuria forskali*, lives out in the open, hauling its fat sausage-like body slowly over rocks and shovelling organic debris into its mouth with short tentacles as it goes.

The 'Cotton Spinner' name has a link to this animal's disregard for shelter, referring to an unusual alternative defensive strategy. If attacked, it directs its anus towards the potential predator and contracts the muscles in its body wall so that special organs connected to its respiratory apparatus are shot out as white threads. These are extremely sticky and readily entangle the assailant, such that a frustrated crab or lobster trying to free its claws from them is a comical sight not to be missed. Occasionally, if particularly threatened, a Cotton Spinner will shoot out its entire alimentary tract and gonad, but all these structures are later regenerated.

Featherstars

Our final group of echinoderms is the featherstars, aptly named primitive animals. Only three species are found around Britain and Ireland, all of which have five feathery arms, each divided in two so it

BELOW: A Cotton Spinner sea cucumber *Holothuria forskali* crawling over the seabed. Behind and below it on the rock, among numerous cup corals, are its distinctive trails of voided, undigested silty material.

appears as though they have 10; some tropical species have even more. The arms are normally held up into the water column, and the small central body has claw-like structures called cirri beneath it that allow the animal to cling on to the seabed. These are particularly long and obvious in the Celtic Featherstar *Leptometra celtica*, a predominantly northern and deeper-water species common off the west coast of Scotland. The Common Featherstar *Antedon bifida* has short, untidy-looking arms around 5cm long and is a widespread species. The tenacious grip of its cirri and the numerous entangling pinnules on the arms are all too obvious if you brush against a reef covered in this featherstar and get any stuck on your diving suit. Trying to remove them without harming these fragile creatures is hard. The similar *Antedon petasus* has longer arms and occurs mostly in the northern Irish Sea and on the west coast of Scotland.

Featherstars are filter-feeders, and the short tube feet on their arms are covered in mucus to help trap suspended food particles. These are then transported down ciliated grooves to the mouth, which unusually is positioned on the top of the central body. Like many of the animals that live by catching drifting food, featherstars thrive in large numbers in current-swept areas. They mainly stay anchored in one spot, but if necessary they can both crawl using their cirri and swim using their flexible arms.

BELOW: A Common Featherstar *Antedon bifida*, its feathery arms catching passing plankton and detritus while clinging to the seabed with its claw-like appendages (cirri).

Getting together while keeping their distance

When starfish stand on tiptoe, sea cucumbers rear up or sea urchins climb to the tops of rocks, you know there is something going on. Such behaviour is a prelude to spawning, and in the summer these animals can sometimes be seen releasing a milky cloud of spawn. Chemicals accompanying the spawn encourage others to do likewise, so you may spot further animals in similar positions nearby doing the same. The sexes are generally separate, and spawning together ensures that eggs and sperm released into the water have the best chance of meeting. Fertilisation typically results in planktonic larvae, but there are species in all five groups of echinoderms that brood their eggs. Like the majority of marine invertebrates, it is difficult to tell the sexes apart, and even their spawn looks similar underwater. This is not surprising, because sexual dimorphism is usually associated with animals that physically mate and need to attract or at least recognise and find a potential partner. However, when a Common Sunstar female stands up to spawn, which in itself is a particularly impressive sight, her unusually large, yolk-filled orange eggs are easy to spot. The larvae of this species are atypical among echinoderms in not feeding during the drifting, planktonic stage, their sustenance instead provided by abundant yolk.

The way the cells arrange themselves in the fertilised eggs of echinoderms as they develop, along with other features, gives us clues about the position of these weird creatures in the animal kingdom – and there is a surprise in store. It turns out that they are grouped (as 'deuterostomes') with chordate animals like us mammals, fish and birds and a small group of worm-like creatures called hemichordates. It is worth noting here that echinoderm larvae have a left and right side, in other words bilateral symmetry, and that the radial symmetry which seems so characteristic of the group only develops in adulthood. The only animals that truly do without bilateral symmetry are found in the more primitive groups such as sponges and cnidarians (sea anemones, corals and jellyfish).

Crustaceans: armoured warriors

Crustaceans are an immensely varied and almost exclusively aquatic group of arthropods, the phylum that includes the predominantly terrestrial insects. Crabs, lobsters, shrimps, prawns, barnacles, amphipods, isopods and copepods are all included. What they and other arthropod groups have in common is a protective outer

Invertebrate variety

covering, the exoskeleton or cuticle. Like insects, they must moult this periodically in order to grow, including the covering of their jointed limbs, another universal arthropod feature. Crustaceans are found in a wide variety of habitats and have already appeared in other chapters, so here we give just one example, of a large and charismatic species.

Spider crabs: travellers and decorators

When diving and snorkelling we tend to see mainly the larger crustaceans, and one of the most impressive of all invertebrates we meet around our shores is the Spiny Spider Crab *Maja brachydactyla*, with a body up to 20cm long and claws twice that length in the males. Despite their stature and economic importance (there is a significant commercial fishery for them), knowledge of their life history remains incomplete, with several mysteries yet to be solved. The most striking thing about these spider crabs is the way they often congregate in great numbers in shallow water close to the coast in the summer, principally in July and August. They sometimes form a dense single layer of crabs that carpets the seabed while, on other occasions, they form a huge heap many crabs high. An aggregation of thousands is an awe-inspiring, if slightly unnerving, spectacle

BELOW: A large moulting aggregation of Spiny Spider Crabs *Maja brachydactyla* and a heap of discarded 'suits of armour' (inset).

that can be surprisingly difficult to photograph because they tend to stir up the seabed as they move around, especially when panicked by a diver trying to get close and capture the perfect shot.

Uncertainties remain about the exact function(s) of these mass gatherings. There is no doubt that moulting takes place in and around the heaps. As the congregation recedes, the seabed scene left behind resembles an eerie battlefield strewn with corpses, although the 'bodies' are of course empty armour suits and not dead crabs. The heaps could therefore have a protective function for the crabs as they go through the dangerous process of extricating themselves from their old armour and hardening the new. We described in Chapter 4 how crabs generally overcome the hazards of moulting by hiding away, particularly from their own potentially cannibalistic peers, so this 'safety in numbers' approach is radically different. By persistently visiting an aggregation near Torbay one summer, Paul was able to film the moulting of several individual crabs. He was struck by how crabs would move around half-moulted, with their 'new' body partly protruding from the old armour before they settled down to complete the process. As expected, the moulting crabs' peers wandered by, apparently oblivious to their struggles. On one occasion, which always gets a laugh when the footage of the moulting is shown (albeit speeded up), a small spider crab clambers up onto the back of a larger one, as if to get a better view of the scenery.

The moult that the crabs undergo when they aggregate is their final one, and whilst they can live for up to another six years, they will never moult again. It also represents the point at which they become sexually mature and is described as the pubertal moult – and herein lies one of the uncertainties. Many references suggest that the aggregations are for mating as well as moulting, and it is certainly tempting to conclude that all these animals are gathered in the ideal situation to take advantage of their new adult status, especially as the female of many crab species is only receptive immediately after emerging soft-bodied from a moult. However, the female Spiny Spider Crab is atypical in being able to copulate while her shell is hard, and there seems to be no evidence of mating by females within the mounds or just after moulting. Instead, it appears to happen later when the crabs have migrated into deeper water. When we have seen isolated mating couples in shallow water, generally in early summer, the females have had shells well encrusted with growths such as worm tubes, which suggests they moulted the previous year or even earlier.

LEFT: Unusually, this Spiny Spider Crab's carapace is adorned with a Snakelocks Anemone *Anemonia viridis* and at least two other small sea anemones, as well as the seaweed normally used.

After Spiny Spider Crabs have struggled free from their old armour, they have another major task to face: redecoration. Their backs are often adorned with growths of seaweed, which the casual observer could assume have resulted simply from fragments catching on the forest of spikes that cover the carapace (and which make picking them up rather uncomfortable). This is until you watch the wonderful process in which they deliberately attach the seaweed to themselves. The crabs show remarkable dexterity in grasping a small piece of weed in a claw, reaching over their back, then rubbing it against their armour until it sticks. It amazes us how easily and accurately they appear to detect that the fragment has stuck (without a make-up mirror) so that they can get hold of another piece and repeat the process. The seaweed does not stick onto the large spines but onto the tiny hooks that surround them (see also *Coats (and hats) of sponge* in Chapter 11), and they don't stop at decorating their carapace, but often assiduously festoon their legs in the same way.

It is quite difficult to watch spider crabs decorating themselves, as they usually stop if disturbed, but Paul once found an unusually laid-back female crab and watched as she carefully rubbed each fragment in her mouthparts before attempting the attachment. This must help the process: think how much easier it would be to attach a stick of celery to Velcro® if you gave it a little chew first. Once attached, the straggly seaweed pieces grow to form luxuriant camouflage. Most divers will have been surprised at some point by seeing what looked like a large clump of seaweed get up and walk away. We do wonder –

and are often asked – what predators such large and spikily armoured animals go to such lengths to evade. We conclude that sharp-toothed seals, otters, sharks and Conger Eels *Conger conger* are all likely contenders. Spiny Spider Crabs are commonest in south and west Britain and Ireland, but have been recorded all around the British Isles. Older references often refer to this species as *Maja squinado*, a very similar crab endemic to the Mediterranean.

Molluscs

Searching for empty seashells along sandy shores is a simple and time-honoured pastime, and we have always found this a good way to learn to identify different species of molluscs. The classification and identification of these animals (marine, terrestrial and freshwater) depends largely on features of their shells, though not all closely related species can be separated in this way and not all molluscs have external shells, though most do. Whilst there are others, the three main groups of molluscs are the bivalves, gastropods and cephalopods (classes Bivalvia, Gastropoda and Cephalopoda). We have already introduced the bivalves in Chapter 1, and the name of this group reflects their hinged, two-part shells, with mussels, oysters and clams as examples of well-known, commercially exploited species.

Gastropods (Gastropoda) are the most biodiverse and numerous of all mollusc groups and include the vegetation-munching terrestrial snails and slugs, a familiar scourge of gardeners. Around our rocky coastline and in shallow water, sea snails such as winkles, limpets and topshells play a similar ecological role, being important seaweed grazers. Sea slugs, on the other hand, are not generally vegetarian like most terrestrial slugs, but are instead almost exclusively carnivorous,

BELOW: The Common or Edible Periwinkle *Littorina littorea* is a typical sea snail, here seen grazing on a kelp stipe.

feeding on sessile animals. They might therefore rank as the world's slowest-moving predators. These animals are also extremely colourful and attractive, and to the many snorkellers and divers who love to photograph and document them, they engender the same passion as birds do for so many people in the terrestrial environment.

The smallest of the three major mollusc groups is exclusively marine. These are the cephalopods, the highly developed and fascinating octopuses, squids and cuttlefishes, and they are the subject of Chapter 10.

Invertebrate variety

Versatile and vibrant: the fabulous sea slugs

No animals fit the 'weird and wonderful' label better than the sea slugs, which exhibit a truly amazing variety of body shapes and behaviours. True sea slugs have no shell at all and belong to an order known as the nudibranchs (Nudibranchia), often affectionately just called 'nudis'. Well over 100 species of nudibranchs are found around the British Isles, with more being discovered all the time to keep nudi-spotters very happy. A number of other similar slug-like molluscs do carry fragile shells, usually hidden by body folds or wholly internal. These are classified in various different orders but are similarly fascinating, and we describe some of them below (see *Nudi or not?*, page 272).

In spite of their often bright colours, the small size of many sea slugs usually means that a close look and a careful search amongst the undergrowth on which they are feeding is necessary to spot them.

BELOW: Impressive variations: four of the 100+ species of nudibranch sea slugs found around the British Isles. Clockwise from top left: Sea Lemon *Archidoris pseudoargus*, Yellow Skirt Sea Slug *Okenia elegans*, Crystal Sea Slug *Antiopella cristata*, Farran's Aeolid *Amphorina farrani*.

As mentioned in Chapter 6, the presence of the more cryptic species is often given away by their distinctive egg masses, usually white or at least pale, making them stand out against the background. The size and shape of the egg masses are distinctive and differ between species, often allowing identification even if no adults are seen. All nudibranchs are simultaneous hermaphrodites, male and female at the same time, so every encounter with another of the same species is a mating opportunity. They can fertilise each other and both subsequently lay eggs, an exemplar of gender equality. The eggs of some nudibranch species hatch into miniature crawling adults, but most produce larvae that drift with the plankton. The settling and development of these larvae is often reliant on them coming across their specific prey, and this searching phase can range from a week up to a few months depending on the species.

Nudibranch defences: picky eating and recycling

The name nudibranch means 'naked gill' and refers to the fact that these molluscs have external gills and no protective shell. Why then are these soft-bodied, slow-moving and generally small animals not rapidly consumed by predators? This is one of the aspects of their lives that we find the most fascinating. In fact, they have a very effective chemical and biological weaponry defence that makes them unpleasant to would-be attackers. In *Living Marine Molluscs*, Yonge and Thompson (1976) describe memorable experiments in the Port Erin Aquarium on the Isle of Man (no longer in existence) where a nudibranch would be taken into the mouth by all the fish in a tank in turn, before being spat out by each one. Paul witnessed such a deterrent working in the wild when he was taking close-up photographs of a resplendent and well-named Yellow Skirt Sea Slug *Okenia elegans*. A large Black Goby *Gobius niger* appeared out of the surrounding seaweed and bit at one of the slug's colourful frontal protuberances before, within a second or two, spitting the intact slug away in apparent disgust.

The chemicals responsible for nudibranch defence include acids (known to be very distasteful to fish) and toxic proteins. They are often generated from compounds in food items consumed by the nudibranchs, or may indeed be the same substances reused without alteration. This remarkable deployment of resources helps to explain why nudibranchs are so specific in their choice of diet. Always carnivorous, each nudibranch species generally feeds on a small range of species, or sometimes only one. Prey are typically sessile invertebrates, chiefly sponges, hydroids, bryozoans and sea squirts. One common species, the Rough-mantled Doris *Onchidoris bilamellata*, is unusual in feeding on barnacles, chewing away the plates on the top of their 'houses' and sucking out their soft inner bodies. When Paul found a patch of boulders covered in completely ravaged barnacles near Oban he thought that unusually thorough crabs might be responsible, until he swam a little further and saw a huge aggregation of these barnacle-eating nudibranchs. Many of them were mating, and their egg ribbons were everywhere. Depositing eggs on their prey is a very common practice among nudibranchs.

ABOVE: Scarlet Lady *Fjordia browni*, one of the nudibranch species that stores the stinging cells of hydroid prey in its cerata to use for defence.

If using chemicals within your food to ward off attackers is not quite impressive enough, some nudibranch species take their resourcefulness to an even higher plane by reusing the intact weaponry of their prey. These slugs eat animals with stinging cells such as hydroids and sea anemones, and they are able to separate the cells from the rest of the meal in their digestive system and transfer them out into sacs at the tips of the many projections on their backs known as cerata (the cerata also act as gills). When a nudibranch with these defences is threatened by a potential predator such as a fish, they usually hold their cerata erect and may even point them towards their assailant. If the fish nips one of the cerata, stinging cells are released and discharge their threads as they meet the seawater, which is usually sufficient to prevent further attack. When Paul describes sea slugs in school talks, he asks children to envisage this astonishing phenomenon as equivalent to them eating wasps and instead of simply getting stung in the mouth, positioning the wasps' stings in their skin where they could deliver a nasty jolt to anyone who grabbed them: a superpower indeed!

Different shades

Releasing noxious chemicals and second-hand stinging cells are only part of the sea slug defence story. Some species, for example, are extremely cryptic and superbly camouflaged when among their prey. The Sea Lemon *Archidoris pseudoargus* looks gaudily coloured out of context, but its mottled colouration makes it very difficult to spot on a sponge when it is feeding, particularly as it tends to withdraw its gill rosette when approached. In Chapter 4 we described the way other nudibranchs living on rocky reefs are equipped to perfectly resemble their soft coral or sea fan prey. The bright colours of some species, however, are so out of keeping with their habitat that they stand out – and it is generally accepted that this is a way of signalling their toxicity or bad taste to potential predators. This mechanism, called aposematism, is of course widespread in animals such as insects, frogs and snakes. A nudibranch's showy cerata may have the alternative function of inviting attention and so diverting a predator's attack away from the slug's more vulnerable and less obvious head region. The slug can afford to have some of its cerata damaged, and they will give the assailant an unpleasant surprise.

Nudi or not?

As already mentioned on page 269, there are non-nudibranch sea slugs living in our shallow seas that do have a shell, but a much reduced one, such that it can have no use as a defensive refuge. These species therefore also rely on chemical defences, and a notable example is the large sea slug *Pleurobranchus membranaceus*, whose skin, if broken, produces sulphuric acid at a sufficient concentration to irritate the hands of anyone who picks it up out of the water. The delightful common name of this species is Highland Dancer, which refers to the way that it will occasionally swim, propelled by the swirling motion of its large, pale foot. The swimming is apparently directionless and is therefore assumed to simply raise the slug up into the water column. While the principal benefit of this could be to evade seabed predators (similar to scallops fleeing from starfish, as

BELOW: Swirling skirt: the dramatic swimming motion of a Highland Dancer sea slug *Pleurobranchus membranaceus*.

described in Chapter 5), this is contradicted by very occasional observations of huge swimming aggregations in the winter. Thompson (1988) reports three in the previous 100 years, and suggests that such swarming may represent migration, preparing for reproduction in the spring.

We have described what is probably the non-nudibranch sea slug encountered most often, the Sea Hare *Aplysia punctata*, and its racy reproductive life in Chapter 6, and the one most noted for swimming, *Akera bullata*, in Chapter 5 (see *Loch Obisary*). Both species are unusual for sea slugs in being vegetarians, as is another wonderfully named animal, the Solar-powered Sea Slug *Elysia viridis*. Like many nudibranchs, it is resourceful in the way it reuses parts of its food, but this time it is the tiny photosynthetic structures (chloroplasts) of its diet of algae that the slug consumes without destroying. These are retained in the animal's tissues and continue to function as they did when in the seaweed, by photosynthesising and generating nutrition with the aid of sunlight.

ABOVE: A small (<1cm) Solar-powered Sea Slug *Elysia viridis* on the green seaweed *Codium* sp. Its colour depends on the hue of its seaweed diet and is usually green. Branches of the digestive system with retained chloroplasts are visible on one of the body flaps (parapodia).

By necessity, all the chapters in this book include only a tiny fraction of the enormous amount of information available on their various subjects. More than any, however, this chapter must 'take the biscuit' for selectivity or perhaps more aptly the 'wooden spoon' for coverage. The first animals on Earth were invertebrates that lived in the sea, and 11 of the 31 phyla of animals currently (2025) listed in the World Register of Marine Species (WoRMS) are exclusively marine, while the rest contain at least some marine representatives. There is therefore a vast array of invertebrate animals living in our coastal seas that we could have chosen to describe. Instead, we have simply highlighted a small handful of particular types to show what fascinating lives they lead. We especially wanted to explain how the forms and habits of animals often regarded as 'primitive,' such as crabs, sea slugs and starfish, are astonishingly complex when examined in detail.

Cunning cephalopods

chapter ten

Those of us lucky enough to meet cuttlefishes or octopuses underwater often have a clear memory of a first, special encounter. We remember the uncanny feeling of watching an animal which, despite seeming so alien, is obviously intelligent and is returning our inquisitive gaze with an equally curious eye.

The cephalopods constitute a group of uniquely sophisticated, fascinating and engaging invertebrate animals, and we have both had very memorable underwater encounters with them. Perhaps surprisingly, they are included in the mollusc phylum but, in terms of their behaviour and interactions, many seem to have more in common with us vertebrates than they do with whelks and oysters. The best indication of their origins probably comes from the *Nautilus*, which, with its beautiful external coiled shell, does at least resemble something like a 'go-faster' version of more conventional molluscs, while the other cephalopods look like different animals entirely. Sadly, in the British Isles, you will only see *Nautilus* as dead shells for sale in curio shops, as all six species – three of them only described in 2023 – live in tropical waters.

Aside from the primitive *Nautilus*, there are three main subgroups of cephalopods, all of which can be found in shallow water around the British Isles: octopuses, which have no shell (though some oceanic species secrete a floating shell in which to lay their eggs); cuttlefishes, with an internal shell known as a cuttlebone; and squids, which have a reduced internal shell or 'pen'. A clue to the form of these amazing animals is in their name. Cephalopod means 'head-footed' and refers to the way that, instead of the typical mollusc's muscular foot, they have a highly developed head equipped with a circle of arms and/or tentacles. The head also has a pair of sophisticated eyes that are

OPPOSITE PAGE:
A Common Cuttlefish *Sepia officinalis* among seagrass showing the 'flamboyant display', with two arms raised. This can aid camouflage, but its main use is to show a potential predator that it has been spotted and so an attack would be fruitless.

structured in a remarkably similar way to those of vertebrate animals, including humans. The eyes do, however, develop very differently and there is no common ancestor that possessed them, so we know that the similarities arose from convergent evolution, a process where natural selection leads to very different organisms coming up with the same answer to a common problem. As you would expect from their behaviour, cephalopods have a large brain. It is positioned between the eyes and, somewhat unusually, forms a ring round the gullet. There are also many neuron-containing ganglia, rather like mini brains, distributed along each of the arms. It is no wonder they are so dexterous.

If you are lucky enough to see a cephalopod when snorkelling or diving, then swim slowly and quietly, as almost all of them are fast movers and liable to disappear rapidly into the gloom. This is all the more remarkable when compared to other molluscs such as the proverbially slow-moving snails. Cuttlefishes and particularly squids can swim rapidly by sucking in and expelling strong jets of water, powered by contractions of their mantle cavity

BELOW: A diver meeting a cuttlefish that is partly buried in the gravelly seabed. Only on close inspection can it be clearly seen (inset). These photographs were taken just a few metres from Porthkerris beach in Cornwall.

Cunning cephalopods

LEFT: This cuttlefish, resting among kelp, is gently blowing water from its siphon, extended just behind its arms. The siphon can be pointed in virtually any direction to enable rapid and versatile jet propulsion.

LEFT: A Curled Octopus *Eledone cirrhosa* next to its lair.

(the mantle is a tough muscular structure that encloses the body organs). The water is expelled through a flexible funnel (siphon) that can be pointed in different directions to move the animal forwards, backwards, up or down. Octopuses generally crawl across the seabed and can even climb up the glass sides of aquaria using powerful suckers on their arms, but they can also use jet propulsion when the situation demands.

Without a hard shell to hide in for protection, most cephalopods have another defensive 'string to their bow' in that they can produce a cloud of ink from a special reservoir that opens into the siphon. A burst of this ink ejected in front of an approaching predator can act as a 'smoke screen' in obstructing its sight, tasting objectionable or numbing its chemoreception senses, but it can also work in a sophisticated visual way. The cloud can appear as a dark object (called a 'pseudomorph') in the water that looks fleetingly like the animal that released it. Meanwhile, the actual animal jets off in an entirely different direction or drops to the seabed unnoticed by the predator and camouflages itself there.

Around the British Isles, octopuses are very occasionally found in rock pools or even crawling over rocky shores and across sandy beaches, possibly caught out by the receding tide or thrown up by storms. Their saliva contains toxins and they can inflict a strong bite, though, in our native species, this is not normally dangerous to humans. However, the same cannot be said for the tiny blue-ringed octopuses (*Hapalochlaena* spp.) found in shallow tropical waters of the west Pacific, whose bite can kill.

Colourful characters

Despite all their other skills, perhaps the most remarkable and engaging aspect of cephalopod behaviour is their incredible ability to change colour and pattern almost instantaneously. They are sometimes called the 'chameleons' of the sea, but this does them a grave injustice. A chameleon can alter its colour within half a minute, but an octopus or cuttlefish can do it in seconds, and their changes are much faster and more varied than the famous reptile's. Many cephalopods use these rapid colour changes for communicating with one another and even for mesmerising their prey, in addition to the obvious function of camouflage against their surroundings. An octopus can disappear before your eyes within seconds, altering not only its colour but also the texture of its skin in order to blend in. A wonderful example of communication is a cuttlefish's ability to use one side of its body to display a 'come hither' message to a potential partner, while the other side sends a 'keep well away' signal to a rival of the same sex. Mixed messages indeed.

These rapid and complex colour changes arise from cells within the animal's skin called chromatophores and iridiophores, which work in concert with each other. Chromatophores contain pigment and can be expanded by the contraction of small muscles around their periphery. They could be visualised as tiny, clear, pigment-containing bags, so their colour is most visible when they are drawn out into a flat plate by the surrounding muscles. Conversely, when the muscles are relaxed, the pigment is concentrated as a tiny dot and the colour is less apparent, helping to explain why a sickly or dead cephalopod often appears virtually white. Chromatophores come in a variety of colours that can occur in different layers or groups within the skin, and in some cephalopods their effect is enhanced by a deeper layer of iridiophores. These are cells that can differentially reflect and polarise light depending on how densely they are packed together. Colour at any spot on the skin and at any one time depends on which chromatophores are expanded and the state of any iridiophores, with cells of a third type, leucophores, acting as further reflectors and contributing to the animals' distinctive white markings.

LEFT: Within seconds, this cuttlefish changed colour as it jetted away from a dark background of kelp onto pale sand.

The chromatophores and iridiophores are under nervous control, operated by an advanced brain, so a cuttlefish presumably finds it as easy to change the colour of a patch of skin as we do to move an arm or a finger. It is still not clear how this is all done, given that cephalopods are conventionally 'colour-blind', but the answer may lie in their impressive ability to detect changes in contrast and, remarkably, tiny variations in the polarisation of light. As a further example of how much there is still to learn about these amazing animals, there is even some molecular evidence that cephalopod chromatophores are photosensitive – so their skin itself might be able to detect light (Kingston *et al.* 2015).

We generally see no more than six cephalopod species around the British Isles, out of approximately 850 worldwide, but, happily, some of these multi-skilled creatures are sufficiently abundant for many divers and snorkellers to experience those special encounters with them.

Meeting the uncommonly talented Common Cuttlefish

Sepia officinalis, the Common Cuttlefish, is the species we generally see underwater, and whose white cuttlebone can be found washed up on beaches in large numbers, particularly after storms. Males can reach a body length of 45cm, females around 30cm. They have the characteristic cuttlefish form of a broad, slightly flattened body with a fringing fin running down each side, an impressive head dominated by a pair of large eyes, plus a cluster of eight arms, behind which lurk two highly extendable tentacles. There are two other smaller species, *S. elegans* (the Elegant Cuttlefish) and *S. orbignyana* (the Pink Cuttlefish), that also occur in the British Isles, but they prefer warmer southern waters and both, especially the latter, are rare inshore.

An encounter with a Common Cuttlefish is much more likely in southern and western parts of Britain and Ireland than in the north and east, and in the warmer spring and summer months. They move into shallow coastal waters to breed in the spring, and whilst youngsters and adults can often be seen as late as November, they generally migrate offshore for the winter and can be found as deep as 200m. However, cuttlefishes are not found in very deep water because the multi-chambered cuttlebone contains gas as part of its advanced buoyancy control function and would implode under extreme pressure.

Interactions

If you snorkel or scuba dive out from a sandy beach, flanked or scattered with rocky areas, in the south or southwest of Britain over the summer months, you stand a reasonable chance of meeting this wonderful creature. Some places are obviously better than others, and Torbay in Devon, with its shelter from prevailing southwesterly winds and many suitable habitats including seagrass meadows, is a particular hotspot for cuttlefish encounters. Such meetings can have a lasting effect on the observer, and this was demonstrated by a friend of Paul's whom he took for a first 'try dive' in a couple of metres of water at Brixham. The stirred-up water close to the beach and long, tangling seaweed fronds were somewhat unappealing to the novice until, once away from the weed, he met a cuttlefish. Instead of jetting away it ran through a repertoire of colour changes right in front of the new diver's eyes. In that moment, Paul's friend was hooked – and, 15 years on, remains an avid scuba diver. Similarly, Frances has never forgotten an encounter with an Australian Giant Cuttlefish *S. apama*. Testing her diving buddy husband's patience, she lay on the sand in front of a small cave where she suspected one might be in residence. Sure enough, after a few minutes of gently wiggling her fingers in the sand, the cuttlefish emerged and reached out a single tentacle to stroke the back of her hand, its innate curiosity finally overcoming its fear.

When cuttlefish are unsettled by an intruding presence, they may simply jet away, but they can also show a particular reaction where two of their arms are raised in what is known as the 'flamboyant display'. Among filamentous algae, it can aid camouflage, but it often appears when the cuttlefish is nowhere near any seaweed. Divers joke that a cuttlefish has given them the V-sign, and it does indeed send a very specific message, roughly as follows: 'hey large predator, I'm watching you and know exactly what you're up to. I'll be able to escape or even damage you if you attack, so it would be much better for you to buzz off and try to catch something else!'

Paul and other underwater photographers even report being deliberately approached by cuttlefish, especially around dusk. They seem eager to take advantage of the divers' camera lights to spot potential prey. At Chesil Beach in Dorset, two cuttlefish waited to grab sandeels that emerged from the sand as Paul moved across the seabed and disturbed them at the start of a dive. Once he had adjusted his buoyancy and stopped stirring up the sand, the cuttlefish lost interest and swam off.

Confusing colours

The more times you meet and spend time with cuttlefishes, the more aspects of their colour-change artistry you see. An individual might descend onto a patch of sand or gravel and instantly match it for colour and pattern, aided by raising bumps in their skin for texture. On other seabed types, such as one with larger stones of different colours, a dramatic pattern may be adopted with a large white square in the centre of the back and matching white bands at the head and tail, which are surprisingly effective in breaking up the animal's outline. Alternatively, a cuttlefish might swim slowly away and, as you cautiously follow it, change colour to blend in with the alternating kelp-covered and sandy areas that it is moving across. Watching them carefully, Paul has observed that they are skilfully matching the background you are seeing them against, rather than simply the seabed that they are directly above. If the cuttlefish crosses paths with a potential competitor, a large wrasse for example, dark rings may appear around its eyes and/or a dark patch on its brow and large spots on the rear of its body, all indicating it is startled or annoyed.

A cuttlefish with the well-known 'white square pattern' that helps obscure its outline. It is resting among some of its less sophisticated molluscan relatives (mussels) under Brighton Pier.

Cuttlefish hunting skills

As with all animals, whether on land or underwater, the most satisfying cuttlefish observations come when they simply ignore you and get on with their lives. With patience and stillness, as long as you are in the right place, their hunting techniques can then be fully appreciated. The best locations seem to be popular dive spots where the local cuttlefish population has had the chance to get used to these clumsy bubbling aliens, and worked out that they mean no harm and may even keep larger predators (such as seals and Conger Eels *Conger conger*) away.

The cuttlefish's equipment for catching its prey is highly effective, with the lobed ends of the two long tentacles and the inner surface of the eight shorter arms all armed with gripping suckers. Once captured, prey is torn up by hard chitinous jaws hidden beneath the arms. The jaws are described as a 'beak' because of their shape, and a cuttlefish bite is accompanied by an injection of venom from salivary glands. A hunting strike starts with the cuttlefish clearly focusing on its prey while changing its body patterning (and sometimes texture), often raising some of its arms and moving into position to line itself up with the potential victim. If that animal is a prawn, shrimp or small fish, the cuttlefish then shoots out its pair of long tentacles to seize it and bring it back to the arms, which then pull it into the mouth. When the prey is a crab, a cuttlefish approaches (usually from behind) and 'jumps' to seize it with partially open arms, without using its tentacles. While their arms and tentacles may be far from mammalian, the stalking technique of cuttlefish certainly makes you realise why they are sometimes called 'cats of the sea'.

Paul's favourite observations of cuttlefish hunting have been at Porthkerris Cove on the Lizard in Cornwall, a superb spot for a dive or snorkel to watch a variety of marine life in action. On this particular occasion, a group of about a dozen cuttlefish were hunting Two-spotted Gobies *Gobiusculus flavescens* amongst seaweed close to the beach. This species is an unusual goby in that, rather than resting on the seabed, it spends most of its time hovering well above it – a dangerous habit when a hungry cuttlefish is around. In addition to getting an excellent view of their stalking technique, Paul was able to

ABOVE: Cuttlefish beaks (jaws) left over from a diner's meal in Spain and kept by Frances as interesting curios, much to the surprise of the waiter.

BELOW: A cuttlefish shooting out its two long tentacles to grasp a hapless goby from a shoal. The action is extremely fast and is rarely captured on camera.

Coastal Seas

LEFT TO RIGHT FROM TOP: This cuttlefish made several rapid colour changes just before grabbing for prey, and then reverted to a more typical 'resting' pattern while it ingested its victim. Altering skin patterns before a strike is thought to distract prey from spotting the cuttlefish's rapidly approaching tentacles (see photo on page 283).

watch how each cuttlefish made rapid colour changes immediately before striking with its tentacles. The nature of these changes varied between individuals: some flashed an overall white colouration, while others ran through a sequence of different shades of mottled brown. Changes like this are thought to function by mesmerising the prey as it watches the patterns on the cuttlefish's back, distracting it from the tentacles that are rapidly approaching from a slightly different direction. The technique certainly worked on those gobies.

What Paul didn't see, but what has been reported from another site by diving biologist friend Nick Owen, was a pair of cuttlefish appearing to work together. Here, one of the individuals grabbed small fish that were being distracted by the other's rapidly changing colour pattern, then they swapped roles so the second could also get a good meal. This type of observation enhances the cuttlefish's deserved reputation for intelligence, and there is plenty of other evidence to back this up. In a recent experimental study by Schnell *et al.* (2021), for instance, cuttlefish demonstrated self-control in terms of learning to wait for a better reward than if they simply seized the first food item that was on offer. The ability to 'delay gratification' in this way demonstrated cognitive capacity comparable to that of the brightest non-human mammals and birds. This fascinating study also showed, for the first time, a link between self-control and learning performance of individuals in an animal other than a primate.

Cuttlefish breeding: courtship, competition and care

To be in with a chance of observing the complexities of cuttlefish courtship in the wild, Paul will often visit the types of habitat they favour for breeding, particularly seagrass meadows (see Chapter 6) and stands of the brown seaweed *Halidrys siliquosa*, often called Sea Oak (a name also used for a different species), both of which provide good attachment for cuttlefish eggs. Cuttlefishes may be intelligent, but when it comes to finding a partner they seem to have trouble identifying male from female. A male cuttlefish starts the whole process by greeting any other individual that he meets (male or female) with a display of intense 'zebra' stripes on his back. At the same time, he extends his outer arm towards his potential mate. By now this is marked with a distinctive signal of very bold stripes running across most of it and characteristic bright white spots nearer to its tip. If the other cuttlefish is male, it returns the same signals and there may be an aggressive contest where the two protagonists circle each other, displaying and even fighting and biting. If, however, the recipient of his 'I am a male' signals does not return them, it is assumed to be female and courtship then proceeds.

The male cuttlefish woos the female by swimming alongside her and showing off plenty more of his bold zebra stripes, while the female responds with a mottled pattern or zebra stripes of her own, but never with an outstretched arm. The male suitor also caresses his

ABOVE: A male cuttlefish showing bold stripes on his arms as he vies for the attention of females. One of the others may also be a male but is not making it obvious in the presence of such a dominant individual.

partner by drawing his arms gently across her head, back and arms. Mating then occurs: he holds her by the head and passes a package of sperm into a receiving oviduct within her mantle cavity. The sight of cuttlefish in this head-to-head embrace is memorable but quite rare, while the fascinating sight of a female subsequently depositing her eggs is much more common. She painstakingly ties each egg to seagrass, seaweeds or even man-made structures such as wrecks with

RIGHT: A pair of mating cuttlefish; the male on the right is grasping the female on the left by her head so he can pass her a packet of sperm, whilst an intruder tries to get in on the action.

LEFT: A male cuttlefish (top) guarding a female as she prepares to lay her eggs. The pair may have mated some time ago, but the female stores the sperm for fertilisation until just before laying. The attentive male will try to repel rivals and thus ensure his paternity.

BELOW: Clusters of cuttlefish eggs attached to brown seaweed.

its own little strap, often carefully blowing away any sediment with a gentle puff of water before each attachment. She is usually accompanied by her male partner, who stays very close and often strokes her back with his arms while she works. This apparent encouragement looks endearing, but there may be a simple biological explanation. The eggs being laid are only fertilised within the female's arms just before she attaches them, with sperm that may have been received many days before and since stored. By staying close by throughout, the male is ready to repel any last-minute approaches from competitors and so guarantee his paternity. The eggs are dyed black with ink, and their size and the way they are placed in bunches makes their name of 'sea grapes' very apt. Unlike octopuses, cuttlefishes do not provide any parental care after egg-laying, and after 2–3 months a perfectly formed miniature cuttlefish breaks out from each egg.

Within the 'sea grapes', it is not just growth that goes on. As they develop with time, the black pigment in each egg case dissipates so it becomes more transparent, and the baby cuttlefishes can observe the world around them from within. An amazing study carried out by researchers in France in 2008 demonstrated that newly hatched

Common Cuttlefish have a preference for prey they have been able to see from inside the egg while they were developing (Darmaillacq *et al.* 2008). Learning from chemical cues detected before birth has been shown in other animals, but these cuttlefish experiments were designed so that only sight could be responsible, and it was the first instance of embryonic visual learning found in any animal. Cuttlefish can also show an awareness of danger within the egg, recognising what might wish to eat them. Observations on embryos of the Indian and Pacific Ocean Pharaoh Cuttlefish *Sepia pharaonis*, facilitated by the totally transparent egg cases of this species, demonstrated both innate and learned responses to predators and non-predators (Mezrai *et al.* 2020).

The adult Common Cuttlefish dies soon after breeding, and one of the most astonishing aspects of their lives is that such advanced and sophisticated animals live for no more than two years.

Fishing for cuttlefish

For those of us who love meeting and watching cuttlefish, a recently returned fishing boat with crates of dead cuttlefish awash with their own ink is a distressing sight. A large fishery operates for them on the south coast of England, with its quarry sometimes called 'black gold' because of their ink and high value, and they are caught by both offshore trawling and inshore traps. The traps are set in areas where cuttlefish come to breed and sometimes use live females as bait. Although trapping is generally regarded as being more selective than trawling, a problem with cuttlefish traps is that the breeding animals may attach their eggs to the pots. This means when they are hauled up and cleaned, the eggs are destroyed. A major concern is that, as of 2024, the fishery remains largely unregulated, with no size limits, closed periods or catch quotas, and it is a particular worry that huge numbers may be caught in trawls before they can breed.

In recognition of the special nature and appeal of cuttlefish, as well as the threat of a burgeoning but poorly controlled fishery, a group of enterprising University of Plymouth

BELOW: 'Black gold': large box containing around 450kg of cuttlefish in a fish market; the black marks all around the box are from cuttlefish ink.

students turned their MSc project into a conservation charity officially registered in 2022. The Cuttlefish Conservation Initiative has helped to raise awareness of these fascinating creatures and the threats they face, created a monitoring scheme for cuttlefish (Project Sepia), supported research on how the fishery can be more sustainable, and campaigned for changes to regulations.

Miniature cuttlefish or bobtail squid?

Observant snorkellers and divers sometimes spot what looks like a tiny cuttlefish on a sandy seabed. It may indeed be a recently hatched Common Cuttlefish but it could, instead, be a more mature Atlantic Bobtail Squid *Sepiola atlantica*. This chubby relative has quite a different form from the Common Cuttlefish, more rounded and with lobe-like fins. It has the endearing habit of peering upwards at you with its bulbous eyes from a part-buried position. It is known more accurately as the 'Little Cuttle', since in spite of its common name, it is not a squid and shares many characteristics with its larger cuttlefish relatives, including the ability to release a cloud of ink. Describing it as a 'cloud' probably overstates the case, and 'blotch' would be more accurate, but it is intriguing to witness how it draws your eye, while the animal itself seems to disappear as it turns pale and jets off in a different direction. Frances has unearthed these charming animals using a wide push net at low water on sandy Cornwall beaches, and Paul has found them with the same method in Norfolk.

BELOW: Atlantic Bobtail Squid or 'Little Cuttle' *Sepiola atlantica* among seagrass (left) and a mating pair (right). One of the delights of these tiny 5cm long cephalopods is that the individual colour cells (chromatophores) controlling their colour show up clearly.

Octopuses: the ocean's intellectuals

While meetings with octopuses in the seas around the British Isles have been (until recently) much rarer than those with cuttlefish, their reputation for intelligence and advanced behaviour is even more lofty. Stories abound of how they learn to tackle puzzles, develop strategies for escaping and getting food, and interact with humans. A resident octopus at the National Marine Aquarium in Plymouth could obviously recognise the staff, because her reaction to different individuals varied dramatically. She seemed to take against some in particular and jet water at them, for instance, when they approached her tank. The preferences persisted with time but were never easily explained by the appearance or behaviour of the people involved. A wonderfully graphic example of positive human interaction with an octopus was depicted in the hugely popular Oscar-winning Netflix documentary *My Octopus Teacher*, released in 2020. It was filmed in South Africa, but the same species, the Common Octopus *Octopus vulgaris*, is found in our waters, as described below.

Which octopus is common?

If you can see the whole of an octopus, its sack-like globular body and eight sucker-bearing arms are unmistakeable, but the precise nature of sightings in the wild around the British Isles has changed with time. Over previous decades most encounters have been with the smaller Curled (or Lesser) Octopus *Eledone cirrhosa*, and these are usually most common around the north of Britain. They tend to be quite secretive and generally hunt at night. Paul remembers meeting six on a single night dive off the Isle of Man. You occasionally see them sitting out in the open, devouring the remains of a crab, but it is more usual to find a collection of dismembered crab parts around an entrance to a rocky crevice or a cavity underneath a large boulder. Deep inside the cavity, the eye or the tentacles of its owner, but no more, might just be visible. One of many remarkable features of octopuses (that is the correct plural) is the way they can squeeze their body, which lacks any hard skeleton, through the narrowest of openings as long as it is wider than their rigid beak jaws.

In some recent years, many more of the larger Common Octopus, very familiar around southern Europe and Africa (hence the name 'Common'), have been found in southwest Britain, particularly

ABOVE: An impressive Common Octopus *Octopus vulgaris*, showing the double row of large suckers on each arm and obvious wart-like bumps on its body.

LEFT: Curled Octopus *Eledone cirrhosa* photographed in the Isle of Man, where sightings on night dives are very common. Its slender tentacles have only a single row of suckers and, as seen here, curl up when at rest.

Cornwall. As well as their size, the clearest distinguishing feature is that they have a double row of suckers on their tentacles, in contrast to the Curled Octopus's single row.

The Common Octopus population increase is not just a recent phenomenon, and big booms, sometimes even described as 'plagues', were reported in 1900 and 1950. The exact reason behind these booms is unclear. Common Octopuses have recently been discovered breeding in Cornwall, but they are generally thought to reach our shores through migration of the adults or by drift of their planktonic young (a notable difference between most octopuses and cephalopods such as the Common Cuttlefish, that hatch into miniature versions of the adult). The distribution of Common Octopus sightings suggests they prefer warmer waters, and it seems that booms may follow unusually mild winters, so we might see them more regularly as a result of the changing climate. Divers have had many wonderful sightings of large Common Octopuses at certain spots, particularly in Cornwall, and some travel from a long way away to see them, although such journeys may end in disappointment. When one group arrived at their destination, they were greeted by being told that a large Grey Seal *Halichoerus grypus* had just been seen at the surface playing with the unmistakeable remains of a large octopus's tentacles.

There is no well-established fishery for octopuses around Britain, although large numbers are caught as bycatch in trawls and pots during population booms. The situation is very different in southern Europe where increasing demand and intensive fishing threaten populations to the extent that octopus 'farming' has even been suggested. These proposals, however, raise grave concerns about the welfare of such sensitive and intelligent animals, which are usually solitary, quite apart from the sustainability of using other marine resources to support raising them in such quantities.

Remote romance but exhausting egg care

Mating in octopuses is often literally done at arm's length. There are no noticeable courtship patterns or postures in *Octopus vulgaris*, and a male either leaps onto a female's body to pass her a packet of sperm with a specialised arm or sits a little distance away and passes it to her with the arm outstretched. Such a lackadaisical approach by a male may leave him open to competition, and two male Common Octopuses have been observed mating with the same female by this method. In their fascinating book, *Cephalopod Behaviour*, Hanlon and Messenger (2018) even report an observation of six male California Two-spot Octopuses *O. bimaculatus* all trying to mate with one female at the same time.

It is interesting that, despite their rather laissez-faire mating habits, octopuses guard their eggs conscientiously, unlike most other cephalopods. After laying her eggs in a sheltered spot, the female Common Octopus never leaves it and stops feeding. She continuously cleans and aerates the eggs for the whole brooding period of 1–3 months, which can be a quarter of her lifetime. Not surprisingly, a female dies soon after her eggs hatch. The last act of care is often to jet water forcefully at her eggs to drive the hatching young out of her lair and into more open water where they are less vulnerable to seabed predators.

Squids

With their slim, approximately cylindrical bodies and more prominent and powerful-looking fins, squids look rather like racing versions of cuttlefish, which is an entirely accurate impression. Worldwide, these rapid open-water swimmers are the most abundant cephalopods, but around the British Isles they are elusive and are seen much more rarely than cuttlefishes or octopuses. The best chance of spotting them seems to be on night dives in certain spots that include wrecks along the Cornish and Dorset coasts. Squids encountered can include the large *Loligo* species, *L. forbesii* (called the Veined or Long-finned Squid) and *L. vulgaris* (the Common or European Squid), plus the smaller and more delicate *Alloteuthis subulata*. Some sources refer to the latter species as the European Common Squid, demonstrating the potential pitfalls of common names.

BELOW: A small squid photographed on a night dive. Squids are important food for many predators, and, although numerous, are elusive and rarely seen by snorkellers and divers. Their speed makes the different species difficult to identify.

Squids can also be attracted to boats at night by shining a powerful light down into the water. Often a buzz of planktonic animals will also follow the beam up, like moths lured to a street lamp. In warmer water, lights are commonly used to attract squids into fishing nets. In British seas, targeted fisheries trawl for squids, mainly the *Loligo* species, around the west of Scotland and the southwest of England. As with Common Cuttlefish, the fisheries are almost completely unregulated, so there are worries about their sustainability and the vulnerability of squid populations.

Whilst divers rarely see adults, it is a different story with their egg capsules. The distinctive white sausage-like egg capsules of *Loligo* squids are often spotted and can regularly be found attached to Pink Sea Fans *Eunicella verrucosa* or in large bunches on the wrecks that the squids visit. The eggs of *Alloteuthis* are smaller, more transparent and much less obvious.

What a nerve

Squids caught around the British Isles have a special place in medical history, as their axons (nerve fibres) have been used in a great deal of the fundamental research on nerve function. The axons are relatively easy to study because they are so thick, up to 1mm across. This allows the fast transmission of nerve signals that is necessary for the squid's rapid, jet-propelled escape to be coordinated. The axons of vertebrate animals are nowhere near as large, because they have evolved an insulating sheath of myelin around the nerve fibres that allow electrical impulses to transmit quickly and efficiently.

Sentience and welfare

In the UK (and EU), aspects of domestic animal welfare have long been included in various laws. In 2021 the Animal Welfare (Sentience) Bill was introduced to parliament. It recognises that vertebrate animals are sentient, with the ability to feel pain and distress. Following various scientific reviews, the Bill was extended to include cephalopod molluscs (plus decapod crustaceans such as crabs, lobsters and the like). Whilst this will not protect cephalopods from being caught, or immediately change fishing methods, their inclusion will hopefully provide a legal way for preventing unnecessary suffering in the future. Cephalopods are also widely used in scientific research, and as far back as 1993 it was deemed likely that the Common Octopus was intelligent enough to feel pain and distress, and so this was the first invertebrate animal to be added to the UK Animals (Scientific Procedures) Act 1986, meaning that its use in research is regulated. A further 2013 amendment to this Act added all remaining living cephalopods. A major concern remains, however, about the way such sophisticated animals are often killed by brutal methods when caught for food. Certainly, having met these remarkable creatures first-hand, neither of us could ever contemplate catching or eating them.

Artistic displays

Cephalopods have featured widely in the art and legends of many different cultures throughout the ages. Octopuses are a common theme in paintings, on ceramics and in Roman mosaics, though often depicted with the wrong number of arms. Octopuses and squids in particular are widely eaten, especially in Mediterranean countries, and this is probably one reason why they feature so much. Back in 1969, Ringo Starr of the Beatles even wrote a song called 'Octopus's Garden', reflecting the habit of these versatile animals of picking up stones and other objects to 'decorate' around their home dens. He apparently learned about this when eating squid.

Perhaps the most widely perpetuated myth concerning cephalopods is that of the Kraken, a giant octopus-like or squid-like creature large enough to envelop and sink sailing ships. Thought to have originated in Scandinavian folklore, this monster famously appears in French author Jules Verne's classic book *Twenty Thousand Leagues Under the Sea*. Similar myths can be found in tales from outside Europe, in Japan, New Zealand and the Caribbean. Such mythical cephalopods were almost certainly inspired by rare sightings of Giant Squid *Architeuthis dux* and other large squid species. The Natural History Museum in London has a preserved specimen 8.6m long (including tentacles). Whilst these live in the ocean depths, specimens or tentacles do sometimes wash up on shores around the British Isles.

Over the centuries, octopuses have featured widely in art, especially around the Mediterranean, as here in an ancient Roman mosaic from Treviso, Italy.

Their evident sophistication and intelligence, coupled with a nature that is somehow alien to us vertebrates, often makes cephalopods the most memorable sea creatures that people meet, whether this is in their natural environment or in an artificial one. An octopus is often seen as the highlight of a visit to a public aquarium, for example, and divers in our seas regularly name the cuttlefish as their favourite marine animal. It is the frequency of encountering the Common Cuttlefish which has made it so prominent in this chapter, especially in terms of photographs showing various aspects of behaviour, but we hope the immense appeal of the whole group has also come across.

Living together: shared lives and unwelcome lodgers

chapter eleven

If you see a caterpillar munching its way through your hard-won crop of cabbages, it will be obvious what the caterpillar is getting out of it. However, the wealth of complex relationships between different organisms, which go far beyond one simply eating another, is one of the most fascinating aspects of natural habitats and ecosystems. Perhaps the best-known example in the marine world, made famous through television and cinema, is 'Nemo', the tropical clownfish beloved of children worldwide, who lives in the safe embrace of a large stinging anemone. However, a wide variety of equally intriguing relationships can be seen and appreciated in our own shallow coastal seas, and there are surely many more waiting to be discovered by any diver, snorkeller or rock-pooler with the time and patience.

When members of two or more different species are normally found together within a long-term relationship, it is known as symbiosis. Historically, and still in everyday language, this has tended to mean that both parties gain from the association. In biology, however, symbiosis is now more generally used as an umbrella term for all such persistent relationships. This includes those where both parties benefit (mutualism), those where one benefits with no harm to the other (commensalism), and those where one gains at the expense of the other (parasitism). Relationships vary greatly in their strength, and there may not be clear distinctions between the different types. 'Costs' and 'benefits' to each party can change depending on their stage of development, and can vary with environmental conditions.

OPPOSITE PAGE:
Small fish (juvenile gadoids) sheltering among the tentacles of a large Lion's Mane jellyfish *Cyanea capillata*.

It is a complex subject! Just because we cannot see or currently understand the benefits or detriments to one of the participants does not mean that there aren't any.

A classic terrestrial example that took many years to untangle is the dependence of the rare Large Blue Butterfly *Phengaris arion* on the red ant *Myrmica sabuleti*. The butterfly caterpillars initially feed on the flower buds of wild thyme *Thymus* spp., but then drop to the ground and are bodily carried by ants into their underground nest. Here they overwinter, feeding on ant grubs and in turn providing the adult ants with an energy-rich sugary secretion, until the caterpillars pupate and emerge in summer as adults. The Large Blue became extinct in the British Isles in 1979, but once the relationship was properly understood it was successfully reintroduced, though it remains globally endangered. Apart from the intrinsic interest of such relationships, this is why we are both happy to spend precious underwater or shore time helping to elucidate them. Effective conservation is not possible without detailed life-history information. In this chapter we describe a small selection of fascinating symbiotic relationships that we have come across over many years and that, with a careful search, can be observed relatively easily in the shallow waters and on shores around the British Isles.

Hermit crabs and their companions

Hermit crabs and their range of 'hangers-on' provide some wonderful and relatively obvious examples of different types and strengths of relationships. But, even before their living partners are considered, these strange but oddly endearing crustaceans are reliant on other species. Their crustacean 'armour' only covers the front part of their body and the soft, unprotected abdomen (rear section) is adapted to cling onto the internal structure of an empty gastropod mollusc (snail) shell whose owner has died and the soft tissues have decayed or been eaten. The shell's quality as a hermit crab home is partly determined by the fate of its previous molluscan owner. If, for example, it perished at the claws of a large crab, the shell may be partially broken. It is interesting to see that badly damaged shells are often occupied by hermit crabs in Scottish sea lochs, whereas on open coasts, where the supply of empty shells is presumably greater, they would be given a wide berth by these normally fastidious animals.

Living together: shared lives and unwelcome lodgers

LEFT: A large male Common Hermit Crab *Pagurus bernhardus* (holding a much smaller mate), equipped with the double defence of a Parasitic Anemone *Calliactis parasitica* on the back of his shell and a colony of hydroids around the front.

The empty gastropod shell serves as a mobile shelter for the hermit crab into which it can withdraw when danger threatens, with its largest claw often forming a barrier at the shell entrance. The shell also provides scope for a variety of travelling companions. True 'hermits' are supposed to live on their own, in isolation, but it seems that hermit crabs rarely live up to their name. The advantage to these partner organisms in living on or in a hermit crab shell, as opposed to the living armour of a 'regular' crab, is that the hermit's shell may be reused by another hermit if the owner outgrows it or dies. So the hitchhikers retain their transport, whereas a 'regular' crab's armour will be abandoned once it has been shed at a moult.

Anemone friends

The most prominent partner of the Common Hermit Crab *Pagurus bernhardus*, found all around the coastline of the British Isles, is the misleadingly named 'Parasitic' Anemone. When attached to a hermit crab's shell home, the anemone benefits from food fragments released during the crab's messy eating. It also gets transported to new feeding locations and may bend over and use its tentacles to pick up food items as the hermit crab walks along. The anemone's name is misleading (and the libel is repeated in its scientific name,

Calliactis parasitica) because it is clearly a mutualistic relationship, with the anemone's stinging cells helping to deter potential predators of the crab; octopuses, for example, learn to avoid crabs carrying the anemone. The partnership is usually quite relaxed, in that both the hermit crab and anemone species involved are often found living apart. It is thought to be generally instigated by the anemone, which reaches over and latches on to the shell occupied by a passing hermit crab using its tentacles, then frees its base from its current attachment and somersaults over onto the new mobile residence. Hermit crabs generally stay still to aid this process but have also been observed prodding the anemone to activate it and promote the transfer.

Paul has noticed how a greater proportion of Common Hermit Crabs in seagrass beds seem to carry Parasitic Anemones, and research with a different, Mediterranean species of hermit crab but the same anemone species could perhaps provide an explanation. In 1979, researchers described how hermit crabs in their experiments eventually stopped showing any activity with anemones after being kept in tanks with no potential predators but regained their enthusiasm for the relationship when they received water that had contained octopuses or cuttlefishes (Ross and von Boletzky 1979). Seagrass beds are often a hunting ground for cuttlefish, so the thought that hermit crabs might sense their presence chemically and more actively seek an anemone partner is intriguing. Furthermore, a

RIGHT: Unusually, this Parasitic Anemone was being carried by a small Hairy Hermit Crab *Pagurus cuanensis* (see seagrass leaves for scale) that was struggling to walk under the weight.

Living together: shared lives and unwelcome lodgers

weakened partnership between hermit crabs and this sea anemone in the absence of predators implies that carrying one does incur some 'cost' for the hermit crab.

The relationship between another hermit crab and sea anemone pair in our home waters is much more intimate regardless of outside encouragement. The Anemone Hermit Crab *Pagurus prideaux* and Cloak Anemone *Calliactis palliata*, both aptly named, are very rarely recorded living apart. This type of association is often termed obligatory. The anemone's base is wrapped around the home shell of its host, so its tentacles are positioned directly below the crab's mouth, in the perfect position to catch dropped food. These crabs have also been observed deliberately feeding their passenger by placing food close to its mouth, but the most remarkable aspect of the relationship is that the anemone uses its base to secrete a hard, chitinous extension to the crab's shell home and so frees it from the usual need to move into a larger shell as it grows. This is obviously a 'win–win' strategy, as the anemone retains the services of its 'chauffeur' and is not abandoned, while the hermit crab is released from the dangers and stresses associated with moving house.

The Cloak Anemone has distinctive pink spots on its base, but these can be obscured by a dusting of silt in the muddy habitats where the crabs often live. In this case, their presence is quickly revealed if a crab collides with any object on the seabed while it is scuttling

BELOW: This pair of Anemone Hermit Crabs *Pagurus prideaux* each has its own Cloak Anemone *Calliactis palliata*, an association thought to be obligatory. The anemone's base is wrapped round the shell occupied by the crab, with its tentacles positioned under the crab's mouth to catch food scraps.

Coastal Seas

ABOVE: The Cloak Anemone on this hermit crab has released its acontia, sticky white threads that carry extra batteries of stinging cells, as a supplementary defence mechanism.

along. When the anemone is nudged in this way, it releases copious sticky white threads (known as acontia) armed with stinging cells as a further deterrent against predatory attack. Even with this extra protection, the defence is not 100 per cent effective. Swimming crabs, with sharp claws well suited to prising a small hermit crab from its home, can occasionally be spotted devouring their prey with a peeled-away and now discarded cloak anemone lying nearby. Look for this hermit–anemone twosome on sublittoral sand and gravel, mixed with stones and shell. Stranded pairs can also be found on the beach after storms, and young anemones are sometimes seen attached to intertidal rocks and shells.

Other hermit crab hitchhikers

The Commensal Ragworm *Neanthes fucata* is another well-known hermit crab companion, partly because of its role as the third character in Julia Donaldson's delightful children's book *Sharing a Shell*. The worm is also a good example of the somewhat mysterious nature of such symbiotic relationships. Up to half of large *P. bernhardus* reportedly play host to one of these worms, which are also found free-living, but it is very unusual to see one. Despite often closely watching and filming hermit crabs while they are feeding, Paul has only ever observed the worms on two occasions. One displayed their typical behaviour, reaching out just far enough from the whelk shell occupied by the hermit crab to snatch a morsel of food from amongst the hermit's mouthparts, before quickly retreating back into the shell. On the other occasion, a hermit crab was walking towards some carrion on the sandy seabed (a large dead spider crab) and its worm extended a large part of its body out and away from the shell. The worm could presumably smell the forthcoming banquet and reacted with enthusiasm. While the behaviour of the worm was different on these two occasions, they did both emerge from exactly the same (and reportedly the 'standard') position in the shell, just behind the crab's head and on its right-hand side.

The relationship between crab and worm starts after a juvenile ragworm, living within its tube in the seabed sediment, senses the vibrations caused by a hermit crab dragging its shell along nearby. The worm then extends much of its body from the burrow to make searching movements and, as soon as the crab is near enough, makes a break for the safe space within the shell, where it secretes a mucus tube in which to live. The worm's eagerness to move house is understandable, as the benefits it obtains are obvious, namely safety and access to plentiful food, but things seem less clear-cut for the hermit crab. It is generally assumed to receive no benefit (hence the worm's 'commensal' name), but it has been tentatively suggested that the worm might perform a cleaning function in preventing the build-up of the crab's faeces in the back of the shell. If, in the absence of a worm, the accumulation of faeces might irritate the crab sufficiently for it to move home and be subjected to all the risks associated with that process, the worm could be providing a valuable service in return for board and lodging after all. Another speculation is that aggressive worms could perhaps deter more damaging parasites from settling with the hermit crabs, along the lines of 'the enemy of my enemy is my friend'. The fact that hermit crabs have been found to recognise and not attack their commensal worm supports these notions.

Obvious and abundant although less familiar co-travellers of hermit crabs include hydroids, which are colonial relatives of sea anemones. There are several closely related hydroid species that live on hermit crabs, but around the British Isles the commonest is Hermit Crab Fur *Hydractinia echinata*. This delicate, centimetre-high

LEFT: A Commensal Ragworm *Neanthes fucata* (see underneath the crab's right eye) living within the shell of a Common Hermit Crab *Pagurus bernhardus*, making a grab for food from the mouthparts of its host.

RIGHT: This small Common Hermit Crab has a furry covering of protective hydroids *Hydractinia* sp.

hydroid can be found growing on rocks and other substrata, but most typically it forms an attractive pale pink 'fur' over the shell occupied by a Common Hermit Crab. The crawling planula hydroid larvae detect hermit crabs on which to settle from their movement, although chemicals produced by a bacterial biofilm are also reported to be involved. The larvae then metamorphose and grow into the colonial encrusting form. As is typical in hydroids, different polyps (individuals) in the colony are specialised for different roles and, interestingly, the presence of the crab and its respiratory currents affects the development and distribution of the different polyp types. Stinging polyps associated with defence, for example, predominate around the mouth of the shell and regress within a few days if the crab is removed experimentally from the shell, but redevelop if the crab is returned. The presence of the hydroid on a host hermit's shell is thought to protect it from losing the shell to a hostile takeover by another hermit crab, in addition to helping to deter predators.

Whilst they seem to have more than their fair share, hermit crabs are not the only ones to carry hitchhikers. Frances came across a tiny example when she dug up a Heart Urchin *Echinocardium cordatum* from its burrow in a muddy sand shore on Tresco in the Isles of Scilly. Attached to the long spines at the rear of the urchin by byssus threads was a small, pale bivalve mollusc called *Tellimya ferruginosa*. Young ones often attach to their host, whilst adults are frequently found in urchin burrows (see photo on page 150).

Living together: shared lives and unwelcome lodgers

Coats (and hats) of sponge

Most sponges grow attached to non-living, hard substrata such as rocks and shipwrecks, but some species of these enigmatic animals grow on a variety of other animals. However, the nature of the relationships between sponges and those that they envelop remains somewhat uncertain. Although firmly belonging to the animal kingdom (see Chapter 1), sponges show little of the behaviour we associate with typical animals, and it is easy to see why they were once considered to be plants. This means that any benefits there may be for the two parties are often difficult to ascertain.

Protective coats

A good example of an arrangement that is thought to benefit both parties concerns sponges such as the Sea Orange *Suberites ficus*, which are normally found growing on rocks but also regularly encrust living Queen Scallops *Aequipecten opercularis*. The theory is that the sponge is raised up from the seabed and is therefore more difficult for a predatory nudibranch (such as the Sea Lemon *Archidoris pseudoargus*) to reach and graze, while the bivalve gets a coat that is less easily grasped by the tube feet of a marauding starfish. This shared protection has

BELOW: Queen Scallop *Aequipecten opercularis* with a typical coat of orange sponge on its shell (perhaps being regarded with envy by the small hermit crab?).

305

(logically) been called protective mutualism. The sponge may well also taste unpleasant, since chemical deterrents are one of their very limited options for self-protection. Another explanation might be that whilst such sponges grow perfectly well on rocks and wrecks, they can expand their distribution, including into sediment areas, by means of the scallops. Whatever the reason, the incidence of sponges encrusting Queen Scallops around the British Isles is higher than would be expected by chance.

Given the helpful defensive attributes bestowed by the sponge, it is not surprising that a variety of molluscs have shells that have become adapted to be particularly attractive to settling sponge larvae. That, however, raises an intriguing follow-up question about the Boring Sponge *Cliona celata*. This is a species that chemically bores into limestone rock, but also into the shells of molluscs. It weakens the molluscs, either physically or in terms of resources, by diverting their energies from reproduction to shell reinforcement. Does the Boring Sponge benefit from an overall molluscan welcome, then 'betray' the favour by damaging its host? The sponge's impact may become more severe in the future, as laboratory experiments suggest that elevated ocean acidity, resulting from increasing levels of carbon dioxide in our atmosphere, could increase bioerosion rates of Boring Sponges on scallop shells (Duckworth and Peterson 2012).

Gastropod shells occupied by small hermit crabs, particularly the Hairy Hermit Crab *Pagurus cuanensis*, are often encased in impressive growths of sponge that in some instances dissolve and replace the shell, becoming the crab's complete replacement home. The mass of sponge can be many times larger than the hermit crab owner, so the crab's movement across the seabed and over obstacles seems to take herculean exertion. The effort appears to be worthwhile, however, because while large Shore Crabs *Carcinus maenas* prey enthusiastically on small hermit crabs by prising them out of their shells with sharp claws, they seem to ignore those enclosed in extensive sponge growths. Once again, questions are raised about the origin of the sponge–host partnership. It is very unusual to find sponge on the shells of the original mollusc shell owner, typically the Netted Dog Whelk *Tritia reticulata*, but, once occupied by hermits, large numbers of the shells are covered with orange or white sponge. Possible explanations are that the hermit crabs are very good at finding sponge-encrusted shells, or that the mollusc can use its greatly extendable foot to remove settling sponge larvae. However, we think it more likely that the sponge

LEFT: Hairy Hermit Crab *Pagurus cuanensis* with its shell encased in an impressive growth of sponge. When carried by a crab, sponges can benefit by being less vulnerable to predation, but this one is being grazed by a Painted Topshell *Calliostoma zizyphinum*.

larvae preferentially settle on shells occupied by hermit crabs. Netted Dog Whelks spend much of their time wholly or partially buried in seabed sediment, but the elevated position provided by a wandering hermit crab in a discarded shell will give the sponge not only better protection from predators but also better opportunities for filter-feeding. It imparts a certain air of unreality when, as a diver, you see a sponge apparently walking over the seabed. Frances has also seen small solitary cup corals *Heterocyathus* and *Heteropsammia* spp. doing something similar in the tropics. In this case the coral has settled and grown over an empty gastropod shell in which a sipunculid worm is living. The coral leaves a small hole at the base through which the worm can protrude and pull its coral home along.

There is much more certainty about how sponges make their way onto the backs of small spider crabs. One of Paul's favourite photographs (because of the story it tells rather than the image quality) shows how one of these crabs, an *Inachus* species, has chiselled out small pieces of the orange sponge on which it is sitting and painstakingly attached them to its armoured body and legs; there is no other possible explanation for what you see in the picture (see page 308). The beauty of this strategy is that the fragments of sponge readily grow into a complete sponge coat – the result of which can be seen on the little crab's neighbour in the photograph – although the process needs to be repeated every time the spider crab goes through a moult and emerges with new armour. The armour

ABOVE: This photograph (one of Paul's favourites) shows the sponge defences of these small *Inachus* sp. spider crabs as a 'work in progress'. The crab on the left has attached small chunks of sponge onto its armour, where they will grow to form a complete coat like that worn by the crab on the right.

is superbly adapted for this protective and camouflaging function, as it is covered in numerous tiny attachment hooks that resemble the sticky part of Velcro® fasteners. Paul likes to tell students at school talks that Velcro® was invented by spider crabs and not by the sportswear manufacturers they might have imagined.

Umbrella hats

We can conclude that sponge has a very valuable protective function for crabs because another species, the Sponge Crab *Dromia personata*, lacks the benefit of Velcro®-equipped armour, but instead devotes two pairs of its walking legs to continually holding a large sponge in position over its carapace. The attachment appears firm and permanent until the usually motionless crab (its alternative common name is Sleepy Crab) walks across the seabed and the sponge can be seen apparently slipping around on its back. Experiments have also shown that if one of these crabs is separated from its sponge 'hat', it can find the right one when offered a choice of similar adornments.

Sponges are of course not the only sessile animals that choose to make their home on a living hard substratum rather than an inert one. Perhaps surprisingly, there are several species of hard corals that live in shallow water around the British Isles, albeit they are small 'solitary' cup corals that do not form reefs. The commonest species is the Devonshire Cup Coral *Caryophyllia smithii*, which adorns vertical and steep rock faces (see Chapter 4). The pleasingly symmetrical oval shape of many individuals in the southwest of the British Isles is distorted by a tiny barnacle, *Adna anglica*. This species only grows attached to cup corals, in warmer southern waters. At just a few millimetres across, the barnacle presumably benefits from being raised above the rock surface, where it can filter-feed more effectively.

Cohabitation

Cooperative living arrangements do not always involve one animal living on another; the partners may just share a space. One well-known example can be seen in the often surprisingly beautiful, soft muddy habitats found in sheltered bays and sea lochs around Scotland's west coast (see Chapter 5). Despite being able to excavate its own burrows by carrying pellets of mud in its mouth, the distinctive Fries's Goby *Lesueurigobius friesii* (named after the Dutch scientist who discovered it) is often found residing in one occupied by a Norway Lobster *Nephrops norvegicus*. This small lobster species can excavate complex burrows, and it seems more likely that the fish benefits from the crustacean's work rather than vice versa. Once they are cohabiting, however, both parties may well gain advantage from the relationship. The goby is likely to obtain scraps that result from the Norway Lobster tearing up its food and may act, albeit unwittingly, as a look-out or sentinel in return. Gobies often rest nervously at the mouth of a burrow but rapidly dart down it at the slightest sign of disturbance. This could warn the crustacean of an approaching predator, such as a cod, skate or catshark, more quickly than its own senses. In tropical waters there is a proven mutualistic association between certain shrimps and gobies, and watching this delightful cooperation has often distracted Frances from her work during reef surveys.

We frequently observe cohabitation in rocky reef crevices and under overhangs between another distinctive, but shy, goby, the Leopard-spotted Goby *Thorogobius ephippiatus*, and the large Common Lobster *Homarus gammarus*. While the goby might similarly benefit from crumbs from the lobster's table, Paul suspects that the main

ABOVE: Sponge Crab *Dromia personata* holding a 'hat' of sponge in place with its rear legs. In the right position, the crab can be extremely difficult to spot among surrounding sponges.

ABOVE: Groups of Common Prawns *Palaemon serratus* often live around the lairs of Conger Eels *Conger conger* (as here) and lobsters, where they presumably live on scraps of food. It is not clear if or how they in turn benefit their large neighbours.

advantage it could receive is from the large crustacean deterring potential goby predators, such as sea scorpions or small Conger Eels *Conger conger*, from entering the crevice. The lobster itself is presumably too slow and clumsy to catch its small, rapid 'lodger', and may not benefit from the arrangement at all.

Fish may sometimes seek food from a crustacean's activity in a very deliberate way. On one memorable occasion while diving in the rich, current-swept habitat of Loch Carron in Scotland, Paul watched in fascination as one, then two Butterfish *Pholis gunnellus* followed a large Shore Crab as it walked across the seabed searching for food. Shore Crabs often hunt by prodding at the sand with their pointed legs as they walk along and are able to detect prey by touch or 'taste'. Once located and unearthed by the probing legs, the hapless prey can be seized by the crab's claws. Presumably in anticipation of this action, the Loch Carron Butterfish were keeping so close to the crab that they were sometimes being struck by its legs. It appeared that this discomfort was outweighed by the opportunity of grabbing a disturbed shrimp or worm before the crab could grasp it. We also give the example of Tompot Blennies *Parablennius gattorugine* getting mussel morsels from crabs under Brighton Pier in Chapter 8, while other small fish, particularly Painted Gobies *Pomatoschistus pictus*, can often be seen darting around any animals that are disturbing a sandy seabed including other fish (see photo on page 225), crabs, sea slugs and even human divers.

Living together: shared lives and unwelcome lodgers

LEFT: These mating Shore Crabs *Carcinus maenas* have attracted a crowd of gobies, presumably seeking any food disturbed from the sand by the crustaceans' amorous activities.

Powerful protectors

Perhaps the most famous example of an obligate association in the marine world, and of cohabitation and mutual benefit, is the one we referred to in the opening paragraph of this chapter, namely where tropical anemonefishes (often called clownfishes) gain protection from certain large sea anemones. While these particular animals are not found around the British Isles, we do have crustaceans that shelter among the tentacles of Snakelocks Anemones *Anemonia viridis*, a common species in shallow water on southern and western coasts of the British Isles. Like the clownfishes, the crustaceans gain protection from their home anemone's powerful stinging cells, but it is uncertain whether they return similar benefits to the anemone, such as cleaning and defence against potential attackers.

The most commonly seen anemone-dwelling crustaceans are the small spider crabs *Inachus* spp. that also diligently decorate their armour with sponge as described on page 307, an interesting case of multi-level protection. In some areas, virtually every Snakelocks Anemone has a crab resident, either sitting among the tentacles or more often sheltering beneath them around the anemone's base. Studies show that a crab can stay with the same host for months at a time and is much more likely to be predated by fish when away from the anemone, so it is easy to see why territorial disputes between the crabs over 'possession' of anemones are commonly observed.

Coastal Seas

ABOVE TOP: Small sponge-coated spider crabs (*Inachus* sp.) often shelter under the stinging tentacles of a Snakelocks Anemone *Anemonia viridis*.

ABOVE: An attractively coloured but hard-to-spot Anemone Shrimp *Periclimenes sagittifer* living permanently among the tentacles of a Snakelocks Anemone.

Another crustacean that lives with Snakelocks Anemones is the beautifully coloured Anemone Shrimp *Periclimenes sagittifer*, but it is hard to spot because of its small size and tendency to dwell deep among the anemone's tentacles. It was known from the Channel Islands and further south but was not recorded on the British mainland coast until Seasearch divers found it at Swanage in 2007 (see Chapter 4). It now appears to be spreading slowly along the south coast, and is also being seen for longer periods of the year. It may well be significant that both the spider crab and the shrimp choose to associate with Snakelocks Anemones: this species rarely retracts its tentacles, unlike most other anemones, and so may offer a much better protection 'deal' to residents.

Snakelocks Anemones are in fact real hotbeds of interspecific associations, because they also host single-celled symbiotic algae called zooxanthellae within their tissues, and this produces the vibrant colours of the green tentacles with purple tips seen in many individuals. In return for a place to live, and possibly essential nutrients, the algae share their photosynthetic products and so supplement the anemone's predatory diet, a similar arrangement to the zooxanthellae found in tropical reef-building corals.

Floating protection

We have already mentioned in Chapter 7 that there are six common species of true jellyfishes found around the British Isles, and that most people try hard to avoid them and their stings. It may seem incredible then that small fish, typically belonging to the cod family, often shelter among the tentacles of jellyfish, especially the Lion's

Mane *Cyanea capillata*. As with the Snakelocks Anemone described opposite, this is a case of defenceless animals gaining safety from another's powerful stinging cells, this time a floating predator. Lurking amongst a jellyfish's dangling tentacles, they are of course protected from larger fish predators, which are deterred by the stinging power of their jellyfish 'guardian'. The reliance on the jellyfish defence is clear to see when you swim close enough to worry the fish, because any of them that are outside the tentacle curtilage will quickly dart back within it. How the fish themselves avoid being stung has been the subject of different theories, but it appears that the skin mucus of the fish somehow becomes altered to send a 'don't sting me, I'm part of you' signal similar to that from the jellyfish's own tissues. This is the mechanism that prevents a jellyfish continually stinging itself as its tentacles inevitably collide with one another when the animal is swimming or drifting along.

Paul has spent a good deal of time, particularly while snorkelling, trying to get clear photographs or video footage to show the relationship. This has generally been a fruitless enterprise because the fish continuously try very hard to keep as much jellyfish as possible between themselves and an intruding camera. An amusing incident once occurred, however, when Paul got so close to a rather sickly Compass Jellyfish *Chrysaora hysoscella* that its accompanying

ABOVE: The small fish that associate with Lion's Mane Jellyfish *Cyanea capillata* usually dive into the protection of their tentacle home when approached.

group of very small Horse Mackerel *Trachurus trachurus* decided that his dangling dive kit looked like a better option and jumped ship. Paul had to swim very close to the jellyfish and persuade the small fish to transfer their allegiance back again, or they would have followed him in to the beach.

Troublesome guests

Mention the word 'parasite' and most people will immediately think of well-known examples such as leeches and tapeworms – but would perhaps be surprised that our seas are also home to a wide variety of parasites. Plants too can be parasitic, but here we are talking about animals that live on (ectoparasites) or inside (endoparasites) other animals and so gain sustenance and somewhere to live, usually to the detriment of their hosts. Marine parasites come in a huge range of sizes and originate from a wide variety of animal groups (both in terms of themselves and their hosts) and often have fascinating lifestyles. Internal parasites are obviously difficult to observe in the wild, though Frances has come across various marine examples in fish, either when dissecting them or when eating them. So we have restricted ourselves here to those a diver, snorkeller or angler might well come across. We find that we are constantly learning more about external parasites that live on fish, because fish are popular photographic subjects for divers.

Bloodsuckers

Who would expect the ecological and size equivalent of a vampire bat to be living in our coastal seas? In fact, there are two, though few people ever encounter them. These are the eel-shaped lampreys, among the largest of all parasites and obvious when spotted firmly clamped onto another fish, though very rarely seen by divers and snorkellers. Paul clearly remembers his only meeting with one when, surrounded by a shoal of large Pollack *Pollachius pollachius*, he became aware of one Pollack moving differently before noticing the strange object attached to it, undoubtedly a lamprey. He managed to snatch a quick photograph before the Pollack, a species always upset by a camera flash, dashed off into the gloom.

Although fish themselves, lampreys belong to a small, primitive and very different class of fish that, instead of jaws, have a circular toothed mouth disc that clamps onto fish and sometimes marine

Living together: shared lives and unwelcome lodgers

LEFT: The fearsome rasping disc of a River Lamprey *Lampetra fluviatilis.*

mammals such as seals. Sharp teeth on the disc rasp a hole in the victim's skin and introduce a substance that dissolves tissue and stops blood from coagulating so that it can be extracted as food. The lamprey encountered by Paul could have been either the Sea Lamprey *Petromyzon marinus* or the smaller River Lamprey *Lampetra fluviatilis*, but more likely the latter given its colour. Despite their 'Sea' and 'River' names, both species have similar lifestyles, spending their adult life feeding parasitically in the sea, then stopping feeding and moving up into rivers to lay their eggs and produce young that ultimately migrate back to coastal waters. River Lamprey tend to remain in and near to estuaries. There are records of both species throughout the British Isles, though mostly from fresh water. Anglers sometimes catch salmon with a lamprey attached, both at sea and in rivers as the salmon migrate upstream to spawn. There are even some photographs of lamprey still clinging firmly to their salmon host as it leaps up a waterfall on its way upriver.

Lampreys have one particular, albeit probably apocryphal, claim to fame. King Henry I is often said to have died from eating 'a surfeit of lampreys', but, whilst he was indeed very fond of a lamprey feast and died suddenly after one, medical experts now think it was unlikely to have been the cause of his death. Lampreys were in fact a popular delicacy for European royalty, but both the Sea and River Lamprey have declined in number around the British Isles and are now listed as UK Biodiversity Action Plan species in need of conservation.

Coastal Seas

ABOVE: Two leeches *Pontobdella muricata* on the rear of a Thornback Skate *Raja clavata*.

So what about the classic, blood-sucking leeches? Most of course live in freshwater ponds and lakes or in wet places such as rainforests. However, around the British Isles there are several marine species large and obvious enough to be spotted by divers, feeding *in situ* on fish. Paul has photographed *Pontobdella muricata*, a species that can reach 20cm long, on a Thornback Skate *Raja clavata*, which is where they are most often reported. Many other species of smaller leeches have been recorded on fish such as Shanny *Lipophrys pholis* and Butterfish in rock pools around the British Isles.

Another group of crustacean ectoparasites that have become far more prominent in our seas in recent years are isopods belonging to the family Cymothoidae. Unlike most isopods, which are free-living (including many shore and shallow-sea species and the terrestrial woodlice), the cymothoids are specialised and well adapted for parasitising fish by feeding on their blood and tissues. Some do this by living within the mouth and gill cavities of fish, and the infamously gruesome 'tongue-biter' of California, *Cymothoa exigua*, gradually destroys its host's tongue by stealing the blood supply, latching on to the resulting stub and then serving as the fish's tongue. These sometimes turn up in fishmongers on imported fish, and a similar tongue-attaching isopod has been recorded on Lesser Weeverfish *Echiichthys vipera* in Cornwall (Horton and Okamura 2002).

Much more widely seen are the cymothoid isopods that cling onto the outside surface of fish by using sharp points on the ends of their seven pairs of legs to pierce the skin. It is these 'skin-attaching' species that have recently become so obvious to snorkellers and divers around the southern coasts of England. They are described as 'rare' in field guides published as recently as 2018, but we now see them clamped onto fish whenever we go underwater around Dorset, Devon and Cornwall. It is thought that the increase may be due to climate change and ocean warming, but more information is needed, particularly on which of the two *Anilocra* species is most prevalent. These are difficult to identify from underwater photographs of affected fish, so specimens from fish caught by anglers are particularly valuable.

The most frequent host of the *Anilocra* lice appears to be the Corkwing Wrasse *Symphodus melops*, and it is sad to see so many of these beautiful fish infested. These are large parasites when compared to the size of the fish. The parasite clearly has an effect on their behaviour, making them more skittish and less bold. This is rather ironic as an early study suggested that the greater abundance of a small leech, *Sanguinothus pinarum*, on rock-pool fish in Scotland, as compared to southwest England, could be due to the lower abundance of Corkwing Wrasse in Scotland (Hussain and Knight-Jones 1995). Corkwings are well known for their parasite-picking efforts as cleaner fish. This species is one of the main targets for the wrasse potting that provides cleaner fish to salmon farms (see Chapter 8), so it is a worry that the fishery could have an exaggerated impact on populations already under stress from the upsurge in parasitism.

ABOVE: Young Corkwing Wrasse *Symphodus melops* with two parasitic isopods *Anilocra* sp. attached in the usual position close to the unfortunate host's eye.

Taking over

The impact of parasites on the lives of their hosts varies greatly, with an extreme version demonstrated by the bizarre Crab Hacker Barnacle *Sacculina carcini* on that of the Shore Crab and some swimming crabs (Portunidae). The planktonic larvae of this weird barnacle settle on the outside of a young crab, but then instead of growing into a normal barnacle, each larva grows into the crab's body as a root-like, absorptive network of tissue that penetrates throughout the crab's body. When the barnacle matures, a reproductive egg-containing sac bursts out of the crab's underside beneath its abdominal flap. A heavy infestation eventually prevents the crab from moulting, so even if the telltale sac cannot be seen, a heavy encrustation of the shell by a variety of sessile organisms is usually a sure sign that a crab has suffered attack by *Sacculina*. The barnacle effectively castrates both male and female crabs, and it also feminises males, which then develop female characteristics. These include smaller claws, but the benefit for the barnacle invader is that the male's normally slim abdomen becomes broader. In a healthy female, this feature enables her to successfully carry and protect a brood of eggs until they hatch, but in

ABOVE: This Shore Crab is parasitised by a Crab Hacker Barnacle *Sacculina carcini*, whose smooth yellow reproductive sac is tucked under the crab's abdomen where it would normally carry its own granular egg mass (see inset). This crab has also lost one of its mouthparts and cannot replace it because the parasite stops it from moulting.

the parasitised and newly feminised male it increases his capacity for carrying the *Sacculina* barnacle's eggs. In a recent Welsh study of over 200 Shore Crabs carried out by the University of Swansea, nearly a quarter were infected with the parasite (determined histologically through microscopic examination of tissues), though only about 10 per cent showed the external sac (Rowley *et al.* 2020).

Size is no barrier

While the large and obvious parasites of host animals such as fish and crabs are relatively easy to see and study, a huge variety of smaller parasites to which we are mostly oblivious are busily taking advantage of hosts great and small in our seas. Copepods are best known as tiny free-living crustaceans that make up a significant part of the zooplankton and are a hugely important part of the oceanic food chain. However, at least a third of all known copepod species are parasites. Some species are well adapted for attaching to the skin and gills of fish but are far less prominent than the isopod fish lice described on page 316. Mostly too small to be seen underwater, fish copepod parasites are often called sealice and are only usually encountered in anglers' catches or when buying whole fish to eat. One that is currently causing problems in the salmon farming industry is *Lepeophtheirus salmonis*. Heavy infestations in crowded fish pens can weaken and even kill fish, and the chemical treatments used to kill sealice can cause environmental damage. Carrying out desk studies of such treatments in the 1990s, Frances was rather shocked to see the range of potent chemicals in use then. Increased infection of wild salmon by sealice is believed to be a contributory factor in the severe decline of this fish in rivers, especially apparent in Scotland. Other copepod parasites burrow into polychaete worms and gastropod sea snails on the seabed.

Copepods and other small planktonic invertebrates are themselves parasitised by nematodes (roundworms), as are many other groups of animals. One genus of marine nematode has a chain of hosts. After breeding in the stomachs of sea mammals such as seals, their eggs pass out in the faeces and the juveniles that hatch are ingested by a range of small invertebrates in the plankton. When these are eaten by a fish or squid that is then preyed upon by a seal, the cycle is complete. People eating raw seafood infested with these nematodes can suffer from anisakiasis, named after the genus *Anisakis* to which they belong, where the roundworms burrow into the intestine causing severe inflammation and bowel blockage.

As well as showing the great variety of relationships between species that live together, this chapter has also demonstrated how much more there is to learn about them. For example, the benefits that are gained or the detriments suffered by the different species involved, can be little more than guesswork in some cases. An intriguing thought is that, with more study, some of the more fanciful ideas about the interactions may prove correct, or that totally new aspects might emerge. A final and sobering consideration here is that the complexity of relationships reminds us that we humans damage and interfere with natural systems and habitats at our peril, an appropriate lead into the next and final chapter.

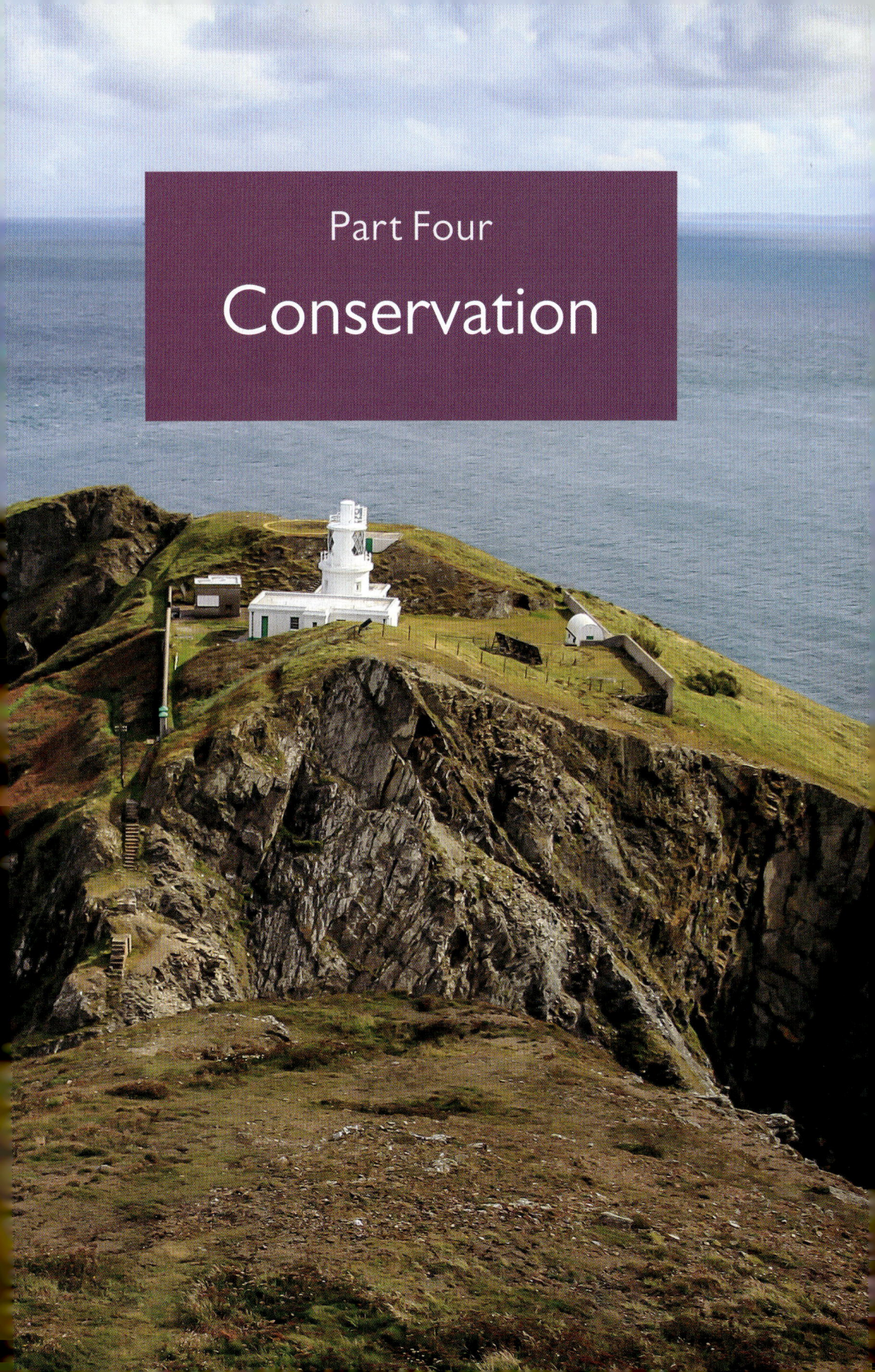

Part Four
Conservation

Protecting our seas

chapter twelve

Most people reading this book will be well aware of the myriad problems facing our planet today. The world is changing but, in the ocean, those changes are not always easily visible. The French proverb *'plus ça change, plus c'est la même chose'* translates as 'the more things change, the more they stay the same', and in this context could reflect both hidden change over time (the concept of 'shifting baselines' described near the start of this book) and the sometimes very slow progress made in mitigating human impact. We are both marine biologists of a certain 'vintage', and by far the most frequent question we are asked when we talk about our passion for the sea is 'what changes have you seen in your lifetime?' – followed by 'what is the state of the seas?'

Our aim throughout this book has been to show through words, and especially images, the surprising variety and beauty of marine communities and species hidden below the surface of coastal seas around the British Isles. While some of the photographs are quite old, many are very recent and virtually all of them could have been taken in the 2020s. As enthusiastic advocates of marine life close to home, and as a follow-up to the questions above, we are sometimes challenged as to how such a 'rosy view' squares with 'doom and gloom' reports of the huge impacts that humans are having on our seas and the damage that is being done to vulnerable species and habitats. A good comparison here might be the Amazon rainforest. Nobody is surprised when documentary film crews return from the Amazon with beautiful footage of amazing wildlife, but neither would they refute the fact that this special place is also being degraded by human activities at an alarming speed. Whether we are talking about South American forests or the coastal seas on our doorstep, it is important to simultaneously recognise the damage being done and cherish what is there, or we risk creating a 'counsel of despair'.

PREVIOUS PAGES:
Lundy in the Bristol Channel, the first statutory Marine Nature Reserve in the UK, is an inspiration to marine conservationists.

OPPOSITE PAGE:
Diver cutting lost fishing line from kelp to prevent animals getting entangled.

In each chapter of this book, we have flagged up some of the issues directly relevant to the communities and species we describe, for example the damage caused to seagrass beds by boat anchors (Chapter 6). We have also described local initiatives led by organisations such as the Wildlife Trusts and by voluntary groups and individuals, designed to provide local solutions. It is not the intention of this final chapter to go through the whole gamut of national and global problems that challenge the integrity of marine communities, species and the worldwide marine ecosystem. Sadly, these issues provide plenty of material for the many books dedicated to them. Between us, over the years, we have collected and counted dead seabirds covered in spilt oil on once pristine shores, surfaced from dives through floating slicks of plastic litter, untangled lost 'ghost' nets full of rotting fish from wrecks and reefs, dived under fish farms, and heard the rumble of raw sewage and seen it emerge underwater adjacent to beautiful beaches. There are certainly plenty of problems. In terms of the impacts we have on our seas, pollution has a high profile, particularly when caused by sewage and the scourge of plastic waste. There are also the insidious effects of climate change causing ocean warming and what is sometimes described as its 'evil twin', ocean acidification. It is, however, unsustainable harvesting of the seas for food, generally known as 'overfishing', that has done and continues to do a large proportion of the damage. It is to this and to the efforts to mitigate this through the development of Marine Protected Areas (MPAs) that we devote most of this final chapter.

Over-exploitation

The historical impact of over-exploitation in the ocean is well summarised in a small book titled *Marine Biology: a Very Short Introduction* (Mladenov 2013). This notes the general assumption that overfishing began in the late 19th century when steam-powered trawlers replaced sailing fishing vessels, and increased urbanisation, coupled with improved transport, drove a much greater demand for seafood. Although these factors had a significant effect by allowing and encouraging more aggressive fishing methods and much bigger nets, the seeds of the tragedy had been sown long before then (see box on page 326). Twenty-first-century developments in GPS and echo-sounding have of course exacerbated the problem. In his summary, Mladenov states that European fish stocks are now estimated to be

Protecting our seas

ABOVE: A busy fish market in the south of England with boxes of recently caught fish ready for onward transport.

LEFT: Atlantic Cod *Gadus morhua* drying on racks in the Lofoten Islands, Norway. This is a particularly important commercial species here, and declining stocks are forcing greater reductions in fishing quotas each year.

a tenth of what they were in 1900, while the total mass of fish in European seas is probably less than 5 per cent of what was there before any human exploitation.

Collateral damage

Sadly, industrial and highly intensive modern fishing does far more than simply remove huge, unsustainable numbers of fish. In heavily fished areas such as the North Sea, some locations are trawled several times in a year. All bottom-towed trawls and other gear inevitably kill and collect animals that are not targets of the fishery, while many do immense damage by scraping and crushing everything in

Plenty more fish in the sea? The birth of the Marine Biological Association of the United Kingdom (MBA)

It is perhaps not surprising that the origins of a major body such as the MBA (detailed by Southward and Roberts in 1984 to mark its centenary) lie in a debate between two eminent scientists about an issue as important as the impact of the fishing industry on our seas and its future sustainability. What strikes us as most remarkable now are, with the benefit of hindsight, the views of one of the protagonists. Professor Thomas H. Huxley was an eminent biologist and such a powerful advocate of the theory of evolution and natural selection that he was often described as 'Darwin's bulldog'. Huxley was also part of a Royal Commission on Sea Fisheries, which reported in 1866 that fears of fishery over-exploitation were groundless and that the prevailing laws on fishing grounds and closed seasons could be abandoned. Regardless of this conclusion, concerns continued to grow around the expanding trade in fresh fish allowed by the railways, the great increase in size and number of fishing boats, and widespread reports about the scarcity of some fish species. When these issues were aired at the International Fisheries Exhibition in London in 1883, however, Huxley repeated in his opening address the view that important fisheries were simply inexhaustible with contemporary fishing methods.

Professor E. Ray Lankester had studied and worked under Huxley and greatly admired him, eventually taking over his role as one of the most influential biologists of the day. That didn't stop him, along with many others who attended that 1883 meeting, disagreeing with the inexhaustibility view – and he summed up their scientific arguments in what Southward and Roberts describe as 'a brilliant essay on what we would now call ecology'. Lankester followed scientific points on the distribution of fish, the disruption of their reproduction and the upsetting of the natural balance with a proposal for a new society to encourage the study of marine life, both for scientific interest and because more information on the biology of food fishes was obviously needed. He suggested that the society should build a coastal facility with seawater tanks, laboratories and close access to boats. A group of influential scientists soon resolved to respond to this proposal, and, in a meeting at the Royal Society in London in 1884, formed what we know as the MBA. Huxley, now apparently persuaded of the importance of such study, was elected as its president and Lankester as its honorary secretary.

It was not just the MBA that emerged from the call for more information about the sea in the late 1800s. It stimulated the establishment of many other marine stations internationally and around the British Isles, such as at Port Erin on the Isle of Man (see box on page 78).

The Marine Biological Association Laboratory in Plymouth.

Protecting our seas

LEFT: Crawfish (or Spiny Lobster) *Palinurus elephas*. Ruinous overfishing by netting and diving through the 1960s and 1970s rendered this species extinct in many areas. It is now finally making a welcome recovery but is still vulnerable to over-exploitation.

their path on the seabed. Available 'before' and 'after' photographs show graphically how it becomes a wasteland. Many of the richest habitats have resulted from the activities of animals like oysters and tubeworms (whose reef-building activities we describe in Chapter 4) and cold-water corals over the millennia, so may take centuries to recover, or may never do so. This all contributes to the 'shifting baselines' issue that we raised in Chapter 1.

Another effect of intense over-exploitation is to change the structure of fish populations. The oldest and largest individuals (and the least numerous) produce a disproportionate number of eggs and young and are generally fished out first. Conversely, the smaller fish survive better, and the genetic composition of a population can therefore be altered. Smaller fish are less able to make up for losses due to other factors, and the reduced scope for recovery makes them less resilient to environmental fluctuations such as those caused by climate change. A good way of expressing these changes is to ask people how big they visualise an adult Plaice *Pleuronectes platessa* to be. Their answer is usually a gesture of the hands indicating the size of a large dinner plate, so they are astonished to hear that Plaice over a metre long were once common. We have never actually seen or even met someone who has seen such a giant; the Plaice is Europe's most commercially important flatfish, and we simply never allow them time to get that large.

Conservation solutions

The answer to this disastrous over-exploitation seems straightforward. Create protected areas as we do on land and reduce the rate at which we fish adjacent open areas. Areas closed to all fishing can bring benefits in many ways, as explained in Callum Roberts' (2007) inspiring but frightening book *The Unnatural History of the Sea*. Fish (and other targeted seafood species) protected from capture in reserves live longer and grow larger so they produce far more young. Whether it is the larvae from this increase in reproduction that drift in the plankton, or more mature fish that naturally move into less crowded areas, populations in areas both inside and outside the reserve are increased. This beneficial 'spillover' can, depending on the species involved, take time to have effect, but ultimately benefits the fishing industry as well as conservation. By allowing the development of more natural age structures, fully protected marine reserves make fish populations more resistant to unfavourable conditions. The larger the protected areas are, the better they will enable recovery.

RIGHT: Stills from remote monitoring video taken in Lyme Bay in 2008 (above) and 2013 (below) by University of Plymouth scientists, show the type of habitat recovery that can occur when the use of towed fishing gear is prevented. Two bright dots (ringed) in the 2013 image are from lasers projected onto the seabed for measurement. Intriguingly, the way some fish chase these dots can be seen in such footage, and can be used to analyse their territorial behaviour.

Proper protection from fishing also allows seabed habitats to recover. Animals that support healthy ecosystems by creating structures and filtering seawater, like sponges, molluscs and sea squirts, can thrive and reproduce more effectively, again increasing the productivity of fish (including commercially important species) as well as restoring beautiful natural environments. Benefits and changes resulting from the establishment of marine reserves in various parts of the world are reviewed in detail by Keith Hiscock (2014).

So much for the theory, but does it truly work, and to what extent have we gone down that path here in the British Isles?

How much is enough?

In his book, Callum Roberts also explains a simple logic behind his assertion that we need to protect sufficiently large areas, stating that around 30 per cent of the sea needs to be covered with reserves in order to lift fish populations to sustainable levels. Other scientists are in broad agreement, having used different modelling assumptions to suggest we should protect between 20 and 40 per cent of the sea from all fishing.

It is important to recognise this consensus and note that calls for action on such a scale are not limited to conservation campaigns. A report on the impact of fisheries by the Royal Commission on Environmental Pollution to the UK Parliament (*Turning the Tide*) in 2004 concluded that a network of MPAs 'should lead to 30% of the UK's exclusive economic zone being established as no-take reserves closed to commercial fishing'.

BELOW: Campaigners for much better protection of our precious but undervalued marine life outside the Houses of Parliament in London.

'Paper parks'

Given the apparent agreement on the way forward, how well are we making progress? At first glance, things look encouraging. By 2023, according to Joint Nature Conservancy Council (JNCC) statistics on its website (updated to July that year), there were 377 MPAs of various types and sizes in all UK waters. JNCC statistics also give the number of inshore MPAs as 329 and offshore MPAs as 78. These two figures do not add up to 377, and the confusing discrepancy in total is because MPAs that have both inshore and offshore components are counted in both figures.

The different types of MPAs included in these figures are Marine Conservation Zones (MCZs), Special Areas of Conservation (SACs) with marine components, Special Protection Areas (SPAs) with marine components, Highly Protected Marine Areas (HPMAs), and Nature Conservation MPAs in Scotland. In total, this complex network of MPAs covered an impressive-sounding 38 per cent of UK waters. For those interested in the details and differences between the various types of MPA, we suggest a visit to the JNCC website.

If you look, however, at what 'protected' actually means, the picture is very much less promising, with great variations in the degree of legal protection afforded. For example, Marine Conservation Zones, many of which are large, are legally designated and intended to protect specific features. They have conservation objectives, designed to maintain or recover those features to a 'favourable condition', but this, frustratingly, does not confer automatic legal protection from potentially damaging activities. Regulation of activities in the sea and at the coast falls to various public authorities, particularly the Marine Management Organisation (MMO) and Inshore Fisheries and Conservation Authorities (IFCAs), both of which are able to establish byelaws to protect features within MCZs.

A detailed and alarming report by the Marine Conservation Society (MCS) laid the issue bare (Dunkley and Solandt 2021). In English seas, only 2 per cent of territorial water was legally protected from bottom trawling, but much of this management was in place to protect inshore reef areas where trawls do not operate for fear of the gear being damaged. For soft seabed habitats where fishing can occur, the MCS calculated that less than 1 per cent was closed to bottom trawling. The situation was similarly bleak in Scotland, where government scientists assessed that only 2.5 per cent of inshore seabed (out to 12 nautical miles) was protected from the use of mobile bottom-fishing gear. Again, when limited to areas where towed gear could actually be operated, the figure was less than 1 per cent. The vast majority of current inshore UK MPAs cover areas that were fished with bottom trawls and dredges prior to MPA designation and fishing with such gear has not since been prohibited. However, byelaws to control such fishing have been introduced in some MPAs, such as around the Thanet and Essex coasts, where byelaws were introduced in 2018 to control the traditional Wash brown shrimp fishery. There are other inshore MPAs still awaiting byelaws to allow productivity to return, and environmental NGOs (non-governmental organisations) such as MCS and the Blue Marine Foundation are keeping track of developing regulations to see if they are fit for purpose.

A dramatic mismatch between the apparent coverage of our MPAs and the amount of habitat properly protected was also highlighted in *Rocky Shores* (Archer-Thomson and Cremona 2019), and that mismatch remains. The lack of protection against the most damaging impacts has led to the areas being widely described as 'paper parks', and the discrepancy is indeed remarkable. When people are asked during public opinion surveys whether they support banning bottom trawling in MPAs, their first reaction is astonishment that it isn't already.

Inching forward

Since that MCS report was published in 2021, there has been some positive but limited progress. In June 2022, the MMO introduced byelaws that banned bottom trawling in the well-known and very large Dogger Bank Special Area of Conservation in the North Sea, although that protection has been legally challenged by other nearby nations. Bottom trawling was also banned in designated habitats within three other offshore (beyond the 12nm territorial limit) MPAs, but there is still concern that the bans only cover parts of those other areas, not to mention the dozens of MPAs with no protection against it at all.

Another welcome step forward was made in March 2024 when new MMO byelaws came into force prohibiting the use of bottom-towed gear within specific areas of 13 more English offshore MPAs (mostly MCZs). The protected areas cover important 'reef' habitats containing vulnerable species and habitats such as worm reefs, sponges and sea fans. The total area covered amounts to nearly 18,000km^2. It remains to be seen whether the then government's programme to protect all English offshore MPAs from fishing activity (or at least especially vulnerable areas within them) is achieved within a meaningful time frame. In Scotland, measures for managing fisheries within offshore MPAs are being considered. A consultation covering 20 protected areas closed in October 2024 and at the time of writing the responses are being analysed and considered. We remain cautiously hopeful that, by the time you read this, more will have been achieved.

Coastal Seas

RIGHT: Efforts to make fishing methods more sustainable include the fitting of small 'escape hatches' to pots used for catching crustaceans. These are intended to reduce damage to undersize juveniles and non-target animals by allowing them to leave the pot before it is hauled up.

RIGHT: Discarded and lost pots, like other fishing gear, continue to 'ghost fish' when abandoned. This one in a rich maerl habitat is now so broken up that the numerous crabs attracted to shelter in it were not trapped. Unfortunately, this is often not the case.

A new legislative mechanism for obtaining better habitat protection is the creation of Highly Protected Marine Areas (HPMAs), which, as stated on the gov.uk website, 'will protect all species and habitats and associated ecosystem processes within the site boundary, including the seabed and water column'. This has moved particularly and painfully slowly, with only three such inshore areas designated in English waters as 'pilots' in July 2023 and only vague commitments to explore further sites being made thereafter. Before the advent of HPMAs, which should be equivalent to full protection against any removal of marine life or damaging activities, there were only three No-Take Zones (NTZs) with legal status in our waters, small areas within larger MPAs where some exploitation is still allowed. The locations and extent of HPMAs and NTZs are shown in the table below.

It is also of great concern to marine NGOs that many of these MPA-style measures, designed to provide protection in specific areas, do not receive enough support for adequate monitoring following designation. This applies equally to large areas of closure to bottom-towed gear, such as at Dogger, and to monitoring fish and invertebrate populations in smaller NTZs and HPMAs. For example, the Blue Marine Foundation told us they have only seen really effective monitoring at five sites since the 1990s: Port Erin, Lundy, Arran, Skomer and Lyme Bay. There are limited public funds to enable monitoring and to communicate the results to stakeholders and resource users so that they can understand what progress is being made. This could be addressed through 'sentinel sites' – sites where monitoring can demonstrate to others in different areas of the UK what biological responses there are to such measures. Only by strategic and well-funded monitoring over perhaps a decade will we be able to understand the true value of these vital interventions. The Blue Marine Foundation recommends that at least 10 sites are supported in this way for at least 10 years.

Whilst we and many others may feel that progress has been and remains slow, we do feel that it is important to acknowledge the incredibly hard work that is being put into trying to attain meaningful MPA-style protection of our seas, by individuals and by both professional and volunteer organisations.

Highly Protected Marine Areas (HPMAs) and No-Take Zones (NTZs) in England as at 2025

Name	Location	Extent (square kilometres)	Year established
Pilot HPMAs			
Allonby Bay	Solway Firth (inshore)	28	2023
Dolphin Head	English Channel (offshore Sussex)	466	2023
North East of Farnes Deep	Berwickshire (offshore)	492	2023
NTZs			
Lundy	Bristol Channel (inshore)	4	2003
Lamlash Bay	Arran, W Scotland (inshore)	2.67	2008
Flamborough Head	Yorkshire (intertidal)	1	2010

Lights at the end of the tunnel

In addition to the yearned-for overall progress, there are other shining and longer-standing examples of successful MPAs around the British Isles, five of which we highlight here, starting with those that include NTZs. While sometimes small in their geographical scale, they provide inspiration and tantalising glimpses of what can be achieved.

Lundy

A pioneer among these gems is Lundy, an island at the entrance to the Bristol Channel. Lundy has led the way in being Britain's first voluntary marine reserve, its first statutory Marine Nature Reserve, its first No-Take Zone and its first Marine Conservation Zone. The no-take area within the reserve, enforced by a fisheries byelaw, is an excellent example of what can be achieved by constructive collaboration between passionate and pragmatic conservationists, fishing regulators (here, the Devon Sea Fisheries Committee, forerunner to the Devon and Severn Inshore Fisheries and Conservation Authority, D&S

RIGHT: Diver monitoring Sunset Cup Corals *Leptopsammia pruvoti* on Lundy, as part of a long-term study.

IFCA) and those engaged in fishing. It is small at only about 4km² but has had significant benefits. There has, for example, been a great increase in the size and abundance of lobsters within the area that has also benefited stocks outside it. The complex and over-50-year story of the journey from the first suggestion of a voluntary marine reserve to a MCZ with a smaller NTZ within it, is a key part of Keith Hiscock and Robert Irving's 2012 book *Protecting Lundy's Marine Life: 40 Years of Science and Conservation*, an essential read for disheartened marine conservationists. A comprehensive marine management plan published by the Lundy Management Forum in 2017 provides a wealth of information, not only on conservation aspects, but also on the natural environment of this tiny island.

While a local fishing community, such as around Lundy, may eventually welcome and support a no-take area, others may not, so ongoing enforcement is always essential. D&S IFCA has been at the forefront of developing and implementing remote electronic monitoring on fishing vessels. This technology uses a combination of GPS and gear sensors with, increasingly, video cameras to track fishing activity. With two coastlines to cover and the largest area of any of the IFCAs, this Authority is particularly reliant on the benefits of such technology in terms of comprehensive coverage and cost-effectiveness.

Arran

This island in the Firth of Clyde is a wonderful demonstration of people-power driving conservation. The Community of Arran Seabed Trust (COAST), a citizen group of volunteer activists, was set up by two local divers in 1995. Howard Wood was motivated by observing, first-hand, the way destructive fishing methods such as scallop dredging were destroying wildlife and damaging the entire seabed ecosystem. Don MacNeish added inspiration from overseas, having seen the effects of MPAs on a visit to New Zealand. COAST then ran a grassroots campaign to establish Scotland's first No-Take Zone in Lamlash Bay, using petitions and community rallies and engaging with public officials, scientists and the local fishing community. Finally, in 2008, a legally enforced NTZ was established and, despite its small extent (less than 3km²), there have been impressive improvements in the abundance and productivity of animals such as lobsters and scallops.

ABOVE: Lamlash Bay on the Isle of Arran, the site of Scotland's first No-Take Zone (NTZ).

COAST's work did not end with the creation and application of the NTZ. They developed and submitted a proposal for a much larger MPA, and this resulted in the announcement, with other MPAs around Scotland, of the South Arran MPA in 2014. A complex management plan for the area (nearly 300km^2) now allows and prohibits different types of fishing within four zones, a small part of Lamlash Bay being the only full NTZ where all fishing is prohibited. A map showing the zones can be found on the COAST website. COAST also supports enforcement in the MPA, since a satellite vessel monitoring system (VMS) helps ensure compliance of large fishing vessels (over 12m long), but, for smaller fishing boats, on-the-ground reporting is required. Furthermore, it is important to note that the rate at which a VMS transponds (sends out a position signal) is not relevant to the size and scale of MPAs in many areas. Vessels only transpond their position once every two hours, meaning that a vessel in a small MPA such as the Lamlash Bay NTZ could fish illegally in the period between signals and then sail out of the area.

General raising of awareness and education are of course essential parts of any conservation effort, with COAST heavily involved there too, and those efforts can even receive global recognition. A Goldman Environmental Prize was awarded to Howard Wood in 2015 and he was delighted to receive it at the White House in Washington, DC.

Flamborough Head

Within the Flamborough Head SAC on the Yorkshire Coast, there is a small NTZ that is the only such fully protected UK site in the North Sea. It is enforced by the North Eastern IFCA and covers fish and all shellfish, both molluscs and crustaceans. The IFCA also works with partners to monitor changes to the extent and distribution of key species, and it is this gathering of information that lay behind the NTZ's creation in 2010. Interestingly, and unusually, the NTZ covers the intertidal area, because Edible Mussels *Mytilus edulis* are important here.

Lyme Bay: the UK's 'Coral Garden'

This large bay straddling the coasts of Dorset and Devon is home to both a wealth of marine biodiversity and a richly complex history of conservation management and research, as described in detail by Renn *et al.* (2024). In the late 1980s, Lyme Bay's fabulous marine life and varied seabed communities were surveyed and recognised as internationally significant. It was then quickly realised they were also very vulnerable to damage from bottom-towed trawls and scallop dredges, particularly as some of the dredging equipment had been adapted to enable operation in low-lying reef areas that had

LEFT: A Yellow Staghorn Sponge *Axinella dissimilis*, an example of a long-lived and slow-growing species benefiting from protection in Lyme Bay (here photographed in Bigbury Bay, Devon).

apparently been avoided previously. Conservation groups, especially Devon Wildlife Trust, raised the profile of damage being done to iconic species such as Pink Sea Fan *Eunicella verrucosa* (see *Out of sight, out of mind*, page 347). A byelaw to protect reefs had been considered by the Southern Sea Fisheries Committee (forerunner to Southern IFCA), but when this was opposed by the operators of the large fishing vessels, a voluntary agreement was instead struck to protect two key areas.

With tireless campaigning and support from conservation bodies, further areas were added until eventually, in 2008, a single MPA of more than 200km^2 was created, through which fishing restrictions could be enforced. Combined with the later (2011) introduction of an overlapping and even larger SAC, the result has been the protection of marine life from towed fishing gear, allowing restoration of the reefs. Fishing with static gear (potting) has continued, with voluntary agreements to limit its impact, the result of years of discussions and implementation between the Blue Marine Foundation and local fishing interests, since this type of fishing can have significant effects through intense and repeated dropping and lifting of pots and their lines. The agreements are reinforced by measures such as additional facilities being provided to those who comply with them, but, while this works well in many instances, further regulation will probably be needed to manage the activities of non-local boats.

Groundbreaking techniques, such as 'flying' and static video arrays that improve data-gathering and minimise seabed disturbance (compared to traditional towed versions), have been used to monitor the recovery of marine life, including Pink Sea Fans, in Lyme Bay. Interestingly, this also showed how the sea fan population recovered much more quickly from damage done by the severe winter storms of 2013/14 than they had from the fishing activity (Sheehan *et al.* 2021). The Lyme Bay monitoring techniques, along with a multidisciplinary approach that has also recorded socioeconomic benefits, have been recognised as best practice, including internationally. All of this is a further example of what can be achieved when conservationists, the local fishing community, regulators and scientists all work together. The work of the Blue Marine Foundation has also been instrumental in supporting both the scientists and the fishing community in addressing this change in how the seas can be managed.

Pembrokeshire

A large SAC covers the beautiful southwestern-most tip of Wales in recognition of the wildlife above and below water, including animals that pass through it as well as those that live within it permanently. A number of different bodies work together to oversee its management, and activities are mainly managed by codes of conduct. Within the wider SAC the waters around Skomer and the adjacent mainland of the Marloes Peninsula became the first (and, as of 2025, only) MCZ in Wales in 2014, with its own specific byelaws. This simple statement belies the importance and long history of marine conservation in this area, as described in the box below.

The byelaws in place within the MCZ prohibit beam trawling, dredging and any taking of scallops, including hand-collection by

---

Skomer MCZ: a hard-won victory

Skomer is the second-largest island in Wales, the largest of Pembrokeshire's islands, and has itself been a terrestrial National Nature Reserve since 1959 (owned by Natural Resources Wales and managed by the Wildlife Trust of South and West Wales). It is of international importance for its breeding seabirds (such as Guillemots *Uria aalge* and Puffins *Fratercula arctica*) and seals. It is the waters around the island and the adjacent mainland of the Marloes Peninsula that form the Skomer Marine Conservation Zone (MCZ).

The current MCZ was preceded by a decades-long history of marine advocacy and a well-fought but frustrating struggle to attain the current degree of protection. The importance of the marine habitats and species in these waters and the damage being done to them by unsympathetic fishing methods were recognised as long as 50 years ago. However, it took until 1976 before agreement was reached for it to become a voluntary marine nature reserve and a further 14 years before it was declared a statutory Marine Nature Reserve (MNR) in 1990. It was one of only two such MNRs ever designated in Britain (the other being Lundy), before that legislation was superseded and it became an MCZ in 2014.

In contrast to most others, Skomer MCZ/MNR is the only British MPA to have a dedicated, full-time management and HSE (Health and Safety Executive) dive qualified monitoring team, and one that has been in place for over 30 years. It has by far and away the most comprehensive suite of biological and hydrographic monitoring (begun in 1982) of any MPA in the UK. As described on page 333, adequate monitoring of MPAs is essential to demonstrate the positive effects of protection measures. The damaging effects of scallop dredging were first shown clearly here, and this was the first MPA to have legal control of such dredging. The scallop population has rebounded spectacularly through such measures, but the initial reason for seeking to prohibit dredging was to protect the sediment habitats and their rich communities – which it has done well. Both habitat and species diversity have recovered significantly (see Skomer Marine Conservation Zone Annual Reports), but it is the scallops that have the popular appeal and in a sense act as 'ambassadors' for marine conservation success.

ABOVE: Three Great Scallops *Pecten maximus* in Martin's Haven, part of the Skomer Marine Conservation Zone, where there are now large numbers of these animals thanks to many years of protection.

divers. The effect of that control on the density of Great Scallops *Pecten maximus* dotted across the sandy seabed is remarkable. When Paul dived there in 2021 he was so impressed that despite his dive time being limited by the weight of air cylinder he was willing to carry up a big hill afterwards, he spent a good part of it seeing how many feeding (and therefore visible) scallops he could fit in a single photograph. More scientifically, the *Skomer Marine Conservation Zone Annual Report 2022/23* documents Great Scallop counts in the monitored areas of the MCZ as 62 per 100m^2, a 12.4-fold increase since the year 2000 (Lock *et al.* 2023). Such increases have also been documented in other protected or well-managed areas such as the Isle of Man.

Voluntary marine nature reserves and conservation areas

In addition to areas with complete or partial statutory protection, there are a variety of voluntary reserves and conservation areas around the British Isles. In many cases, smaller voluntary areas aiming for a higher level of protection lie within more formally designated MPAs, so there may already be statutory protection from some activities. With the voluntary areas intended to add protection, the situation can be quite complicated, such that some activities may be prohibited and others merely 'discouraged', but the overall aim is always to encourage good practice in caring for the marine environment and foster a wide appreciation of its wildlife.

One of the best known is the Berwickshire Marine Reserve in the southeast of Scotland, covering the coast around the fishing towns of Eyemouth and St Abbs. This has been a popular dive site for many years and we have both enjoyed visits there, as well as an introduction to the famous resident Wolf Fish, as described in Chapter 8. It has codes of conduct promoting responsible recreational activities alongside a sustainable commercial fishery. At nearly the opposite end of the British mainland in Dorset, Kimmeridge Bay Marine Reserve is a voluntary no-take zone with a visitor centre run by Dorset Wildlife Trust. The Wembury Marine Conservation Area in neighbouring Devon similarly has education about marine life and habitats at its heart, with a centre run by the Devon Wildlife Trust. Situated just a few miles from the large city of Plymouth, the centre has links with many local schools and plays a significant role in instilling a love for the sea and its inhabitants in their pupils. In Cornwall, there is a network of 'Your Shore' groups established by the Wildlife Trust and run by passionate local volunteers, with many of them (such as at Looe, Helford, Polzeath and St Agnes) supporting specific Voluntary Marine Conservation Areas.

LEFT: Typical information board in a Voluntary Marine Conservation Area, aiming to raise awareness of the wildlife that lives there and encourage its protection.

'Take only photos …'

For some divers and snorkellers, getting underwater means an opportunity to collect a delicious dinner. This can include spearfishing, which in the British Isles and the EU is now limited by law to snorkelling. Divers also sometimes hand-collect molluscs (mainly scallops) and crustaceans such as crabs and lobsters. When done by experienced hunters, these methods can be highly specific to what is going to be eaten and so are potentially among the most sustainable forms of fishing. Unfortunately, spearfishing in particular is sometimes taken up by those with insufficient knowledge, and it is very frustrating when you come across (as we have) novices who kill 'sitting duck' Corkwing Wrasse *Symphodus melops* nest-builders without realising they are inedible, or undersized Bass *Dicentrarchus labrax* because they failed to take account of the magnifying effect of a diving mask.

Early in our diving careers, we both occasionally collected scallops or picked up the odd lobster for supper (outside conservation areas, we must add!), but stopped doing so long ago. Part of this is personal; we get so much pleasure from watching animals in their natural habitat that putting some in a bag to haul up to the surface would spoil our enjoyment. While we don't think there is anything intrinsically wrong with underwater hunting, since it can be tightly targeted and humans are naturally predatory creatures, we believe there is also a wider issue worth considering. It sends out a very powerful message to other users of the sea when the people who venture into the underwater world are so impressed at what they find that they come back only with photographs, observations and memories.

Sustainable seafood

Whether or not they have 'hands-on' involvement with the sea, everyone can contribute to marine conservation. In addition to making personal changes that minimise the waste we produce and our 'carbon footprint', which will all help the sea, we can use our power as consumers to specifically encourage less harmful fishing practices. Making sure that you only buy seafood from sustainable sources can be tricky, but helpful information is available. The best known is the detailed *Good Fish Guide* produced online by the Marine Conservation Society, and another well-researched, but more specific, online guide is the *Cornwall Good Seafood Guide* by Cornwall Wildlife Trust. There are also certification schemes such as that operated by the Marine Stewardship Council, where particular products carry their logo. Some uncertainty and disagreement about choices is inevitable but we feel that anything that helps to drive the move towards more sustainable fishing is positive, even if it results in an awkward conversation in a restaurant.

ABOVE: These tins of wild-caught tuna and sardines carry the Marine Stewardship Council (MSC) label, indicating that the fisheries have met certified sustainable standards.

Hatching a plot for lobsters

Supporting a particular commercial species is an intriguing way of protecting stocks and helping conservation. A growing number of hatcheries for the Common Lobster *Homarus gammarus* have been set up, including those at Padstow (the National Hatchery) in Cornwall, Whitby in Yorkshire, North Berwick on the Firth of Forth and Wells in Norfolk. Anglesey Sea Zoo and the Lake District Coast Aquariums also include lobster hatcheries.

In the wild, it has been estimated that only about one in 20,000 of the eggs produced by a female lobster survives through the planktonic larval phase to become a miniature lobster living on the seabed.

The idea of hatcheries is to boost natural populations by taking eggs from captured lobsters and 'seeing them through' this very dangerous phase before releasing the juveniles, which then have a much better rate of survival through to adulthood. In addition to expertise in rearing larval lobsters, care is also needed on that final step into the wild. Paul's partner Teresa's most memorable job as a scientific fisheries research diver was acting as a 'bodyguard' for tiny lobsters as they were released. Without divers to keep the gathering throng of hungry fish away, most of them would be snaffled before they had a chance to burrow into the seabed.

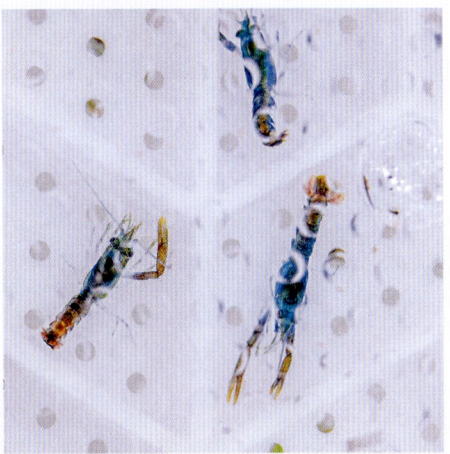

A special tray for rearing juvenile lobsters in a hatchery and preventing cannibalism before release.

ABOVE: Salmon farm in a Scottish sea loch. Aquaculture may appear to solve over-exploitation, but it can cause pollution and, through the escape of fish, weaken the genetics of wild populations. A major issue is that vast numbers of wild fish are often caught to feed those being farmed.

RIGHT: A line of pots used to catch wrasse in Devon for transport to Scottish salmon farms. The wrasse are used as 'cleaner fish' for removing parasites from the caged salmon. There is concern over the removal of large numbers of such territorial fish from reef ecosystems (see Chapter 8).

It is an undoubted mark of progress when you see the entire side of a lorry emblazoned with a supermarket's claim that all its seafood comes from sustainable sources. Can you imagine space being given to such an advertisement a few decades ago?

Warmer waters: 'winners' and 'losers'

The seas around the British Isles are blessed with an abundance of marine life, with over 10,000 different organisms in the Marine Species of the British Isles and Adjacent Seas (MSBIAS) database. In addition to the impressively wide range of habitats that surround our relatively small islands, a major reason for this richness is that we are in the happy position of lying across a biogeographical transition zone, with warmer subtropical (Lusitanian) waters to the south and cooler Arctic ones to the north, meaning we tend to get 'the best of both worlds' in terms of species variety. This also places us at the edge of the temperature tolerances for many organisms, so as our waters become warmer due to climate change there are inevitably 'winners' and 'losers'. Some warmer-water species are extending their range northward into our waters, whilst other already northern species may find life too warm and move further north beyond the British Isles.

Long-term datasets and observations are an essential tool in determining whether a species really has expanded its range northward. As discussed in Chapter 8, mobile species such as Grey Triggerfish *Balistes capriscus* have long been known as summer visitors to our southern waters. They may die (as is probably the case with Grey Triggerfish) or return south in winter. This is a familiar scenario in the bird world, and to a lesser extent in the insect world: Painted Lady butterflies *Vanessa cardui* migrate over to us from the continent in summer but die out over winter. When such species start to remain and breed, then this is evidence of a true range extension. There is a small amount of (still inconclusive) evidence to suggest Grey Triggerfish may now be breeding in UK waters, while we see the Variable or Ringneck Blenny *Parablennius pilicornis* now brooding large batches of eggs here (see Chapter 8).

Fish and seabirds are mobile species, but what about slow-moving and bottom-living sessile invertebrates? Sea slugs are not noted for their athletic abilities and yet, much to the delight of the divers and shore searchers who spot them, several colourful species have turned up in our waters since 2020. Although small, these are not easily overlooked cryptic species and appear to be genuinely new arrivals. Patterned with purple, red, pink and yellow, *Babakina anadoni* is distributed along the Atlantic coast of France, Spain and Portugal and at least a short way into the Mediterranean. It was first recorded from the Isles of Scilly and southern Cornwall in 2022, and then Paul's family found one at Wembury, Plymouth, in August 2024. According to Bernard Picton and Christine Morrow's beautiful nudibranch book (2023) it is thought to feed on the tiny hydroid *Candelabrum cocksii*. A quick check of the NBN Atlas shows that most UK records for this hydroid come from the southwest peninsula of England, although it is

Coastal Seas

RIGHT: The so-called 'Rainbow Sea Slug' *Babakina anadoni* was first recorded from around the British Isles in 2022 and is gradually being spotted more often, this one (about 2cm long) by Paul's family in Devon.

so small it is easily overlooked. However, if the hydroid itself expands its range northward, perhaps *Babakina* will do so too. The story of this and other new arrivals is often complex.

When a new species is found in a particular location, or another appears to lose its foothold, it is sometimes too easy to immediately conclude that it is due to climate change, when another factor or factors are mainly responsible. The effect of gradually warming seas, however, is complicated, so if a further factor is at play, or the timing of similar observations suggests a different cause, it does not necessarily mean that climate change is *not* playing its part. A good example is

RIGHT: The Comber *Serranus cabrilla* has a Mediterranean and southern distribution and is a recent arrival to the Channel Islands and the south coast of England. This is a juvenile from Plymouth Sound, which may indicate the fish is now breeding here.

the warm-water Common Octopus *Octopus vulgaris* that, as we note in Chapter 10, has been seen much more often in the southwest of England in recent years. This might immediately suggest climate change, while finding historic references to a 'plague' of this species around 1900 implies it is not climate change. The explanation may be subtle, with spasmodic increases occurring after unusually mild winters because of the way the octopus young develop, travel and grow. Occasional mild winters have always been with us, although they are becoming much more frequent.

Out of sight, out of mind

Marine conservationists often emphasise the fact that the environmental impacts of human activities in the sea receive much less attention than those on land because the effects inevitably go unseen by the great majority of people – including, crucially, politicians and lawmakers. The Wildlife Trusts, for example, highlighted this contrast in their campaign for better protection of UK marine habitats through a Marine Bill in 2006. Under the heading 'If only the destruction of our seas were this obvious ...' they used an image of a large digger destroying a forest to show how we are horrified by such activity on land, but seem oblivious to the equivalent under the sea, and happy to allow it.

Another illustration of this difference can be seen in the cooling-water infrastructure at coastal power stations, which take in huge volumes of seawater to remove heat from their steam condensers during the generation of electricity. The intake of one of the nuclear stations now being constructed in Britain, for example at Hinkley Point C, will use a flow equivalent to one of our major rivers. Millions of fish are drawn in and killed at power-station intakes, despite some developments in making them more 'fish-friendly'. In calling for the use of alternative cooling methods, or at least the use of all available technology to minimise fish kill, marine conservationists highlight how different our reaction would be if an equivalent number of birds were killed on cooling fans. The power industry's defensive comparisons with the impact of fishing are misleading because fishing can at least be altered or stopped depending on its impact. In contrast, once operational, a cooling-water intake will run for decades. Many power stations are also close to particularly sensitive habitats that are protected by law.

Dead fish washed from a cooling-water intake screen in a coastal power station.

Other problems

If we were able to instantly solve the problem of overfishing described above and implement meaningful and appropriate levels of protection for all the varied MPAs around our coastline, would our marine conservationists be out of a job? The answer, of course, is no. We have touched on some other specific threats (and possible solutions) at relevant places in the various chapters of this book, but sadly there are many more widespread problems, including the 'elephant in the room', climate change. Here we briefly describe some currently topical issues. A great deal more information is available on the web and in accessible texts such as the Wildlife Trusts' *Britain's Living Seas* (Rudd 2023) and more detailed texts such as *Elements of Marine Ecology* (Dipper 2022).

Invasive species

'Invasive', 'alien', 'non-native' – these are all terms applied, often rather dramatically, to species that have arrived in the British Isles, brought here outside their natural range in a myriad of different ways through human activities. Alien, or more correctly non-native, species do not always become established or invasive, whether in terrestrial, freshwater or marine settings, and some may even have positive impacts. What would childhood be without conkers and conker fights, yet Horse-chestnut trees *Aesculus hippocastanum* are a non-native species brought here in the 17th century from Turkey. However, those arrivals that find ideal conditions and a lack of controlling influences (such as grazers and predators) can become invasive and have significant impacts on native biodiversity through competition, habitat invasion and introduction of disease. As well as ecological effects, there may also be significant economic repercussions – on land, Japanese Knotweed *Reynoutria japonica* immediately springs to mind.

According to Christine Wood from the Marine Biological Association (MBA) in Plymouth, who researches and collates information on marine non-native species, there are just over 90 established, benthic non-native animal species plus a further 30 or so algae recorded to date from around the British Isles. Some of these have now become widespread and common. There are also many other non-native species that have arrived, but that have not (yet) established self-sustaining populations. Non-natives include

ABOVE: A beach near Portsmouth covered in the empty shells of the invasive Slipper Limpet *Crepidula fornicata*.

seaweeds, molluscs, bryozoans, crustaceans, annelid worms, sponges and cnidarians. The data on relevant marine species, curated at the MBA, is fed into the GB Non-native Species Information Portal (NNSIP), which provides a wealth of information on individual species including identification guides.

Widespread and familiar non-natives that are with us to stay include Slipper Limpet *Crepidula fornicata*, Wireweed *Sargassum muticum* and Pacific Oyster *Magallana gigas*. There is a connection between these species, in that the first two are thought to have reached the British Isles through imports of the non-native oysters, either attached to their shells or contained in the shipment and later discarded in the sea. Current efforts to restore native European Flat Oyster *Ostrea edulis* beds may be affected by *Crepidula*, which in large numbers can smother and compete for planktonic food with oysters (both native and non-native).

When Wireweed first appeared in the Isle of Wight in 1973, considerable efforts were made to eradicate it, and Frances remembers always having to look out for it on shore and diving surveys. The classic way of identifying it then was to hold a collected specimen at either end: if the side branches hung down like washing on a line, it was Wireweed. It filled rock pools and even caused problems for

RIGHT: 'It's an ill wind'... a trio of Sea Hares *Aplysia punctata* take advantage of non-native Wireweed *Sargassum muticum* for acrobatic mating activity.

boats in sheltered harbours where it grew particularly thickly. It is now found as far north as the Outer Hebrides. It definitely fits the description of invasive, growing quickly and with the ability to spread by floating fragments, but has not been the ecological disaster that was once expected. It does not tolerate long periods of exposure to the air and this restricts its intertidal habitat to rock pools. Here, it might shade out other algae, much as blanketweed does on freshwater ponds, and its long fronds float on the surface of shallow pools so that it looks as though it is covering a large area. However, when the tide returns, it can stay upright, providing far less shade. It has a high light requirement and rarely grows below 5m depth but it can form dense forests in shallow water, potentially outcompeting native species such as Sea Oak *Halidrys siliquosa* that grow under similar conditions. Growing over 2m long, it can in some circumstances also interfere with fishing, aquaculture and recreational activities.

Wireweed could be considered as both invasive and now naturalised, but not all widespread non-native species deserve the 'invasive' label. The Australian or Modest Barnacle *Austrominius modestus* (previously *Elminius modestus*), originating from Australasia, is found on intertidal hard substrata all around the British Isles. It was already widespread in the 1940s and in some areas or parts of shores, especially in southern England, is now the dominant barnacle. In this respect it should be considered invasive, but barnacle-dominated shores with this species appear little different to others in terms of ecology, at least superficially. A 2015 study on the Isle of Cumbrae in Scotland showed that, even after 60 years, *Austrominius* had not outcompeted native barnacles at this site, which is near its northern distributional limits (Gallagher *et al.* 2015). We have included this intertidal invader because it is a prime example of something creeping in under the radar, but also because we have a soft spot for it as the only species of barnacle that as students we both found easy to identify.

The Carpet Sea Squirt *Didemnum vexillum* is an example of a potentially worrying invasive species. It is a priority invasive species, which means that if you find it, it would be helpful to photograph and report it to the Biological Records Centre. This is a colonial didemnid sea squirt that, as its English name suggests, can cover and smother large areas of rock and hard substratum. On vertical surfaces such as mussel aquaculture cages, it can hang down as long, pendulous lobes that break off and help it spread. In that sense it is a bit like a buff to dull-orange version of the 'green slime' in the 1980s cult comedy film *Ghostbusters*, though in fact it has a relatively leathery consistency. Occurrences remain scattered and, as with many marine non-natives, mostly in marinas and at aquaculture sites, but it has also been found on some shores and on wrecks in deeper water. It poses a significant problem and cost to shallow-water, standing aquaculture facilities.

Sewage pollution

Huge progress has been made in tackling sewage pollution since the days when Parliament was unable to sit in 1858 due to the 'great stink' from the River Thames. However, a lack of investment in outdated sewerage systems and a lack of government control has led to a continued and unacceptable pollution of shorelines and shallow seas with sewage-related debris (SRD). This material enters rivers (or goes directly into the sea) from combined sewer overflows, a system where raw sewage is discharged, bypassing treatment plants. Such discharges are permitted to a limited extent during severe storms, when the volume of water is too high for treatment plants to cope, but increased monitoring has shown that this is happening shockingly often in many locations. With the increased frequency of storms, and operating companies regularly exceeding their permitted limits, the problem is becoming worse.

Oil exploration

The oil boom in the North Sea peaked in 1999. The UK and other bordering European countries are now making significant moves away from fossil fuel production, but there are still over 180 offshore oil rigs in this area, and new exploratory wells are still being drilled (2025). Accidental oil spills from North Sea oil rigs are not rare, and though many are small, there were significant spills of between 100 and 200 tons in 2011 and 2016. The effects of oil spills, particularly those that reach the coast, are well documented. Rafts of seabirds at sea, such as auks, are particularly vulnerable. On the plus side (though in our eyes it's a small plus), well-established oil rig legs provide 'artificial reefs' for settlement of marine organisms.

Wind farms

The UK has played a leading role in the development of wind power, including inshore and offshore wind farms (though sadly many of the components are not manufactured here). Wind power accounted for nearly 28 per cent of the UK's electricity generation in 2022, the majority of which came from offshore. The North Sea is home to several of the largest offshore wind farms in the world.

Moving away from fossil fuels towards renewable energy is of huge importance in combating climate change. But of course it comes with its own problems. Construction causes at least localised seabed disturbance, and operation generates underwater noise. Above the water and on land, migrating birds are at risk from collision. Many wildfowl and waders use the Eastern Atlantic Flyway, which extends from the Arctic to South Africa. In the UK there is a tentative World Heritage Site (i.e. one being considered), the 'East Coast Flyway', that includes a series of coastal wetland sites along the east coast of the British Isles designated for their international avian importance. The expanding network of wind farms in the North Sea poses a potentially increased threat to seabirds. However, we would certainly argue that careful and considered development of wind farms at sea has far fewer downsides than continued oil and gas exploration. There is also the intriguing prospect of wind farms becoming incidental marine reserves because fishing will not be allowed near the turbines.

Whilst some of the statistics and lack of progress in protecting our coastal seas, which we have flagged up in this final chapter, are both frustrating and depressing, there are undoubtedly some shining examples out there of just what can be and has been achieved. The MPAs around Lundy, Arran and Skomer Island are outstanding examples. These successes could not have been achieved without the input of dedicated, visionary scientists and individuals and the involvement of conservation charities such as the Marine Conservation Society, the Landmark Trust and the regional Wildlife Trusts. Our hard-pressed and cash-strapped statutory conservation agencies come under a lot of fire (some would say rightly so) when things that really should happen, don't, at least within a reasonable time frame. But within them are many dedicated conservationists, and, as we said earlier in this chapter, it is important to acknowledge the hard work being put in by individuals both professional and volunteer. We are certainly not in the 'doom and gloom' camp.

Excluding overseas territories, there are currently 32 World Heritage Sites in the UK, including places such as Stonehenge that are recognised by UNESCO as having universal value for humanity. Two of the 32 are natural areas of coastline: the Dorset and East Devon Coast, and the Giant's Causeway in Northern Ireland. A few World Heritage Sites, such as Australia's Great Barrier Reef, encompass sublittoral areas, but as far as we know there are none anywhere in the world that do not also include a terrestrial element easily visible to humankind. That is a pity, because we would consider fully submerged natural habitats such as maerl, seagrass and offshore cold-water coral reefs to be equally precious, but their importance is not fully recognised. They remain hidden, 'out of sight, out of mind'. We hope that by sharing our experiences of exploring the shallow waters around the British Isles coastline, we have been able to bring some of those hidden gems to light. Knowing that something exists, recognising its importance, and caring about it, is a prerequisite for nature conservation.

Acknowledgements

We would particularly like to thank Katy Roper, at Bloomsbury, for entrusting us with the commission of this book and giving us the chance to share our knowledge, photographs and experiences with others. We would also like to thank all our friends and colleagues who generously provided selections of their amazing photographs for us to choose from: Kirsty Andrews, Lin Baldock, Peter Bardsley, Dan Bolt, Sarah Bowen, John Buckley, Charlotte Cumming, Sue Daly, Jacca Deeble, Iain Dixon, Matt Doggett, Tim Harvey, Douglas Herdson, Keith Hiscock, Rohan Holt, Patrick Joel, Phil Lightfoot, Shannon Moran, Teresa Naylor, Malcolm Nimmo, Martin Palmer, Todd Palmer, Bernard Picton, Joe Redfern, Nick Robertson-Brown, Aaron Sanders, Emma Sheehan, Rob Spray, Andy Turnpenny, Sue Watson-Bate.

Our sincere thanks also go to the following for reading and commenting so constructively on various sections and chapters: Holly Baigent, Lin Baldock, John Bishop, Blue Marine Foundation (Jean-Luc Solandt), Charlotte Bolton, Blaise Bullimore, Anne Bunker, Lisa Chilton, Alix Harvey, Keith Hiscock, Kate Lock, Penny Martin, Seb Shimeld, Christine Wood.

References and further reading

Asterisks (*) denote books that we feel may be particularly useful to readers who wish to explore these topics further.

Ackers, R. G., Moss, D., Picton, B. E., Stone, S. M. K., Morrow, C. 1992. *Sponges of the British Isles ('SPONGE V'): a Colour Guide and Working Document*. Marine Conservation Society, Ross-on-Wye, and Ulster Museum, Belfast. Reset with modifications, 2007. www.habitas.org.uk/marinelife/sponge_guide/sponge5.pdf

Alleway, H. K., Klein, E. S., Cameron, L. et al. 2023. The shifting baseline syndrome as a connective concept for more informed and just responses to global environmental change. *People and Nature* 5: 885–896.

*Archer-Thomson, J. and Cremona, J. 2019. *Rocky Shores*. British Wildlife Collection 7. Bloomsbury, London.

Atkinson, R. J. A. and Pullin, R. S. V. 1996. Observations on the burrows and burrowing behaviour of the red band-fish, *Cepola rubescens* L. *Marine Ecology* 17: 23–40. https://doi.org/10.1111/j.1439-0485.1996.tb00487.x

Atkinson, R. J. A., Pullin, R. S. V. and Dipper, F. A. 1977. Studies on the Red band fish *Cepola rubescens*. *Journal of Zoology* 182: 369–384. https://doi.org/10.1111/j.1469-7998.1977.tb03916.x

*Balcombe, J. 2016. *What a Fish Knows: the Inner Lives of Our Underwater Cousins*. Oneworld Publications, London.

Bowen, S., Goodwin, C., Kipling, D. and Picton, B. E. 2018. *Sea Squirts and Sponges of Britain and Ireland*. Princeton University Press (Wild Nature Press), Princeton and Oxford.

Cousteau, J. Y. 1953. *The Silent World*. Hamish Hamilton, London.

Darbyshire, T. 2024. Status and distribution of Eyelash Worms (*Myxicola* spp.) in the UK. *Bulletin of the Porcupine Marine Natural History Society* 21: 10–18.

Darmaillacq, A.-S., Lesimple, C. and Dickel, L. 2008. Embryonic visual learning in the cuttlefish *Sepia officinalis*. *Animal Behaviour* 76: 131–134. https://doi.org/10.1016/j.anbehav.2008.02.006

Dipper, F. 1991. Colonisation and natural changes in a newly established 'artificial reef' in Gulf waters. In *Estuaries and Coasts: Spatial and Temporal Intercomparisons ECSA 19 Symposium*, edited by M. Elliott and J.-P. Ducrotoy, pp. 259–264. Olsen and Olsen, Fredensborg.

*Dipper, F. 2016. *The Marine World: a Natural History of Ocean Life*. Princeton University Press (Wild Nature Press), Princeton and Oxford. Revised reprint, 2019.

*Dipper, F. 2021. *Seals*. RSPB Spotlight series. Bloomsbury, London.

*Dipper, F. 2022. *Elements of Marine Ecology*, 5th edition. Butterworth Heinemann, Oxford.

Dobbs, H. E. 1977. *Follow a Wild Dolphin: the Story of an Extraordinary Friendship*. Souvenir Press, London.

Donaldson, J. 2004. *Sharing a Shell*. Macmillan, London.

Duckworth, A. R. and Peterson, B. J. 2012. Effects of seawater temperature and pH on the boring rates of the sponge *Cliona celata* in scallop shells. *Marine Biology* 160: 27–35. https://doi.org/10.1007/s00227-012-2053-z

Dunkley, F. and Solandt, J.-L. 2021. *Marine unProtected Areas: a Case for a Just Transition to Ban Bottom Trawl and Dredge Fishing in Offshore Marine Protected Areas*. An online report from the Ocean Recovery Department, Marine Conservation Society. https://doi.org/10.13140/RG.2.2.35655.52645

Eger, A. M., Layton, C., McHugh, T. A, Gleason, M. and Eddy, N. 2022. *Kelp Restoration Guidebook: Lessons Learned from Kelp Projects Around the World*. The Nature Conservancy, Arlington, VA. https://kelpforestalliance.com/TNC-KFA-kelp-guidebook-2022.pdf

Gallagher, M. C., Davenport, J., Gregory, S., McAllen, R. and O'Riordan, R. 2015. The invasive barnacle species, *Austrominius modestus*: its status and competition with indigenous barnacles on the Isle of Cumbrae, Scotland. *Estuarine, Coastal and Shelf Science* 152: 134–141. https://doi.org/10.1016/j.ecss.2014.11.014

Gamble, C., Debney, A., Glover, A. et al. (eds) 2021. *Seagrass Restoration Handbook*. Zoological Society of London, London.

Goncalves, I. B., Mobley, K .B., Ahnesjö, I., Sagebakken, G., Jones, A. G. and Kvarnemo, C. 2010. Reproductive compensation in broad-nosed pipefish females. *Proceedings of the Royal Society B* 277(1687): 1581–1587. https://doi.org/10.1098/rspb.2009.2290

Gosse, P. H. 1860. *Actinologia Britannica: a History of the British Sea-Anemones and Corals*. Van Voorst, London.

*Hanlon, R. T. and Messenger, J. B. 2018. *Cephalopod Behaviour*, 2nd edition. Cambridge University Press, Cambridge.

Harries, D. B., Moore, C. G., Porter, J. S., Sanderson, W. G., Ware, F. J. and Kamphausen, L. 2018. *The Establishment of Site Condition Monitoring of the Sea Caves of the St Kilda and North Rona Special Areas of Conservation with Supplementary Data from Loch Eriboll*. Scottish Natural Heritage Research Report 1044.

*Hayward, P. J. 2016. *Shallow Seas of Northwest Europe*. New Naturalist 131. William Collins, London.

*Hayward, P. J. and Ryland, J. S. 2017. *Marine Fauna of North-West Europe*, 2nd edition. Oxford University Press, Oxford.

Hickman, J., Richards, J., Rees, A. and Sheehan, E. V. 2024. Shipwrecks act as de facto Marine Protected Areas in areas of heavy fishing pressure. *Marine Ecology* 45: e12782. https://doi.org/10.1111/maec.12782

*Hiscock, K. 2014. *Marine Biodiversity Conservation: a Practical Approach*. Routledge, London.

*Hiscock, K. 2018. *Exploring Britain's Hidden World: a Natural History of Seabed Habitats*. Princeton University Press (Wild Nature Press), Princeton and Oxford.

Hiscock, K. and Irving, R. A. 2012. *Protecting Lundy's Marine Life: 40 Years of Science and Conservation*. Lundy Field Society, UK.

Hiscock, K., Sharrock, S., Highfield, J. and Snelling, D. 2010. Colonization of an artificial reef in south-west England: ex-HMS 'Scylla'. *Journal of the Marine Biological Association of the United Kingdom* 90: 69–94. https://doi.org/10.1017/S0025315409991457

*Holland, P. 2011. *The Animal Kingdom: a Very Short Introduction*. Oxford University Press, Oxford.

Horton, T. and Okamura, B. 2002. The distribution of *Ceratothoa steindachneri* (Crustacea: Isopoda: Cymothoidae) parasitic in *Echiichthys vipera* in the north-east Atlantic. *Journal of the Marine Biological Association of the United Kingdom* 82: 415–417. https://doi.org/10.1017/S0025315402005660

Howson, C. and Picton, B. 1985. A sublittoral survey of St Kilda. British Sub Aqua Club / Marine Conservation Society expedition to St Kilda, 7th to 20th July 1984. Report to the Nature Conservancy Council.

Howson, C. M., Clark, L., Mercer, T. S. and James, B. 2012. Marine biological survey to establish the distribution and status of fan mussels *Atrina fragilis* and other Marine Protected Area (MPA) search features within the Sound of Canna, Inner Hebrides. Scottish Natural Heritage Commissioned Report 438.

Hussain, N. A. and Knight-Jones, E. W. 1995. Fish and fish-leeches on rocky shores around Britain. *Journal of the Marine Biological Association of the United Kingdom* 75(2): 311–322. https://doi.org/10.1017/S0025315400018191

Jackson, E. L., Higgs, S., Allsop, T., Cathray, A., Evans, J. and Langmead, O. 2011. Isles of Scilly Seagrass Mapping. Natural England Commissioned Report NECR087.

Jacoby, D. M. P., Fear, L. N., Sims, D. W. and Croft, D. P. 2014. Shark personalities? Repeatability of social network traits in a widely distributed predatory fish. *Behavioral Ecology and Sociobiology* 68: 1995–2003. https://doi.org/10.1007/s00265-014-1805-9

Kaplan, S. W. 1983. Intrasexual aggression in *Metridium senile*. *The Biological Bulletin* 165: 416–418. https://doi.org/10.2307/1541206

Kingston, A. C. N., Kuzirian, A. M., Hanlon, R. T. and Cronin, T. W. 2015. Visual phototransduction components in cephalopod chromatophores suggest dermal photoreception. *Journal of Experimental Biology* 218: 1596–1602. https://doi.org/10.1242/jeb.117945

Kuqo, A. and Mai, C. 2023. Flexible insulation mats from *Zostera marina* seagrass. *Journal of Natural Fibers* 20(1). https://doi.org/10.1080/15440478.2022.2154303

Lesser, M. P., Carleton, K. L., Böttger, S. A., Barry, T. M. and Walker, C. W. 2011. Sea urchin tube feet are photosensory organs that express a rhabdomeric-like opsin and PAX6. *Proceedings of the Royal Society B* 278: 3371–3379. https://doi.org/10.1098/rspb.2011.0336

Lock, K., Burton, M., Jones, J. and Massey, A. 2023. *Skomer Marine Conservation Zone, Annual Report 2022/23*. National Resources Wales Evidence Report 657. NRW, Cardiff.

Lundy Management Forum 2017. *Lundy Marine Management Plan 2017*. Written by Rebecca

MacDonald and revised by Robert Irving. Produced for Natural England by the Landmark Trust, UK.

Macdonald, R. 2011. *The Darkness Below*. Whittles Publishing, Dunbeath.

Mezrai, N., Arduini, L., Dickel, L., Chiao, C-C. and Darmaillacq A.-S. 2020. Awareness of danger inside the egg: evidence of innate and learned predator recognition in cuttlefish embryos. *Learning and Behaviour* 48: 401–410. https://doi.org/10.3758/s13420-020-00424-7

*Mladenov, P. 2013. *Marine Biology: a Very Short Introduction*. Oxford University Press, Oxford.

Moore, C. G., Harries, D. B., James, B. et al. 2018. *The Distribution and Condition of Flame Shell Beds and Other Priority Marine Features in Loch Carron Marine Protected Area and Adjacent Waters*. Scottish Natural Heritage Research Report 1038.

Munster Technological University (MTU) 2022. *Socio-Economic Study of Seaweed Harvesting in Ireland*. A report prepared by the Clean Technology Centre and the Circular Bioeconomy Research Group, MTU and Benton Ecological Solutions and Technology. Ireland.

Naylor, E. 2015. *Moonstruck: How Lunar Cycles Affect Life*. Oxford University Press, Oxford.

*Naylor, P. 2021. *Great British Marine Animals*, 4th edition – with special focus on their behaviour. Sound Diving Publications, Plymouth.

Naylor, P., Naylor, T., Hammond, L. and Jacoby, D. M. P. 2022. From sneaker to bourgeois male: long-term observations on recognised tompot blenny *Parablennius gattorugine* individuals reveal new information on their biology. *Journal of Fish Biology* 102: 542–545. https://doi.org/10.1111/jfb.15285

Naylor, T. 2013. *Benny the Blenny's Shallow Sea Adventure*. Tompot Publications, Plymouth.

Papastamatiou, Y. P., Bodey, T. W., Caselle, J. E. et al. 2020. Multiyear social stability and social information use in reef sharks with diel fission–fusion dynamics. *Proceedings of the Royal Society B* 287: 20201063. https://doi.org/10.1098/rspb.2020.1063

Pauly, D. 1995. Anecdotes and the shifting baseline syndrome of fisheries. *Trends in Ecology and Evolution* 10: 430.

Picton, B. and Morrow, C. 2023. *Nudibranchs of Britain, Ireland and Northwest Europe*, 2nd edition. Princeton University Press (Wild Nature Press), Princeton and Oxford.

Potts, G. W. 1985. The nest structure of the Corkwing Wrasse, *Crenilabrus melops* (Labridae: Teleostei). *Journal of the Marine Biological Association of the United Kingdom* 65: 531–546. https://doi.org/10.1017/S002531540005058X

Renn, C., Rees, S., Rees, A. et al. 2024. Lessons from Lyme Bay (UK) to inform policy, management, and monitoring of Marine Protected Areas. *ICES Journal of Marine Science* 81: 276–292. https://doi.org/10.1093/icesjms/fsad204

*Roberts, C. 2007. *The Unnatural History of the Sea*. Island Press, London.

Rosenqvist, G. and Johansson, K. 1995. Male avoidance of parasitized females explained by direct benefits in a pipefish. *Animal Behaviour* 49: 1039–1045. https://doi.org/10.1006/anbe.1995.0133

Ross, D. M. and von Boletzky, S. 1979. The association between the pagurid *Dardanus arrosor* and the actinian *Calliactis parasitica*. Recovery of activity in 'inactive' *D. arrosor* in the presence of cephalopods. *Marine Behaviour and Physiology* 6: 175–184. https://doi.org/10.1080/10236247909378564

Rowley, A. F., Davies, C. E., Malkin, S. H. et al. 2020. Prevalence and histopathology of the parasitic barnacle, *Sacculina carcini* in shore crabs, *Carcinus maenas*. *Journal of Invertebrate Pathology* 171: 107338. https://doi.org/10.1016/j.jip.2020.107338

Royal Commission on Environmental Pollution. 2004. *Turning the Tide: Addressing the Impact of Fisheries on the Marine Environment*. HMSO, London.

*Rudd, H. 2023. *Britain's Living Seas*. The Wildlife Trusts. Bloomsbury, London.

Sanchez-Vidal, A., Canals, M., de Haan, W. P., Romero, J. and Veny, M. 2021. Seagrasses provide a novel ecosystem service by trapping marine plastics. *Scientific Reports* 11: 254. https://doi.org/10.1038/s41598-020-79370-3

Schnell, A. K., Boeckle, M., Riviera, M., Clayton, N. S. and Hanlon, R. T. 2021. Cuttlefish exert self-control in a delay of gratification task. *Proceedings of the Royal Society B* 288: 20203061. https://doi.org/10.1098/rspb.2020.3161

Schoenrock, K. M., O'Callaghan, T., O'Callaghan, R. and Krueger-Hadfield, S. A. 2019. First record of *Laminaria ochroleuca* Bachelot de la Pylaie in Ireland in Béal an Mhuirthead, County Mayo. *Marine Biodiversity Records* 12: 9 (2019). https://doi.org/10.1186/s41200-019-0168-3

Sheehan, E. V. and Cousens, S. L. 2017. 'Starballing': a potential explanation for mass stranding. *Marine Biodiversity Records* 47: 617–618. https://doi.org/10.1007/s12526-016-0504-3

Sheehan, E. V., Rees, A., Bridger, D., Williams, T. and Hall-Spencer, J. M. 2017. Strandings of NE Atlantic gorgonians. *Biological Conservation* 209: 482–487. https://doi.org/10.1016/j.biocon.2017.03.020

Sheehan E. V., Holmes L. A., Davies B. F. R., Cartwright A., Rees A. and Attrill M. J. 2021. Rewilding of protected areas enhances resilience of marine ecosystems to extreme climatic events. *Frontiers in Marine Science* 8: 671427. https://doi.org/10.3389/fmars.2021.671427

*Sherwood, A. 2017. *Top 100 British Shore Dives*, revised edition. Aquapress, Southend-On-Sea.

Sims, D. W. 2005. Differences in habitat selection and reproductive strategies of male and female sharks. In *Sexual Segregation in Vertebrates: Ecology of the Two Sexes*, edited by K. E. Ruckstuhl and P. Neuhaus, pp. 127–147. Cambridge University Press, Cambridge.

Sims, D. W., Berrow, S. D., O'Sullivan, K. M. et al. 2022. Circles in the sea: annual courtship 'torus' behaviour of basking sharks *Cetorhinus maximus* identified in the eastern North Atlantic Ocean. *Journal of Fish Biology* 101: 1160–1181. https://doi.org/10.1111/jfb.15187

Smith, P. and Nunny, R. 2012. Mapping of sedimentary marine biotopes around Lundy, UK. *Journal of the Lundy Field Society* 3: 41–69.

Southward, A. J. and Roberts E. K. 1984. The Marine Biological Association 1884–1984: one hundred years of marine research. *Report and Transactions of the Devonshire Association for the Advancement of Science*: 116: 155–199. Available as Marine Biological Association of the United Kingdom Occasional Publication Number 3.

*Taylor, E. and Taylor, G. 2025. *Snorkelling Britain: 100 Marine Adventures*. Wild Things Publishing Ltd, Bath.

Thompson, T. E. 1988. *Molluscs: Benthic Opisthobranchs (Mollusca: Gastropoda)*. Synopses of the British Fauna New Series 8 (Second Edition). Published for the Linnean Society of London and the Estuarine and Brackish-water Sciences Association. Brill/Backhuys, Leiden.

*Trewhella, S. and Hatcher, J. 2015. *The Essential Guide to Beachcombing and the Strandline*. Princeton University Press (Wild Nature Press), Princeton and Oxford.

Trewhella, S. and Hatcher, J. 2017. *In the Company of Seahorses*. Princeton University Press (Wild Nature Press), Princeton and Oxford.

Unsworth, R. K. F., Green, A., Chadwick, M. A. and Jones, P. J. S. 2021. Seagrass meadows shrank by 92% in UK waters – restoring them could absorb carbon emissions and boost fish. *The Conversation*, 4 March 2021. https://theconversation.com/seagrass-meadows-shrank-by-92-in-uk-waters-restoring-them-could-absorb-carbon-emissions-and-boost-fish-156459

Yonge, C. M. and Thompson, T. E. 1976. *Living Marine Molluscs*. Collins, London.

*Seasearch series marine identification guides Britain and Ireland, Princeton University Press (Wild Nature Press): *Inshore Fishes* (2023), *Marine Life* (2018), *Sea Squirts and Sponges* (2018), *Seaweeds* (2017), *Sea Anemones and Corals* (2013), *Bryozoans and Hydroids* (2012).

Websites of organisations mentioned in the book

Chapter 1
Marine Habitat Classification for Britain and Ireland
mhc.jncc.gov.uk

Chapter 2
National Biodiversity Network Atlas
nbnatlas.org
Sherkin Island Marine Station
sherkinmarinedata.ie
South-West Marine Ecosystems
swmecosystems.co.uk

Chapter 3
Kelp Forest Alliance
kelpforestalliance.com
Sussex Kelp Recovery Project
sussexkelp.org.uk

Chapter 4
ATLAS project
eu-atlas.org
National Trust for Scotland
nts.org.uk
The SHIPS Project (Liberty 80 Project)
shipsproject.org/Liberty70

Chapter 5
Blue Natural Capital
letstalk.cornwall.gov.uk/bluecarbon
Seasearch Reports – Fireworks Anemones
seasearch.org.uk/seasearch-report-fireworks

Chapter 6
The Green Blue
thegreenblue.org.uk
Life Recreation ReMEDIES
saveourseabed.co.uk/the-project

References and further reading

Ocean Conservation Trust
  oceanconservationtrust.org
SeagrassSpotter
  seagrassspotter.org
Seahorse Trust
  theseahorsetrust.org

Chapter 7
Irish Basking Shark Project report a sighting
  baskingshark.ie/report-a-sighting
Joint Nature Conservation Committee volunteer seabird recording
  jncc.gov.uk/our-work/volunteer-seabirds-at-sea-surveys
Manx Whale and Dolphin Watch report a sighting
  mwdw.net/report-a-basking-shark
Manx Whale and Dolphin Watch solitary dolphins
  mwdw.net/moonlight-starlight-solitary-dolphins
MARINElife
  marine-life.org.uk
Shark Trust Basking Shark project
  sharktrust.org/basking-shark-project
UK Cetacean Strandings Investigation Programme
  UKstrandings.org/csip-publications

Chapter 8
Black Bream Project
  mattdoggett.com/the-black-bream-project
Glasgow University Hunterian Museum
  gla.ac.uk/hunterian/collections
IUCN Red List
  iucnredlist.org
Shark Trust Fisheries Advisories
  sharktrust.org/pages/category/fisheries-advisories
Sussex Inshore Fisheries and Conservation Authority regulations
  sussex-ifca.gov.uk/regulations#kingsmere
Undulate Ray Project
  undulateray.uk

Chapter 9
World Register of Marine Species (WoRMS)
  marinespecies.org

Chapter 10
Cuttlefish Conservation Initiative
  cuttlefishconservation.com

Chapter 12
Berwickshire Marine Reserve
  berwickshiremarinereserve.org.uk
Biological Records Centre
  brc.ac.uk
Blue Marine Foundation
  bluemarinefoundation.com
COAST (Community of Arran Seabed Trust)
  arrancoast.com
COAST map of the South Arran MPA conservation zones (click 'Welcome to Arran's MPA' in the list on the right)
  arrancoast.com/south-arran-mpa
Cornwall Good Seafood Guide
  cornwallgoodseafoodguide.org.uk
GB Non-native Species Information Portal (NNSIP)
  nonnativespecies.org/non-native-species/information-portal
GB Non-native Species Secretariat species sheets
  nonnativespecies.org/non-native-species/id-sheets
Marine Species of the British Isles and Adjacent Seas (MSBIAS)
  marinespecies.org/msbias
MCS Good Fish Guide
  mcsuk.org/goodfishguide
National Biodiversity Network Atlas
  nbnatlas.org

Websites providing MPA information

jncc.gov.uk/our-work/offshore-mpas.
  Lists 39 offshore MPAs in English and Scottish waters, with links to individual site information centres.
jncc.gov.uk/our-work/marine-protected-area-mapper.
  An interactive resource containing information on the MPAs designated in UK and Crown Dependency waters. It also has useful links to descriptions of the different types of MPAs.
wildlifetrusts.org/marine-protected-areas/england.
  An easy-to-use interactive map of MPAs within English waters.
jncc.gov.uk/our-work/UK-marine-protected-area-network-statistics.
  Summary statistics, updated July 2023.

Illustration credits

All photographs and figures are copyright © Paul Naylor or are understood to be out of copyright, except for those listed below.

Bloomsbury Publishing would like to thank those listed below for providing illustrations and for permission to reproduce copyright material within this book. While every effort has been made to trace and acknowledge copyright holders, we would like to apologise for any errors or omissions, and invite readers to inform us so that corrections can be made in any future editions.

Key: T = top; B = bottom; C = centre; L = left; R = right; TL = top left; TR = top right; BL = bottom left; BR = bottom right

1 Shannon Moran; 9 L John Buckley; 22 Malcolm Nimmo; 24 Rob Spray; 28 Frances Dipper; 31 Wild Nature Press; 32 Frances Dipper; 37 B Frances Dipper; 39 Wild Nature Press; 41 Sarah Bowen; 44 Frances Dipper; 54 T, 54 B, 55 T Frances Dipper; 55 B Sue Watson-Bate; 56 L Frances Dipper; 57 John Buckley; 59 B Malcolm Nimmo; 60 Keith Hiscock; 61 Frances Dipper; 64 Phil Lightfoot; 67 Teresa Naylor; 78 Frances Dipper; 82, 85 T Shannon Moran; 86 L Frances Dipper; 87 Iain Dixon; 88 TL Malcolm Nimmo; 88 TR Kirsty Andrews; 90 T, 90 C, 90 B Jacca Deeble; 91 L, 91 R Malcolm Nimmo; 93 Frances Dipper; 94 Iain Dixon; 95 C Frances Dipper; 97 L, 97 R Iain Dixon; 99 Tim Harvey; 102 Khun Ta/Shutterstock; 104 Kirsty Andrews; 109 Iain Dixon; 114 T, 115 Rohan Holt; 121 Rob Spray; 122 Lin Baldock; 126 Sarah Bowen; 129 Kirsty Andrews; 130 Rob Atherton/Shutterstock; 131 T Kirsty Andrews; 131 B Shannon Moran; 136 Kirsty Andrews; 144 Keith Hiscock; 146, 150 B, 153 (all), 163 TR, 163 BR Frances Dipper; 163 TL Iain Dixon; 163 BL Shannon Moran; 166, 168, 169 L Frances Dipper; 170 Andi111/Shutterstock; 175 T Bernard Picton; 177 L, 177 R, 180 Frances Dipper; 183 Farrah Fortnam/RYA The Green Blue. Reproduced by kind permission of the LIFE Recreation ReMEDIES project and The Green Blue, the environmental programme of the RYA; 188 Keith Hiscock; 193 Malcolm Nimmo; 194 BR Keith Hiscock; 195 L, 196 T Malcolm Nimmo; 197 B Keith Hiscock; 198 Peter Bardsley; 200 Nick Robertson-Brown; 202 Kirsty Andrews; 205 Rohan Holt; 207 Aaron Sanders; 209 T, 209 C Rohan Holt; 209 B Sue Daly; 212/213 Todd Palmer; 224 Matt Doggett; 233 T Kirsty Andrews; 248 L Martin Palmer; 250 Lin Baldock; 252, 261, 269 BL, 269 BR, 271 Malcolm Nimmo; 273 Charlotte Cumming; 274 Shannon Moran; 283 T Frances Dipper; 283 B Kirsty Andrews; 286 T, 286 B Dan Bolt; 288 Douglas Herdson; 289 L Shannon Moran; 289 R, 291 T Aaron Sanders; 291 B Sue Daly; 293 Shannon Moran; 295 Boerescu/Shutterstock; 315 Gena Melendrez Shutterstock; 318 B Frances Dipper; 320/321 Havelock Photography/Shutterstock; 322 Shannon Moran; 325 T Douglas Herdson; 325 B Frances Dipper; 326 RogerMechan/Shutterstock; 328 T, 328 B Emma Sheehan/University of Plymouth; 329 MCS Patrick Joel; 336 jimmonkphotography/Shutterstock; 343 T Frances Dipper; 343 BL, 343 BR Joe Redfern/Whitby Lobster Hatchery; 347 Andy Turnpenny.

Index

Page numbers in **bold** refer to illustrations.
Page numbers in *italics* refer to tables.

Acrocnida brachiata 143
Acromegalomma vesiculosum 23
Actinia equina 113
Actinothoe sphyrodeta 135
Adna anglica 309
Advanced Mooring Systems (AMS) 183, **183**
Aeolid, Farran's **269**
Aequipecten opercularis 132, 152, 305–306, **305**
Aequorea 195, **195**
Akera bullata 273
Alaria esculenta 40, 97, 103
Alcyonium
  digitatum 47, **49**, 110, 132
  glomeratum 110, **110**
  hibernicum 113, **114**
Alitta virens 153, 154
Alloteuthis subulata 293
Alosa fallax 38
ambush predators 152, 231–232, **232**
Ampelisca 149
amphipods 22, 91, **121**, 149, 155, 167, 169
Amphiura filiformis 143
Amphorina farrani **269**
Anarhichas lupus 76, 232, **233**, 341
anchor damage 183–184, **183**
Anemone
  Beadlet 113
  Burrowing 141, **141**, 176
  Cloak 301–302, **301**, **302**
  Clock Face 151, **151**
  Dahlia 37, **37**, 79
  Daisy **175**, 176
  Elegant 109, **109**
  Fireworks **136**, 140–141, **140**
  Green Snakelocks 177, **177**
  Jewel 40, 79, 106–107, **107**
  Parasitic 299–300, **299**, **300**
  Plumose 79, 107–109, **108**, 132
  Sea Loch 77, **81**
  Snakelocks 94, **160**, 311–312, **312**
  White-striped 135
  Yellow Cluster **110**, 133
anemones 21, **21**
  muddy seabeds **136**, 140–141, **140**, **141**
  reproduction 26, 107, **107**, 108, 109
  rocky reefs **104**, 106–109, **107**, **108**, **109**
  sandy seabeds 151, **151**
  sea caves 113
  seagrass meadows **160**, 171, **175**, 176, 177, **177**
  in spring 48, **51**
  stinging cells 108, 271, 300, 302, **302**
  symbiotic relationships 299–302, **299**, **300**, **301**, **302**, 311–312, **312**
  and tidal currents 34, **35**
Anemonia viridis 94, **160**, 177, **177**, 311–312, **312**
Angler 152, 231–232
Anglesey 77, *185*
  see also Menai Strait
Anguilla anguilla 97, 135
Anilocra 316–317, **317**
animal-constructed reefs 123–127
  flame shell reefs 125–126, **126**, 138
  mussel reefs 124–125
  oyster reefs 123–124
  tubeworm reefs 127, **127**
animal welfare 294
Anisakis 319
annelid worms
  boring 44
  predatory 153–154
  seagrass meadows 167, **175**
  sediment seabeds 153–154, 158–159
  tubeworms 22–23, 27, 34, **35**, 127, **127**, 147–149, **148**, **149**
Antedon
  bifida **263**
  petasus 263
Anthus petrosus 208
Antiopella cristata **269**
ants 298
Aphrodita aculeata 153–154
Aplysia punctata **169**, 273, **350**
aposematism 272
Apus apus 201
Archidoris pseudoargus **269**, 272, 305

Architeuthis dux 295
Arenicola 158
Aristotle's lantern 92, **93**, 261
Arran, Argyll and Bute 77, *333*, 335–336, **336**
arrow worms 191
artificial reefs 128–135
  piers 75, 133–135, **133**, **134**, 221–222, **221**
  shipwrecks 36, 77, 128–133, **129**, **130**, **131**
Ascidia mentula 193
Ascophyllum nodosum 93, 97, 101
asexual reproduction 25–26, 107, **107**, 108, 193
Aslia lefevrei 117, 262
Asterias rubens **25**, 132, 135, **254**, **256**, 257, 258, 259–260
Asterina gibbosa **116**, 259
Astropecten irregularis 152–153, **153**
Atherina presbyter 134–135, **203**
Atkinson, Jim 235
Atrina fragilis 144, **144**
Aurelia aurita 192–193, **193**
Austrominius modestus 350–351
Axinella dissimilis **337**
axons, squids 294

Babakina anadoni 345–346, **346**
Balaenoptera
  acutorostrata 42, 199, 205
  musculus 42
  physalus 42
Balanophyllia regia 122
Balanus crenatus 37, 40
Balistes capriscus 247–249, 345
Balistoides viridescens 249
Bandfish, Red 147, 234–236, **235**
Barnacle
  Australian 350–351
  Crab Hacker 317–318, **318**
barnacles **17**, 22, 37, 40
  artificial reefs 132
  invasive species 350–351
  larvae 26, 27, 317
  parasitic 317–318, **318**
  as prey 56, **254**, 271

reproduction 24, **24**
symbiotic relationships 309
Bass 135, 342
beachcombing 53–56, **54**, **55**, **56**
Beachwatch 71
Bellamy, David 69, 90
Bembridge, Isle of Wight 75
benthos, defined 14
Berwickshire Marine Reserve, Scotland 341
Bib **131**, 134, 135, 203, 242
Big Seaweed Search 71
biofuel 102
biogenic reefs *see* animal-constructed reefs
bioluminescence 190–192, **191**
biotopes 40
birds 170, **170**, 208–211, **209**, 239, 352
bivalve molluscs 18–20, 268
  boring 44, **44**, 45
  flame shell reefs 125–126, **126**, 138
  invasive species 349
  larvae 26, 27, 124
  oyster reefs 16, 123–124
  as prey 56, **56**, 255–256, **256**, 259
  sediment seabeds 152, 158, **158**
  siphons **17**, 19, 44, 158, **158**, 234
  symbiotic relationships **150**, 304, 305–306, **305**
  see also mussels
Blenny
  Black-faced 113–114, 134
  Blackfaced **6**
  Red 249–251
  Tompot 48, 75, **116**, 117, 135, **214**, 216, 218–222, **218**, **219**, **221**, **222**, 240, 310
  Variable 247, 248, **248**, 345
Blue Marine Foundation 331, *333*, 338
Bolinopsis infundibulum 197
boring animals 44–45, **44**
Branta bernicla 170, **170**
breeding *see* reproduction
Brighton Pier, Sussex 75, 133–135, **133**, 221–222, **221**

361

Coastal Seas

Brill 228
British Sub-Aqua Club (BSAC) 62, 69
Brittlestar
    Black 81, 260
    Common 260, **261**
brittlestars 21, 23–24, **35**, 143, 152, 257, 259, 260, **261**
brown seaweeds 32, 41, 93–94, 98–99, **99**, 101–102, *172*, 285
    see also kelp/seaweed forests; kelps
Bryozoan, Potato Crisp 121
bryozoans 21–22, 37
    epiphytic 47, 85, 86, **87**
    kelp forests 85, 86, **87**, 90
    larvae 26
    reproduction 26
    seagrass meadows 170, 171, *172*
bubble shells 175, **175**
Buccinum undatum 55, **55**, 152
Butterfish 310
Butterfly, Large Blue 298
By-the-wind Sailor 197–198, **197**

Calliactis
    palliata 301–302, **301**, **302**
    parasitica 299–300, **299**, **300**
Callionymus **212–213**
    lyra 134, **225**
Calliostoma zizyphinum **307**
Callistephanus pallida 111
Calvadosia campanulata **171**
cameras 67–68, **67**, **68**
Cancer pagurus 118, 119, **119**, 120–121, 135
Candelabrum cocksii 345–346
Candiella odhneri 111
Canna, Hebrides 76–77
caprellid shrimps 89
carbon sinks 84, 157, 161, 164
Carcharhinus amblyrhynchos 224
Carcinus maenas 58, **59**, 89, **89**, 118, **119**, 135, 306, 310, 317–318, **318**
Caryophyllia inornata 122
Catshark, Small-spotted 54, **82**, 216, **217**, 224–225
Centrolabrus exoletus 236, 241, **241**, 242
cephalopods 268, 275–280
    in art 295
    colour changes 278–280, **279**
    ink clouds 277–278
    jet propulsion 276–277, **277**
    octopuses 275, 277, **277**, 278, 290–293, **291**, 294, 347
    sentience and welfare 294
    squids 275, 276–277, 293–294, **293**

see also cuttlefishes
Cepola macrophthalma 147, 234–236, **235**
Cereus pedunculatus **175**, 176
Cerianthus lloydii 141, **141**, 176
Cetacean Strandings Investigation Programme (CSIP) 207
cetaceans 42, 199, 204–205, **205**, 207
Cetorhinus maximus **59**, 199–201, **200**, 217, 234
Charadrius hiaticula 208
Chesil Cove, Dorset 74
    see also Fleet Lagoon
Chink Shell, Banded 169, **169**
chitons 91
Chorda filum 45
chromatophores 278–280
Chrysaora hysoscella **193**, 194, **194**, 313–314
Ciona intestinalis 20–21, **21**, 25, 146
citizen science projects 54, **54**, 68–72, **69**, 71, 210, 216, 245–246
Clathrina coriacea 40, **41**
Clavelina lepadiformis 25
'cleaner fish' 218, 241–242, **241**, 317, **344**
climate change 247, 316, 324, 344–347, **346**
    see also carbon sinks
Clingfish, Shore 91
clingfishes 90, **90**, 91
Cliona celata 44–45, **46**, 306
Clupea harengus 42, 201–202, 234
cnidae 106
cnidarians 21
    sea pens 141–142, **142**
    stinging cells 106, 108, 271
    see also anemones; bryozoans; hydroids; jellyfish; soft corals
Cod 42
comb jellies 191, 196–197, **196**
Comber 346
Community of Arran Seabed Trust (COAST) 77, 335–336
Conger conger 117, **131**, 135, 310, **310**
conservation problems and solutions 323–324
    anchor damage 183–184, **183**
    climate change 247, 316, 324, 344–347, **346**
    hunting by divers 342
    invasive species 98–99, **99**, 123, 348–351, **349**, **350**
    lobster hatcheries 343, **343**
    oil exploration 352
    overfishing 100, 324–327, **325**, **327**

power station cooling-water infrastructure 347, **347**
restoration projects 100–101, 184–186, *185*
salmon farming 241, 317, 319, **344**
sewage pollution 351–352
spearfishing 342
sustainable seafood 342–344, **343**
wind farms 352–353
see also Marine Protected Areas (MPAs)
copepods 234, 318–319
Coral
    Scarlet and Gold Star 122
    Southern Cup 122
    Sunset Cup **110**, 121–122
corals see hard corals; soft corals
Cornwall Seal Group Research Trust 71, 207
Cornwall Wildlife Trust 71, 73, *185*, 186, 341, 343
Corymorpha nutans 151
Corynactis viridis 40, 79, 106–107, **107**
Corystes cassivelaunus 149–150, **150**
Cotton Spinner 262, **262**
Cousteau, Jacques 13, 61, 234
Crab
    Angular 147
    Broad-clawed Porcelain 89–90
    Brown 118, 119, **119**, 120–121, 135
    Flying 174
    Great Spider 87–88, **88**
    Harbour 177
    Masked 149–150, **150**
    Shore 58, **59**, 89, **89**, 118, **119**, 135, 306, 310, 317–318, **318**
    Spiny Spider 56, 74, 118, 135, 152, 174, **174**, 265–268, **265**, 267
    Sponge 308, **309**
    Velvet Swimming **116**, 135, **218**, 222
    Wrinkled Swimming 174
crabs 265–268
    artificial reefs 135
    crevice-dwellers 116, **116**, 310
    fisheries 120–121, 265
    kelp forests 87–90, **88**, **89**
    moulting 55–56, 89, **89**, 118–120, **119**, 265, 266–267
    muddy seabeds 147
    Norfolk chalk-reef 118–121, **119**, **120**
    parasites 317–318, **318**
    sandy seabeds 149–150, **150**, 152
    seagrass meadows 167,

167, 174, **174**, 177
    symbiotic relationships 307–308, **308**, **309**, 311, **311**
    see also hermit crabs
Crangon crangon 58
Crawfish **131**, **327**
Crepidula fornicata 123, 349, **349**
Cromer Shoal Chalk Beds Marine Conservation Zone 118
Crossaster papposus **81**, **252**, 258, **258**, 264
crustaceans 264–265
    amphipods **22**, 91, **121**, 149, 155, 167, 169
    copepods 234, 318–319
    isopods 91, 169, 316–317, **317**
    shrimps 89, 167, 169, 309, 312, **312**
    see also barnacles; crabs; hermit crabs; lobsters
Ctenolabrus rupestris 236–237, 241, 242
cup corals **92**, **110**, 113, 121–122, **262**, 307, 308–309, **334**
Cushion Star **116**, 259
    Red 259
cuttlebones 55
Cuttlefish
    Australian Giant 280
    Common **73**, 74, **173**, **274**, 280, 288
    Elegant 280
    Pacific Ocean Pharaoh 288
    Pink 280
Cuttlefish Conservation Initiative 71, 289
cuttlefishes 66, 275, **276**, 280–289
    colour changes 278–280, **279**, 282, **282**
    cuttlebones 55
    egg masses 172–173, *172*, *173*, 287–288, **287**
    embryonic visual learning 287–288
    fisheries 288–289, **288**
    hunting skills 282–285, **283**, **284**
    ink clouds 277–278
    intelligence 285
    jet propulsion 276–277, **277**
    'Little Cuttle' 289, **289**
    reproduction 172–173, *172*, *173*, 285–288, **286**, **287**
Cyanea
    capillata **67**, 194–195, **194**, **296**, 312–313, **313**
    lamarckii **194**, 195
Cyclopterus lumpus 216, 238
Cylista elegans 109, **109**
Cymothoa exigua 316

Index

cymothoid isopods 316–317, **317**
Cystophora cristata 205
Dab 158, 227, 228, 234
Dabberlocks 40, 97, 103
Darbyshire, Teresa 148–149
Dasyatis pastinaca 230, 231
Dead Man's Fingers 47, **49**, 110, 132
Delphinus delphis 204, **205**, 207
Dendrodoa grossularia 40, **41**
Dermochelys coriacea 198
Desmarestia aculeata 41
Desmarestia ligulata 41
Devon Wildlife Trust 338, 341
diatoms 32, 96, 171
Diazona violacea 48
Dicentrarchus labrax 135, 342
Didemnum vexillum 351
dinoflagellates 32, 191, 192
Dipturus
  batis 230, 246
  intermedius 230–231, 246
Dobbs, Horace 206
Doggett, Matt 242
Dolphin
  Bottlenose 204, 206, 207
  Common 204, **205**, 207
Doris, Rough-mantled 271
Dorset Wildlife Trust **54**, 179, 341
Dory, John 134, **134**
Dragonet, Common 134, **225**
Dromia personata 308, **309**
Dugong 170
Dugong dugon 170
Dulse 86

Eagle, White-tailed 77, 210–211
Earll, Bob 71
EAST Marine Ecosystems (EASTME) 72
Echiichthys vipera 225, **227**, 316
Echinocardium cordatum 150, **150**, 304
echinoderms 22, 23–24, **23**, 254–257
  bilateral symmetry 264
  brittlestars **21**, 23–24, **35**, 143, 152, 257, 259, 260, **261**
  featherstars 23, **23**, **85**, **252**, 262–263, **263**
  larvae 264
  pedicellariae 256–257
  radial symmetry 254–255, **254**, 260–261, 264
  reproduction **25**, 264
  sea cucumbers 23, 117, 142–143, **143**, 151, **156**, 167, 255, 261–262, **262**, 264
  tube feet 255–256, **255**

see also sea urchins; starfish
Echinus esculentus 81, 92, **92**, 100, **255**, 261
Eel
  Conger 117, **131**, 135, 310, **310**
  European 97, 135
Eelgrass 162
  Dwarf 161–162
eelgrasses *see* seagrass meadows
egg capsules, squid 293–294
egg cases
  gastropod molluscs 55, **55**, 159
  skate and shark 54, 70, 223, 231, 236, 245–246, **245**
egg masses
  cuttlefish 172–173, **172**, **173**, 287–288, **287**
  sea slugs 111, 172, 173, 175, 270
Eigg, Hebrides 76–77
Electra pilosa 86, **87**
Eledone cirrhosa **277**, 290, **291**
Elysia viridis 273, **273**
Enhydra lutris 206
epibenthic organisms
  defined 14
  see also sessile and sedentary animals
epiphytes
  kelp/seaweed forests 47, 85–87, **85**, **86**
  seagrass meadows 171, 172
Ericaria selaginoides 246
Erignathus barbatus 205
Eunicella verrucosa 72, 110–111, **111**, 121, **121**, 122, 294, 338
Euspira catena 56, 154, **154**, 158, 159

Falls of Lora, Argyll and Bute 36–37
Featherstar
  Celtic 263
  Common **263**
featherstars 23, **23**, **85**, **252**, 262–263, **263**
File Shell, Gaping 125–126, **126**, 138
Fish
  Tadpole 116
  Wolf 76, 232, **233**, 341
fish 215–251
  ambush predators 152, 231–232, **232**
  artificial reefs 128, **131**, 134–135, **134**
  benthic fishes 225–231, **225**, **227**, **228**, **230**
  'cleaner fish' 218, 241–242, **241**, 317, **344**
  and climate change 247, 345, **346**

courtship, nests and egg-guarding 236–240, **237**, **238**, **239**, 242–244, **243**, **244**
crevice-dwellers 116–117, **116**, 309–310, **310**
egg cases 54, 70, 223, 231, 236, 245–246, **245**
finding food 152, 231–236, **232**, **233**
as individuals 216–225, **217**, **219**, **220**, **221**, **222**
kelp forests 87, **88**
new residents and summer visitors 247–251
open sea 198–204, **198**, **200**, **202**, **203**
parasites 314–317, **315**, **316**, **317**, 318–319
reproduction 48, 114, 181, 219–221, **220**, 231, 236–240, **237**, **238**, **239**, 242–246, **243**, **244**
sea caves 113–114
seagrass meadows 176–178, **178**, 180–181, **181**
sediment seabeds 145, 147, 152, 157–158
in spring and summer 48, 50
swim bladders 42
symbiotic relationships **296**, 309–310, **310**, 311, **311**, 312–314, **313**
venomous spines 227, **227**
fisheries
  crabs 120–121, 265
  cuttlefishes 288–289, **288**
  lobsters 120–121, 145–147
  octopuses 292
  overfishing 100, 324–327, **325**, **327**
  oysters 124
  squids 293
  trawling 111, 122, 125, 129, 138, 145–147, 156, 236, 288, 292, 293, 325–327, 330–331
  wrasses as 'cleaner fish' 241, 317, **344**
  see also Marine Protected Areas (MPAs)
Fjordia browni **271**
Flamborough Head, Yorkshire **333**, 337
flame shell reefs 125–126, **126**, 138
flatfishes 226–229, **228**
Fleet Lagoon, Dorset 74, 169, 179–180, **179**
Flounder 228
Flustra foliacea 22, **55**
Fucus
  serratus 26
  vesiculosus 93, **94**
Fulmar **209**, 210
Fulmarus glacialis **209**, 210

Funiculina quadrangularis 142, **142**
Furbellows 90–91, **90**, **97**

Gadus morhua 42
Gagnan, Émile 61
Galathea squamifera 119
Galathea strigosa 116
Gannet, Northern **209**, 210
Gasterosteus aculeatus 243–244
gastropod mollusc shells, as hermit crab homes 298–299, 306–307
gastropod molluscs (sea snails) 268
  egg cases 55, **55**, 159
  invasive species 123, 349, **349**
  kelp forests 91–92, **91**
  as predators 56, **56**, 152, 154, **154**, 242
  seagrass meadows 169
  see also sea slugs
Gobius
  cruentatus 250, **250**
  gasteveni 244
  niger **46**, 270
Gobiusculus flavescens 87, 283–284
Goby
  Black **46**, 270
  Fries's 145, 309
  Leopard-spotted 232, 251, **251**, 309–310
  Painted **225**, 310
  Red-mouthed 250, **250**
  Steven's **244**
  Two-spotted 87, 283–284
Goneplax rhomboides 147
Goose, Brent 170, **170**
Gosse, Philip 68
Grass, Neptune 168, **168**, 187
Great Eggcase Hunt 70, 71, 245
Guillemot 210
Gulf of Corryvreckan, Hebrides 36
Gulf Stream 33
Gulosus aristotelis 239
gurnards 234

Haematopus ostralegus 208
Haliaeetus albicilla 77, 210–211
Halichoerus grypus 79, 113, 205, 207, **207**, 292
Halichondria panicea 37
Haliclystus auricula **196**
Halidrys siliquosa 285, 350
Haminoea navicula 175, **175**
Hampshire & Isle of Wight Wildlife Trust *185*
Hannafore Point, Looe, Cornwall 73
Hapalochlaena 278
hard corals 106
  cup corals **92**, 110, 113, 121–122, **262**, 307,

308–309, **334**
reef-building 123
harvesting
  kelp/seaweed forests 101–102
  seagrass meadows 186–187
Hatcher, Julie 181
Helford Estuary, Cornwall 73, 156, 157, 166, 186
hermaphrodites 24, 173, 270
Hermit Crab
  Anemone 301–302, **301**
  Common **17**, 299–300, **299**, 302–303, **303**, 304, **304**
  Hairy **300**, 306–307, **307**
Hermit Crab Fur 303–304, **304**
hermit crabs 152, 157, 158
  symbiotic relationships 298–304, **299**, **300**, **301**, **302**, **303**, **304**, 306–307, **307**
Herring 42, 201–202, 234
Heterocyathus 307
Heteropsammia 307
hexacorals 106
  see also anemones; hard corals
Highland Dancer 272, **272**
Highly Protected Marine Areas (HPMAs) 330, 332–333, *333*
Himanthalia elongata 48, 93–94, **95**, 98, 105
Hippocampus
  guttulatus 180–181, **181**, *182*, 215, 244
  hippocampus 180–181, 244
Hiscock, Keith 34, 126, 132, 329, 335
Holland, Peter 254
Holothuria forskali 262, **262**
Homarus gammarus 56, 117, 145, 309–310
Hornwrack 22, **55**
Huxley, Thomas H. 326
Hyas araneus 87–88, **88**
Hydractinia echinata 303–304, **304**
Hydrobia 169
Hydroid
  Nodding 151
  Oaten Pipes **22**, 37
hydroids 21, **22**
  and climate change 345–346
  epiphytic 85, 86
  kelp forests 85, 86, 90
  larvae 195, 304
  life stages 195, **195**
  open sea 195, **195**, 197–198, **197**
  reproduction 26, 195
  sea caves 113
  seagrass meadows 170, 171, 172, *172*
  sediment seabeds 151

in spring 48, **51**
stinging cells 271, 304
symbiotic relationships **299**, 303–304, **304**
in winter 48
Hymedesmia 118

Inachus 307–308, **308**, 311
infauna, defined 14
Inshore Fisheries and Conservation Authorities (IFCAs) 242–243, 330, 334–335, 337, 338
insulation materials, made from seagrasses 187
intelligence
  cuttlefishes 285
  octopuses 290, 294
invasive species 98–99, **99**, 123, 348–351, **349**, **350**
iridiophores 278–280
Irish Basking Shark Group (IBSG) 201
Irving, Robert 335
Isles of Scilly 165, 166, 178–179
isopods 91, 169, 316–317, **317**

Jellyfish
  Barrel **188**, **194**, 195
  Blue **194**, 195
  Compass **193**, 194, **194**, 313–314
  Kaleidoscope **196**
  Lion's Mane **67**, 194–195, **194**, **296**, 312–313, **313**
  Moon 192–193, **193**
jellyfish 50, **188**, 189, 192–196, **193**, **194**
  bioluminescence 191, **191**
  life stages 192–193
  reproduction 193
  stalked **171**, 196, **196**
  stinging cells 313
  symbiotic relationships 312–314, **313**

Kelp
  Californian Giant 103
  Forest 30, 47, 83, **84**, 85–86, **86**, 89, 91, 96, **97**, 99–100, 103
  Golden 98
  Sugar 96, 103
kelp/seaweed forests 50, 83–103, **84**, **85**
  epiphytes 47, 85–87, **85**, **86**
  Golden Kelp forests 98
  harvesting 101–102
  herbivores 91–92, **91**, **92**, 93
  holdfasts 89–91, 92
  kelp farming 102–103, **102**
  light levels and depth 30–31, **30**, **31**, 83–84
  natural destruction 99–100

non-native species 98–99, **99**
predators 86, 87–89, **87**
restoration 100–101
Thong Weed forests 48, 93–94, **95**
variations in form 96–97, **97**
wrack forests 93, **94**, 101
kelps
  citizen science project 69
  holdfasts **84**, 85, 89–91, 92
  and tidal currents 35
  in winter 47
  see also kelp/seaweed forests
Kimmeridge Bay Marine Reserve, Dorset 75, 341
Kitching, Jack 60–61
Kittiwake 210
Kraken 295

Labrus
  bergylta **73**, **92**, 134, 236, 237, 241–242, **241**
  mixtus **30**, **51**, 72, 236, 237, **237**, **238**, **238**
Labyrinthula zosterae 182
Lacuna vincta 169, **169**
Laminaria
  digitata 83, 87, 96, 99, 100
  hyperborea 30, 47, 83, **84**, 85–86, **86**, 89, 91, 96, **97**, 99–100, 103
  ochroleuca 98
Lampetra fluviatilis 38, 315, **315**
Lamprey
  River 38, 315, **315**
  Sea 315
lampreys 314–315, **315**
Lanice conchilega 23, 147–148
Lankester, E. Ray 326
larvae, planktonic 26–27, 33–34, 48–50, 106, 117, 124, 195, 264, 270, 304, 306–307, 317
leeches 316, **316**
Lepadogaster purpurea 91
Lepeophtheirus salmonis 319
Leptometra celtica 263
Leptopsammia pruvoti **110**, 121–122
Lesueurigobius friesii 145, 309
Liberty Ships 130, **130**, 132
light underwater 27–32
  depth and zonation 30–31, **30**, **31**, 83–84
  seaweed colours 31–32, **32**
  underwater visibility 27–28, **29**, 65–66
  wavelengths of light 28–29
lighting, underwater 68, **68**
Limacia clavigera 86, **87**
Limanda, limanda 158, 227, 228, 234
Limaria hians 125–126, **126**, 138

Limpet
  Blue-rayed 91–92, **91**
  Slipper 123, 349, **349**
limpets 56, 91–92, **91**, 123, 349, **349**
Lithophyllum dentatum 79, 156
Lithothamnion
  corallioides 156
  glaciale 38, 156
Littorina littorea 169, **268**
Lobster
  Common 56, 117, 145, 309–310
  Leach's Squat 119
  Norway **136**, 145–147, 309
  Spiny Squat 116
lobsters
  crevice-dwellers 116–117, 309–310
  fisheries 120–121, 145–147
  hatcheries 343, **343**
  moulting 56
  muddy seabeds **136**, 145–147
  Norfolk chalk-reef 119, 120–121
  symbiotic relationships 309–310
Loch Carron, Ross and Cromarty 76, **76**, **81**, 88, 125, 126, 310
Loch Obisary, Hebrides 146, **146**
Loch Sween, Argyll and Bute 38, 164
Loligo
  forbesii 293
  vulgaris 293
Lophius piscatorius 152, 231–232
lugworms 158
Luidia ciliaris 259
Lumpsucker 216, 238
Lundy, Devon 72, 138, 139, 206, 210, 235–236, **321**, *333*, 334–335
Lutra lutra 206
Lyme Bay, Dorset 74, 121–122, **122**, 337–338

Macdonald, Rod 36
machair beaches 157
Mackerel
  Atlantic 201–202, 203
  Atlantic Horse 201–202
  Horse 314
MacNeish, Don 335
Macrocystis pyrifera 103
Maerl
  Celtic 38, 156
  Northern 38, 156
  Southern 156
  Stone Rose 79, 156
maerl beds 35, 38, 76, 77, **81**, 154–157, **155**, **156**
Magallana gigas 349
Maja brachydactyla 56, 74,

118, 135, 152, 174, **174**, 265–268, **265**, **267**
mammals, marine 42, 199, 204–208, **205**, **207**
Man-of-war, Portuguese 197–198, **197**
Mareca penelope 170
Marine Biological Association (MBA) 200, 201, 326, **326**, 348–349
Marine Conservation Society (MCS) 69, 70, 71, 195, 330–331, 342, 353
Marine Conservation Zones (MCZs) 73, 118, 181–182, 242–243, 330, 331, 334, 335, 339–340
Marine Management Organisation (MMO) 330, 331
Marine Protected Areas (MPAs) 38, 74, 126, 138, 185, 199, 246, 328–340
  Arran 77, *333*, 335–336, **336**
  Flamborough Head *333*, 337
  Lundy *333*, 334–335
  Lyme Bay 122, 337–338
  Pembrokeshire 77, 339–340
  voluntary reserves and conservation areas 340–341, **341**
Marine Species of the British Isles and Adjacent Seas (MSBIAS) database 344
marine stations 78, **78**, 79, 326
Marine Stewardship Council 343, **343**
Marine Strandings Network 71, 207
Marthasterias glacialis 152, 257–258, **257**, **258**, 259
Mauve Stinger 191, **191**
Maxmuelleria lankesteri 158–159
Megaptera novaeangliae 42, 205
Membranipora membranacea 86
Menai Strait, Wales 37, **37**
mermaid's purses 54, 70, 223, 231, 236, 245–246, **245**
Metridium senile 79, 107–109, **108**, 132
Mitchell, Maura 206
Modiolus modiolus 123, 124–125
Mola
  alexandrini 199
  mola 198–199, **198**
molluscs 268
  see also bivalve molluscs; cephalopods; gastropod molluscs
moon 25
Morus bassanus **209**, 210

moulting, crabs 55–56, 89, **89**, 118–120, **119**, **265**, 266–267
Muck, Hebrides 76–77
muddy seabeds 136, 139–147
  anemones **136**, 140–141, **140**, **141**
  brittlestars 143
  crabs and lobsters **136**, 145–147
  fish 145, 147
  sea cucumbers 142–143, **143**
  sea pens 141–142, **142**
  signs of animal activity 157–159, **158**
Mullet, Red 232–234, **233**
Mullus surmuletus 232–234, **233**
mushroom anemones 106
Mussel
  Edible **17**, 19–20, **19**, 56, 124, 135, 221–222, **221**, 337
  Fan 144, **144**
  Horse 123, 124–125
mussels **17**, 19–20, **19**
  artificial reefs 135, 221–222, **221**
  larvae 26
  mussel reefs 124–125
  as prey 56, **56**, 255–256, **256**, 259
  reproduction 25, 26
  'sea silk' 144, **144**
Myliobatis aquila 231
Myrmica sabuleti 298
Mytilus edulis **17**, 19–20, **19**, 56, 124, 135, 221–222, **221**, 337
Myxicola infundibulum 148–149, **148**

Natural History Museum, London 70, 71, 250, 295
Nautilus 275
Naylor, Ernest 25
Neanthes fucata 302–303, **303**
Necklace Shell, Common 56, 154, **154**, 158, 159
Necora puber **116**, 135, **218**, 222
nekton, defined 14
nematocysts 106
nematodes 319
Neopentadactyla mixta 151, **156**
Nephrops norvegicus **136**, 145–147, 309
'Neptune balls' 168, **168**
Nicol, Edith 146
no-anchor zones 181–183, 184
No-Take Zones (NTZs) 77, 138, 332–333, *333*, 334, 335–336, **336**, 337, 341

Norfolk chalk-reef 75, 117–121, **119**, **120**, **121**
North Wales Wildlife Trust *185*
notochord 20
Nucella lapillus 56, **56**
nudibranchs 268, 269–272, **269**
  and climate change 345–346, **346**
  defences 270–272, **271**
  egg masses 111, 172, 270
  kelp forests 86, **87**
  larvae 270
  reproduction 172, 173, 270
  rocky reefs 106, 110, 111
  seagrass meadows 172
Nursehound **245**, 246

Oban, Argyll and Bute 77
Ocenebra erinacea 56
octocorals 110
  see also sea pens; soft corals
Octopus
  California Two-spot 292
  Common 290–293, **291**, 294, 347
  Curled **277**, 290, **291**
Octopus
  bimaculatus 292
  vulgaris 290–293, **291**, 294, 347
octopuses 275, 277, **277**, 278, 290–293, **291**, 294, 347
oil exploration 352
Okenia elegans **269**, 270
Onchidoris bilamellata 271
open sea 189–211
  bioluminescence 190–192, **191**
  blue-water diving 190
  fish 198–204, **198**, **200**, **202**, **203**
  hydroids 195, **195**, 197–198, **197**
  jellyfish **188**, 189, 191, **191**, 192–195, **193**, **194**
  marine mammals 42, 199, 204–208, **205**, **207**
  seabirds **209**, 210, 239, 352
Openshaw, Martin 216, 223–224, 242
Openshaw, Sheilah 216, 223–224
Operation Kelp 69
Ophiocomina nigra **81**, 260
Ophiothrix fragilis 260, **261**
Ophiura 260
Orca 205
Orcinus orca 205
Ostrea edulis 16, 20, 123–124, 349
Otter 206
  Sea 206
overfishing 100, 324–327, **325**, **327**

Oyster
  European Flat 16, 20, 123–124, 349
  Pacific 349
oyster reefs 16, 123–124
Oystercatcher 208
oysters 20, 27, 349

Pachycerianthus multiplicatus **136**, 140–141, **140**
PADI (Professional Association of Diving Instructors) 62
Padina pavonica 75
Pagellus erythrinus 247
Pagophilus groenlandicus 205
Pagrus pagrus 247
Pagurus
  bernhardus **17**, 299–300, **299**, 302–303, **303**, 304, **304**
  cuanensis 300, 306–307, **307**
  prideaux 301–302, **301**
Palaemon serratus 310
Palinurus elephas **131**, 327
Palmaria palmata 86
Pandora, Common 247
Parablennius
  gattorugine 48, 75, **116**, 117, 135, **214**, 216, 218–222, **218**, **219**, **221**, **222**, 240, 310
  pilicornis 247, 248, **248**, 345
  ruber 249–251
Paracentrotus lividus 92
parasites 314–319
  barnacles 317–318, **318**
  copepods 318–319
  isopods 316–317, **317**
  lampreys 314–315, **315**
  leeches 316, **316**
  nematodes 319
Parazoanthus axinellae 110, 133
Patella pellucida 91–92, **91**
Pauly, Daniel 16
Pawsonia saxicola 117, 262
Peachia cylindrica 151, **151**
Peacock's Tail 75
Pecten maximus 152, 156, 177, 340, **340**
Pelagia noctiluca 191, **191**
Pembrokeshire 77, 185, *185*, 339–340
Pennatula phosphorea 142, **142**
Pentapora foliacea 121
Periclimenes sagittifer 135, 312, **312**
Periwinkle, Edible 169, **268**
Petromyzon marinus 315
Phengaris arion 298
Phoca vitulina 205
Phocoena phocoena 204, 207
Pholas dactylus 45
pholasin 45
Pholis gunnellus 310

Coastal Seas

photography, underwater 64–68, **67**, **68**
Phyllophora pseudoceranoides 146
Phymatolithon calcareum 38, 156
Physalia physalis 197–198, **197**
Physeter macrocephalus 42
Piddock, Common 45
piddocks 44, **44**, 45
piers 75, 133–135, **133**, **134**, 221–222, **221**
Pink Sea Fingers 113, **114**
pinnipeds see seals
Pipefish, Deep-snouted 176–178, **178**
Pipit, Rock 208
Plaice 226, 228, **228**, 229, 327
plankton 32, 189, 234
  bioluminescence 190–192, **191**
  comb jellies 191, 196–197, **196**
  defined 14
  plankton blooms 27, 48, 50, 191, 192
  see also jellyfish
planktonic larvae 26–27, 33–34, 48–50, 106, 117, 124, 195, 264, 270, 304, 306–307, 317
plastic pollution 122, 168, 197
Platichthys flesus 228
Pleurobrachia pileus **196**, 197
Pleurobranchus membranaceus 272, **272**
Pleuronectes platessa 226, 228, **228**, 229, 327
Pliny the Elder 45
Plover, Ringed 208
Pollachius
  pollachius 204, 215, 314
  virens **202**, 204
Pollack 204, 215, 314
Polybius
  corrugatus 174
  depurator 177
  holsatus 174
Polycera quadrilineata, 86
Polydora ciliata 44
Pomatoschistus pictus **225**, 310
Pondweed, Fennel 146
Pontobdella muricata 316, **316**
Porania pulvillus 259
Porcellana platycheles 89–90
Porcupine Marine Natural History Society (PMNHS) **54**, 71, 98, 177
Porpoise, Harbour 204, 207
Port Erin Marine Laboratory, Isle of Man 78, **78**
Porthkerris, Cornwall 72–73, **73**, 283
Portland Harbour, Dorset 74, **179**
Posidonia oceanica 168, **168**, 187

Potamogeton pectinatus 146
Potts, Geoff 239–240
power station cooling-water infrastructure 347, **347**
Prawn, Common 310
predators
  ambush predators 152, 231–232, **232**
  gastropod molluscs 56, **56**, 152, 154, **154**, 242
  kelp forests 86, 87–88, **87**, **88**
  overfishing of 100
  sandy seabeds 152–154, **153**
  starfish 152–153, **153**, 255–256, **256**, 257–259, **257**
Prionace glauca 59
Project Seagrass 167
Project Sepia 71, 289
Protanthea simplex 77, **81**
protection see conservation problems and solutions; Marine Protected Areas (MPAs)
Psammechinus miliaris **116**, 132, 169, 257, 261, **261**
Psolus phantapus 142–143, **143**
Puffinus puffinus 210
Pullin, Roger 235
Pusa hispida 205

Ragworm
  Commensal 302–303, **303**
  King 153, 154
Raja
  clavata **156**, 229, **230**, **316**
  undulata 216, 223–224, **224**
Raniceps raninus 116
rays 231
Red Sea Fingers 110, **110**
red seaweeds 32, 146
  epiphytic 85, 86
  maerl beds 35, 38, 76, 77, **81**, 154–157, **155**, **156**
'red tides' 192
reefs see animal-constructed reefs; artificial reefs; rocky reefs
ReMEDIES project 183, 185, *185*
reproduction
  asexual 25–26, 107, **107**, 108, 193
  cuttlefishes 172–173, **172**, **173**, 285–288, **286**, 287
  echinoderms **25**, 264
  fish 48, 114, 181, 219–221, **220**, 231, 236–240, **237**, **238**, **239**, 242–246, **243**, 244
  hermaphrodites 24, 173, 270
  hydroids 26, 195
  jellyfish 193

octopuses 292–293
planktonic larvae 26–27, 33–34, 48–50, 106, 117, 124, 195, 264, 270, 304, 306–307, 317
sea slugs 172, 173, 270
seagrasses 162–163, **163**
seaweeds 94, **95**, 98
sessile and sedentary animals 24–27, **24**, **25**, 48–50
restoration projects
  kelp/seaweed forests 100–101
  seagrass meadows 184–186, *185*
Rhincodon typus 217
Rhizostoma octopus **188**, **194**, 195
Rissa tridactyla 210
Rissoa 169
Roaringwater Bay, Ireland 79
Roberts, Callum 329
Rock Cook 236, 241, **241**, 242
rock-pooling 57–58, **57**
rock seabeds 42–45
  boring animals 44–45, **44**
  see also rocky reefs
rocky reefs **104**, 105–122
  anemones **104**, 106–109, **107**, **108**, **109**
  crevice-dwellers 116–117, **116**, 261–262, 309–310, **310**
  Lyme Bay Reefs 121–122, **122**
  Norfolk chalk-reef 75, 117–121, **119**, **120**, **121**
  sea caves 113–115, **114**
  soft corals **104**, 110–111, **110**, **111**, **122**
  sponges **104**, 112, **112**, 118
roundworms 319
Royal Yachting Association (RYA) 185
Rum, Hebrides 76–77, 211
Ruppia maritima 162

Sabella
  pavonina 37, **121**, 148, **149**, 175
  spallanzanii 148, **148**
Saccharina latissima 96, 103
Saccorhiza polyschides 90–91, **90**, 97
Sacculina carcini 317–318, **318**
Saithe **202**, 204
Salmo
  salar 38
  trutta 38
Salmon, Atlantic 38
salmon farming 241, 317, 319, **344**
salt 41–42
Sand Star 152–153, **153**
sandeels 203, **203**
sandy seabeds 139, 147–154

coarse sand and shell gravel 151, **151**
crustaceans 149–150, **150**
predators and scavengers 152–154, **153**
signs of animal activity 157–159, **158**
tubeworms 147–149, **148**, **149**
Sardina pilchardus 42
Sardine 42
Sargassum muticum 98–99, **99**, 349–350, **350**
Scallop
  Great 152, 156, 177, 340, **340**
  Queen 132, 152, 305–306, **305**
Scapa Flow, Orkney 128
Scarlet Lady **271**
Scinaia 41
Scomber scombrus 201–202, 203
Scophthalmus maximus 228
Scophthalmus rhombus 228
Scottish Association for Marine Science (SAMS) 103
Scottish Wildlife Trust 76, 155
scuba diving **52**, 60–68
  blue-water 190
  equipment 61–62, **61**
  photography 64–68, **67**, **68**
  recording 64–65, **64**
  safety stops 190
  sea conditions 63, **63**
  training 62
  underwater lighting 68, **68**
  underwater visibility 65–66
Scyliorhinus
  canicula 54, **82**, 216, **217**, 224–225
  stellaris **245**, 246
Scylla (ship) 131–133
sea anemones see anemones
sea caves 113–115, **114**
Sea Cucumber
  Gravel 151, **156**
  Pink-spotted 142–143, **143**
sea cucumbers 23, 117, 142–143, **143**, 151, **156**, 167, 255, 261–262, **262**, 264
Sea Fan
  Northern 111
  Pink 72, 110–111, **111**, 121, **121**, 122, 294, 338
sea fans 23, **30**, 110–111, **111**, 121, 122, **122**
sea firs see hydroids
Sea Gooseberry **196**, 197
  Common Northern 197
'sea grapes' 172–173, **172**, **173**, 287–288, **287**
Sea Hare **169**, 273, **350**
Sea Lemon **269**, 272, 305
Sea Mat 86
sea mosses see bryozoans

Index

Sea Mouse 153–154
Sea Oak 350
Sea Orange 18, 305–306, **305**
Sea Pen
  Phosphorescent 142, **142**
  Slender 142
  Tall 142, **142**
sea pens 141–142, **142**
Sea Scorpion, Long-spined 87, **88**, 212–213, 217, 231, **232**
'sea silk' 144
Sea Slug
  Crystal **269**
  Orange-clubbed 86, **87**
  Solar-powered 273, **273**
  Yellow Skirt **269**, 270
sea slugs 268, 269–273, **269**
  and climate change 345–346, **346**
  defences 270–272, **271**
  egg masses 111, 172, 173, 175, 270
  kelp forests 86, **87**
  larvae 270
  non-nudibranch sea slugs 173, 175, **175**, 272–273, **272**, **273**
  reproduction 172, 173, 270
  rocky reefs 106, 110, 111
  seagrass meadows 172, 173, 175, **175**
sea snails *see* gastropod molluscs
Sea Squirt
  Baked-bean 40, **41**
  Carpet 351
  Football 48
  Light-bulb 25
  Yellow-ringed 20–21, **21**, 25, 146
sea squirts **6**, 20–21, **21**
  invasive species 351
  jellyfish polyps on 193
  kelp forests 90
  larvae 26
  reproduction 25, 26
  sea caves 113
  seagrass meadows 171
  in spring **51**
  in wave-surge areas 40, **41**
  in winter 48
sea urchins 23, 260–261, **261**
  artificial reefs 132
  feeding structure 92, **93**, 261
  kelp forests 91, 92, **92**, 100
  pedicellariae 256–257
  radial symmetry 260–261
  reproduction 264
  sandy seabeds 150, **150**
  seagrass meadows 169
  symbiotic relationships **150**, 304
  tube feet 255, **255**, 256
sea-wash balls 55, **55**
seabirds **209**, 210, 239, 352
Seabream
  Black 236, 242–243

Couch's 247
seagrass meadows 30, 32, **160**, 161–187
  in British Isles 73, 74, 75, 77, 79, 165–166, **166**, 178–182
  comparison with terrestrial grasses 162–163, **163**, **164**
  detritus cycle 167–169, **167**, **168**
  diseases 182
  ecosystem 163–165, **164**
  egg masses laid on 172–173, **172**, **173**, 175
  grazers 169–170, **169**, **170**
  harvesting 186–187
  and oyster reefs 124
  physical damage 183–184, **183**
  reproduction 162–163, **163**
  resident and visiting animals 171–178, **171**, *172*, **174**, **175**, **177**, **178**
  restoration projects 184–186, *185*
  and tidal currents 34
Seahorse
  Long-snouted 180–181, **181**, 182, 215, 244
  Short-snouted 180–181, 244
seahorses 180–181, **181**, 182, 244
Seal
  Bearded 205
  Common 205
  Grey 79, 113, 205, 207, **207**, 292
  Harp 205
  Hooded 205
  Ringed 205
sealice 318–319
seals 113, 205, 207–208, **207**
Seaquest Southwest 71
Seasearch **64**, 65, 69, 70, 71, 98, 118, 126, 132, 141, 144, 247, 312
seasons 47–50
seaweeds
  colours 31–32, **32**
  holdfasts 35, **84**, 85, 89–91, 92
  light levels and depth 30–31, **30**, **31**, 83–84
  reproduction 94, **95**, 98
  rock seabeds 43–44
  in spring and summer 48, 50
  and tidal currents 34, 35
  vegetative dispersal 45
  and waves 39–41
  in winter 47
  see also brown seaweeds; kelp/seaweed forests; kelps; red seaweeds

sediment seabeds 42–43, 45–47, 137–139
  see also animal-constructed reefs; maerl beds; muddy seabeds; sandy seabeds; seagrass meadows
sentience 294
Sepia
  apama 280
  elegans 280
  officinalis 73, 74, **173**, **274**, 280, 288
  orbignyana 280
  pharaonis 288
Sepiola atlantica 289, **289**
Serpula vermicularis 127, **127**
Serranus cabrilla **346**
sessile and sedentary animals
  basic biology 16–24
  boring animals 44–45, **44**
  larvae 26–27, 33–34, 48–50, 106, 117
  light levels and depth **30**, 31, **31**
  reproduction 24–27, **24**, **25**, 48–50
  rock seabeds 43–45
  in spring and summer 48–50, **49**, **51**
  and tidal currents 33–34
  tubeworms 22–23, 27, 34, **35**, 127, **127**, 147–149, **148**, **149**
  and waves 39–40, **41**
  in winter 47–48, **49**
  see also anemones; barnacles; bivalve molluscs; bryozoans; hydroids; sea squirts; soft corals; sponges
Severn Estuary 33, 38
sewage pollution 351–352
Shad, Twaite 38
Shag 239
shallow coastal seas, defined 14–15
Shark
  Basking **59**, 199–201, **200**, 217, 234
  Blue **59**
  Grey Reef 224
  Whale 217
Shark Trust 71, 199, 201, 245, 246
sharks, egg cases 54, 70, 236, 245–246, **245**
Shearwater, Manx 210
sheep, North Ronaldsay 101
Sheringham, Norfolk 75, 118
Sherkin Island, Ireland 79
'shifting baselines' concept 15–16, 327
shipwrecks 36, 77, 128–133, **129**, **130**, **131**
Shoresearch 71
Shrimp
  Anemone 135, 312, **312**

Brown 58
shrimps 89, 167, 169, 309, 312, **312**
Sims, David 201
sirenians 170
Skate
  Blue 230, 246
  Flapper 230–231, 246
  Thornback **156**, 229, **230**, 316, **316**
  Undulate 216, 223–224, **224**
skates **156**, 216, 223–224, **224**, 226, 229–231, **230**
  egg cases 54, 70, 223, 231, 245–246
The Skelligs, Ireland 78–79
Skomer, Wales 77, 138, 166, 339, 340, 353
slime moulds 182
Smelt, Sand 134–135, **203**
snorkelling 58–59
  equipment **59**, 62
  photography 64–68
  recording 64–65
  sea conditions 63, **63**
soft corals 21, **30**
  reproduction 26
  rocky reefs **104**, 110–111, **110**, **111**, 121, 122, **122**
  sea caves 113, **114**
  sea fans **23**, **30**, 110–111, **111**, 121, 122, **122**
  in spring and summer 48, **49**, **51**
  and tidal currents 34, **35**
  in winter 47, **49**
Solaster endeca 258–259
Sole 227
Solea solea 227
South-West Marine Ecosystems (SWME) 71–72
spearfishing 342
Special Areas of Conservation (SACs) 77, 115, 122, 124, 157, 180, 185–186, *185*, 330, 331, 337, 338, 339
Spinachia spinachia **243**, 244
Spondyliosoma cantharus 236, 242–243
Sponge
  Boring 44–45, **46**, 306
  Breadcrumb 37
  White Lace 40, **41**
  Yellow Staghorn **337**
sponges **6**, **18**, **18**, 37
  boring 44–45, **46**, 306
  epiphytic 85
  identification of species 70
  kelp forests 85, 90
  larvae 26, 306–307
  reproduction 24, 26
  rocky reefs **104**, 112, **112**, 118
  sea caves 113
  in spring **51**
  symbiotic relationships 305–

308, **305**, **307**, **308**, **309**
in wave-surge areas 40, **41**
Sprat, Atlantic 201–202
Sprattus sprattus 201–202
Squid
  Bobtail 289, **289**
  Giant 295
squids 275, 276–277, 293–294, **293**
St Abbs, Berwickshire 76
St Kilda 28, 97, **114**, 115, **115**
Starfish
  Common **25**, 132, 135, **254**, **256**, 257, 258, 259–260
  Seven-armed 259
  Spiny 152, 257–258, **257**, **258**, 259
starfish 23, 257–260
  artificial reefs 132, 135
  number of arms **258**
  as predators 152–153, **153**, 255–256, **256**, 257–259, **257**
  radial symmetry 254–255, **254**
  reproduction **25**, 264
  sediment seabeds 152–153, **153**
  'starballing' 259–260
  strandings 259–260
  tube feet 255–256, **256**
Starr, Ringo 295
Stickleback
  Fifteen-spined **243**, 244
  Three-spined 243–244
Stingray, Common 230, 231
stony corals 106
  cup corals **92**, **110**, 113, 121–122, **262**, 307, 308–309, **334**
  reef-building 123
Strongylocentrotus droebachiensis 100
Studland Bay, Dorset 180–182, **180**, 184
Suberites ficus **18**, 305–306, **305**
Sunfish
  Bumphead 199
  Ocean 198–199, **198**
Sunstar
  Common **81**, **252**, 258, **258**, 264
  Purple 258–259
Sussex Kelp Recovery Project 100
sustainable seafood 342–344, **343**
Swanage Pier, Dorset 75, 133–135, **134**
Swift 201
Symbion pandora 145
symbiotic relationships 297–314
  anemones 299–302, **299**,

300, **301**, **302**, 311–312, **312**
barnacles 309
bivalve molluscs **150**, 304, 305–306, **305**
crabs 307–308, **308**, **309**, 311, **311**
cup corals 308–309
fish **296**, 309–310, **310**, 311, **311**, 312–314, **313**
hermit crabs 298–304, **299**, **300**, **301**, **302**, **303**, **304**, 306–307, **307**
hydroids **299**, 303–304, **304**
jellyfish 312–314, **313**
lobsters 309–310
sea urchins **150**, 304
shrimps 312, **312**
sponges 305–308, **305**, **307**, **308**, **309**
see also parasites
Symphodus melops 134, 236, 238–240, **239**, 241, 317, **317**, 342
Syngnathus typhle 176–178, **178**

Tasselweed, Beaked 162
Taurulus bubalis 87, **88**, **212**–**213**, 217, 231, **232**
Tellimya ferruginosa **150**, 304
Tetronarce nobiliana 231
thigmotropism 128
Thorogobius ephippiatus 232, 251, **251**, 309–310
Thurlestone, Devon 74
tidal currents, rapids and races 33–38
Topknot 228, **228**
Topknot, Eckström's **88**, 227
Topshell, Painted **307**
Torbay, Devon 74
Torpedo marmorata 231
Trachurus trachurus 201–202, 314
trawling 111, 122, 125, 129, 138, 145–147, 156, 236, 288, 292, 293, 325–327, 330–331
Tresses, Mermaid's 45
Trewhella, Steve 181
Triggerfish
  Grey 247–249, 345
  Titan 249
Tripterygion delaisi **6**, 113–114, 134
Trisopterus luscus **131**, 134, 135, 203, 242
Tritia reticulata 152, 306–307
Tritonia hombergii 110
Trout, Sea 38
tube-dwelling anemones **136**, 140–141, **140**, **141**, 176
tubeworms 22–23, 27, 34, **35**, **127**, **127**, 147–149,

148, 149
Tubularia indivisa **22**, 37
tunicates *see* sea squirts
Turbot 228
Tursiops truncatus 204, 206, 207
Turtle, Leatherback 198
turtles 170, 198

Undaria pinnatifida 99
Underwater Conservation Year 69
Urchin
  Common Heart 150, **150**, 304
  Common Sea **81**, 92, **92**, 100, **255**, 261
  Green Sea **116**, 132, 169, 257, 261, **261**
  Purple Sea 92
Uria aalge 210
Urticina felina 37, **37**, 79

Velella velella 197–198, **197**
Verne, Jules 295
Virgularia mirabilis 142
visibility, underwater 27–28, **29**, 65–66
voluntary reserves and conservation areas 340–341, **341**
Volunteer Seabirds at Sea (VSAS) 210

Wakame 99
water currents 33–38
waves and wave surges 38–41, **39**
Weed
  Desmarest's Flattened 41
  Desmarest's Prickly 41
  Oar 83, 87, 96, 99, 100
  Thong 48, 93–94, **95**, 98, 105
Weeverfish, Lesser 225, **227**, 316
Wembury Marine Conservation Area, Devon 60, **63**, 73, 240, 246, 341
West Runton, Norfolk 75
Whale
  Blue 42
  Fin 42
  Humpback 42, 205
  Killer 205
  Minke 42, 199, 205
  Sperm 42
whales and dolphins 42, 199, 204–205, **205**, 206, 208
Wheeler, Alwyne 250
Whelk
  Common 55, **55**, 152
  Dog 56, **56**
  Netted Dog 152, 306–307
whelks 55, **55**, 56, **56**, 152,

242, 306–307
Whitley Bay, Tyneside 75
Wigeon 170
Wildlife Trusts 71, 72, 222, 324, 347, 353
wind farms 352–353
Winkle, European Sting 56
Wireweed 98–99, **99**, 349–350, **350**
Wood, Christine 348
Wood, Howard 335
World Heritage Sites 353
World Register of Marine Species (WoRMS) 273
Worm
  Eyelash 148–149, **148**
  Mediterranean Fan 148, **148**
  Organ Pipe 127, **127**
  Peacock **37**, **121**, 148, **149**, **175**
  Sand Mason 23, 147–148
  Sentinel Fan 23
  Volcano 158–159
worms
  boring 44
  predatory 153–154
  seagrass meadows 167, **175**
  sediment seabeds 153–154, 158–159
  tubeworms 22–23, 27, 34, **35**, **127**, **127**, 147–149, **148**, **149**
Wrack
  Bladder 93, **94**
  Egg 93, 97, 101
  Rainbow 246
  Serrated 26
wrack forests 93, **94**, 101
Wrasse
  Ballan **73**, **92**, 134, 236, 237, 241–242, **241**
  Corkwing 134, 236, 238–240, **239**, 241, 317, **317**, 342
  Cuckoo **30**, **51**, 72, 236, 237, **237**, 238, **238**
  Goldsinny 236–237, 241, 242
wrasses 50, 74, 216, 232
  as 'cleaner fish' 241–242, **241**, 317, **344**
  courtship, nests and egg-guarding 236–240, **237**, **238**, **239**

Zeugopterus 228, **228**
  punctatus 228, **228**
  regius **88**, 227
Zeus faber 134, **134**
zooxanthellae 123, 312
Zostera
  marina 162
  noltei 161–162
  see also seagrass meadows